Chile's Transformation Amidst Crisis

Kenneth Bunker

Chile's Transformation Amidst Crisis

The Theseus Paradox

palgrave
macmillan

Kenneth Bunker
Department of Economics, Business,
and Government
San Sebastian University
Santiago, Chile

ISBN 978-3-031-96462-6 ISBN 978-3-031-96463-3 (eBook)
https://doi.org/10.1007/978-3-031-96463-3

This Palgrave Macmillan imprint is published by the registered company Springer Nature Switzerland AG
The registered company address is: Gewerbestrasse 11, 6330 Cham, Switzerland

For Anna
To Olivia Maria and Luca Leon

Preface

In October 2019, Chile—a country long celebrated as a beacon of stability and progress in Latin America—was suddenly thrust into the global spotlight for reasons few could have anticipated. What began as a modest fare increase in Santiago's metro system ignited a wave of protests that quickly spread across the nation. The demands were urgent and wide-ranging, accompanied by an unprecedented surge of violence now known as the *estallido social* (social outburst). At the heart of the crisis lay a profound contradiction: how could a nation that had been so often hailed as a model erupt so suddenly into mayhem?

What followed was a dramatic and unlikely chain of events. Chile embarked on an ambitious journey to redefine itself through a new constitution, raising hopes for a fundamental transformation of its political system and social landscape. However, despite the momentum for change, voters ultimately rejected two proposals—first a progressive one and then a conservative one—effectively reaffirming the constitution originally drafted under the dictatorship of Augusto Pinochet. This underscores a second contradiction: how can a country that had been so determined to fully overhaul its structure reject not one but two proposals to reform its foundational charter?

The purpose of this book is to examine the circumstances that led to the social outburst and then the failure of two constitutional processes. It delves into the structural conditions and moments that transformed Chile while leaving much of what had once been presented as a problem in place. By exploring this "Theseus Paradox," of sorts, this book seeks to provide a candid and unique account of Chile's recent history, offering lessons for other developing democracies grappling with crises and contemplating reform, and examining in detail how much things really changed in Chile between 2019 and 2023.

The primary source of insight for this book comes from my experience as a political columnist for *Las Últimas Noticias* and *Ex-Ante*, two leading Chilean media outlets where I published hundreds of articles throughout the four-year ordeal. These columns, written in real-time, in the heat of the moment, offered a window into the experience of those navigating the crisis and served as theoretical placeholders while events still unfolded. Since many of the original ideas have withstood the test of time, they are woven into the text here, adding a perspective rooted in the immediacy of the events.

This work is further informed by my extensive engagement with both local and international media outlets attempting to make sense of the unfolding crisis. Speaking to journalists from global platforms such as *TIME*, *The Wall Street Journal*, and *The Economist*, as well as traditional Chilean outlets like *El Mercurio*, *Diario Financiero*, and *TVN*, helped me identify the most contentious points of the rapidly evolving situation. Because I believe these interactions helped me understand the multidimensional nature of the events, many of those articles are included in the references as additional context.

Yet a third source of input comes from the numerous conversations I had with foreign investors and decision-makers. These dialogues illuminated the global significance of Chile's upheaval and challenged me to explain the complex transformation that Chile was going through to an audience heavily invested in the country's future. Since the concerns raised in these discussions helped refine by own stance on the situation at hand, I made sure to provide an account that was capable of addressing both the local and international spheres of the situation.

Finally, this book is shaped by my experience in academia. Attending and presenting at seminars, labs, research groups, and discussion forums across universities in the United States, Chile, and Italy, where much of this work was conducted, provided me with a deeper understanding of a problem that is, by nature, not only complex, but universal. The nuances of what is undeniably a delicate political situation are reflected not only in the multilayered analysis but also in its broad applicability across a diverse range of contexts.

The book is written for anybody interested in understanding the unexpected series of events that disrupted an otherwise stable and predictable country. It offers an accessible narrative that sheds light on Chile's trajectory, providing both background and an original account of the crisis and its aftermath.

Readers with little to no prior knowledge of Chile are encouraged to begin with Part I (Chapters 2–5), which provides a clear historical and conceptual foundation for understanding the issues at stake. While many of the topics covered here are explored in greater depth elsewhere, this section brings them together in a concise and accessible format, offering a coherent starting point for engaging with the more detailed analysis that follows.

Those already familiar with the Chilean case may prefer to start directly with Part II (Chapters 6–10), which examines the interplay of structural and contingent factors that ultimately triggered the social outburst. This section will be particularly relevant for risk analysts and country specialists, as it uncovers meaningful trends in the evolution of the party system and shifts in voter-party linkages through quantitative methods. These insights are complemented by a close reading of political discourse, shedding light on how competing narratives framed the crisis and influenced public perception.

Academics, in turn, may find value in Part III (Chapters 11–17), which traces the trajectory of the two constitutional processes and examines the factors behind their eventual failure as well as the events that took place in between. Scholars—especially political scientists and historians—will have access not only to original data and replication code but also to a rich set of supplemental materials, including a unique archive of documents that chronicle the unfolding of this pivotal chapter in Chile's recent history.

Finally, Part IV (Chapters 18–19), will be of particular interest to policymakers and stakeholders. These readers, who often focus more on the future than the past, will find a succinct synthesis of the key turning points that irreversibly reshaped the country's trajectory. These chapters are designed to stand alone and can be read independently of the rest of the book, offering a streamlined overview for those seeking a quick yet comprehensive understanding of the core arguments.

Readers interested in exploring supplementary materials, such as images, datasets, code, documents, and additional resources referenced throughout the book, are encouraged to visit the companion website at https://kennethbunker.github.io/theseus. There, they will find a curated collection of files designed to complement and expand upon the topics discussed in each chapter, offering further depth and opportunities for independent analysis.

My hope is that this work will not only help make sense of Chile's experience but also encourage deeper reflection on the broader tensions between stability, crisis, and the choice to pursue reform amidst uncertainty.

Santiago, Chile

Kenneth Bunker

Acknowledgments I would like to express my sincere gratitude to all those who contributed to this project. Special thanks to the Tresquintos team for their diligent data collection of roll-call votes during both constitutional processes, and their invaluable efforts in gathering data on voting intentions and presidential approval ratings over the years. I am also grateful to the members of the Laboratorio Democracia y Gobierno of the Universidad San Sebastián for their research support, coordination of activities, and general assistance throughout the process. Among others, these include Fernanda Arrieta, Hasan Basaran, Camila Daza, Emilio Espinosa, Lorena Galdames, Benjamín Valdés, Maximiliano Vargas, and Joselyn Vilches.

I also appreciate the support from friends and colleagues at Universidad San Sebastián, particularly Alejandro Weber, Dean of the Department of Economics, Business, and Government, for providing the conditions that made it possible to complete this work. I am also in debt to José Miguel Cabezas, Chair of the School of Government, for his support, and to Luz Poblete, Secretary General of the department, for her insightful discussions regarding politics and society. I am thankful to Anice Saud and Hugo Jofré for their backing, and Cristóbal Castro for his strategic vision and coordination. I am especially grateful to Diego Jiménez, whose thoughtful feedback significantly enhanced the quality of this book.

The project also benefited from the generous institutional support of the Vicerrectoría de Investigación y Doctorados of the Universidad San Sebastián, through the Fondo USS-FIN-25-FATE-02, and the Agencia Nacional de Investigación y Desarrollo (ANID), under grant NCS2024_007 (Núcleo Milenio MEPOP). Their contributions made this work possible.

I thank the editors and publishing staff at Springer Nature and Palgrave Macmillan for carrying this book through the production process, as well as the friends, colleagues, beta readers, and anonymous reviewers who carefully looked over and commented on several pre-publication drafts. Their collective input helped shape the book's structure, arguments, and style.

I warmly acknowledge Benedetta Calandra of the University of Bergamo for offering me a visiting position and inviting me to speak about the events unfolding in Chile in seminars in Bergamo, Milan, and Rome. I am also grateful to Luigi Curini for hosting me as a visiting professor at the University of Milan, and to Alessandro Bucciol for receiving me at the University of Verona. I owe special thanks to Gianluca Pasarelli for his kind offer to visit the Political Science Department at Sapienza University in Rome, shortly before any of these events began to unfold.

I am thankful to *Las Últimas Noticias*, Chile's last nationally circulating printed newspaper, for their trust and support over the years. Special thanks go out to Gerardo Cañas, as well as to Luis Miranda and Orietta Santa María for offering fresh perspectives on the country's direction in uncertain times. In the same vein, I also appreciate the thoughtful exchanges with Cristián Bofill and Alfonso Peró of *Ex-Ante* regarding some of the more contentious developments that sparked, and were sparked by, the social outburst.

I am grateful to the many financial and political analysts who generously shared their insights in private meetings, public seminars, academic forums, and informal exchanges over the years. While I am unable to mention them individually for confidentiality reasons, their perspectives greatly enriched my understanding of the complex relationship between politics and markets. I especially appreciate those who offered reflections on institutional risk, investor sentiment, and public finance, as well as those "on the ground" in Chile whose real-world experience added essential context to this research.

I am equally appreciative of the journalists whose timely and probing questions helped uncover subtle yet important dynamics shaping public discourse. Through hundreds of interviews, chats and conversations—both in Chile and abroad—I was often challenged in ways that helped refine my thinking. While there are far too many of these interactions to mention individually here, I've done my best to document them on my website as a small way of recognizing their value.

I extend my thanks to the research colleagues with whom I collaborated on projects that intersected with the themes explored in this book during the period in which it was written. The research undertaken with Gabriel Negretto on electoral systems relates to some of the discussion presented in Chapter 6, while the work with John Polga-Hecimovich on cleavage theory relates to some of the ideas discussed in Chapter 7. In turn, the work on ideological polarization, carried out with Stéphanie Alenda and Miguel Ángel López, is more directly connected to the analysis of extremism and related dynamics presented in Chapter 12.

Although these collaborations emerged from distinct contexts, they each contributed meaningfully.

In the same vein, I am also grateful to those who, over the years, indirectly and maybe unknowingly, contributed in different ways to many of the thoughts and ideas scattered across this book. Among others, my thanks go out to Jaime Abedrapo, Marcel Aubry, Cristóbal Bellolio, Francisco Birke, Daniel Brieba, Juan Pablo Capomassi, Ryan Carlin, Sebastián Carrasco, María de los Ángeles Fernández, Yarela Flores, Arturo Fontaine, Valentina Fuentes, Germana González, Javier González, Pablo Jamett, Cristóbal de la Maza, Jaquelin Morillo, Francisco Muñoz, Patricio Navia, Ciara Nugent, Jaime Ojeda, Tito Olavarría, María Luisa Puig, Javiera Quiroga, David Sánchez, Luis Oro Tapia, and Pilar Tavella.

So then, with that, here begins the account offered to the reader: a necessarily incomplete but deliberately straightforward interpretation of the events that profoundly and perhaps permanently altered the course of Chile. Written over time and shaped by chance, it is now as ready as it ever will be to be released into the sea. Any and all errors are mine, and mine alone.

Competing Interests The author has no competing interests to declare that are relevant to the content of this manuscript.

Contents

About the Author

Kenneth Bunker is an academic, consultant, and columnist with a PhD in Government and a Master of Research in Political Science from the London School of Economics. His research focuses on electoral systems, political parties, and electoral forecasting in new democracies. His work has been featured in leading political science journals, such as Party Politics, Electoral Studies, and the Journal of Political Ideologies. He is an Associate Professor in the Department of Economics, Business, and Government and Director of the Democracy and Government Lab at San Sebastián University. He has held visiting appointments at Sapienza University of Rome and the University of Milan in Italy. He is currently affiliated with the University of Verona. Dr. Bunker is the creator and director of Tresquintos, a Chilean political consulting firm, as well as the leading political columnist for Chilean daily Las Últimas Noticias and online news platform Ex-Ante. He is a frequent political commentator in Chilean and international outlets. His website is: https://kennethbunker.github.io/

Abbreviations

AFPs	Administradoras de Fondos de Pensiones
AHV	Acción Humanista Verde (Green Humanist Action)
AMA	Amarillos (Yellows)
AMP	Amplitud (Amplitude)
AN	Acción Nacional (National Action)
ANI	Alianza Nacional de los Independientes (National Alliance of Independents)
APEC	Asia-Pacific Economic Cooperation
CH1	Chile Primero (Chile First)
CEP	Centro de Estudios Públicos
CIU	Ciudadanos (Citizens)
COM	Comunes (Commons)
CPI	Consumer Price Index
CS	Convergencia Social (Social Convergence)
DC	Democracia Cristiana (Christian Democratic Party)
DEMO	Demócratas (Democrats)
DR	Democracia Regional (Regional Democracy)
DRP	Democracia Regional Patagónica (Patagonian Regional Democracy)
ECO	Ecologistas (Ecologists)
ENP	Effective Number of Parties
Evópoli	Evolución Política (Political Evolution)
FA	Frente Amplio (Broad Front)
FDN	Fuerza del Norte (Force of the North)
FECH	Federación de Estudiantes de la Universidad de Chile
FEUC	Federación de Estudiantes de la Pontificia Universidad Católica

FP	Frente Popular (Popular Front)
FREP	Frente Regional y Popular (Popular and Regional Front)
FRNV	Fuerza Regional Norte Verde (Northern Green Regional Force)
FRV	Frente Regional Verde (Green Regional Front)
FRVS	Federación Regionalista Verde Social (Social Green Regionalist Federation)
GDP	Gross Domestic Product
HDI	Human Development Index
IC	Izquierda Cristiana (Christian Left)
IMF	International Monetary Fund
ISAPREs	Instituciones de Salud Previsional
LAPOP	Latin American Public Opinion Poll
LOCE	Ley Orgánica Constitucional de Enseñanza
LV	Los Verdes (The Greens)
MAPU	Movimiento de Acción Popular Unitario (Popular Unitary Action Movement)
MAS	Movimiento Amplio Social (Broad Social Movement)
MIRA	Movimiento Independiente Regionalista Agrario y Social (Independent Agrarian and Regionalist Social Movement)
MIR	Movimiento de Izquierda Revolucionaria (Revolutionary Left Movement)
NAP	Nueva Alternativa Popular (New Popular Alternative)
NT	Nuevo Tiempo (New Time)
OECD	Organisation for Economic Co-operation and Development
PAIS	Partido Amplio de Izquierda Socialista (Country)
PAVP	Partido Alianza Verde Popular (Popular Green Alliance Party)
PCC	Partido Conservador Cristiano (Christian Conservative Party)
PC	Partido Comunista de Chile (Communist Party of Chile)
PEC	Partido Ecologista (Ecologist Party)
PEV	Partido Ecologista Verde (Green Ecologist Party)
PEVN	Partido Ecologista Verde del Norte (Green Ecologist Party of the North)
PH	Partido Humanista (Humanist Party)
PI	Partido Igualdad (Equality Party)
PL	Partido Liberal (Liberal Party)
PN	Partido Nacional (National Party)
PNC	Partido Nacional Ciudadano (Citizen National Party)
POD	Poder (Power)
PP	Partido Popular (People's Party)
PPD	Partido por la Democracia (Party for Democracy)
PRI	Partido Regionalista Independiente (Independent Regionalist Party)
PR	Partido Radical (Radical Party)

PRM	Partido Regionalista de Magallanes (Regionalist Party of Magallanes)
PRO	Partido Progresista (Progressive Party)
PRSD	Partido Radical Socialdemócrata (Social Democrat Radical Party)
PSC	Partido Social Cristiano (Social Christian Party)
PSD	Partido Socialdemócrata (Social Democratic Party)
PS	Partido Socialista (Socialist Party)
PSCH	Partido Socialista Chileno (Chilean Socialist Party)
PTR	Partido de Trabajadores Revolucionarios (Revolutionary Workers' Party)
PPP	Purchasing Power Parity
SERVEL	Servicio Electoral de Chile
SQM	Sociedad Química y Minera de Chile
RD	Revolución Democrática (Democratic Revolution)
REP	Partido Republicano (Republican Party)
RN	Renovación Nacional (National Renewal)
SAY	Somos Aysén (We Are Aysén)
SUR	Partido del Sur (Southern Party)
TODOS	Todos (Everybody)
UCC	Unión de Centro Centro (Center-Center Union)
UDI	Unión Demócrata Independiente (Independent Democratic Union)
UNICEF	United Nations International Children's Emergency Fund
UP	Unidad Popular (Popular Unity)
URD	Unidos Resulta en Democracia (United Results in Democracy)
W	Wallmapuwen (Mapuche Nation)
WB	World Bank
WHO	World Health Organization
WTO	World Trade Organization
UNDP	United Nations Development Programme
UNICEF	United Nations International Children's Emergency Fund

List of Figures

List of Tables

CHAPTER 1

From Stability to Upheaval

1.1 From Stability to Upheaval

On October 8, 2019, Chilean President Sebastián Piñera declared his country to be "a true oasis" of stability and progress. Compared to its neighboring countries—many of whom were mired in political crises, economic decline, and social unrest—he was right. Chile had become a symbol of success: a functioning democracy, a growing economy, and a society that appeared to be advancing steadily. For decades, it had been viewed as a model for Latin America and the Global South, demonstrating the potential to balance economic development with democratic governance.

But just ten days later, the image came crashing down. A modest increase in Santiago's Metro fare triggered protests that quickly escalated into a nationwide movement. In the mornings, tens of thousands would take to the streets to peacefully voice their frustration over high living costs, low wages, and deep-seated inequality. By nightfall, however, the scene would descend into chaos and violence, as *encapuchados* (lit. "hooded figures") and radicals would clash with police and government forces.

In response to systemic demands and as an attempt to quell the violence, Chile's political class convened to initiate a historic constitutional reform process. Over the next four years, this effort would dominate the political sphere and culminate in two failed reform attempts.

K. Bunker, *Chile's Transformation Amidst Crisis*,
https://doi.org/10.1007/978-3-031-96463-3_1

In 2022, Chileans would reject a left-leaning proposal drafted by progressives and independents. And just a year later, they would dismiss a second, more conservative alternative.

By 2024, Chile had seemingly returned to where it was five years earlier. It had undergone political upheaval, a leftward shift, a conservative correction, and, ultimately, reaffirmed the very Constitution that had seemingly sparked the 2019 protests. Global media highlighted the irony: the document that had triggered mass demonstrations not only remained in place but was, in effect, ratified twice—once through the rejection of the progressive draft and again with the rejection of the right-leaning one. What began as an effort to overturn a Constitution born under dictatorship—associated with rigidity and neoliberalism—ended up reaffirming the very system it meant to replace.

This raises critical questions. How could a country so often regarded as a success story descend into widespread unrest, with citizens questioning the very foundations that led them to stand out? And, if constitutional change was essential to addressing the demands behind the social outburst, how can the rejection of not one but two proposed alternatives be interpreted? And finally, were the four years of social upheaval, political turmoil, and economic disruption ultimately worth it?

1.2 A Model for Developing Nations

To address these questions, it is essential to step back and examine the historical foundations of Chile's transition, which rested on two key pillars: political stability and economic development.

On the political front, Chile's democratization was notably orderly and peaceful, setting it apart from other Latin American countries where transitions were often marred by violence, conflict, or military resistance. The process formally began with the 1988 national referendum, in which Chileans voted to end Augusto Pinochet's dictatorship. This turning point was followed by presidential and legislative elections in 1989, where the opposition secured victory. The smooth, peaceful changeover earned Chile international praise and cemented its reputation as a beacon of democratic governance in the region.

Economically, Chile implemented market-oriented reforms that drove significant growth and development. While not without criticism, its model demonstrated that consistent, pragmatic policies could yield extraordinary results. In comparison to nations struggling with stagnation or crisis after experimenting with heterodox solutions, Chile offered a compelling alternative. In fact, its commitment to trade liberalization, fiscal discipline, and global economic integration prompted many to reconsider their economic strategies.

Over the next two decades, under successive governments led by the center-left *Concertación* coalition and later the center-right *Alianza*, Chile transformed from a dictatorship with a struggling economy into a thriving democracy with a competitive global market. Few countries in the region had achieved such a harmonious blend of political stability and economic success. Chile's two-party system and disciplined legislative framework minimized political fragmentation, reducing the risk of dysfunction and gridlock. Meanwhile, its responsible economic management insulated it from the populist waves and financial crises that disrupted its neighbors, allowing for sustained growth, poverty reduction, and improved living standards.

By 2010, Chile's progress was internationally recognized when it joined the Organisation for Economic Co-operation and Development (OECD), marking its entry into the ranks of more developed economies. Shortly after, it consistently began ranking at the top of democracy indices in Latin America. Chile's pragmatic approach—balancing political consensus, economic openness, and social development—became a blueprint for emerging economies striving to combine growth with good governance.

By 2019, the year the "storm" erupted, Chile had consolidated its status as a model for new democracies and emerging economies alike, proving that sustained political stability and economic progress were not only achievable but mutually reinforcing. In no uncertain terms, Chile stood as an example of what was possible when institutions, governance, and markets aligned effectively.

However, the events that followed—the social outburst, the constitutional processes, and their aftermath—inevitably raised questions about whether the trade-offs were justified. While the protests exposed cracks in the system, they also served as a warning against discarding what had been one of the region's most successful frameworks for stability and growth. Rather than resolving Chile's core challenges, the upheaval deepened political polarization and economic uncertainty, undermining decades of progress.

Precisely because Chile was regarded as a model of success leading up to 2019, its trajectory offers a valuable case study. It provides key lessons on building strong institutions, fostering growth, and maintaining stability. At the same time, it serves as a stark warning about the risks of embracing rupturist narratives that offer easy fixes at the expense of proven solutions. Understanding the chain of events is thus crucial to assessing the consequences of dismantling pillars of stability and attempting to rebuild from scratch—a trade-off that, in Chile's case, ultimately proved not to be worth the cost.

This book analyzes the sequence of occurrences that both preceded and followed the 2019 crisis. The conclusion is clear: what Chile accomplished in the three decades before 2019 remains a remarkable achievement, deserving of recognition and praise. Yet what followed serves as a cautionary tale for new democracies and emerging economies, illustrating the dangers of abruptly attempting to tear down long-established systems and the risks of trying to push sweeping change without regard for historical evidence or institutional track records.

1.3 The Core Thesis

The core thesis of this book is that Chile's development model and institutional framework, while imperfect, were not as fundamentally flawed as portrayed during the height of the 2019 social outburst. Although legitimate grievances over inequality and exclusion existed, the dramatic characterization of Chile's system as a wholesale failure ignored decades of measurable progress in economic stability and democratic institution-building. The events surrounding and following 2019 reflected the influence of a heightened politicization and an overly critical narrative rather than a fair assessment of the system's strengths and weaknesses. This book aims to restore balance to a discussion often dominated by hyperbole, highlighting the achievements and challenges of Chile's development path.

A key component of this thesis is the recognition of the structural gains achieved under Chile's model. For decades, the country was a regional leader in governance and economic management, successfully combining political stability with sustained growth. However, this success also created expectations that outpaced the system's ability to adapt. While inequality and perceived unfairness became rallying points for protests, the data indicate that Chile made consistent progress in reducing poverty and improving social indicators over time. The issue was not the failure of the model itself but the growing disconnect between its achievements and the evolving demands of Chilean society.

The roots of the 2019 social outburst lie in a combination of structural and contextual factors. The increasing fragmentation of the political system, coupled with an increasingly disengaged electorate and eroded trust in institutions, created fertile ground for discontent. This structural disconnect was further exacerbated by economic anxieties stemming from previous financial crises, which exposed vulnerabilities in Chile's development model. At the same time, the ambition of a younger generation of leaders, many shaped by the student protests of 2006 and 2011—fueled demands for systemic change. These pressures, amplified by the structural reforms introduced under Michelle Bachelet's second administration, opened the door to a rupturist discourse that deeply resonated with the public.

This book challenges prevailing critiques that label Chile's development model and political system as inherently flawed. Many critics embraced the notion that "the model is the problem," advocating for sweeping political and economic reforms under the assumption that greater political openness would lead to a stronger democracy. However, this perspective often overlooks the unintended risks of dismantling structures that had provided decades of stability and progress. Rather than dismissing the need for reform, this book argues that change should be pragmatic and incremental, leveraging the strengths of the existing system rather than undermining it.

The failure of the constitutional process that followed the initial political upheaval stemmed from its inability to connect with the median voter, who remained skeptical of both extremes of the political spectrum. The first constitutional process faltered due to ideological extremism, overreach, and an ambition reinforced by an admitted sense of moral superiority within the government and the generation that led it. This dynamic pushed the process too far to the left, alienating moderates who favored incremental, pragmatic changes over sweeping reforms.

In contrast, the second constitutional process failed because it did not move sufficiently toward the center. Although the proposal sought to correct some of the overreach of the first attempt, it remained rigid on divisive moral issues, such as abortion rights, which ultimately hindered consensus. Compounding these challenges was widespread "constitutional fatigue," as the electorate, weary of repeated reform efforts, dismissed the second draft as irrelevant to their immediate concerns.

A closer examination of both constitutional failures reveals a fundamental misdiagnosis of the public discontent. The notion that Chile's development model was inherently broken does not hold up against the evidence. If the model had been the root cause of the crisis, voters would have eagerly embraced at least one of the proposed alternatives. Instead, their rejections reflect a broader realization: while Chile's system may have had its flaws, it was still preferable to plunging into deeper uncertainty. The electorate's decision underscored not that Chile's system was exceptional, but that it could be far worse—a sobering recalibration that tempered calls for sweeping transformation.

This conclusion offers a forward-looking perspective. Chile's experience highlights the need to balance the urgency of addressing societal demands with the imperative of maintaining stability. The rapid embrace of self-critical narratives by the political class and the upheavals of the 2019–2023 constitutional process underscore the risks posed by fragmented party systems, rupturist discourse, ideological overreach, and extended and the failure to retreat in time. Chile's experience serves as a compelling example that to achieve long-term reform, stability, representation, and consensus are as important as the alignment between the ambitions of the elite and the priorities of the citizen.

1.4 Outline of the Book

Chapter 2 examines the origins, structure, and enduring impact of Chile's 1980 Constitution, drafted under the military regime of Augusto Pinochet in the aftermath of the 1973 coup. It explores how the Constitution was shaped by two priorities: consolidating centralized authority to ensure political stability and embedding neoliberal principles such as privatization and minimal state intervention to guide economic policy. The chapter details how the drafting process, led by Jaime Guzmán and influenced by the *Chicago Boys*' market-driven ideas, produced a framework designed to institutionalize these priorities and extend their influence beyond the dictatorship.

The chapter highlights how the 1980 Constitution pursued these objectives through a combination of centralized governance and economic liberalization. Politically, it concentrated power in the executive branch, curtailed the role of Congress, and formalized military oversight to safeguard stability. Economically, it codified a neoliberal framework by privatizing key social services, strengthening protections for private property, and emphasizing deregulation. This integration of authoritarian governance with market-oriented policies sought to create long-term order and economic growth in a country previously marked by instability and turmoil.

The chapter concludes by tracing the origins of key criticisms against the Constitution, which, while not widely prominent at the outset, later evolved into major points of contention. It argues that, from an early stage, critics shifted their focus away from assessing the Constitution's performance and instead targeted two foundational flaws: its lack of democratic legitimacy and its rigidity. The legitimacy critique highlighted the Constitution's authoritarian origins, while the rigidity critique underscored procedural barriers to reform. The discussion provides a framework for understanding the validity of these concerns and their role in shaping the greater push for constitutional overhaul.

Chapter 3 establishes a working definition of neoliberalism and examines its role as the foundational framework of Chile's 1980 Constitution and subsequent economic reforms. It defines neoliberalism as a market-oriented model that prioritizes privatization, deregulation, and minimal state intervention, emphasizing its implementation by the *Chicago Boys* under the Pinochet regime. The chapter focuses on three key sectors—pensions, healthcare, and education—to illustrate how these principles were embedded in Chile's institutional design, transforming traditionally public domains into systems shaped by competition and individual choice.

The chapter demonstrates how neoliberalism reshaped these sectors in significant and lasting ways. In pensions, a privatized, individual capitalization model replaced the previous state-managed system. In healthcare, a dual structure emerged, dividing service provision between public and private insurers. In education, a voucher-based model decentralized funding and expanded parental choice. These reforms marked a departure from state-led development and introduced a new governance logic. While they addressed certain inefficiencies and allowed for institutional innovation, they also generated persistent concerns over equity, access, and long-term outcomes—making them recurrent sites of public debate.

The chapter concludes that although neoliberalism has been subject to sustained criticism, especially in moments of heightened political pressure, its institutional foundations largely endured. In the cases of pensions and healthcare, reforms conducted as late as 2025 ultimately reinforced core aspects of the existing systems. Education, by contrast, underwent more substantial changes, yet with mixed results that reopened debates about quality and structure. Rather than offering a definitive endorsement or rejection, the analysis highlights the model's adaptability and continued relevance in shaping Chile's development.

Chapter 4 examines how the political and economic framework established by the 1980 Constitution functioned upon Chile's return to democracy, focusing on the period dominated by the *Concertación* coalition. Rather than dismantling the neoliberal model inherited from the dictatorship, successive social democratic governments worked to consolidate and deepen it. Under the leadership of Patricio Aylwin, Eduardo Frei Ruiz-Tagle, Ricardo Lagos, and Michelle Bachelet, the coalition balanced institutional rebuilding, economic governance, and democratic consolidation.

The chapter demonstrates that the *Concertación* administrations effectively managed and advanced the inherited economic model, achieving significant advances in poverty reduction, economic growth, international integration, and horizontal democratization. Aylwin prioritized political stability and human rights, while Frei Ruiz-Tagle positioned Chile as a regional leader. Lagos modernized the country, as Bachelet expanded social policies and inclusivity during her first term. However, by the end of the *Concertación*'s dominance in 2010, doubts regarding its position in reference to the neoliberal model began to emerge. These concerns stemmed primarily from political fractures within the coalition rather than from the grassroots, marking a critical turning point in Chile's post-transition political trajectory.

The key takeaway is that while the *Concertación* governments successfully navigated Chile's post-dictatorship period, early signs of fatigue within the model were evident by the late 2000s. The coalition's inability to adapt to evolving societal demands, coupled with increasing critiques from the left, opened the door for a deeper questioning of the constitutional, social and economic framework. This marked the beginning of a shift: from this point forward, the 1980 Constitution became vulnerable to criticism, not only due to its rigidity but also as part of a political strategy by the left to regain power. These dynamics set the stage for the broader political narrative that would unfold in the years to come.

Chapter 5 explores the paradox at the core of Chile's economic trajectory: how a nation that excelled in key developmental metrics could be thrust into widespread unrest. It investigates the roots of this "paradox of progress" by analyzing metrics such as inequality, intergenerational mobility, and other commonplace progress indicators. By assessing Chile's achievements in the broader Latin American context, it highlights the strengths of the country's developmental model alongside the structural and societal tensions that fueled public discontent. It finishes by looking at the nature and origin of the critics and their criticism, evaluating their incentives and their arguments.

While the dominant narrative attributes the unrest to entrenched inequality and the failures of neoliberalism, this chapter challenges these assumptions. Decades of decreasing income inequality, increasing upward mobility, and declining poverty rates contradict the notion that inequality had been worsening or that the model had fundamentally failed. Instead, this chapter suggests that the widespread adoption of this critique represents a politically convenient narrative advanced by political elites. It contends that Chileans' frustrations were not necessarily rooted in outright rejection of the model but can be better understood through complementary factors that align more closely with the observed data.

The chapter concludes by proposing moderating explanations for the unrest in the country, emphasizing the interplay of systemic financial vulnerabilities, entrenched perceptions of *desigualdad de trato* ("unfair treatment" or "inequality of treatment"), and frustrations with the distribution and pace of the model's benefits. It reframes the critique of capitalism, suggesting that the issue is not the system itself but rather its perceived inability to equitably meet citizens' expectations. These factors—presented as complementary rather than mutually exclusive—highlight the importance of adopting a nuanced approach to understanding Chile's social challenges. By revisiting the data and reframing the debate, the chapter lays the foundation for understanding the argument in favor of abandoning Chile's developmental framework.

Chapter 6 shifts focus to examine the political context leading to Chile's 2019 social outburst, analyzing the evolution of the party system through a historical and longitudinal perspective. Beginning with an overview of Chile's political cycles since 1833, the chapter zooms in on the fifth political cycle, which it proposes begins with the return to democracy in 1990. Drawing on a novel study that employs the effective number of parties (ENP) index and a dataset cataloging every party that ever competed in a major district-level election in Chile, it offers a fresh understanding of the party system's development, challenging conventional views that until this point have obscured its true trajectory.

In this vein, the chapter introduces three novel ideas that enhance understanding of the structural landscape leading to the social outburst. First, it contends that the party system was already undergoing significant fragmentation by 2010, at least five years earlier than previously established, with this trend only intensifying in subsequent years. Second, it demonstrates that the political system experienced a distinct leftward shift during this period, as more new parties emerged on the left than on the right, creating an imbalance that favored progressive ideas in the lead-up to the 2019 events and their aftermath. Third, it highlights the asymmetric evolution of the party system, with fragmentation occurring primarily among left-wing parties and polarization intensifying within the right. This asymmetry weakened the conservative sector's ability to counter the advance of its opposition effectively.

The key takeaway of this chapter is that even minor institutional reforms can have substantial consequences for political stability. The reforms of the early 2000s, although seemingly incremental, significantly lowered barriers in the context of a repressed multiparty system. By the late 2010s, Chile's party system had become so fragmented that it could no longer effectively absorb or mediate societal tensions. This fragmentation led to a proliferation of parties offering rapid solutions to an ever-increasing range of demands, thereby creating an unstable political landscape. Ultimately, the chapter argues, this rapidly shifting party system left Chile's political institutions vulnerable to instability, paving the way for the social and political crisis that erupted in 2019.

Chapter 7 builds on the previous discussion by examining the state of Chilean democracy in the post-transition years, particularly focusing on the erosion of voter–party linkages. Shifting the lens from parties to voters, it explores the evolving nature of political attitudes, engagement, and trust in institutions. The chapter highlights how the 2011 electoral reform, which introduced voluntary voting, not only exposed but also intensified the deepening disconnect between voters and parties. By analyzing long-term trends in voter disengagement, declining turnout, and collapsing trust in political institutions, the chapter explains how these dynamics eroded the democratic foundation and heightened the fragility of Chile's political system.

The chapter examines three key processes that illustrate the erosion of voter–party linkages in the years preceding the social outburst. The first process was the steady decline in electoral participation, with voter turnout dropping to historic lows as citizens increasingly withdrew from the formal democratic process. The second was the collapse of trust in parties, which became hollow institutions disconnected from their constituencies and unable to effectively respond to societal demands. The third was the rise of "ghost" parties and "zombie" party members, reflecting a political system increasingly functioning as a vehicle for elite ambitions rather than genuine representation.

This chapter's significance lies in its introduction of the concept of representation backsliding, which describes the intertwined processes of party system fragmentation and the erosion of voter–party linkages. While fragmentation allowed new actors to enter the system, the lack of genuine societal demand for many of these parties weakened Chilean democracy's representative capacity. This breakdown hollowed out the relationship between citizens and their representatives, creating fertile ground for radical discourse and destabilizing rhetoric. Ultimately, the chapter demonstrates how these dynamics played a crucial role in undermining Chile's political stability, setting the stage for subsequent crises of governance and representation.

Chapter 8 shifts focus from the structural factors discussed in the two previous chapters to the short-term determinants that catalyzed a transformative and rupturist discourse in Chilean politics. While the former chapters examine how party fragmentation and the erosion of voter–party linkages created structural vulnerabilities for instability, this chapter explores how these fractures coalesced into political and ideological momentum for change. It identifies critical moments when transformation ideas began to crystallize, analyzing how narratives gained traction through shifting rhetoric, emerging leadership, and political ambition. By narrowing the lens to short-term developments, the chapter demonstrates how the cumulative pressures of fragmentation and disengagement laid the groundwork for a rupturist narrative to take hold in the lead-up to the 2019 crisis.

The chapter highlights three interconnected turning points that fueled this transformative discourse. First, the internal divide within the *Concertación* coalition between *autoflagelantes*—who demanded radical reforms—and *autocomplacientes*, who defended gradualism, exposed the limits of incremental change. Second, Michelle Bachelet's second government (2014–2018) implemented a decisive program of structural reforms in education, taxation, and the electoral system, proving that systemic transformation was possible. Third, the rise of a younger generation of leaders, shaped by the 2006 and 2011 student protests, brought clarity of purpose and a readiness to challenge established norms. Figures such as Camila Vallejo, Giorgio Jackson, and Gabriel Boric rejected the compromises of the past and embraced an unapologetic vision for structural change, drawing a clear distinction between their agenda and the incrementalism of earlier generations.

This chapter's relevance lies in its explanation of how these forces—ambition, determination, and transformation—reshaped Chile's political narrative in the years leading up to the 2019 crisis. While previous chapters trace the structural cracks to Chile's political system, this chapter illustrates how short-term dynamics, including the rise of new leadership and shifts in political discourse, filled the void left by fragmentation and disengagement. Ultimately, the combination of these factors created fertile ground for a rupturist discourse to flourish. By the time the 2019 crisis erupted, the new and emboldened generation had already laid the ideological groundwork for change.

Chapter 9 recounts the explosive events of October 18, 2019, when a modest fare hike in Santiago's Metro system served as the immediate catalyst for a wave of protests that quickly escalated into a nationwide movement. It details how an act of fare evasion by high school students evolved into massive mobilizations driven by apparent deep-seated political grievances. The chapter traces the unfolding events, from peaceful daytime demonstrations to destructive nighttime violence, illustrating how protesters targeted both physical infrastructure and symbols of the state authority alike. Rather than representing the culmination of a single grievance, the protests embodied the convergence of multiple frustrations, none necessarily more significant than the other.

The chapter identifies two key elements that explain the transformative nature of the protests. First, the massive demonstrations symbolically delegitimized existing power structures by eroding public confidence in state institutions. The government became increasingly marginalized and was denounced in ways that rendered it incapable of effectively managing the crisis. Second, the protests and their aftermath created a point of no return, locking political actors and supporters into entrenched positions. For those aligned with the movement, demands for systemic change became non-negotiable. For detractors, opposing the unrest carried significant political and social costs. This polarization deepened the crisis, making it nearly impossible for decision-makers to retreat as the economic and human toll continued to mount.

The significance of this episode lies in how it marked a definitive rupture in Chile's political and social trajectory. The social outburst not only delegitimized traditional power structures but also fundamentally altered the political landscape, creating a vacuum of legitimacy and forcing a reckoning with the unsustainability of the status quo. At the same time, the protests amplified societal polarization, as political actors became increasingly entrenched in their stances. This dual effect—undermining existing power while solidifying divisions—ensured that the unrest would leave a lasting imprint on Chile's political process and profoundly influence the constitutional process that followed.

Chapter 10 explores how Chile's constitutional process emerged in response to the social unrest, reflecting both an institutional effort to manage this unrest and a societal demand for systemic transformation. The chapter examines how the *Acuerdo por la Paz Social y la Nueva Constitución* ("Agreement for Social Peace and a New Constitution") marked a critical turning point, where political elites attempted to channel widespread frustration into formal reform. It identifies two key developments: the overwhelming approval for a new constitution in the October 2020 plebiscite and the electoral upheaval in the May 2021 Constitutional Convention elections.

The chapter then delves into each of these critical developments. First, it argues that the October 2020 plebiscite signified a decisive break from the traditional order, as nearly 80% of voters supported drafting a new constitution, signaling a rejection of the Pinochet-era framework. Second, it argues that the May 2021 elections revealed a deep distrust of traditional parties, with independents and anti-system forces securing an unprecedented share of seats. This outcome was, in part, enabled by ad-hoc rules, such as lower barriers for party registration, gender parity, and reserved Indigenous seats, which all favored nontraditional actors. These factors combined effectively to amplify the electorate's demand for new voices and signaled a dramatic shift away from establishment politics.

The chapter's contribution lies in its portrayal of this moment as a decisive break that reshaped Chile's political balance. The results not only sidelined the political right but also empowered the left and anti-establishment forces, creating a fragmented and uncertain environment. The redistribution of power revealed both the depth of societal frustration and the challenges of building consensus for reform. While the process offered hope for renewal, it also highlighted the risks of instability, as dismantling the old order opened a door for untested actors to take the reins of Chile's political future.

Chapter 11 examines the pivotal intersection of the 2021 presidential election and the ongoing constitutional process, illustrating how Gabriel Boric's rise and his coalition's success reshaped Chile's political landscape. At its core, the chapter argues that the 2021 election presented Chileans with a critical choice: to embrace the radical change fueled by the social outburst or to preserve the continuity and stability of the established order. In selecting the former, voters not only rejected the legacy of traditional parties but also affirmed the dominance of the emergent far-left coalition, *Apruebo Dignidad*, led by the leftist Lower Chamber deputy Boric.

The chapter highlights how the constitutional process provided the backdrop to the presidential contest, intertwining institutional reform with the electoral debate. Boric's victory reflected the same forces that empowered independent and leftist voices in the May 2021 Constitutional Convention elections. His unexpected rise, especially his triumph over the Communist Party's Daniel Jadue in the primaries, positioned Boric as the serendipitous leader of a generational movement that combined grassroots momentum with institutional ambitions. This new discourse, radical in tone and transformative in scope, resonated with voters eager to break from an era they perceived as stagnant.

The primary contribution of this chapter lies in its analysis of how extremist rhetoric, legitimized through Boric's campaign and coalition, translated into institutional effects. The electoral victory of the far left symbolically decapitated Chile's traditional power structures while ushering in tangible political change. Boric's presidency, supported by a young and ideologically cohesive cabinet, sidelined the center-left and right, indicating a definitive rupture with past coalitions. This shift increased public expectations of the constitutional process while embedding the rhetoric of transformation into Chile's institutions. In choosing Boric, Chile embraced the instability and cost of radical change, preparing for a new and different but still uncertain political future.

Chapter 12 examines the formation, inner workings, and ideological trajectory of the 2021–2022 Constitutional Convention, a historic yet ultimately futile attempt to replace Chile's foundational charter. It describes the Convention's tumultuous inauguration, the structural and procedural rules that influenced its work, and the dominance of progressive and independent representatives in drafting the final proposal. It asses the rise and relevance of Elisa Loncon and Jaime Bassa. The chapter outlines how the Convention navigated internal challenges and political fragmentation throughout its tenure.

The chapter details how electoral rules influenced the composition of the Convention, resulting in a left-leaning majority, with over two-thirds of members aligning with progressive forces. This extreme coalition secured key leadership positions and adjusted procedural rules, enabling them to pass most articles with minimal opposition. The proposed constitution introduced 383 articles, including provisions for plurinational recognition, environmental protections, and expanded social rights, marking a sharp departure from Chile's constitutional tradition. The chapter also presents ideological maps and voting patterns, illustrating how the independent-left bloc dominated decision-making, while the fragmented right struggled to exert influence.

Finally, the chapter examines the evolution of public sentiment toward the process, demonstrating how initial optimism gave way to growing skepticism. Polling data from early 2022 indicated a sharp decline in support for the draft, with rejection surpassing approval about six months in. The chapter concludes by showing that the September 2022 plebiscite resulted in 62% of voters rejecting the proposal, marking the most significant electoral defeat of any constitutional project in Chilean history.

Chapter 13 analyzes the rejection of Chile's 2022 constitutional proposal in the national plebiscite and the political recalibration that followed. It explores the key factors behind the proposal's failure, focusing on both long-term ideological misalignment and short-term contextual challenges.

The chapter posits that the primary reason for the proposal's defeat was the ideological disconnect between the draft and the electorate's priorities. The proposed constitution introduced transformative provisions that aligned with progressive ideals but alienated moderates and those favoring incremental reform. Furthermore, it argues that several moderating variables deepened public skepticism, including leadership transitions within the Convention, heightened media scrutiny, perceptions of disorder, economic instability, rising crime, and growing distrust in the Boric administration. These factors eroded public support, ultimately leading to the proposal's resounding rejection.

While contextual challenges—such as economic instability, rising crime, and leadership transitions—did not determine the rejection, they exacerbated doubts at a critical moment. Taken together, these factors reinforce the idea of an elite misdiagnosis from the outset. The chapter's key takeaway is that successful constitutional reform requires moderation, broad-based consensus, and an approach that balances bold aspirations with societal pragmatism. The failure of the 2022 draft highlights the risks of ideological overreach.

Chapter 14 examines the political recalibration that followed the rejection of Chile's constitutional proposal in 2022 and focuses on the government's decision to initiate a second constitutional process under less favorable conditions. Despite the scale of the defeat, the Boric administration viewed continued reform as a political necessity and a democratic obligation, citing the plebiscite's mandate in 2020. This chapter explores the immediate fallout from rejection, strategic adjustments to regain public trust, and how negotiations between a weakened left and a resurgent right shaped the second constitutional effort.

The chapter describes key structural changes to address the shortcomings of the first process. These changes include the exclusion of independent candidates, the formation of a smaller and more disciplined Constitutional Council, and the establishment of committees to provide technical oversight. With the right controlling the terms of the process, electoral rules were redesigned to favor party-affiliated representatives, reduce fragmentation, and reinforce ideological cohesion. This chapter also examines the May 2023 Constitutional Council election in which right-wing parties surprisingly secured more than 56% of votes and 34 out of 50 seats.

The chapter underscores the influence of political pragmatism and compromise on Chile's second constitutional attempt and presents broader insights into the challenges of rebuilding public trust, balancing ideological divides, and sustaining momentum for reform in both fragmented and unstable landscapes. By analyzing shifts in political hegemony and voter sentiment, the chapter lays the groundwork to show that, no matter how meticulously institutional design is controlled, it remains impossible to predict outcomes in volatile political climates and shifting social conditions.

Chapter 15 examines how political ambition, governance failures, and a growing disconnect between leadership and public priorities shaped the period surrounding Chile's constitutional process. It traces how the political left, first as opposition and later as government, contributed to an environment of institutional fragility, economic anxiety, and social unrest. Rather than focusing on the constitutional process itself, the chapter explores how the broader deterioration of trust and state capacity of the time influenced the fate of reform and reshaped the greater political landscape.

The chapter argues that strategic decisions—both during the opposition's effort to delegitimize the previous administration and in the early part of the new government—amplified public disillusionment and undermined institutional credibility. Repeated impeachment attempts, inflationary pension withdrawals, and anti-police rhetoric created instability that the incoming administration was unable to contain. Once in power, symbolic gestures, ideological rigidity, and key missteps further distanced the government from public priorities. The result was not only the rejection of a constitutional proposal, but a deepened, albeit unacknowledged, crisis of governance.

The chapter shows how the overambitious push for structural reform ultimately backfired. Rather than rebuilding confidence or channeling demands for change, the effort exacerbated instability and exposed the disconnect between political leadership and the population. In trying to reshape the system without first addressing basic concerns like security, migration, and inflation, the left-leaning leadership undermined its own credibility and ultimately sank any hope of producing long-lasting change in their desired direction.

Chapter 16 analyzes the 2023 Constitutional Council as a disciplined and structured response to the failure of the first constitutional process. The chapter begins by explaining how a pre-drafted text by an Experts Committee, along with oversight by the Technical Admissions Committee, set a framework for predictability and moderation. The council, led by conservative Beatriz Hevia and social democrat Aldo Valle, operated under strict rules and a shortened timeline. In contrast to the 2021–2022 Convention, the chapter describes how this second iteration was more centralized and controlled.

The main findings focus on how the process produced legislative efficiency but revealed persistent political divisions. The Council's smaller size, lower quorum, and thematic committee system led to more consensus—over 80% of provisions were approved. However, internal tensions, particularly between the far-right Republican Party and the more moderate *Chile Vamos*, shaped key debates on judicial independence, social rights, and governance. Although the left was unified, it lacked the numbers to shape the draft and mostly acted in a defensive capacity. Despite these divisions, the process delivered a relatively coherent and moderate proposal that leaned toward conservative principles with centrist adjustments.

The key takeaway is that while the second constitutional process successfully addressed many organizational and procedural flaws of the first attempt, it failed to engage or inspire the broader public. The chapter describes how the December 2023 plebiscite resulted in a 56% rejection, not only because of ideological backlash but also widespread apathy and a sense that the process had disconnected from voters' pressing concerns. Ultimately, it underscores that no matter how efficient or well-structured a constitutional process may be, it cannot succeed without public trust and elite alignment.

Chapter 17 turns to examine the failure of Chile's second constitutional proposal. It provides an analysis of the process leading to the December 2023 referendum, detailing how this second draft, despite being more orderly and institutionally stable, failed to secure key societal rights and reassure an increasingly skeptical electorate. The chapter explores the ideological shift from the overtly progressive first draft to a more conservative second proposal and considers how ambiguities surrounding issues such as abortion contributed to its rejection.

In particular, it argues that three key factors underpinned the proposal's failure. The first is that because the draft failed to safeguard established societal gains, it created uncertainty about whether the proposal was rolling back on cornerstone policy. While intended as a moderate alternative to the first proposal, it retained enough elements of partisan rigidity to make it vulnerable to the opposition's campaign. This allowed critics to frame it as a step backward, contributing to its rejection by 56% of voters—a narrower margin than the first plebiscite but still a decisive outcome. The second key factor was the backdrop of *constitutional fatigue* and shifting voter calculations. After four years of political debates, economic struggles, and rising crime, many Chileans had grown disillusioned with the entire reform process. Third, a *trade-off mindset* had taken hold. The second referendum forced voters to decide whether constitutional change was worth the risk at all, and in such a position, faced with the dilemma, the majority decided to end the process entirely.

The chapter ends by highlighting the uniqueness of the experience and the limitations of conducting institutional reform under unstable conditions. It describes the reasoning of the Boric administration to shelve the constitutional question, much like President Piñera did in early 2018, and move on to more pressing issues. It then circles back briefly to the original sin, the elite misdiagnosis, highlighting the underlying irony of the failure. Finally, it argues that, in retrospect, it is likely that a minimalist proposal—one ideologically void and focused on simple yet broad concepts, might have succeeded where both ambitious proposals failed.

Chapter 18 provides a stand-alone summary of Chile's four-year constitutional journey, framed around the first two questions posted above: how could a country long praised for its democratic stability descend into mass unrest? And if constitutional change was the proposed solution, how can the rejection of not one, but two new drafts be understood?

The first part of the chapter examines the slow erosion of Chile's political system—a fragmenting party system, deteriorating linkages, and a declining trust in institutions—left the country increasingly incapable of mediating social demands; and how contextual shifts, such as the rise of a rupturist discourse, transformed discontent into a demand for foundational change. The second part turns to the constitutional process itself, showing how both conventions failed: the first by overreaching ideologically, and the second by arriving too late to restore legitimacy.

The core argument of this chapter is that Chile's crisis was not about a society rejecting reform, but about a political system no longer capable of delivering it. Both constitutional drafts failed not simply because of their contents, but because the broader process had lost credibility, as the country began to spiral. They had converted what had once been seen as a historic opportunity for renewalin to exhaustion and then resignation.

Chapter 19 concludes with the third, outstanding question presented above: was the social upheaval, political turmoil, and economic uncertainty that followed the 2019 outburst ultimately worth it? Through the lens of the Theseus Paradox, it assesses whether the country ultimately changed or remained the same, proposing that if Chile was truly transformed, then the journey may very well be justified. But if not, then costs may instead outweigh the benefits.

To examine this more philosophical question, the chapter traces what remained and what changed after four years of upheaval. The first half focuses on institutional outcomes. While the Constitution itself remained intact after two failed referendums, a crucial procedural shift occurred:

amendment quorums were lowered, introducing greater flexibility into an otherwise rigid system. This may be enough to break even. In turn, the second half turns to social sentiment. Chileans who once demanded rupture began to reassess the value of what had been done before.

The main takeaway is that Chile both changed and stayed the same. It did not adopt a new constitution, but it returned from the journey with a new outlook: more cautious, more discerning, and arguably more appreciative of its own past. The process reaffirmed the difficulty of transformation without institutional cohesion or public trust. For other nations contemplating deep reform in unstable conditions, Chile's experience serves as both a lesson and a warning: change is not always progress, reform does not guarantee success, and things can, in fact, always get worse.

Part I: Model

CHAPTER 2

The 1980 Constitution

2.1 Introduction

The Chilean 1980 Constitution—often described as one of the most rigid and controversial constitutions in modern Latin America—was written during a period of intense political and economic upheaval. Drafted in the aftermath of the 1973 military coup that overthrew President Salvador Allende's government, the constitution reflected the military regime's dual priorities: restoring political stability through a "protected democracy" and embedding free-market principles as the foundation of Chile's governance. Under General Augusto Pinochet, the military dictatorship sought to consolidate its authority while establishing an enduring institutional framework that would prevent a return to the fragmentation and ideological polarization of the Allende years.[1]

[1] For a foundational account of the political fragmentation and ideological polarization of the Allende years, see Arturo Valenzuela, *The Breakdown of Democratic Regimes: Chile* (1978, Baltimore, MD: The Johns Hopkins University Press), which portrays a democracy increasingly strained by the disintegration of the centrist coalition, deepening societal polarization, and the politicization of traditionally neutral institutions. See also Bernardino Bravo Lira, *Régimen de gobierno y partidos políticos en Chile, 1924–1973* (1986, Santiago: Jurídica de Chile), who highlights how the decline of traditional, negotiation-based parties and the rise of ideologically driven ones in the 1960s contributed to a rigid party-statism that ultimately overwhelmed Chile's institutional framework.

K. Bunker, *Chile's Transformation Amidst Crisis*,
https://doi.org/10.1007/978-3-031-96463-3_2

The origins of the 1980 Constitution must be understood in the context of the breakdown of Chile's democratic tradition and the regime's desire to impose a stable and efficient system.[2] Allende's government, as the first Marxist administration elected in a Western democracy, introduced transformative reforms—such as the nationalization of key industries and land redistribution—which, while ambitious, also deepened social and political divisions. Severe economic challenges, including hyperinflation and shortages, combined with escalating political unrest, created conditions that enabled the military to seize power.

Once in control, the *Junta* dismantled democratic institutions, banned political parties, and concentrated authority in the executive. However, its ambitions extended beyond seizing power. Under the guidance of Jaime Guzmán and the *Chicago Boys*, the regime viewed the creation of a new constitution as essential to securing long-term stability and institutionalizing the subsidiary role of the state. In their view, the new constitution needed to prioritize privatization, deregulation, and protect private property while embedding structural safeguards, such as military oversight and high reform thresholds, to insulate its fundamental principles from future changes.

This chapter provides a basic understanding of the 1980 Constitution, focusing on its architects, key political and economic objectives, and its departure from the 1925 Constitution. It does not aim to offer a comprehensive account of a complex historical process, but rather to provide enough context to understand developments that would unfold decades later. In this effort, it explores how the framework designed to stabilize Chile also planted seeds of future tensions, as its authoritarian origins and rigidity became an easy target for the organized opposition. Ultimately, this chapter sets the stage for understanding how the Constitution's setup was linked to the frustrations that, in different ways, surfaced during the 2019 protests and opened space for calls for constitutional change.

[2] Readers should note that although the Constitution was officially enacted in 1980 under military rule, it underwent multiple reforms throughout the 1980s, most notably the 1989 reform package approved by plebiscite, which amended over 50 articles to strengthen civil liberties and make the charter more acceptable for democratic transition, before becoming the governing constitution of restored democracy in 1990.

2.2 The Making of a "Protected Democracy"

The drafting of the 1980 Constitution was a highly controlled and carefully orchestrated process, designed by the military regime to ensure that its principles would endure well beyond the dictatorship itself. This was not an ordinary constitutional exercise but rather an effort to institutionalize a "protected democracy"—a framework that would maintain governance with stability and order while limiting the scope of popular participation. Some have described it as a recipe for a *democracia semisoberana* (lit. "semi-sovereign democracy"), as it sought to establish institutional safeguards against the economic and political instability that had characterized the Allende years.[3]

At the heart of this process was Jaime Guzmán, a young lawyer, conservative theorist, and close confidant of Pinochet, who served as the chief architect of the document. Drawing from corporatist and authoritarian traditions in European political thought, Guzmán envisioned a constitution that would stabilize Chile by preserving the regime's accomplishments while limiting democratic participation. In his view, governance required order and predictability, which could only be secured by curbing popular politics and concentrating decision-making power in a strong executive. Thus, the Constitution was designed to guide society "from above," shielding it from disruptive political forces.

The drafting process unfolded through a series of controlled commissions, beginning with the *Comisión Ortúzar*, established in 1973 and chaired by Enrique Ortúzar. Composed of legal experts sympathetic to the regime, the commission's task was to produce a document aligned with the *Junta*'s political and economic objectives. This initial draft was subsequently refined by a smaller group of handpicked advisors, including Guzmán, who ensured that key provisions would be resilient to future political changes. At no point was there an effort to include broader public input or consult opposition groups. This exclusion was deliberate, as the regime viewed consensus-building as a threat to its authority and long-term vision.

The economic model embedded in the Constitution (detailed in Chapter 3) was heavily influenced by the *Chicago Boys*, a group of

[3] For more on the origin of this concept and the safeguards imposed by the 1980 Constitution, see: Huneeus, C. 2014. *La democracia semisoberana: Chile después de Pinochet*. Santiago: Taurus.

Chilean economists trained under Milton Friedman at the University of Chicago. Their proposals emphasized neoliberal principles such as privatization, deregulation, and fiscal discipline. Guzmán and the *Chicago Boys* understood that for these reforms to endure, they needed to be enshrined in the constitutional framework, effectively shielding them from reversal by future governments. By codifying the subsidiary role of the state, the Constitution ensured that government intervention would occur only when private actors were incapable of meeting societal needs, thereby prioritizing market-oriented solutions in sectors such as pensions, education, and healthcare.

To solidify these changes, the Pinochet regime sought to legitimize the Constitution through a national plebiscite in 1980.[4] However, the conditions under which this vote took place severely undermined its credibility. Voter registration was limited, media access for opposition voices was restricted, and the visible presence of the military at polling stations created an atmosphere of coercion. Despite these irregularities, the regime declared an overwhelming victory, using the plebiscite as evidence of popular approval.

While the 1980 Constitution successfully institutionalized the regime's political and economic vision, it introduced a rigidity that became increasingly contentious in later years. Notably, mechanisms designed to protect the Constitution from significant reform stood out. These included supermajority requirements for constitutional amendments and the establishment of institutions such as the *Consejo de Seguridad Nacional* ("National Security Council"), which ensured military oversight of civilian governance.

By the late 1980s, as Chile transitioned toward democracy, revisions were introduced to address governance and legitimacy concerns.[5]The

[4] For a detailed account of the origins and consequences of the 1980 constitutional process—widely regarded as illegitimate due to its lack of transparency, absence of electoral safeguards, and tight control by the military regime—see: Cavallo, A., O. Sepúlveda, and M. Salazar. 1988. *La historia oculta del régimen militar: Chile 1973–1988*. Santiago: Uqbar Editores. See also: Fuentes, C. 2013. *El fraude: Crónica sobre el plebiscito de la Constitución de 1980*. Santiago: Hueders.

[5] This defining feature of Chile's transition—marked by mutual recognition between the military regime and the democratic opposition that a negotiated exit was necessary—makes it one of the clearest examples of a transición pactada in Latin America. The tradeoff was explicit: the opposition accepted key institutional safeguards for the outgoing regime, such as Pinochet's appointment as a senador vitalicio and the preservation of the 1978 Amnesty

1989 referendum amended aspects of the Constitution, including rebalancing executive powers and modifying some of its more controversial provisions. However, these reforms were carefully calibrated to preserve the essence of the original text, ensuring that the military's influence and the economic principles it enshrined remained largely intact. For instance, during this period, reforms were introduced to regulate legislative elections, including *senadores designados* (lit "designated senators") and the adoption of the unique *sistema binominal* (lit. "binomial system").

2.3 Balancing Stability and Economic Order

The 1980 Constitution was designed to achieve a dual purpose: to safeguard Chile's democratic system by providing a framework of political stability and to establish a lasting foundation for economic modernization.

As outlined above, these two objectives—political stability and economic liberalization—were pursued through measures that concentrated authority in the executive, formalized a clear separation of powers, and embedded structural protections to limit the risks of instability and populism. At the same time, the Constitution *Constitution* institutionalized a subsidiary role for the state, prioritizing privatization, deregulation, and protections for private property, which the regime viewed as essential for long-term economic prosperity.

2.3.1 Protected Democracy

At the political level, the Constitution sought to address the governance challenges that had plagued Chile in the years preceding the military government. The final years of the Allende administration had been characterized by legislative gridlock, political polarization, and economic crisis, creating an environment of instability that ultimately led to the collapse of the democratic system in 1973. To prevent a resurgence of such turmoil, the Constitution concentrated power in the executive branch, establishing the presidency as the central authority in Chilean governance. The president was granted extensive powers, including the ability to appoint and remove ministers, dissolve Congress under specific

Law, in exchange for constitutional reforms and an agreed path toward democratic elections. See: Godoy, O. 1999. "La transición chilena a la democracia: pactada." *Revista de Estudios Públicos* 15: 79–106.

circumstances, and rule by decree in exceptional cases. The design reflected a desire for a streamlined and effective decision-making process, ensuring that political deadlock would not impede governance or threaten stability.

In tandem with the strengthening of the executive, the Constitution redefined the role of Congress to align with its vision of stability. Legislative powers were restricted, particularly in matters of public finance and taxation, which were reserved for the executive. This limitation not only reinforced the president's authority but also insulated fiscal and economic policy from excessive political interference.

The judiciary, while formally independent, was similarly aligned with the principles of order and stability. Judicial appointments remained under executive influence, ensuring that the courts operated within the framework established by the Constitution and did not become a source of political confrontation. Collectively, these measures were framed as necessary corrections to the perceived weaknesses of Chile's previous system, which had struggled to manage divisions and conflict in earlier decades.

A key feature of the Constitution's political design was the inclusion of structural protections aimed at safeguarding the democratic system while ensuring a gradual and stable transition. Central to this effort were mechanisms that prevented any single political force from gaining undue dominance. For instance, the introduction of designated senators allowed for the appointment of nonelected members to the Senate, many of whom represented institutional actors such as the military or conservative political factions.[6] This provision was intended to create a stabilizing influence

[6] Article 45 of the Constitution held that, in addition to the 38 elected senators, the Senate would include nine designated senators, appointed by various institutions: the Supreme Court was to name two former justices and a former Comptroller General; the National Security Council appointed former commanders-in-chief of the Army, Navy, Air Force, and a former Director General of *Carabineros*; and the President of the Republic selected a former state university rector and a former minister of state. The Senate also included *senadores vitalicios* (lit. "lifetime senators"), consisting of former presidents who had completed a full six-year term. Augusto Pinochet himself became a designated senator on March 11, 1998—just one day after stepping down as Commander-in-Chief of the Army. He held the position until July 4, 2002, when he resigned citing health reasons, under mounting legal and public pressure both domestically and internationally. The only other former president to assume a lifetime seat was Eduardo Frei Ruiz-Tagle, who joined the Senate ten days after leaving office on March 21, 2000, and served until 2006, when the position was formally abolished through constitutional reform (see Chapter 4).

within Congress, ensuring that legislative outcomes reflected a balance of perspectives rather than being shaped by transient majorities.

The Constitution also established high legislative quorums for constitutional amendments, requiring a broad consensus for significant changes. This measure aimed to protect the foundational principles of the Constitution from being overturned by narrow political coalitions, ensuring that any reform would require widespread political agreement. By embedding this safeguard, the designers sought to create a layer of stability that would endure beyond the transition to civilian rule.[7]

The binomial system further reinforced the principles of balance and stability. By favoring the two largest political coalitions, the system's designer sought to encourage cooperation and moderation, reducing the likelihood of fragmentation and extreme political outcomes. While this system was meant to limit the representation of smaller parties, it was designed to promote stability by ensuring that governance reflected broad, centrist agreements rather than the ideological divisions of the past.[8]

[7] Article 118 of the Constitution established special quorum rules for certain constitutional reforms. Amendments that sought to modify rules on plebiscites, reduce presidential powers, or expand congressional authority required the agreement of the President and a two-thirds majority in both chambers. Reforms to Chapters I, VII, X, XI, and XV also required a two-thirds majority. Other constitutional chapters, such as those regulating Congress or the judiciary, could be amended with a three-fifths majority. Additionally, the enactment or modification of leyes orgánicas constitucionales (LOCs)— which governed areas such as elections, political parties, education, and the Armed Forces—originally required a three-fifths majority. This was significantly revised in the 2005 constitutional reform (see Chapter 4): among other changes, the quorum for most LOCs was lowered from three-fifths to four-sevenths, while the quorum for certain core areas—such as the foundations of institutional order, fundamental rights and duties, the Constitutional Court, the National Security Council, and constitutional amendments—was raised from three-fifths to two-thirds.

[8] Article 43 of the Constitution established that the Chamber of Deputies would be composed of 120 members, elected in districts defined by a corresponding LOC. Article 45 applied the same principle to the Senate, stipulating that each region of the country would elect two senators, also according to rules set by an LOC. In the 2005 constitutional reform, all detailed provisions regarding electoral districts and seat allocation were removed from the constitutional text and placed into LOCs, thus reducing the formal rigidity of those rules. Although the quorum for most LOCs was lowered from three-fifths to four-sevenths (as mentioned above), this specific case retained the three-fifths requirement—meaning it was no longer subject to the two-thirds quorum previously required for constitutional provisions, but also not included among those LOCs that could be modified with just four-sevenths. Ultimately, the binominal system was abolished

2.3.2 *Economic Liberalization*

Parallel to its political objective, the Constitution formalized a vision for Chile's economic future, grounded in the principles of the subsidiary state. Drawing on the ideas of the *Chicago Boys*, the document enshrined neoliberal economic policies that prioritized market efficiency, privatization, and the protection of private property. It established clear limits on state intervention, stipulating that the government would act only when private initiatives proved insufficient. This principle laid the foundation for the privatization of education, healthcare, and pensions, shifting responsibility for these services to private actors and significantly reducing the state's direct role in their provision. By embedding these economic principles into the constitutional framework, the architects sought to ensure that Chile's economic policies remained stable and resistant to short-term political pressures (which they did—see Chapter 5).

The protection of private property was another cornerstone of this economic vision. The Constitution included strong safeguards against expropriation, reflecting a commitment to fostering a secure and predictable environment for both domestic and foreign investment. This emphasis on property rights was seen as essential for promoting economic growth and modernization, aligning with the broader goals of stability and prosperity. While the specifics of these policies are explored further in Chapter 3, it is important to note that the constitutional framework significantly altered the course of Chile's economic trajectory.

by the 2015 electoral reform, which introduced a system of proportional representation (see Chapter 6). For a discussion regarding the political and strategic origins of the binomial system, see: Pastor, D. 2004. "Origins of the Chilean binominal election system." *Revista de Ciencia Política* 24(1): 38–57. For additional context regarding the institutional effects of the electoral rules, see: Alemán, E., and S. M. Saiegh. 2007. "Legislative preferences, political parties, and coalition unity in Chile." *Comparative Politics* 39(3): 253–272; Fontaine, A., C. Larroulet, J. Navarrete, and I. Walker. (Eds.). 2009. *Reforma al sistema electoral chileno.* Santiago: PNUD, CEP, Libertad y Desarrollo, ProyectAmérica, and Cieplan; Guzmán, E. 1993. "Reflexiones sobre el sistema binominal." *Estudios Públicos*, 51: 303–324; Huneeus, C. (Ed.). 2006. *La reforma al sistema binominal en Chile. Propuestas para el debate.* Santiago: Catalonia; Magar, E., M. R. Rosenblum, and D. Samuels. 1998. "On the absence of centripetal incentives in double-member districts: The case of Chile." *Comparative Political Studies* 31(6): 714–739; Nohlen, D. 2006. "La reforma del sistema binominal desde una perspectiva comparada." *Revista de Ciencia Política* 26(1): 191–202; Valenzuela, J. S. 2005. "¿Hay que eliminar el sistema binominal? Una propuesta alternativa." *Política* 45: 53–66.

2.4 Legitimacy, Rigidity, and Tension

While debates about the content of the 1980 Constitution certainly took place, critics often sidestepped substantive issues. Instead, they concentrated on two defining characteristics of the document: its legitimacy of origin and its legal rigidity. These critiques purposely avoided arguments about the Constitution's performance. The idea was that by shifting the focus from content to nature, critics could avoid divisive debates over whether the system was delivering results. This, in turn, would allow them to argue that the Constitution's very foundation rendered it inherently unsuitable for a democratic society. And, as such, the text needed to be replaced not because of the policies it enshrined, but because its setup precluded a fair and inclusive public debate about those policies in the first place.

Supporters of the Constitution viewed this approach as an unfair and implicit tactic. They argued that any evaluation should consider not the Constitution's origin and rigidity but instead the political stability and economic results it fostered (explored here in Chapters 4 and 5). Accordingly, they saw no need for major revisions; what mattered was that the Constitution functioned and delivered results.

2.4.1 *The Legitimacy of Origin Issue*

The major contention regarding the legitimacy of the 1980 Constitution stemmed from the circumstances of its creation. Critics argued that the document was conceived under a dictatorship, drafted by regime-appointed commissions without public input, and ratified through a flawed plebiscite. While these concerns were significant from the outset, they gained greater prominence over time as Chile transitioned to democracy and demands for a more inclusive and representative constitutional process intensified.

This critique rested on two main elements. First, the dictatorship under which the Constitution was created precluded any possibility of democratic participation in its drafting. By excluding opposition voices and bypassing societal consensus, the regime ensured that the document reflected its priorities rather than the collective will of the Chilean people. And second, the 1980 plebiscite, intended to confer legitimacy upon the Constitution, was widely regarded as fraudulent. Conducted under conditions of political repression, with restricted media access for opposition voices and a conspicuous military presence, the vote failed to meet basic democratic standards. Together, these two factors rendered the document a product of imposition rather than deliberation.

This line of argument proved particularly effective because it was grounded in historical facts rather than ideological disputes over the Constitution's content. By framing the issue as one of process rather than performance, in line with the reasoning laid out above, critics would be able to appeal to a broad audience, including those who might otherwise support the economic and political outcomes of the Constitution. The focus on legitimacy effectively shifted debates away from thematic provisions and toward the foundation of order.

2.4.2 *The Rigidity Issue*

Equally contentious was the rigidity of the 1980 Constitution, which was criticized for creating structural obstacles to meaningful reform. While this rigidity was intended to protect the document's foundational principles from abrupt political changes, it also led its critics to accuse it as a door stop for progress. They argued that from its inception, the Constitution embedded mechanisms that made amendments extremely difficult, only to ensure that its core features remained intact, even in the face of popular dissatisfaction.

The argument against rigidity was built on three primary elements. First, the requirement of supermajority quorums for constitutional amendments made it nearly impossible to enact substantial changes, even with broad political support. Second, the binomial electoral system reinforced political gridlock by favoring the two largest coalitions, thereby limiting the representation of small parties and reducing the scope of representation. And third, the inclusion of designated senators, many appointed by the military or conservative institutions, created an additional barrier to change by embedding unelected actors into the legislative process. Together, they argued, these elements insulated the Constitution from democratic scrutiny, fostering perceptions of institutional inertia and exclusion.

Like the legitimacy argument, the rigidity critique avoided ideological entanglements by focusing on procedural fairness rather than policy outcomes. By emphasizing structural barriers to reform, critics sidestepped debates regarding the performance of the framework and instead appealed to a shared frustration regarding the political system's inability to adapt in time and properly represent the people.

2.5 Conclusion

This chapter examined the origin, design, and long-term impact of the 1980 Constitution, highlighting its development in the aftermath of the 1973 coup under the control of the military regime of Augusto Pinochet. Very different from a traditional or consensus-driven legal document, the Constitution was crafted as a tool for institutionalizing the political and economic agenda of its designer.

While unique as a political document, the Constitution successfully laid the groundwork for Chile's political stability and economic development—outcomes that would fully materialize in the years following the democratic transition (as explored in Chapters 4 and 5). Nonetheless, the very features that enabled this success would also become the source of its eventual contestation. Nearly forty years after its debut, doubts about its authoritarian origin and its built-in resistance to change would come to the forefront of the political debate.

CHAPTER 3

Neoliberalism: Problem or Solution?

3.1 Introduction

This chapter examines the economic foundations of Chile's 1980 Constitution by focusing on its adoption of neoliberalism as a guiding framework and the evolution of this model over subsequent decades. This is particularly relevant, as neoliberalism has been considered both a driver of Chile's economic growth and stability, as well as a source of social tension—especially in key areas such as pensions, healthcare, and education. The 2019 social outburst (described in Chapter 9) brought these issues to the forefront, prompting widespread critiques of what would come to be known as "the model."

However, rather than being dismantled, neoliberal institutions would show remarkable resilience, with ups and downs, but evolving and consolidating over time. Even after the rise to power of its main ideological detractor (see Chapter 11) and aconstitutional processes that attempted to abolish it altogether (see Chapter 12), neoliberalism was not only able to endure, but ultimately become stronger.

The chapter begins by defining neoliberalism. It situates Chile's adoption of this framework within the broader global context of economic reform and compares its trajectory to that of other Latin American countries. The analysis then turns to three key sectors—pensions, healthcare, and education—where neoliberal principles were most profoundly applied. The discussion section, in turn, considers how, over time, public

K. Bunker, *Chile's Transformation Amidst Crisis*,
https://doi.org/10.1007/978-3-031-96463-3_3

dissatisfaction and reform efforts have led to adjustments rather than full-scale rejection of neoliberal principles. While critiques revealed important flaws—particularly related to equity, access, and regulation—the broader framework remained in place. The chapter reflects on these developments to raise broader questions about how market-driven systems evolve under pressure and how their legacies are assessed.

3.2 Neoliberalism as a Model

Neoliberalism is an economic framework that prioritizes free markets, privatization, and minimal state intervention, viewing these as the most effective mechanisms for driving economic efficiency and growth. While rooted in broader capitalist principles, neoliberalism represents a more radical interpretation, wherein market forces extend beyond traditional economic sectors to influence public governance and social policies.

Historically, neoliberalism emerged in response to the perceived failures of Keynesian economics and state-led development models in the mid-twentieth century. Proponents, such as Friedrich Hayek and Milton Friedman, argued that government intervention distorted market efficiency and led to economic stagnation. Instead, they advocated for deregulation, fiscal discipline, and a diminished public-sector role in favor of private enterprise.

These ideas gained traction in the late twentieth century, particularly in the United States and the United Kingdom, where Ronald Reagan and Margaret Thatcher championed policies emphasizing tax cuts, privatization, and deregulation. Chile, however, adopted these principles under unique circumstances (those described in Chapter 2), making it one of the earliest and most prominent case studies of neoliberalism in practice.[1]

[1] Many of the core ideas that would later define Chile's neoliberal transformation were formulated in *El Ladrillo*, a policy document whose drafting began in August 1972. Its principal authors included economists such as Andrés Sanfuentes, Juan Villarzú, and José Luis Zabala Ponce. Although the document was not yet finalized, substantial portions were presented to the military junta as early as the third week of September 1973, just days after the coup. This rapid delivery reflects how well-developed the neoliberal framework already was at the time. *El Ladrillo* proposed a sweeping restructuring of the Chilean economy based on trade liberalization, low and uniform tariffs, the elimination of price controls and subsidies, and the privatization of key sectors such as pensions, energy, and telecommunications. These principles would go on to form the ideological backbone of the economic policies implemented under the Pinochet regime. [This document, *El Ladrillo*, is available on the author's website.]

Neoliberalism's emphasis on reducing the state's role contrasts with mixed economic models, such as those in Western Europe, which balance capitalist markets with strong welfare protections. Within the neoliberal framework, individual responsibility and market competition take precedence over state intervention, which is limited to addressing market failures when necessary. This principle underpins neoliberal policies such as the privatization of public services, trade liberalization, and industry deregulation, all aimed at maximizing economic efficiency by fostering competition and reducing government influence.

Chile's adoption of neoliberalism was notably distinct in scope and consistency. Compared with neighboring countries such as Argentina, Brazil, and Peru, which experimented with heterodox economic strategies blending state intervention with elements of market liberalization, Chile pursued a more orthodox neoliberal trajectory.[2]

For example, Argentina's reliance on interventionist policies led to repeated bouts of hyperinflation and fiscal instability in the 1980s and 1990s. In contrast, Chile successfully controlled inflation, fostered sustained economic growth, and secured financial stability. Similarly, Brazil and Peru faced periods of stagnation and currency crises during their experiments with state-led approaches. Chile's consistent adherence to neoliberal principles distinguished the country within the region, positioning it as an early pioneer of the *Washington Consensus*, a framework that later codified these principles as essential for economic reform in developing nations.[3]

[2] Notable examples of heterodox experimentation include Argentina's short-lived *Austral*, Brazil's succession of the *Cruzeiro* and *Cruzado Novo*, and Peru's *Inti*—currencies adopted and later discarded in turbulent attempts to tame economic and political instability.

[3] John Williamson first introduced the concept of the "Washington Consensus" in 1990, outlining ten economic policy reforms he believed reflected the prevailing views of Washington-based institutions at the time. The term was meant to describe a pragmatic, technocratic agenda—not an ideological doctrine. See: Williamson, J. 1990. "What Washington Means by Policy Reform." In *Latin American Adjustment: How Much Has Happened?*, edited by J. Williamson, 5–20. Washington, DC: Institute for International Economics. In a later reflection, he responded to mounting criticism by emphasizing that the Consensus was not intended as a one-size-fits-all model and stressed that democratic legitimacy was essential for successful economic reform. See: Williamson, J. 1993. "Democracy and the 'Washington Consensus.'" *World Development* 21(8): 1329–1336.

The Pinochet regime's authoritarian nature facilitated the rapid adoption of neoliberal reforms that might have encountered significant resistance in a democratic context. Unlike democratic governments, where major policy changes require public debate and consensus-building, the Pinochet government leveraged its authority to enact sweeping economic transformations with minimal opposition. These included privatizing key industries, reforming the pension system, and liberalizing trade.

The adoption of neoliberalism in Chile both reflected and reinforced deep ideological divisions. Proponents, aligned with conservative sectors of society and supported by the political right and the *Chicago Boys* (economists trained at the University of Chicago), viewed market-oriented reforms as a remedy to the inefficiency and stagnation of the early 1970s. For them, liberalization promised modernization, financial stability, and integration into the global economy. In contrast, left-leaning movements rooted in Latin American protectionist traditions of the 1950s and later shaped by the ideological currents of the 1960s criticized neoliberalism for intensifying inequality and eroding systems of social protection. They instead advocated a statist developmental model that sought to expand citizens' rights through a robust welfare system, even if this required sustaining a high fiscal burden and economic insulation.

3.3 The Implementation of Neoliberalism

The implementation of neoliberalism in Chile under the Pinochet regime extended far beyond economic policy adjustments; it restructured the country's institutional foundations, embedding market-oriented principles into the 1980 Constitution, as discussed in Chapter 2. This marked a clear departure from earlier models that had prioritized state-led development and the public provision of services.[4]

[4] Readers should note that neoliberalism, both as a theoretical construct and as it developed in Chile, has been widely studied elsewhere. The objective here is to provide a limited contextual understanding, insofar as it relates to the 2019 crisis. For more detailed treatments, see for example David Harvey, *A Brief History of Neoliberalism* (Oxford University Press, 2005); Wendy Brown, *Undoing the Demos: Neoliberalism's Stealth Revolution* (Zone Books, 2015); Michel Foucault, *The Birth of Biopolitics: Lectures at the Collège de France, 1978–1979* (Palgrave Macmillan, 2008); and Simon Springer, Kean Birch, and Julie MacLeavy (eds.), *The Handbook of Neoliberalism* (Routledge, 2016). For scholarship on Chile, see for example Sebastián Edwards, *The Chile Project: The Story of the Chicago Boys and the Downfall of Neoliberalism* (Princeton University Press, 2024); Alfredo

Three key sectors—pensions, healthcare, and education—became central to this transformation. These areas not only reflected the ideological ambitions of the neoliberal agenda but also emerged as cornerstones of the ongoing public debate. The remainder of this section outlines how these sectors shifted from state-centered systems to market-oriented structures, detailing the main mechanisms introduced under the new framework.

3.3.1 Pensions: The Rise of the AFPs

The transformation of Chile's pension system in 1981 marked one of the most ambitious and controversial applications of neoliberal principles. Before the reform, the pension system operated on a pay-as-you-go structure, in which current workers' contributions were pooled to fund retirees' benefits, with variations depending on their employment sector. This system relied heavily on state oversight and redistribution, but by the late 1970s, it was increasingly criticized for inefficiency, fiscal unsustainability, and insufficient coverage.

The new framework replaced the state-managed system with a privatized, individual capitalization model, administered by private pension fund managers known as *Administradoras de Fondos de Pensiones* (AFPs, "Administrators of Pension Funds"). Under this model, workers were required to contribute a fixed percentage of their salaries to personal retirement accounts, which were then invested in financial markets. The underlying assumption was that private management and market competition would generate higher returns, reduce the state's fiscal burden, and create a more sustainable system.[5]

Joignant and Nicolás Somma (eds.), *Social Protest and Conflict in Radical Neoliberalism: Chile, 2008–2020* (Palgrave Macmillan, 2024); Patricio Silva, *In the Name of Reason: Technocrats and Politics in Chile* (Penn State University Press, 2008); and Modesto Gayo and María Luisa Méndez, *The Politics of the Elite: Ideological Orientations, Mothering, and Social Mobilities in Neoliberal Chile* (Routledge, 2023).

[5] The architect of the reform, José Piñera (brother of President Sebastián Piñera, and independent presidential candidate in 1993—see Appendix), recounts the ideological foundations and political circumstances under which the new pension system was implemented in his personal account. He envisioned the system as a cornerstone of economic freedom and individual responsibility, expecting it to not only depoliticize pensions but also foster higher returns and long-term savings through market discipline. See: Piñera, J. 1991. *El cascabel al gato*. Santiago: Zig-Zag.

By embedding the privatized pension model into the 1980 Constitution, the reforms effectively insulated it from political reversals.[6] Although the system faced ongoing criticism for low replacement rates and unequal outcomes—particularly for women, informal workers, and low-income earners—it continued to be regarded by some as a forward-looking model. Variants of Chile's pension structure were later adopted or studied by other countries seeking to reform unsustainable public systems. While it did not deliver the broad results originally projected, it remained a significant and influential policy shift.

3.3.2 Healthcare: A Two-System Solution

Healthcare in Chile underwent a similarly profound transformation under the neoliberal framework. Before the reforms, the system was predominantly state-managed, emphasizing universal access and equity. Public healthcare services were funded through general taxation and employer contributions, ensuring comprehensive coverage for all citizens. However, questions regarding quality, economic pressures, and inefficiencies in service delivery would eventually create momentum for reform.

The neoliberal restructuring introduced a dual system that combined public and private providers.[7] The public system, known as *Fondo Nacional de Salud* (FONASA, "National Health Fund"), continued to

[6] The evolution of Chile's pension system can be divided into three main phases: the structural reform (1981–2008), during which the privatized AFP model was consolidated; the re-reform period (2008–2015), marked by incremental adjustments aimed at expanding coverage and introducing solidarity-based mechanisms; and a third phase following the 2015 Presidential Commission, which produced a comprehensive set of reform proposals intended to address persistent shortcomings and guide future reforms. See: Mesa-Lago, C., and F. Bertranou. 2016. "Pension reforms in Chile and social security principles, 1981–2015." *International Social Security Review* 69(1): 25–45. A fourth phase can be identified following the 2019 social outburst, during which political and constitutional efforts sought to weaken or dismantle the AFP-based model; however, as discussed in Chapter 12 and 15, these initiatives ultimately failed to alter its core structure.

[7] Early research shows that Chile's health indicators rank among the best in Latin America and approach those of industrialized countries. This progress is often attributed to sustained government commitment to maternal and child healthcare since the 1950s, alongside improvements in education and sanitation. See a discussion of the system's evolution in: Manuel, A. 2002. "The Chilean health system: 20 years of reforms." *Salud Pública de México* 44(1): 60–68.

serve the majority of the population, while private health insurers, introduced as *Instituciones de Salud Previsional* (ISAPREs, "Health Provision Institutions"), catered to those who could afford higher premiums—primarily the upper and middle socioeconomic classes. This segmentation aimed to reduce the state's financial burden by encouraging those with greater resources to opt for private coverage, thereby fostering competition and improving service quality.

Over time, this segmented structure became even more unequal as access and service quality began polarizing. In any case, because of developments explained later in the book, it is clear that the private sector played an important role in expanding capacity and relieving pressure on the public system. While the original reforms did not fully resolve the challenges they aimed to address, they *were* able to establish a durable mixed model.

3.3.3 Education: The Subsidiary System

The education system in Chile followed a similar trajectory as it transformed into a decentralized model. Before the reforms, education was centrally managed by the state, with a primary focus on ensuring equal access and standardized quality. Public schools formed the foundation of the system, receiving direct funding and remaining accessible to all.

The introduction of a subsidiary system fundamentally altered this dynamic.[8] Under the new model, public funding was distributed among families in the form of vouchers that could be used to enroll children in either public or private schools. The goal of the model was to foster competition among schools, with market forces expected to drive improvements in quality and efficiency. Decentralization further shifted administrative control from the central government to municipalities, reducing the state's direct role in managing education.

The reforms expanded parental choice and led to a proliferation of private schools; however, as above, they also showed mixed results—at

[8] Before the reform, an estimated 80% of schools in Chile were public, with only 20% privately run. Research suggests that educational policies implemented between the early 1980s and late 1990s were, at the time, considered among the most radical pro-market and pro-choice reforms ever undertaken on a national scale. See: Cox, C., and M. J. Lemaitre. 1999. "Market and state principles of reform in Chilean education: policies and results." In *Chile: Recent Policy Lessons and Emerging Challenges*, edited by G. Perry and D. M. Leipziger, 149–188. Washington, DC: World Bank Publications.

least in principle, considering the difficulty of forecasting the counterfactual scenario. Wealthier families were better positioned to supplement vouchers with additional resources, thus gaining access to higher-quality private education. Meanwhile, public schools, particularly those in low-income areas, struggled with inadequate funding and declining enrollment. Nonetheless, the model persisted, as *colegios particular subvencionados* (lit. "mixed private-state schools") and *liceos tradicionales* (lit. "traditional public high-schools") were able to demonstrate strong academic outcomes over time.

3.3.4 Other Areas of Influence

Beyond pensions, healthcare, and education, neoliberal principles were extended to other sectors of Chilean public life as well. These reforms followed the same logic of privatization, deregulation, and limited state intervention, reshaping areas such as natural resources, infrastructure, and labor relations.

For example, water rights were privatized under the 1981 Water Code, which established a market for water use through tradable, permanent rights. While this framework encouraged investment and legal clarity, it also generated debate over access, ownership concentration, and environmental sustainability. Similarly, major infrastructure projects—particularly highways—were built through concession models that introduced user tolls and attracted private capital. In labor markets, reforms promoted flexibility and reduced the influence of collective bargaining, aiming to stimulate productivity and lower costs.

These changes extended the reach of market mechanisms into areas traditionally managed by the state. They brought investment and institutional innovation, but also sparked questions about long-term equity, regulation, and the balance between private interest and public need.

3.4 Reassessing the Neoliberal Model

Before closing, it is important to return to neoliberalism in hindsight, to underscore how difficult its evaluation has proven to be. To this end, it is useful to recall the phrase that propelled Gabriel Boric to global recognition during his 2021 presidential bid, after the 2019 crisis and before the 2022 constitutional referendum: "*Si Chile fue la cuna del neoliberalismo, también será su tumba*" ("If Chile was the cradle of neoliberalism, it will also be its grave")[9]. For many, it marked a historic turning point and a reckoning with privatization, deregulation, and the state's limited role. Its resonance may have even contributed to Boric's presidential bid and eventual victory, while also lending credibility to the constitutional process. Yet, in retrospect, a reassessment of neoliberalism suggests that the claim was not only overstated but ultimately misguided—neoliberalism was not dying but, in important respects, consolidating.[10]

Without delving into the details (both to respect the chronological underpinning of this account, and because it is told in more detail in upcoming chapters), it is important to say that the reform processes that followed unfolded unexpectedly. This is the case of the AFPs, for example, that had long been the subject of criticism, particularly for failing to ensure equitable retirement incomes for lower-income and informal workers. Yet, despite calls to replace the system outright, including during constitutional debates and in public campaigns,[11] what ultimately emerged was not dismantlement but consolidation.[12] The expansion

[9] After assuming the presidency, Boric was asked directly about the phrase and doubled down on it, even as he signaled a U-turn on several other issues. See: Nugent, C. 2022. "Transcript: Chilean President Gabriel Boric on Democracy, Climate Change, and Inequality." *TIME*. August 16. https://time.com/6209557/gabriel-boric-transcript/. By then, academic and policy debate had already underscored the difficulties of fully eradicating neoliberalism. See: Mellado, B. 2022. "¿Fin del neoliberalismo?: Expertos aseguran que en Chile "no están las condiciones para matarlo" y analizan su evolución." *Emol*. November 25. https://www.emol.com/noticias/Economia/2022/11/25/1079324/neoliberalismo.html/. Nonetheless, even five years after the social outburst, left-leaning intellectuals continued to insist on its persistence and transformation. See: Nogales, D. 2025. "Joseph Stiglitz critica la influencia de Milton Friedman en Chile y cita a Boric sobre "la tumba del neoliberalismo." *La Tercera*. July 22. https://www.latercera.com/pulso/noticia/joseph-stiglitz-critica-la-influencia-de-milton-friedman-en-chile-y-cita-a-boric-sobre-la-tumba-del-neoliberalismo/

[10] The remainder of this section discusses trends and outcomes that unfolded after the constitutional process. Readers who wish to avoid potential spoilers about later developments may prefer to skip ahead to the next chapter before continuing.

[11] See the countermovement #ConMiPlataNo, which emerged as a response of sorts to No + AFP within the framework of the constitutional process, aiming to preserve the integrity of the pension system. See: Román, C., and I. Guerra. 2021. "'Con mi plata no': Iniciativa para proteger ahorros previsionales superó las 15 mil firmas y se discutirá en la Convención." *Emol*. December 30. https://www.emol.com/noticias/Nacional/2021/12/30/1042630/iniciativa-ahorros-15000-firmas-convencion.html/

[12] By the end of the first constitutional process, the share of people supporting the private pillar of the pension system had increased to a historical maximum, while support for expanding the state-run scheme had dropped to a historical minimum. A poll

of the *Pilar Solidario* (lit. "Solidarity Pillar") and later the *Pensión Garantizada Universal* (lit. "Universally Guaranteed Pension") offered a complementary safety net, rather than a departure from the capitalization model.[13] Similarly, the COVID-19 era pension withdrawals (explained in Chapter 15), while highlighting gaps in the system's design, reinforced the perceived benefit of individual ownership of savings. In the end, it would ironically be President Boric who would "rescue" the AFP system by further expanding its participation in the pension pool.[14] Even if the

conducted in late 2022 showed that a clear majority preferred directing the proposed 6% increase in contributions to individual accounts rather than to a solidarity-based public fund—reflecting a marked shift in public attitudes amidst the ongoing constitutional debate. See: Gallardo, P. 2022. "Sondeo muestra preferencia para que el 6% de cotización adicional vaya a cuentas individuales." *El Mercurio*, November 2.

[13] David Bravo, director of the UC Center for Surveys and Longitudinal Studies, described the replacement of the Pilar Solidario with the Pensión Garantizada Universal (PGU) as "one of the most important reforms associated with President Piñera's second term." The reform, which expanded the state's role in guaranteeing a basic pension regardless of contribution history, marked a turning point in Chile's social protection architecture. See: Marusic, M. 2024. "Cómo se gestó la Pensión Garantizada Universal que impulsó Piñera y la valoración de los expertos." *La Tercera*. February 7. https://www.latercera.com/pulso-pm/noticia/como-se-gesto-la-pension-garantizada-universal-que-impulso-pinera-y-la-valoracion-de-los-expertos/EJBWM6RS2JEVFBGUSY5D2TUV4Q/

[14] While the reform passed under President Boric introduced a new employer-side contribution—broadening the scope of social security—it also significantly expanded the role of the AFPs, increasing private pension savings by an estimated 60%. This unexpected outcome was even praised by José Piñera, the architect of the original AFP system, who welcomed the reform as a major boost to the private model. See: González, A. 2025. "José Piñera celebra reforma previsional de Boric que expandió en 60% el modelo de ahorro privado." *Biobio Chile*. March 13. https://www.biobiochile.cl/noticias/nacional/chile/2025/03/13/jose-pinera-celebra-reforma-previsional-de-boric-que-expandio-en-60-el-modelo-de-ahorro-privado.shtml/. Before passing the reform, in early 2025, the Boric administration had been heavily criticized after proposing a pension model in which retirees would lend a portion of their savings to the state. See: *The Clinic*. 2024. "Encuesta Panel Ciudadano-UDD: 68% no está de acuerdo en prestarle al Estado parte de sus ahorros previsionales." October 10. https://www.theclinic.cl/2024/10/10/encuesta-panel-ciudadano-udd-68-no-esta-de-acuerdo-en-prestarle-sus-fondos-de-pension-al-estado/

original promise of high returns and self-sufficiency fell short, the structure proved durable, superior to that in neighboring countries, and for many, preferable to uncertain or failing alternatives.[15]

Healthcare followed a comparable pattern. The dual system—public FONASA and private ISAPREs—was also subject to heavy criticism for entrenching unequal access and quality. Proposals for a universal public system gained visibility but struggled to take hold. Part of the challenge stemmed from the limited scope of ISAPREs: only around 15% of the population were enrolled, and for the majority, the experience of healthcare remained defined by the public system.[16] As FONASA faced longer wait times and growing demand, the idea of folding ISAPRE users into the public system raised concerns about further overcrowding and diminished quality.[17] In this context, ISAPREs came to be seen less as the

[15] In 2020, Chile was found to have the strongest pension system in Latin America, according to the *Melbourne Mercer Global Pension Index*. See: *Deutsche Welle*. 2020. "Chile tiene el mejor sistema de pensiones de América Latina, según el índice global Melbourne Mercer." October 21. https://www.dw.com/es/chile-tiene-el-mejor-sistema-de-pensiones-de-am%C3%A9rica-latina-seg%C3%BAn-el-%C3%ADndice-global-melbourne-mercer/a-55338272/. This perceived relative strength helped reinforce support for the AFP model, especially when compared to the strained public systems in countries like Germany and Spain. The severity of these European challenges had already become clear by 2020, but the problems persisted even five years later—by which point Chile's own pension debate had already been settled. See: Ben Knight. 2025. "Will Germany Raise Retirement Age Beyond 67?" *Deutsche Welle*. August 1. https://www.dw.com/en/will-germany-raise-retirement-age-beyond-67/a-73472863/

[16] The share of the population enrolled in ISAPREs has fluctuated significantly over time, reflecting broader shifts in Chile's health system. In 1990, 17.1% of Chileans were covered by ISAPREs; this figure rose to a peak of 30.7% in 1997 before entering a gradual decline. By 2024, enrollment had dropped to a historic low of 14.6%. These shifts mirror changing perceptions of public versus private healthcare, as well as policy and market dynamics. See: *CNN Chile*. 2024. "Los sistemas de salud frente a frente: cómo ha variado la cantidad de usuarios de Isapres y Fonasa." July 20. https://data.cnnchile.com/salud/isapre-vs-fonasa-2/

[17] In 2023, Chile reached a grim milestone: the number of people who died while on public healthcare waiting lists hit its highest recorded level. In just the first four months of the year, over 10,000 individuals died awaiting medical attention—a stark indicator of systemic strain in the health sector. See: Canales, I. 2023. "Morir esperando: Minsal informa que más de 10 mil personas fallecieron estando en alguna lista de espera durante el primer cuatrimestre." *La Tercera*. July 12. https://www.latercera.com/nacional/noticia/morir-esperando-minsal-informa-que-mas-de-10-mil-personas-fallecieron-estando-en-alguna-lista-de-espera-durante-el-primer-cuatrimestre/KKFJB47S65DZLKVNPHPGX6XV2U/

root of the problem and more as a pressure valve for an overstretched public infrastructure. Notably, the Boric administration's surprising decision to support ISAPREs during a period of financial stress signaled a tacit recognition of their ongoing role in the system.[18] As with the AFPs, the broader structure endured with minor adjustments.

The case of education is more complex. Unlike pensions and healthcare, education had already undergone major reforms before the most recent period of political change. Under President Michelle Bachelet in 2014 (see Chapter 8), a series of laws sought to curb profit-making in private schools, expand public investment, and increase state oversight. These reforms were aimed at making the system more equitable and reducing the role of the market in determining educational access. However, the long-term results were mixed. Although the new framework addressed certain inequalities (in principle), performance indicators—such as standardized test scores—deteriorated over the following decade.[19] Iconic public institutions like the *Instituto Nacional* saw sharp declines in outcomes, and many families expressed growing concern over the declining quality of public education.[20] By contrast, subsidized private

[18] In 2024, President Boric urged Congress to pass a short-term rescue bill that would allow ISAPREs to repay their court-mandated debts over an extended period. Without this legislative lifeline, the private health insurance system faced imminent collapse—an outcome that would have forced FONASA to absorb the entire patient population virtually overnight. The government framed the measure as a necessary intervention to prevent systemic failure, while emphasizing its intent to avoid a blanket bailout. See: Aranda, A. 2024. "Presidente Boric destaca aprobación de la ley corta de Isapres y afirma que la postura del gobierno era evitar un 'perdonazo'." *La Tercera*. May 14. https://www.latercera.com/politica/noticia/presidente-boric-destaca-aprobacion-de-la-ley-corta-de-isapres-y-afirma-que-la-postura-del-gobierno-era-evitar-un-perdonazo/IXYZMFC2QFG6PMYSXA7KQS3FBU/

[19] In 2024, it was estimated that eighth-grade students had lost the equivalent of over a decade of progress in mathematics learning. According to the international TIMSS assessment, average test scores for Chilean 8th graders had regressed to levels not seen in 12 years—a dramatic setback attributed to the long-term impact of pandemic-era school closures and structural weaknesses in the education system. See: Leyton Ojeda, S. 2024. "Aprendizajes de escolares de 8° básico en matemáticas retrocedieron 12 años en Chile, dice Estudio TIMSS." *Chilevisión*. December 5. https://www.chilevision.cl/noticias/nacional/aprendizajes-escolares-matematicas-retrocedieron-doce-anos-estudio-timss/

[20] In 2024, the deep crisis in Chile's public education system was starkly reflected in the national PAES rankings: only one municipal (public) school made it into the top 100 schools with the highest standardized test scores. Of the remaining institutions, 98 were private and fee-paying, and just one was subsidized. The results highlighted not inequality, but the persistent failure of the public system to deliver competitive academic

schools, while not without flaws, continued to deliver comparatively stronger academic results. This raised questions about the long-term viability of the reformed model and whether dismantling the previous voucher-based approach had truly achieved its intended goals.

Taken together, the experiences across these three sectors illustrate the complexity of evaluating Chile's neoliberal legacy. In pensions and healthcare, the outcome was not the collapse or abandonment of market-oriented systems, but rather their consolidation. In education, efforts to reverse the perceived negative effects of privatization were notable, yet not only did they fail to yield improvements, in many cases they made the problems worse. If attempts at reform produced worse outcomes, and those most committed to its eradication proved unable to enact meaningful change once in power, then perhaps the issue lay less in the model itself than in the rhetoric surrounding it.

3.5 Conclusion

This chapter examined the role of neoliberalism in shaping Chile's economic and institutional foundations, particularly through its codification in the 1980 Constitution. By tracing the implementation of market-oriented reforms in key sectors—pensions, healthcare, and education—it explored how these principles were embedded into the state's structure and how they evolved in response to criticism over time. The chapter also considered whether public discontent and reform efforts in recent years signaled a fundamental rejection of neoliberalism or a more complex process of adjustment within its framework.

A working definition of neoliberalism was offered as a model based on privatization, deregulation, and limited state intervention, drawing a clear contrast with previous approaches rooted in state-led development. These principles were applied most directly in pensions, healthcare, and education, where they produced notable changes in access, structure, and delivery. Each sector illustrated how neoliberal logic reshaped institutional practices while also giving rise to persistent tensions and public scrutiny.

outcomes. See: Galvéz, R., and E. González. 2025. "Ranking de los 100 mejores colegios de la PAES: un municipal, un subvencionado y 98 particulares pagados." *La Tercera*. January 6. https://www.latercera.com/nacional/noticia/ranking-de-los-100-mejores-colegios-de-la-paes-un-municipal-un-subvencionado-y-98-particulares-pagados/VQKUADHIP5DFFNI2ZHKON74LPY/

As the chapter showed, however, the long-term trajectory of these reforms does not support a simple narrative of failure or rejection. In both pensions and healthcare, efforts to reform the system often resulted in its consolidation, with new mechanisms introduced to correct specific shortcomings without overturning the overall model. Education presented a more ambiguous situation, in which the shift away from market logics produced troubling outcomes, casting doubt on the effectiveness of alternative models.

To answer the question in the title: neoliberalism can be understood as either a problem or a solution, depending on one's perspective. Ultimately, the answer seems to be political, context dependent, and shaped by the timeframe one is willing to consider (as suggested in Chapter 5). What can be said of "the model" itself is that it was gradually refined and adjusted over time, demonstrating not only the perils of its dismantlement, but also its capacity to draw support from the most unlikely of places.

CHAPTER 4

Two Decades of Stability

4.1 Introduction

Chile's transition following the Pinochet dictatorship has been widely regarded as a success, characterized by political stability, sustained economic growth, and the peaceful consolidation of democratic institutions. Central to this achievement was the *Concertación* coalition, which governed Chile for two decades and guided the country through its post-authoritarian phase. This coalition oversaw significant progress, including the restoration of democratic governance, poverty reduction, and Chile's emergence as a regional economic leader. However, alongside these accomplishments, it preserved much of the neoliberal framework inherited from the dictatorship. While this approach initially ensured stability and economic credibility, it gradually exposed tensions between institutional continuity and the growing demands for social and economic reform.

This chapter explores how the *Concertación* governments navigated these challenges, focusing on the balance they struck between maintaining political stability and pursuing systemic reform. Each administration played a crucial role in shaping Chile's democratic trajectory: Patricio Aylwin prioritized rebuilding democratic institutions and addressing human rights violations; Eduardo Frei Ruiz-Tagle emphasized economic growth and global integration; Ricardo Lagos championed modernization and enacted significant constitutional reforms; and Michelle

K. Bunker, *Chile's Transformation Amidst Crisis*,
https://doi.org/10.1007/978-3-031-96463-3_4

Bachelet advanced social equity through targeted policies. Collectively, they strengthened Chile's global reputation and domestic governance structures, cementing the *Concertación*'s legacy as a stabilizing force.

However, by the late 2000s, cracks had emerged within the coalition's political and ideological foundation. The tensions between incremental progress and a growing demand for structural transformation led to rising elite dissatisfaction and internal divisions. Criticism from progressive factions and external leftist movements questioned the coalition's commitment to meaningful reform, ultimately contributing to its decline. This paved the way for Sebastián Piñera's victory in the 2009/2010 election, marking the end of the *Concertación* era and the beginning of a new phase in Chile's political landscape.

This chapter argues that while the *Concertación* succeeded in consolidating democracy and fostering economic growth, its failure to acknowledge its own contribution as well as its inhability to address internal political rifts ultimately weakened its position. By analyzing the coalition's rise and fall, the chapter offers critical insights into the evolution of Chile's political dynamics over two decades, highlighting the context that would ultimately lead the country toward the 2019 political and social crisis.

4.2 The Concertación: The Most Successful Coalition in Chilean History

To understand how Chile's post-dictatorship economic and political framework became entrenched during its transition to democracy, it is essential to examine the governance of the *Concertación* coalition. Each of its administrations contributed uniquely to consolidating the existing model, navigating a delicate balance between the need for stability and the pressures for reform. The coalition's leaders, instrumental in reinforcing the neoliberal framework during the early years of democracy, would later confront its limitations as Chilean society evolved. A closer examination of these governments not only explains why their policies appeared effective and necessary at the time but also reveals how these very policies laid the groundwork for future debates and criticism.[1]

[1] Readers may find it useful to consult the ideological maps in the Appendix (Figures A1, A2, and A3), which illustrate the general positions occupied by the coalitions, parties, and presidential candidates discussed in this chapter.

4.2.1 Rebuilding Democracy and Confronting the Past

Modern Chile cannot be understood without considering the significant role of Patricio Aylwin. A towering figure in Chilean politics for most of his life, he is rightly regarded as the founding father of the country's modern democracy. Aylwin was an emblematic member of the Christian Democratic Party and served as president of the Senate until the breakdown of democracy in 1973. During the military dictatorship that followed, he emerged as the leader of the institutionalized resistance, consistently advocating for a peaceful transition back to democratic governance.

As the dictatorship neared its end, Aylwin became the leader of the *Concertación de Partidos Políticos por el No*, a coalition of 17 political parties and movements that campaigned for a return to democracy during the 1988 plebiscite. This referendum asked Chileans whether they wanted Pinochet to remain in power for another eight years or to transition to democratic elections. The coalition's unity and effective campaign led to a historic victory for the "*No*" vote, paving the way for the *Concertación* to take over the reins of the country.

Aylwin's role was central to this success. He was not only a leader for the center-left but also a unifying figure who inspired confidence across the political spectrum, including among the center-right. His ability to bridge political divides made him the natural choice to become Chile's first democratically elected president after Pinochet, in the 1989 election.

Aylwin's electoral victory was decisive, reflecting widespread support for his leadership. Unlike most of his successors, he won outright in the first round without requiring a runoff. Once in office, his administration focused on rebuilding democratic institutions from the ground up, creating a governance framework that had been dismantled during the dictatorship. Perhaps Aylwin's most defining contribution, however, was his work on addressing the human rights violations committed under Pinochet's regime. His administration established the *Comisión Rettig* and the *Comisión Valech*, which documented and registered human rights abuses that occurred between 1973 and 1990. These commissions represented a critical step in acknowledging and addressing the legacy of the dictatorship, securing Aylwin a lasting place in the country's collective memory.

Amid these pressing challenges, economic policy and the neoliberal model inherited from the dictatorship were not immediate priorities for Aylwin's government. Rebuilding institutions, ensuring political stability, and managing a delicate relationship with the military—still under Pinochet's command as commander-in-chief—took precedence. By the time Aylwin left office in 1994, Chile's economy was performing exceptionally well, achieving growth rates that remained unprecedented even 30 years later (see Chapter 5). This success further reduced the urgency to engage in debates about constitutional or economic reform. Although discussions about the neoliberal model persisted in some political circles, they remained largely peripheral. At this early stage of the transition, such debates were viewed as niche concerns, and there was little appetite among the broader public or political elite to challenge a system that, while still fragile and potentially reversible, was delivering tangible benefits.

4.2.2 *Economic Growth and Global Reintegration*

Eduardo Frei Ruiz-Tagle,[2] who succeeded Patricio Aylwin as president in 1994, also prioritized other pressing matters over altering Chile's economic model. Like Aylwin, Frei Ruiz-Tagle secured the presidency with an outright victory in the first round, reflecting widespread public support.[3] Once in office, he focused on reintegrating Chile into the global economy and reshaping its international image. This would eventually lead him to become recognized as the president who internationalized and rebranded the country. During his administration, Chile's economy grew at an impressive average rate of 6% per year—slightly below Aylwin's 7%, but also unmatched since. This period marked a significant leap forward for the nation, positioning it as a distinct leader in the region.

[2] The second surname, Ruiz-Tagle, is often used to distinguish President Eduardo Frei Ruiz-Tagle (1994–2000) from his father, Eduardo Frei Montalva, who served as president from 1964 to 1970, both representing the Christian Democratic Party. Neither should be confused with Arturo Frei Bolívar, a 1999 independent presidential candidate (see Figure A3 in the Appendix), that was a nephew of Frei Montalva, and a cousin of Frei Ruiz-Tagle.

[3] In the post-transition era, only Aylwin and Eduardo Frei Ruiz-Tagle secured the presidency outright in the first round. All other presidents have required a second-round runoff to be elected.

While many of the benefits of Frei Ruiz-Tagle's efforts would only materialize in subsequent years, it was already clear in the late 1990s that the international trade deals he was signing would leave a lasting effect on Chile's economic structure.[4]

Frei Ruiz-Tagle's tenure, however, was not without challenges. In 1998, Augusto Pinochet was detained in London on charges related to human rights violations, triggering a major political and diplomatic crisis.[5] Frei Ruiz-Tagle's government faced the delicate task of negotiating Pinochet's release and return to Chile. Domestically, this sparked intense debate: some believed Pinochet should stand trial in Chile, while others argued that any form of justice—even abroad—was preferable to none. This incident underscores the division within Chilean society at the time regarding how to reconcile with its authoritarian past.

The Frei Ruiz-Tagle administration also encountered economic headwinds with the onset of the 1998 Asian financial crisis, which severely impacted Chile's economy.[6] The crisis abruptly ended the robust growth of Frei Ruiz-Tagle's early years, ushering in a period of economic decline.

[4] Frei Ruiz-Tagle's administration consolidated an open, investment-friendly economic model, signing 12 free trade agreements—including with Canada, Mexico, Central America, Peru, and Mercosur. His government also secured Chile's entry into the WTO and APEC, laying the groundwork for future agreements with the United States and China. See: Milet, P. V. 2002. "La política exterior del gobierno de Eduardo Frei Ruiz-Tagle." In *El periodo del presidente Frei Ruiz-Tagle*, edited by O. Muñoz and C. Stefoni, 403–419. Santiago: Editorial Universitaria.

[5] The 503 days Augusto Pinochet spent under house arrest in London—shuttling between his secluded Virginia Water residence and The London Clinic—have been the subject of several detailed academic studies and journalistic accounts. These chronicles capture not only the legal drama surrounding his detention, but also the diplomatic tensions and media spectacle it provoked. See: Brody, R., and M. Ratner, eds. 2000. *The Pinochet Papers: The Case of Augusto Pinochet Ugarte in Spain and Britain*. London: Martinus Nijhoff Publishers; and Pérez, M., and F. Gerdtzen. 2000. *Augusto Pinochet: 503 días atrapado en Londres*. Santiago: Los Andes; Sugarman, D. 2024. "The hidden histories of the Pinochet case." *Journal of Law and Society* 51(4): 459–490.

[6] For a political perspective on how the Asian financial crisis affected Chile's economy—including its impact on investment flows, growth expectations, and state response—see: Insulza, J. M. 1998. "Los efectos de la crisis asiática y su impacto en la economía chilena." *Serie de Publicaciones Análisis Político Coyuntural Fundación Friedrich Ebert* (3)98: 13–18. For a broader discussion and trends, see: Moguillansky, G. 2000. *La inversión en Chile: ¿El fin de un ciclo de expansión?* Santiago: Fondo de Cultura Económica and Cepal; Velasco, A. 2000. "Instituciones, Credibilidad y Manejo Macroeconómico en Chile." *Estudios Públicos* 77: 1–31; Covarrubias R., A. 2002. "El manejo de la economía chilena frente a la crisis asiática 1997-2001." *Panorama Socioeconómico* 24: 1–13.

While the global economic downturn was largely beyond his control, its effects intensified the pressures on his government. Nevertheless, Chile's reputation as a stable and forward-looking nation remained intact, and the country's political leadership continued to prioritize long-term progress over short-term political disputes.

As a result, there was little political momentum to challenge or reevaluate the neoliberal economic model.[7]The prevailing consensus among Chile's political elite largely favored maintaining the status quo. While some academic discussions critiqued aspects of the development model, these debates failed to gain significant traction within the political sphere.[8] Instead, the challenges of Frei Ruiz-Tagle's presidency prompted broader reflections on leadership and governance *within* the *Concertación*. The economic and political developments of the 1990s created opportunities for the coalition to explore a more distinctly social democratic approach—an avenue that had seemed improbable during the early years of Chile's transition to democracy.

4.2.3 Constitutional Reform and Modernization

As the decade (and the century) came to a close, the Christian Democrats passed the baton of leadership to Ricardo Lagos, representing the *Partido por la Democracia*. Lagos had established his political credentials over

[7] Some analysts argue that the absence of a serious challenge to the neoliberal model during Frei Ruiz-Tagle's presidency cannot be explained solely by economic orthodoxy or external constraints. A key but often overlooked factor was the political backlash following the 1997 parliamentary elections, in which the governing coalition suffered serious setbacks. This weakened the government's mandate and discouraged any bold structural departures. See: Heine, J. 2001. "Modernización y malestar: la segunda fase de la transición chilena." *Perspectivas* 4(2): 353–361.

[8] Felipe Portales contends that the *Concertación*'s failure to reform the 1980 Constitution or challenge core elements of the neoliberal economic model—such as the AFP and ISAPRE systems—was not merely the result of opposition obstruction. Rather, it reflected a conscious political strategy: to pursue only those reforms that had prior agreement with the right. This logic came to define the so-called democracia de los acuerdos ("democracy of agreements"), a hallmark of the post-authoritarian consensus. Portales also argues that this approach explains why the *Concertación* accepted constitutional amendments—approved in the June 1989 plebiscite—that effectively ceded control of key legislative initiatives to the right via Articles 65 and 68. See: Portales, F. 1999. *Chile: Una democracia tutelada*. Santiago: Sudamericana.

decades as a prominent figure in the anti-Pinochet institutional resistance. His extensive background included serving as Minister of Public Works and Minister of Education, making him a seasoned political actor by the time of his presidential bid. After winning the center-left primary against Christian Democrat Andrés Zaldívar, Lagos became the *Concertación*'s presidential candidate for the 1999/2000 election. While he secured a first-round victory, his narrow margin over Joaquín Lavín of the *Unión Demócrata Independiente* necessitated a runoff. Lagos ultimately won by just 80,000 votes, signifying the first signs of weakness in the *Concertación's* previously unchallenged dominance.

Despite this, Lagos's administration began on a strong note and is often regarded as one of the most transformative of the post-transition period. Under his leadership, Chile further solidified its position on the global stage. Among other major achievements was the completion of two free trade agreements with the United States and China, building upon the efforts initiated by Frei Ruiz-Tagle. These agreements bolstered Chile's reputation as an open and reliable trading partner. Domestically, Lagos introduced significant political reforms, including the separation of mayoral and council elections and the enactment of new transparency laws, both of which would have a lasting effect on the transformation of the broader party system (see Chapters 6 and 7).

The defining legacy of Lagos's administration, however, lies in the first major reform of the 1980 Constitution. The initiative for reform gained momentum following a corruption scandal that took place between 2003 and 2004, which created an opening for dialogue between Lagos's administration and the opposition.[9] This crisis, which exposed issues of accountability and governance, paved the way for constitutional negotiations.

[9] The 2005 constitutional reform is widely seen as the last major political agreement of the *Concertación* era—an effort to modernize Chile's institutional framework without fundamentally altering its post-authoritarian structure. The process was triggered in part by the legitimacy crisis sparked by the MOP-Gate corruption scandal, which created political pressure to demonstrate a renewed commitment to democratic transparency and accountability. The resulting agreement led to the removal of several authoritarian enclaves from the 1980 Constitution, including the elimination of designated senators and military influence in the *Consejo Nacional de Seguridad* ("National Security Council"). Yet despite these advances, critics argued that the reforms remained firmly within the boundaries of the inherited model. See: Gaggero, R. 2015. "El paso a paso del último gran acuerdo político sellado tras el caso MOP-Gate." *El Líbero*. March 15. https://ellibero.cl/actualidad/el-paso-a-paso-del-ultimo-gran-acuerdo-politico-sellado-en-2003-tras-el-caso-mop-gate/

Recognizing the moment as an opportunity to address broader political concerns, Lagos worked to build consensus with the opposition[10].

This compromise required concessions on both sides. In what has since been referred to as the *acuerdo Lagos-Longueira* (lit. "Lagos-Longueira agreement"), the opposition agreed to support substantial constitutional reforms, while Lagos's administration committed to increasing the quorum required for future amendments. Ultimately, the process culminated in 2005 with the enactment of 58 constitutional reforms that redefined key aspects of Chile's institutional framework.[11]

In any case, it is worth mentioning that none of them challenged the neoliberal economic framework solidified since the 1980s. Instead, discussions centered on political representation, governance fairness, and improving quality of life, favoring incremental progress over sweeping ideological shifts.

By the end of the Lagos presidency in 2006, Chile had made significant strides toward overcoming underdevelopment. The constitutional and political reforms, combined with strategic international trade agreements, solidified Lagos's legacy as a leader who prioritized modernization and institutional strengthening. At the time, these reforms were widely viewed as a natural step in Chile's democratic evolution. However, as time passed, they became a focal point of historical debates, raising a fundamental question: was Chile still governed by the 1980 Pinochet Constitution,

[10] Lagos's opposition counterpart was UDI Lower Chamber Deputy Pablo Longueira. He had previously been elected to three terms representing the outskirts of Santiago (District 13) before shifting to a more populous district in the city center (District 17). Longueira also served as president of the UDI and was part of Joaquín Lavín's campaign team during the 1999/2000 presidential election. After winning reelection in 2001 and securing the agreement with Lagos, he was elected senator in 2005 (to serve 2006–2014). He ran for president in 2013 but dropped out of the race and subsequently retired from politics altogether.

[11] In 2005, President Ricardo Lagos ordered the publication of a new edition of the 1980 Constitution, incorporating the 58 reforms recently approved by Congress. Most notably, his signature appeared in the foreword, replacing that of Augusto Pinochet. While the legal continuity of the 1980 text remained intact, this symbolic act—paired with Lagos's public framing of the moment as one of "unity and reconciliation with history"—sparked ongoing debate over whether the revised document could be considered a new constitution or merely a softened version of its authoritarian predecessor. See: *El País*. 2005. "El Congreso aprueba 58 reformas a la Constitución de Pinochet: Lagos califica el día de 'unidad y reencuentro con la historia.'" August 17. https://elpais.com/internacional/2005/08/17/actualidad/1124229603_850215.html/

or had the reforms effectively ushered in a new "2005 Lagos Constitution?" This lingering uncertainty underscored the ongoing tension surrounding the depth and impact of these changes—a question that would resurface prominently in the final phases of the second constitutional process (see Chapter 17).[12]

4.2.4 *Social Policies and Continuity*

Following Ricardo Lagos's transformative presidency, Michelle Bachelet emerged as the candidate best positioned to advance the modernization and progress associated with the *Concertación* coalition. A committed socialist and the daughter of an Air Force general who was imprisoned and tortured during the Pinochet regime, Bachelet's life story resonated deeply with a nation still grappling with the legacy of dictatorship. Her tenure as Health Minister and later as Defense Minister under Lagos showcased her pragmatic leadership style and reinforced her reputation as a capable and empathetic figure. While her candidacy represented continuity with the *Concertación*'s achievements, her emphasis on equity and social policies marked a shift toward addressing long-standing grievances.

In the 2005/2006 presidential election, Bachelet faced strong competition from two formidable right-wing candidates: Sebastián Piñera and Joaquín Lavín. Despite their challenge, she emerged victorious, securing a decisive lead in the runoff against Piñera. Her victory was historic, making her the first woman to be elected president of Chile. It also underscored the continued dominance of the *Concertación* coalition, even as early signs of fragmentation within its elite began to appear.

During her administration, Bachelet prioritized social policies aimed at reducing inequality and promoting equity. She introduced significant

[12] The issue would reemerge in the campaign cycle of the 2023 plebiscite (see Chapter 17 for an assessment of its relevance). In an effort to reframe the outcome and deny the political right a symbolic victory, former minister Francisco Vidal suggested that Chile was not governed by Pinochet's 1980 Constitution, but rather by "the Constitution signed by President Ricardo Lagos." His comment underscored both the lingering ambiguity over the constitutional legacy and the political stakes of how that legacy is narrated. See: Aranda, A. 2023. "Tras triunfo del 'En contra': Francisco Vidal dice que Carta Magna vigente es 'la Constitución firmada por el Presidente Ricardo Lagos'." *La Tercera*. December 20. https://www.latercera.com/politica/noticia/tras-triunfo-del-en-contra-francisco-vidal-dice-que-carta-magna-vigente-es-la-constitucion-firmada-por-el-presidente-ricardo-lagos/BHTWN4LS2NC4BNIEDEBXHWTMVQ/

programs, such as expanding access to healthcare and education and launching *Chile Crece Contigo* (lit. "Chile Grows With You"), an integrated system to support early childhood development. These initiatives sought to bridge gaps in social services and improve the quality of life for marginalized communities. Despite these advancements, her administration nonetheless operated firmly within the institutional framework established by the 1980 Constitution. Like her predecessors, she did not challenge what had by this point come to be known as "the model," leaving the overarching neoliberal governance structure intact throughout her four years in power.

4.3 The Birth of Criticism

By the end of the last *Concertación* government, the political landscape had changed substantially. Two decades after the democratic transition, while the coalition had achieved steady economic growth, poverty reduction, and institutional consolidation, internal criticism had begun to intensify. Smaller, more organized groups started articulating compelling arguments that the *Concertación* had not done enough to move beyond the legacy of the Pinochet regime. Although the general population largely supported the coalition's stability-focused approach, dissent within like-minded sectors was driven by frustrations over the perceived lack of ambition in addressing deeper structural changes.[13]

[13] While internal differences are to be expected in any broad coalition, this was not entirely the case within the *Concertación*, where official lines were maintained with notable discipline. Both political leaders and economic authorities—particularly finance ministers and their technocratic teams—consistently upheld adherence to "the model." For example, Ricardo Ffrench-Davis defended the model's achievements by drawing a dividing line at 1989, framing the benefits as beginning with the return of democracy under the Concertación rather than being rooted in the earlier economic framework. The further the country moved away from that year, however, the harder it became to maintain the idea that (1) economic success was due solely to the Concertación, as a longer-term pattern was clearly emerging, and (2) that if that success was indeed theirs, then the failures or declines had to be theirs as well—especially considering that the coalition's experts had "established" its performance. See: Ffrench-Davis, R. 2002. "Entre el neoliberalismo y el crecimiento con equidad." *Revista de Economía Política* 22(4): 594–612; Ffrench-Davis, R. 2001. *Tres décadas de política económica*. Santiago: Dolmen Ediciones; and Ffrench-Davis, R. 2005. *Economic Reforms in Chile: From Dictatorship to Democracy*, 4th ed. Ann Arbor, MI: University of Michigan Press.

Two main forces pushed for change from within. The first source of criticism emerged from inside the coalition itself, as minority factions voiced increasingly strong objections to its direction. These groups argued that by this stage, the *Concertación* had the resources and political capital to address inequality and implement more ambitious reforms. In their view, the failure to take meaningful steps toward fairer wealth distribution was a missed opportunity and a sign of an unwillingness to challenge elite interests. This lack of bold action, they contended, reflected broader stagnation in the coalition's leadership.

The second force for change came from the far left, including grassroots movements, radical factions, and satellite parties such as the Communist Party, which occasionally cooperated with the *Concertación* but were not formal partners.[14] These groups had long felt alienated by the coalition's cautious strategies. They had envisioned the democratic transition as a transformative moment that would dismantle Pinochet's institutional and economic legacy entirely. Instead, they saw the *Concertación* embracing continuity over change, maintaining the neoliberal model, and failing to address deep structural inequalities. Their criticism reflected a growing frustration with what they perceived as the coalition's lack of commitment to transformative justice.

These criticisms eventually gave rise to two ideological camps within the *Concertación*: the *autoflagelantes* and the *autocomplacientes*.[15] The *autoflagelantes*, or "self-flagellants," argued that the coalition had grown complacent and failed to tackle Chile's deeper structural issues. They

[14] Cooperation between the Communist Party and the *Concertación* began in the 2008 municipal elections through pactos por omisión, where both sides agreed not to compete in selected districts to improve their chances against right-wing candidates. In 2009, the alliance deepened under the banner *Concertación y Juntos Podemos por más Democracia*, with the Communist Party allocated nine candidacies in winnable districts—securing their first three deputies since the return to democracy (Hugo Gutiérrez in District 2, Lautaro Carmona in District 5, and Guillermo Teillier in District 28). Full integration came in 2013 with the formation of the *Nueva Mayoría* coalition. See Chapter 6 for more on the evolution of the Chilean party system.

[15] While the exact origin of the terms *autocomplaciente* and *autoflagelante* remains debated, political analyst Antonio Cortés-Terzi traces the earliest internal disputes within the *Concertación* to 1997, when differing views over the coalition's legacy and direction began to crystallize. These labels would later come to define two opposing self-perceptions among center-left elites: one focused on defending the transition's achievements, the other on confronting its limitations. See: Cortés-Terzi, A. 2000. *Progresismo desafiado: Hegemonía y Poder*, (vol. 36). Santiago: Centro de Estudios Avance.

called for a more confrontational agenda to challenge the neoliberal framework and pursue greater equity. The *autocomplacientes*, or "self-satisfied," on the other hand, defended the coalition's strategy of gradualism, highlighting Chile's sustained economic stability, poverty reductions, and international prestige as evidence of success. For the *autocomplacientes*, radical reforms risked jeopardizing the achievements the *Concertación* had worked hard to secure. This division is further explored in Chapter 8.

While ideological divisions had always existed to some degree, by the end of Michelle Bachelet's first term, they had become a defining feature of left-of-center politics. While the *autoflagelantes* pushed for the coalition to rediscover its progressive roots and take a stronger stance against inequality, the *autocomplacientes* remained committed to stability and incremental progress.

The debate underscored a deeper question about the coalition's long-term vision: was the *Concertación*'s gradualist strategy sufficient to achieve the social and economic transformation many had hoped for, or had it fallen short of its promise? This tension would not only grow to shape the coalition's legacy but also to foreshadow many of the shifts that Chile's political landscape would take part of in the years to come.

4.4 A Critical Turning Point

The 2009/2010 presidential election marked the disintegration of the *Concertación*'s once-dominant coalition. By this point, internal divisions within the *Concertación* had become increasingly evident. The fractures within the Socialist Party, a key pillar of the coalition and Michelle Bachelet's political base, were particularly pronounced. Thousands of party members and activists defected to support alternative candidates, rejecting the official *Concertación* nominee, Frei Ruiz-Tagle.

Frei Ruiz-Tagle was perceived as emblematic of the coalition's reluctance to break away from the neoliberal model associated with the Pinochet era. His candidacy was viewed as a continuation of the same centrist, stability-focused policies that had long defined the *Concertación* but had increasingly alienated its more progressive base. This perception was particularly strong among younger voters and left-leaning intellectuals, who demanded a more decisive response to issues of inequality and the enduring shadow of the dictatorship.

The fragmentation within the *Concertación* reached its peak in early 2009 with the emergence of two prominent alternative candidacies: Marco Enríquez-Ominami and Jorge Arrate. Both were recently resigned members of the Socialist Party who launched independent campaigns to challenge the dominant political and economic paradigm represented by Frei Ruiz-Tagle. Enríquez-Ominami, in particular, captured the imagination of younger voters and those disillusioned with traditional party politics, offering a vision of modernization and renewal that stood in stark contrast to Frei Ruiz-Tagle's more conventional approach.[16] Meanwhile, Arrate appealed to the far-left segments of the electorate, emphasizing a sharp critique of the neoliberal framework and advocating for policies aimed at addressing deep-seated inequalities.

The split was not merely a matter of political ambition; it exposed the magnitude of the ideological and generational tension within the *Concertación*. Furthermore, the leadership's inability—or unwillingness—to address these tensions ultimately undermined the coalition's unity. Although the combined votes for left-leaning candidates in the first round exceeded 50%, the fractured nature of the coalition prevented any single candidate from posing a credible challenge to Sebastián Piñera, the conservative candidate representing the right-wing coalition, *Alianza* .[17]

Frei Ruiz-Tagle's second-place finish, with just over 29% of the vote, underscored the *Concertación*'s declining appeal and its failure to mobilize its once-unified base. Enríquez-Ominami's strong performance, securing nearly 20% of the vote, further highlighted the electorate's appetite for an alternative vision. These results reflected a dramatic shift in Chilean politics: the center-left was no longer the uncontested voice of opposition to the right. The ideological rift within the *Concertación*,

[16] Several studies examine the complementary dynamic between Marco Enríquez-Ominami and Eduardo Frei Ruiz-Tagle during the 2009 presidential race, often framing it as a tension between political novelty and institutional continuity. For a comparative analysis situating Enríquez-Ominami among other Latin American presidential candidates labeled as "outsiders," see: Bunker, K., and P. Navia. 2013. "Latin American Political Outsiders, Revisited: The Case of Marco Enríquez-Ominami in Chile, 2009." *Journal of Politics in Latin America* 5(2): 3–35.

[17] Structurally, this mirrors the 2005–2006 election, when the right was divided between Sebastián Piñera and Joaquín Lavín in the first round—ultimately allowing a unified *Concertación* to secure victory with Michelle Bachelet in the second round. In 2009, the dynamic was reversed: the center-left was fractured, paving the way for Piñera's win despite the left collectively receiving over half the vote.

compounded by its reliance on familiar figures like Frei Ruiz-Tagle, marked the end of an era of dominance and cohesion.

In retrospect, it is clear that the *Concertación*'s defeat in 2010 did not occur by chance.[18] It was the culmination of years of unresolved tensions and growing disillusionment among its core supporters. At the same time, the opposition understood the challenge ahead and recognized how to appeal to an increasingly skeptical electorate. When the opportunity arose to make a decisive push for power, they did so with determination.

4.5 The Rise of Sebastián Piñera

The rise of Sebastián Piñera, a businessman and former Senator of Santiago (1990–1998) from *Renovación Nacional*, in the 2009/2010 election denoted a profound shift in Chile's political trajectory. For the first time since the country's transition to democracy in 1990, a candidate from the right-wing *Alianza* coalition had won the presidency. Piñera's victory symbolized the decline of the *Concertación* as well as the emergence of a new political dynamic in which the left no longer held a monopoly on governance.

Piñera's campaign promised pragmatism, economic expertise, and a fresh perspective to Chile's leadership. A billionaire and former presidential candidate in 2005/2006, he positioned himself as a technocrat capable of steering Chile through global economic challenges while maintaining its status as one of Latin America's most stable and prosperous nations. His campaign resonated with middle-class voters who sought change but feared the instability that more radical proposals from the left might bring.

In the second round, Piñera successfully consolidated support from conservative and moderate voters, defeating Frei Ruiz-Tagle with 52% of the preferences. This result exposed the inability of the *Concertación* to

[18] For contrasting accounts of the political landscape leading up to the 2010 defeat, see: Tironi, E. 2010. *Radiografía de una derrota: O cómo Chile cambió sin que la Concertación se diera cuenta*. Santiago: Uqbar Editores, for a perspective from within the *Concertación*; and Allamand, A., and M. Cubillos. 2010. *La estrella y el arco iris: Cómo después de 20 años fue derrotada la Concertación*. Santiago: Aguilar, for a view from the *Alianza*. For an analysis of the *Concertación*'s electoral fragmentation and the *Alianza*'s successful appeal to the political center, see: Bunker, K. 2010. *The 2009 Presidential Election in Chile*, (MA Thesis). San Diego,CA: San Diego State University

present a coherent alternative, leaving the left in disarray and strengthening the conservative alliance.

The aftermath of the election rendered the center-left coalition grappling with an identity crisis. Previously a symbol of unity and stability, the *Concertación* appeared fragmented and directionless. Many of its leaders struggled to reconcile the centrist approach of the coalition with increasing demands from its progressive factions. Meanwhile, figures such as Enríquez-Ominami emerged as credible challengers to the *Concertación*'s hegemony on the left, which further complicated its efforts to regroup.[19]

Piñera's victory marked a turning point in the public's perception of the left. For decades, the *Concertación* had been considered natural stewards of Chilean democracy and credited with guiding the country through a peaceful transition from dictatorship. However, the 2009/2010 election shattered this narrative, which, in retrospect, reveals the coalition's vulnerability and its inability to adapt to a changing political landscape. With the *Concertación* in disarray, Piñera's presidency ushered in a period in which the right became a viable and competitive force in Chilean politics.

The left's response to Piñera's presidency was characterized by introspection and experimentation. Recognizing the limitations of previous strategies, many individuals within the *Concertación* and its broad network explored alternative approaches to regain public trust. This period of political recalibration brought a series of significant changes in Chile's political landscape, as the left sought to rebuild its identity and chart a new path forward (these changes are described in Chapter 8).

[19] After losing in the first round, Marco Enríquez-Ominami refused to endorse Eduardo Frei Ruiz-Tagle in the runoff, declaring that neither he nor Sebastián Piñera represented "the hope for a different Chile." His decision to leave his supporters free to vote as they wished not only destabilized the *Concertación*'s second-round strategy but also signaled a deeper fracture within the Chilean left—a moment that raised broader questions about leadership, legitimacy, and generational renewal. See: Charpentier, D. 2009. "ME-O deja en libertad de acción a sus adherentes y manifiesta que ni Frei ni Piñera son la esperanza de un Chile distinto." *Biobio Chile*. December 13. https://www.biobiochile.cl/noticias/2009/12/13/me-o-deja-en-libertad-de-accion-a-sus-adherentes-y-manifiesta-que-ni-frei-ni-pinera-son-la-esperanza-de-un-chile-distinto.shtml/

4.6 Conclusion

This chapter explored the trajectory of the *Concertación* and its two decades of governance when it became the most successful political coalition in the history of Chile. Each of the four *Concertación* presidents played a significant role in the formation of the country's post-authoritarian progress. Patricio Aylwin prioritized the restoration of democratic institutions and reconciliation over human rights abuses; Eduardo Frei Ruiz-Tagle fostered significant economic growth and positioned Chile as a regional leader; Ricardo Lagos modernized the country through key constitutional reforms and infrastructure development; and Michelle Bachelet focused on the advancement of social equity and inclusivity. Together, these leaders ensured that Chile's transition from dictatorship to democracy was stable, peaceful, and economically prosperous.

The *Concertación*'s approach was centered on the maintenance of stability while avoiding significant disruption to the neoliberal framework inherited from the dictatorship. The lack of large-scale constitutional or economic challenges afforded a sense of predictability and continuity that appealed to domestic and international audiences. By the time of Lagos's constitutional reforms in 2005, Chile had achieved unprecedented economic growth, institutional consolidation, and poverty reduction, which reaffirmed the pragmatic approach of the coalition to governance.

However, the limitations of the coalition's strategy became increasingly evident with the evolution of societal expectations and internal rifts. The emergence of modern demands, arising naturally as Chilean society adapted to global and generational change, revealed that the Concertación's sense of strength and sufficiency was more fragile than it appeared. Elite divisions further fragmented the coalition, undermining its ability to present a unified response and a clear path forward. These tensions culminated in the 2009/2010 election in which the rise of Sebastián Piñera signaled a dramatic shift in the political landscape in Chile and the end of two decades of social democracy.

The *Concertación*'s legacy is one of triumph and constraint. While its governments successfully guided Chile through a critical period of democratic consolidation and economic transformation, its greater inability to evolve within the framework of the neoliberal model rendered it obsolete. Tensions from within not only shaped the eventual decline of the coalition but also led to the political and social transformations that would define Chile in future decades. As demonstrated in subsequent chapters, the transition from *Concertación* hegemony to a fragmented and contentious political system marked a fateful turning point in Chile's modern history.

CHAPTER 5

The Paradox of Progress

5.1 Introduction

The economic and political model implemented in Chile between 1990 and circa 2014 represents a remarkable success story. Across these decades, the country achieved sustained economic growth, addressed poverty, and maintained macroeconomic stability, such that it earned international recognition as a development leader within Latin America. Even more impressively, this progress defied traditional tradeoffs between growth and equity: Chile steadily decreased inequality in income while maintaining a robust GDP growth, which challenged assumptions about the inevitability of such tradeoffs in developing economies.[1]

Yet despite this trajectory of progress, a major social uprising still erupted in 2019. While this event is examined in greater detail later in the

[1] A substantial body of economic literature explores the relationship between growth and inequality, often emphasizing a tradeoff wherein pro-growth reforms—such as financial liberalization or market deregulation—tend to exacerbate income disparities, particularly in early stages. See: Ostry, J. D., A. Berg, and S. Kothari. 2021. "Growth–equity trade-offs in structural reforms." *Scottish Journal of Political Economy* 68(2): 209–237. However, more recent research suggests this relationship may be nonlinear, with inequality initially rising but subsequently declining as reforms mature and institutional capacity strengthens. Chile exemplifies this trajectory: over two decades, it combined sustained economic growth with a gradual decline in income inequality. See: Parro, F., and L. Reyes. 2017. "The rise and fall of income inequality in Chile." *Latin American Economic Review* 26(3): 1–31.

K. Bunker, *Chile's Transformation Amidst Crisis*,
https://doi.org/10.1007/978-3-031-96463-3_5

book, it must be acknowledged here, as it was widely seen as a direct backlash against the very model that had brought Chile its apparent success. (Readers wishing to avoid spoilers may prefer to skip ahead to Chapter 9 and return to this point afterward.)

This tension gives rise to what has been called the paradox of progress.[2] How could a nation that excelled across nearly every developmental metric still experience such profound public discontent? Understanding this puzzle, thus, requires moving beyond quantitative indicators to consider the role of elite interests—interests that may have found both incentive and reassurance in promoting a discourse of systemic failure that largely attributed the country's problems to the economic model.

At least, this would be consistent with the pattern that emerged in the immediate aftermath of the 2019 outburst, when the dominant narrative quickly attributed the unrest to deep-seated inequality and the failure of Chile's neoliberal framework. However, as this chapter suggests, the explanation lacks strong empirical support. Decades of declining inequality challenge the idea that the general situation was worsening or intractable. Rather than a reflection of measurable trends, this standard account, advanced by leftist intellectuals and elites, functioned more as a politically expedient critique than an evidence-based diagnosis. This chapter explores alternative factors that provide a nuanced understanding of the unrest, including perceptions of economic vulnerability, systemic unfairness, and dissatisfaction with the pace of progress.

By addressing these dynamics, the chapter challenges oversimplified narratives and provides essential context for understanding the debates that were taking place in Chile in this tumultuous period. In addition, it considers the influence of the framing of the unrest, which simultaneously shaped both the context that led to the demand for reform as well as

[2] The idea of a "contradiction" in Chile's development was present in public debate well before the 2019 social outburst—at least since the emergence of the *autoflagelantes* described in Chapter 4. However, the term takes on more analytical precision in the work of Sebastián Edwards, who explicitly framed it as a paradox grounded in a specific set of developmental metrics. His early contributions to both public and academic discourse following the 2019 events helped clarify the tension between Chile's strong macroeconomic performance and the widespread public dissatisfaction it failed to prevent. Edwards emphasized how measurable gains in poverty reduction and inequality could coexist with deep perceptions of unfairness and exclusion. See: Edwards, S. 2019. "The Reality of Inequality and Its Perception: Chile's Paradox Explained." *Promarket*. November 19. https://www.promarket.org/2019/11/19/the-reality-of-inequality-and-its-perception-chiles-paradox-explained/

the greater trajectory of the constitutional debates. At its core, the chapter proposes that a misreading of the root causes of the social outburst may have not only influenced public discourse but also contributed to the ultimate rejection of the alternative solutions proposed (an idea that is discussed in greater detail with the benefit of hindsight in Chapter 18).

5.2 Undeniable Macroeconomic Success

Between 1990 and 2014, Chile stood out as an exceptional performer in Latin America, as it achieved remarkable results in conventional economic indicators. As mentioned in Chapter 3, its levels of economic growth (as captured by its Gross Domestic Product, GDP) were among the highest in the region, positioning it as a regional leader in terms of per capita income. Figure 5.1 illustrates the steady upward trajectory of Chile's GDP per capita, which increased nearly fourfold from 1960 to 1990, and almost eighfold from 1990 to 2024 (from $4,400 to $34,600). This rapid growth transformed Chile into the wealthiest large country in Latin America, underscoring its remarkable progress over only a few decades.

Economic growth in Chile was driven by a combination of structural reforms, sound fiscal policies, and export-led development strategies. As presented in Chapter 3, the country embraced open trade policies, which facilitated its integration into global markets. In particular, copper export became a critical pillar of the Chilean economy as it provided a stable source of revenue and foreign exchange. This explains the consistency of its growth even during periods of global economic uncertainty. Apart from copper, Chile diversified its economy by expanding other sectors, such as agriculture, wine production, and salmon farming, which also contributed to its sustained economic performance and improved resilience against commodity price fluctuations.

Inflation, a long-standing issue in Chile, was also brought under control during this period. In the 1970s and early 1980s, inflation rates often exceeded 100% annually, severely undermining economic stability. However, by the 1990s, Chile had achieved remarkable success in stabilizing prices. As shown in Fig. 5.2, consumer prices declined steadily, eventually stabilizing at single-digit levels. While this is considered normal now, it was seen as a major achievement at the time, making a small developing country like Chile comparable to the performance of advanced economies. The success was largely attributed to the independent *Banco*

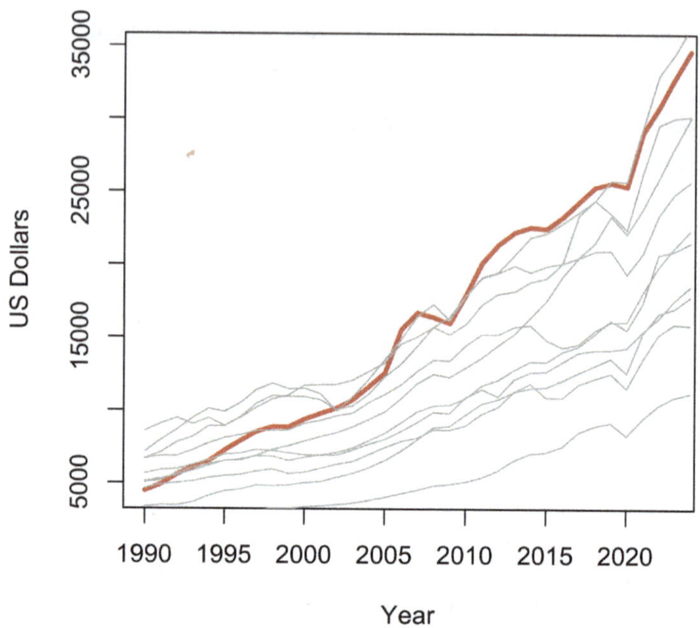

Fig. 5.1 Economic growth, 1990–2023 (*Note* Gross Domestic Product (GDP) per capita (divided by midyear population) converted to current international dollars using Purchasing Power Parity (PPP). The red line represents the evolution of the GDP in Chile. The grey lines represent the evolution of the GDP in Argentina, Bolivia, Brazil, Colombia, Costa Rica, Ecuador, Mexico, Paraguay, Peru, and Uruguay. *Source* Author with data from World Bank [NY.GDP.PCAP.PP.CD])

Central (Central Bank of Chile), which implemented disciplined monetary policies focused on inflation targeting (see Chapter 15 for the development of this indicator in the aftermath of the social outburst). The stability of prices not only protected purchasing power but also created a predictable economic environment that encouraged long-term investment and consumer confidence.

One of the most celebrated achievements of Chile's economic performance, however, was its dramatic poverty reduction. In the late 1980s, more than half of the population lived below the poverty line. By 2010, this figure had fallen below 8%, representing one of the most significant poverty reductions in Latin America. Figure 5.3 illustrates this

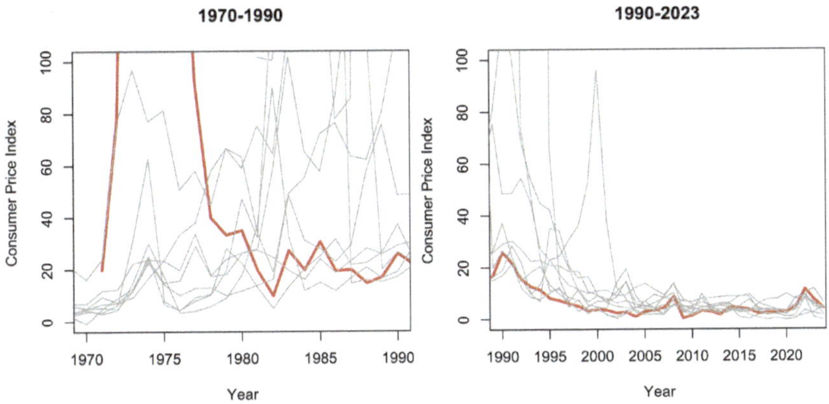

Fig. 5.2 Inflation, 1970–2023 (*Note* Consumer Price Index (CPI). The left panel covers 1970–1990, and the right panel covers 1990–2023. The red line represents the evolution of the CPI in Chile. The grey lines represent the evolution of the CPI in Bolivia, Brazil, Colombia, Costa Rica, Ecuador, Mexico, Paraguay, Peru, and Uruguay. No data was available for Argentina. *Source* Author with data from World Bank [FP.CPI.TOTL.ZG]))

extraordinary result, showing how sustained growth, combined with targeted policies, significantly improved the quality of life for millions of Chileans. Social programs such as conditional cash transfers, including *Chile Solidario* (lit. "Solidary Chile"), introduced by President Lagos, were instrumental in ensuring that benefits reached the most vulnerable populations (see Chapter 4).

Several other indicators support the narrative. Employment opportunities expanded significantly during this period.[3] Steady economic growth translated into a consistent rise in formal sector jobs, while unemployment rates fell to historically low levels. Investments in infrastructure and public works projects further contributed to job creation, particularly in urban

[3] During the first decade following the return to democracy, Chile's unemployment rate remained consistently below 10%, reaching a notably low 5.3% in 1997. This marked a sharp contrast with the 1976–1986 period, when unemployment was persistently above 10%, underscoring the labor market improvements tied to the democratic transition and market reforms. See: Micco, A., C. Pages-Serra, and K. Cowan. 2004. *A Diagnosis of Chilean unemployment*. Series *Estudios Económicos y Sociales*, (Research Paper No. RE1-04-012). Washington, DC: Inter-American Development Bank.

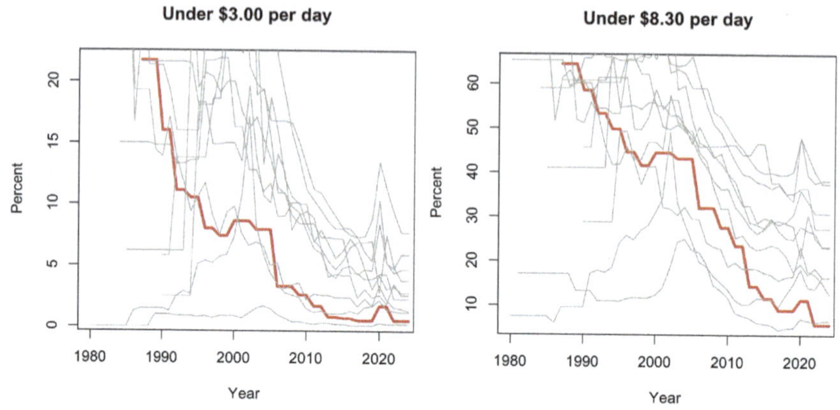

Fig. 5.3 Poverty, 1980–2023 (*Note* Poverty headcount ratio based on international poverty lines. The left panel shows the proportion of the population living on less than $3.00 a day (2021 PPP), and the right panel shows those living on less than $8.30 a day (2021 PPP). The red line represents poverty levels in Chile. The grey lines represent levels in Argentina, Bolivia, Brazil, Colombia, Costa Rica, Ecuador, Mexico, Paraguay, Peru, and Uruguay. *Source* Author with data from World Bank [SI.POV.DDAY; SI.POV.UMIC])

areas where much of the country's economic activity was concentrated. The expansion of these opportunities was crucial in lifting households out of poverty, maintaining economic momentum, and generating a cycle of prosperity.

By the end of this period, Chile's economic performance had earned international recognition. Organizations such as the *World Bank* (WB) and the *International Monetary Fund* (IMF) frequently cited Chile as a model for effective economic governance and development. Therefore, it was no surprise when, in **2009**, Chile became the first South American nation invited to join the *Organisation for Economic Co-operation and Development* (OECD), an acknowledgment of its achievements in economic reform, institutional strength, and policy innovation.[4]

[4] On December 15, 2009, Chile received a formal invitation to join the Organisation for Economic Co-operation and Development (OECD), becoming the second Latin American country after Mexico to be extended this honor. Following congressional ratification in 2010, Chile officially became the OECD's 31st member—a milestone reflecting

Revisiting "the model" detailed in Chapter 3 is pertinent to contextualize these results. If the objective during the 1980s was to establish economic liberalization as the prevailing paradigm that propelled the nation toward sustained development, then Chile successfully exemplified this vision. By 2000, Chile had emerged as a global leader in economic liberalization, likely allowing it to achieve many of the substantial results highlighted above. Figure 5.4 illustrates that Chile's rapid ascent in this measure. It shows that by 2010, Chile had reached the top ten of the Fraser Institute's *Economic Freedom of the World Index*, tied with the United Kingdom, ranking alongside leading nations such as the United States, Switzerland, Austria, and Australia—and above several others such as Canada, Ireland, Japan, and the Nordic countries.[5]

5.3 A Path Toward Development

Notwithstanding all of the above, these macroeconomic achievements raise a deeper question: did the success translate into tangible improvements in societal well-being? Beyond growth and fiscal stability, were there meaningful gains in public health, quality of life, and human development? To assess this, three fundamental indicators serve as useful benchmarks: access to clean drinking water, life expectancy, and the Human Development Index (HDI).

The first benchmark, access to clean drinking water, is a relevant indicator because it has direct implications for public health and quality of

its international credibility in economic reform and institutional governance. See: Saunders, E. 2009. "Chile Invited to Join OECD." *Financial Times*. December 15. https://www.ft.com/content/936dd770-bbf3-3abf-97ab-5d9d8d2cb701/

[5] The Fraser Institute's *Economic Freedom of the World Index* evaluates the extent to which a country's institutions and policies are consistent with economic freedom, using indicators such as the size of government, legal system, and property rights, access to sound money, freedom to trade internationally, and regulatory efficiency. Higher scores reflect closer adherence to classical liberal economic principles. Other measures, though based on different methodologies, show consistent results. For instance, the Heritage Foundation's *Index of Economic Freedom* assesses similar themes through a distinct framework, emphasizing rule of law (property rights, judicial effectiveness, government integrity), government size (tax burden, government spending, fiscal health), regulatory efficiency (business, labor, and monetary freedom), and market openness (trade, investment, and financial freedom). Despite these differences, both indices have consistently ranked Chile among the top performers in Latin America and often within the ranks of advanced economies such as the United States, Canada, and the United Kingdom.

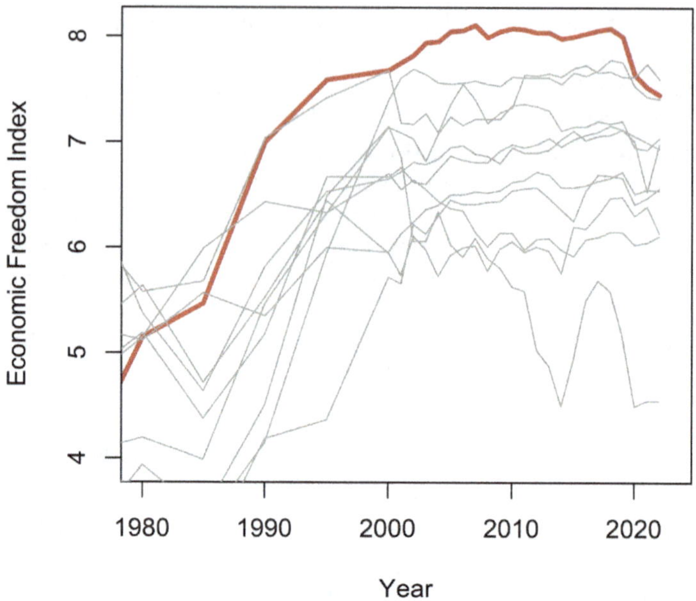

Fig. 5.4 Economic Freedom Index, 1980–2023 (*Note* Economic Freedom of the World Index, a composite measure of five key areas: size of government, legal system and property rights, sound money, freedom to trade internationally, and regulation. The red line represents the evolution of Economic Freedom in Chile. The grey lines represent the evolution of Economic Freedom in Argentina, Bolivia, Brazil, Colombia, Costa Rica, Ecuador, Mexico, Paraguay, Peru, and Uruguay. *Source* Author with data from Fraser Institute [Fraser_EFW_Index])

life. If Chile had championed economic freedom but lacked access to clean tap water, the problem would be evident. However, this was not the case. Chile stood out as a regional leader, achieving near-universal access to safely managed drinking water well ahead of its peers. As shown in Fig. 5.5, Chile's success in this area reflects its strategic investment in public utilities and rural outreach programs. By 2020, Chile had become the *only* Latin American country to provide safe water access to nearly its entire population, setting an example in infrastructure development and public health.

The second benchmark is life expectancy, widely regarded as a key indicator of societal development because it reflects the overall health and

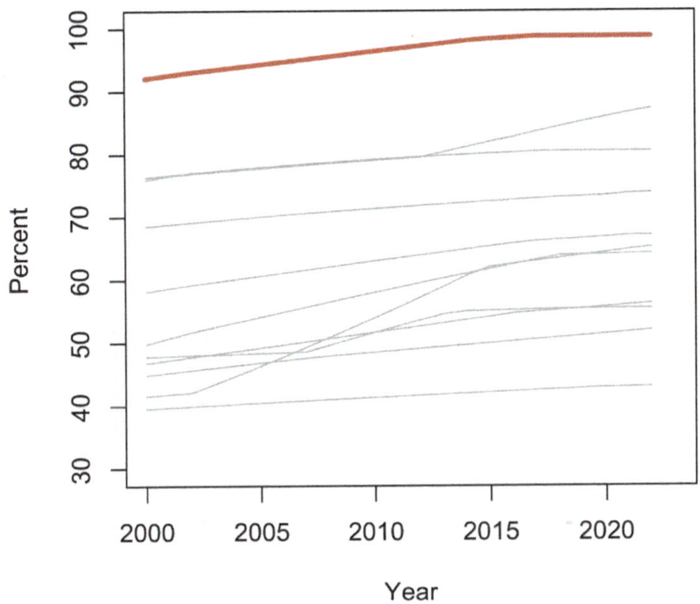

Fig. 5.5 Access to drinking water, 2000–2023 (*Note* Share of the population with access to drinking water includes access to sanitation, and hygiene (WASH). The measurement is based on a ladder-based system that classifies service levels by quality, safety, and accessibility. The red line represents the evolution of access to drinking water in Chile. The grey lines represent the evolution of access to drinking water in Brazil, Colombia, Costa Rica, Ecuador, Mexico, Paraguay, and Peru. No data was available for Argentina, Bolivia, or Uruguay. *Source* Author with data from World Health Organization (WHO) and United Nations International Children's Emergency Fund's (UNICEF) Joint Monitoring Programme for Water Supply, Sanitation and Hygiene (JMP) [SDG6.1.1; SDG6.2.1a; SDG6.2.1b])

living conditions of a population. In this regard, Chile's life expectancy rose steadily throughout the observed period, surpassing its regional peers and approaching levels seen mainly in high-income countries. As illustrated in Fig. 5.6, these gains were driven by improvements in healthcare infrastructure, better nutrition, and the reduction of preventable diseases.

Finally, the third is the HDI, a well-known composite indicator of life expectancy, education, and income that offers a multidimensional view of societal progress. As shown in Fig. 5.7, Chile consistently ranked at the

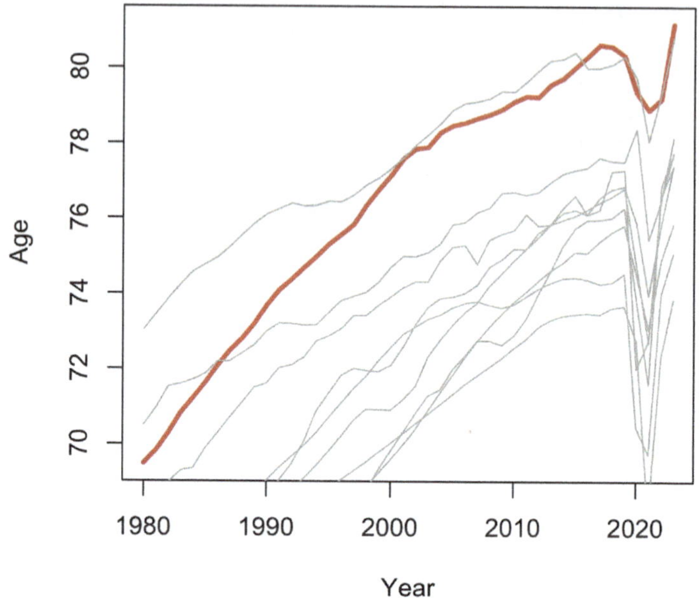

Fig. 5.6 Life expectancy at birth, 1980–2023 (*Note* Life Expectancy at Birth (measured in years of age). The red line represents the evolution of life expectancy in Chile. The grey lines represent the evolution of life expectancy in Argentina, Bolivia, Brazil, Colombia, Costa Rica, Ecuador, Mexico, Paraguay, Peru, and Uruguay. *Source* Author with data from United Nation Human Development Programme (UNDP) Human Development Reports [UNDP/HDR/69206])

top of Latin America in HDI, demonstrating steady improvement over several decades. By the early 2000s, Chile's HDI levels were comparable to those of developed nations, underscoring the broad-based nature of its progress.

Taken together, these achievements demonstrate that Chile had successfully translated its macroeconomic success into tangible societal progress. They underscore how sustained economic growth, along with targeted investments in health and education, laid the foundation for long-term development, ultimately allowing Chile to distinguish itself from the broader Latin American trajectory.

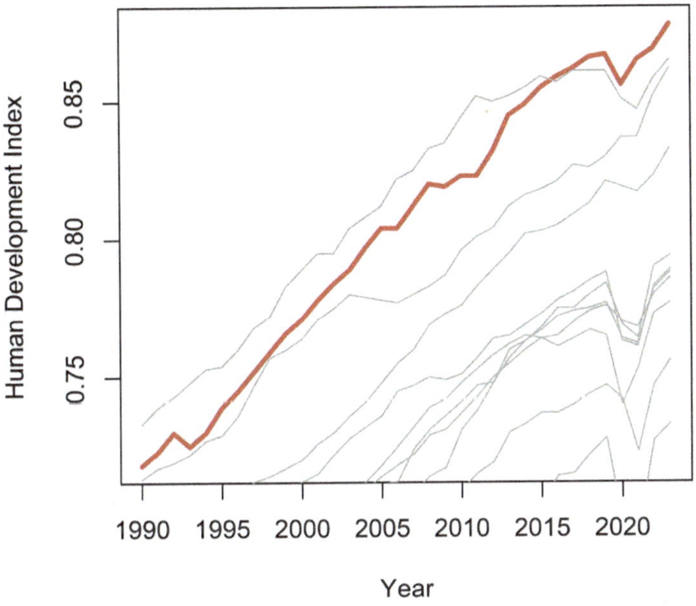

Fig. 5.7 Human Development Index, 1990–2023 (*Note* Human Development Index (HDI) is a composite measure that captures average achievements in health, education, and standard of living. It combines indicators of life expectancy, educational attainment, and gross national income per capita. The red line represents the evolution of the HDI in Chile. The grey lines represent the evolution of the HDI in Argentina, Bolivia, Brazil, Costa Rica, Colombia, Ecuador, Mexico, Paraguay, Peru, and Uruguay. *Source* Author with data from United Nations Development Programme (UNDP) Human Development Reports [HDI composite indicator])

Politically, this progress reflects the consistent commitment of different governments to health and social investments, which complemented the benefits of economic growth. Continuity in public policy across successive administrations (see Chapter 4) ensured that macroeconomic stability transformed into improved living conditions, longer life expectancies, and healthier lives for Chileans. If nothing else, these achievements highlight how sustained growth can elevate not only income levels but also overall quality of life. Furthermore, they emphasize the critical importance of maintaining a unified vision across governments to sustain progress, as exemplified by the policies of the *Concertación* coalition across two decades and continuity provided by the Piñera administration in 2010–2014.[6]

5.4 Rethinking the Problem

Despite Chile's undeniable macroeconomic success and its progress toward development, Chileans were evidently only partially satisfied. The social unrest that erupted that fateful day in October of 2019 serves as a stark indicator of this dissatisfaction, which, in turn, poses pressing questions: What are the flaws in this development model that led to discontent among Chileans? Why did a population that benefited from significant improvements in quality of life take to the streets to challenge and endeavor to dismantle a model that, by many measures, delivered tangible progress?

While many observers attributed the unrest to economic inequality, an in-depth analysis points to doubts about whether inequality was indeed the root cause of public discontent. This section presents and evaluates the standard explanation developed *before* the social unrest, tailored to explain it *after* its occurrence, and used as a justification for structural overahaul throughout the first constitutional process (2021–2022). It then examines evidence that points to a fundamental contradiction in the theory and proposes a nuanced alternative account before explaining why the standard explanation gained so much traction.

[6] Debates surrounding President Sebastián Piñera's first term (2010–2014) often centered on the extent to which his administration represented a departure from, or continuation of, the policy trajectory established by the *Concertación* coalition. Some observers, including analysts like Juan Carlos Hidalgo, contended that Piñera's policies aligned more closely with social democratic traditions than with conservative ones. See: Lago, S. 2013. "Las políticas de Piñera no difieren de la de los gobiernos de la Concertación." *Diario Financiero*. March 25. https://www.df.cl/economia-y-politica/actualidad/las-politicas-de-pinera-no-difieren-de-las-de-los-gobiernos-de-la. Former President Ricardo Lagos added to this debate by jokingly remarking that Piñera could be considered "the fifth government of the Concertación," a comment he later acknowledged was somewhat exaggerated. See: Muñoz, C. 2014. "La crisis argentina no afecta a Chile, pero puede afectar a Brasil." *ABC de España*. January 29. https://www.abc.es/internacional/20140129/abci-crisis-argentina-afecta-chile-201401282133.html/

5.4.1 *The Standard Explanation*

So, the standard explanation for the social unrest in Chile stems from the belief that the country's economic and political model was fundamentally flawed.[7] In simple terms, critics viewed the unrest as a rejection of neoliberalism, attributing public anger to the systemic failures within Chile's capitalist framework. According to their argument, decades of market-driven policies not only entrenched inequality but also excluded significant portions of the population from meaningful opportunities. And, it was this exclusion that ultimately drove people to the streets in October 2019.

At the heart of the argument is the idea that income inequality was the primary driver of discontent. The logic put forward was that Chile's economic model produced palpably unequal outcomes, with wealth visibly concentrated in the hands of a privileged few, while the majority struggled to access basic services or achieve upward mobility. In turn, this dynamic fueled resentment—not only toward the elite beneficiaries of the system but also toward the structural foundations of the model itself. Privatized pensions, healthcare, and education, combined with other more immediate issues (such as stagnant wages and rising household debt), became potent symbols of systemic exclusion and dissatisfaction

[7] A substantial body of literature identifies income inequality as the principal driver of Chile's 2019 social unrest. This book acknowledges *that* explanation as the dominant narrative in both academic and policy circles. However, rather than assuming its validity, the analysis treats it as a null hypothesis—a default position to be rigorously tested rather than uncritically accepted. This approach allows for a more open and systematic inquiry: if evidence emerges that contradicts the inequality explanation or reveals alternative factors of greater explanatory power, then the standard narrative must be revised or rejected. In this sense, the goal is not to reaffirm the conventional wisdom but to subject it to critical scrutiny, thereby encouraging a more nuanced understanding of the causes behind Chile's social upheaval. Readers seeking key signposts in the debate over Chile's economic model can see: Moulian, T. 1997. *Chile actual: anatomía de un mito*. Santiago: Lom Ediciones; Larraín, L. 2012. *El regreso del modelo*. Santiago: Libertad y Desarrollo; Garretón, M. A. 2012. *Neoliberalismo corregido y progresismo limitado: los gobiernos de la Concertación en Chile, 1990–2010*. Santiago: Arcis/CLACSO; Opplinger, M., and E. Guzmán. 2013. *El malestar de Chile ¿Teoría o Diagnóstico?* Santiago: Ediciones Universidad Diego Portales; Mayol, A. 2012. *El derrumbe del modelo: la crisis de la economía de mercado en el Chile contemporáneo*. Santiago: Lom Ediciones; Atria, F., G. Larraín, J. M. Benavente, J. Couso, and A. Joignant. 2013. *El otro modelo: del orden neoliberal al régimen de lo público*. Santiago: Debate; Kaiser, A. 2015. *La tiranía de la igualdad*. Santiago: El Mercurio/Aguilar; Ffrench-Davis, R. 2018. *Reformas económicas en Chile, 1973–2017*. Santiago: Penguin Random House Grupo Editorial.

(often referred to in discourse as *malestar*, meaning "dissatisfaction" or "unease").

Importantly, this explanation was not a post hoc theory created to explain the unrest; it had been gradually developed over many years. For its proponents, the social outburst seemed to confirm a long-standing hypothesis about the neoliberal model's failings. Some even framed it as the fulfillment of their predictions. However, the theory required significant adjustment to align with the unfolding events, which raises questions about its accuracy.

If the hypothesis—that neoliberalism or the broader capitalist framework was "the root cause"—were correct, it would have been logical for the public to embrace *any* alternative in subsequent political decisions. One would have expected, for example, overwhelming support for the first constitutional proposal, which represented a stark departure from the existing model. However, as Chapter 13 shows, this did not occur. The proposal was decisively rejected, calling into question the validity of this explanation and prompting a need for a more nuanced understanding of the unrest's causes.

5.4.2 *Shortcomings in the Diagnosis*

Without examining the rejection of the constitutional proposal, which will be addressed later in the book (see Chapter 13), it is safe to say that the standard explanation of inequality as the root cause of the social outburst was not only widely circulated for political clout, but also used to justify the first constitutional proposal. Thus, if the process ultimately failed, the very premises that justified the need for reform must also be called into question. And when this is done, significant weaknesses in the theory become apparent.

Perhaps the most problematic of the issues stems from the claim that worsening inequality was driving grievances. The widespread argument was based on several key assumptions. Among them, three stand out: that inequality was worsening, that this trend emerged at the expense of economic growth, and that systemic barriers to socioeconomic mobility were entrenched and visible. However, the available data challenge all three of these assumptions, which in turn undermines the validity of the overarching theory.

First, data does not support the claim that inequality was worsening. Figure 5.8 depicts that Chile's Gini coefficient (i.e., a standard measure of income inequality) steadily declined from the 1990s onward. This progress likely reflects intentional policy efforts, including programs that targeted poverty reduction (e.g., conditional cash transfers initiated by Lagos and continued by Bachelet and Piñera), progressive taxation, and general investment in social services. By 2015, inequality levels in Chile were significantly lower than those of regional peers such as Bolivia, Brazil, Colombia, Costa Rica, Ecuador, Mexico, and Paraguay (only Peru and Uruguay had lower Gini coefficients than Chile that year, according to the World Bank). Contrary to the claim that inequality was entrenched or worsening, the evidence indicates that Chile was not only on a trajectory of steady improvement in income distribution, but also making progress faster than that of comparable countries with similar levels of inequality when Chile first adopted "the model."

Second, the assumption that inequality persisted at the expense of economic growth lacks theoretical coherence. Development economics frequently posits that efforts to reduce inequality involve tradeoffs, which potentially slow down GDP growth. However, Fig. 5.9 indicates that Chile overcame this trend. Across several decades, the country managed to reduce inequality and sustain robust economic growth at the same time. If economic growth were driving inequality, then one would expect to observe widening disparity alongside increasing GDP; however, evidence demonstrates the opposite.[8] Data demonstrate that Chile achieved measurable progress in both aspects, thus contradicting the argument that the model prioritized growth at the expense of equality.

Figure 5.10 presents that the tradeoff between inequality reduction and growth did not stagnate, at least until Bachelet's first administration. For the first three governments after 1990, significant success was observed in striking a balance between GDP growth and inequality reduction. This again calls into question the notion that the model was fundamentally flawed from the outset. If the diagnosis foretelling the collapse of Chile's developmental model had been correct, then

[8] This pattern aligns with early research suggesting that sustained high levels of inequality in Chile did not necessarily correspond to lower overall welfare. Dante Contreras, for instance, found that during the period of rapid economic growth from 1990 to 1996, poverty declined significantly even as inequality remained relatively stable. His analysis showed that economic expansion improved conditions for both the poor and the wealthy, indicating that broad welfare gains were possible without a proportional reduction in inequality. See: Contreras, D. 2003. "Poverty and inequality in a rapid growth economy: Chile 1990–96." *The Journal of Development Studies* 39(3): 181–200.

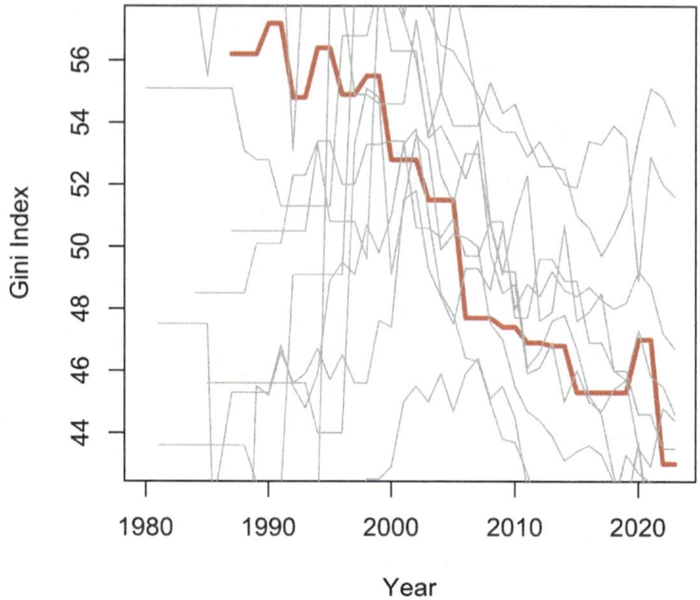

Fig. 5.8 Income inequality, 1980–2023 (*Note* The Gini Index (or coefficient) measures income inequality within a country, based on the distribution of income among its population (0 = perfect equality, 100 = maximum inequality). The red line represents the evolution of the Gini Index in Chile. The grey lines represent the evolution of the Gini Index in Argentina, Brazil, Costa Rica, Colombia, Ecuador, Mexico, Paraguay, Peru, and Uruguay. *Source* Author with data from World Bank [SI.POV.GINI])

the warning signs would have been evident beforehand, particularly in measures such as growth and equality. But no such signs were present. It was only after the social outburst that any meaningful reversal in key indicators took place. Indeed, the only instance in the entire post-1990 period where both indicators moved sharply in the wrong direction at the same time did not occur until 2020, *after* the social outburst, not *before*. That year, GDP fell from 25,611 to 25,350 USD, and the Gini coefficient rose from 45.9 to 47. It is ironic, perhaps, that the "symptoms" only appeared after the "disease" had been diagnosed.

Finally, Chile is often described as exhibiting "sticky floors and sticky ceilings"—that is, persistent barriers to escaping poverty or moving into

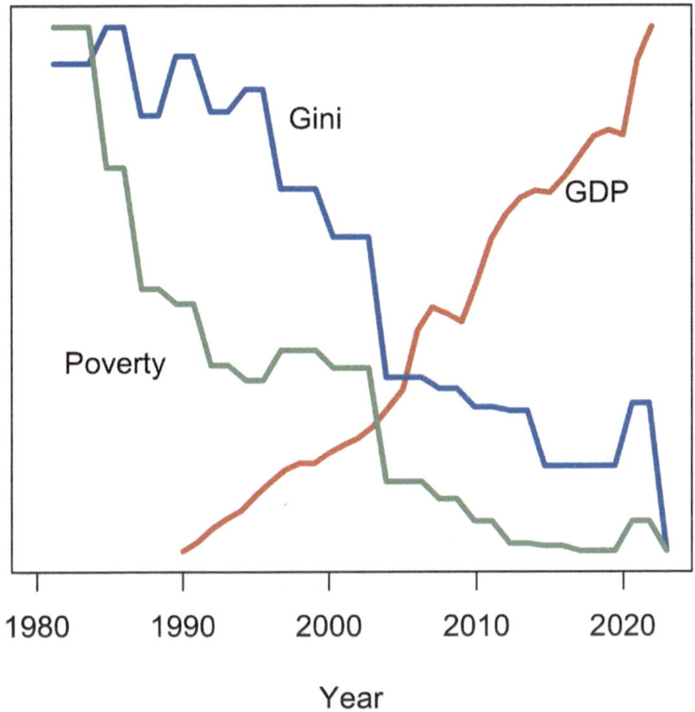

Fig. 5.9 Inequality, growth, and poverty in Chile, 1980–2023 (*Note* Composite visualization of three development indicators in Chile: GDP per capita, income inequality, and extreme poverty. GDP is measured in current international dollars (PPP); inequality is measured using the Gini Index (0 = perfect equality, 100 = maximum inequality); poverty is measured as the share of the population living on less than $3.00 per day (2021 PPP). Lines reflect trends over the 1980–2023 period. For actual values, refer to the respective figures in this chapter. The red line shows GDP per capita, the blue line shows the Gini Index, and the green line shows the percentage of the population living in poverty. *Source* Author with data from World Bank [NY.GDP.PCAP.PP.CD; SI.POV.GINI; SI.POV.DDAY])

top income brackets. However, this diagnosis is typically made through

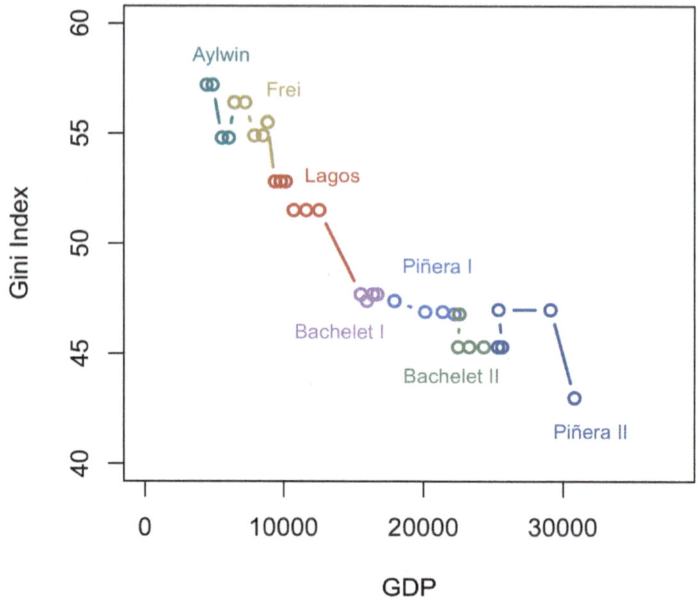

Fig. 5.10 Inequality vs growth by government, 1990–2023 (*Note* Relationship between income inequality and economic growth in Chile across presidential administrations from 1990 to 2023. GDP per capita is measured in current international dollars (PPP), and income inequality is measured using the Gini Index (0 = perfect equality, 100 = maximum inequality). Each colored line traces the evolution of GDP and Gini Index during one administration. The horizontal position shows average income level; the vertical position shows income inequality. Lines reflect temporal sequences but use distinct axes: GDP is measured on the horizontal axis, Gini Index on the vertical axis. For underlying values, see Figures 5.1 and 5.8. *Source* Author with data from World Bank [NY.GDP.PCAP.PP.CD; SI.POV.GINI])

comparisons with other OECD countries.[9] In that context, Chile's

[9] Social mobility refers to the extent to which individuals or families can move between different income or social strata over time, both across generations (intergenerational mobility) and within a person's lifetime (intragenerational mobility). High mobility implies a dynamic society where opportunities are broadly accessible, while low mobility—often described through metaphors like "sticky floors" (entrenched poverty) and "sticky ceilings" (barriers to top income levels)—indicates structural rigidity. Chile has been diagnosed with

patterns do not necessarily reflect a complete lack of mobility, but rather limited mobility within a select group of advanced economies. Chile fares poorly compared to the world's most developed nations, but this reflects the high benchmark as much as Chile's own performance. Even limited mobility within such a group, given certain conditions, can still be considered a form of success.

To avoid cherry-picking international benchmarks, it is useful to compare Chile to itself. And when this is done, a more nuanced picture emerges. According to the 2024 UNAB study on multidimensional social mobility,[10] a considerable share of Chileans—particularly those starting from disadvantaged positions—achieved upward mobility across key areas such as education, housing quality, and access to consumption.[11] While there is significant room for improvement, the data suggests that Chile is not defined by rigid class immobility, as generally denounced, but by a dynamic context where meaningful advancement is achievable under the right set of circumstances.[12]

both phenomena when compared to other OECD countries. For a detailed comparative analysis and methodological discussion, see: Organisation for Economic Co-operation and Development (OECD). 2018. *A broken social elevator? How to promote social mobility*, 79–80. Paris: OECD Publishing.

[10] For the complete study and methodological overview, see: Universidad Andrés Bello (UNAB), Instituto de Políticas Públicas. 2024. *Estudio UNAB de movilidad social multidimensional*. Santiago: Universidad Andrés Bello. This report offers a multidimensional framework for assessing social mobility, incorporating indicators beyond income—such as education, housing quality, consumption, and neighborhood security—to capture a more holistic picture of intergenerational advancement in Chile.

[11] The UNAB study reports a national average of 12% net upward mobility across all measured dimensions. Disaggregated data show notably higher rates in specific areas: 52.4% in education, 48% in housing quality, and 31.9% in access to consumption. However, mobility in neighborhood security declined by 42.7%, substantially lowering the composite index. These results indicate that while certain structural challenges—particularly in safety—remain, they are not insurmountable. The data suggest that targeted policy interventions can meaningfully enhance mobility outcomes when enabling conditions (such as education access, infrastructure, and services) are present.

[12] One emerging explanation for observed upward mobility highlights the unexpected positive role of Chile's private higher education system. Recent empirical work shows that access to elite universities can enable low-status students to accumulate and transmit social capital to their children, not through academic outcomes, but through social networks and status reproduction. This challenges traditional critiques of private education's role in intergenerational inequality. See: Barrios-Fernández, A., C. A. Neilson, and S. D. Zimmerman. 2024. *Elite universities and the intergenerational transmission of human and social capital*, (IZA Discussion Papers 17252). Bonn: Institute of Labor

Taken together, these indicators challenge the narrative that inequality was the primary driver of the social unrest. While public dissatisfaction with the economic model was evident, data do not fully support claims that inequality was worsening, intractable, or directly associated with Chile's growth trajectory. This does not dismiss the relevance of inequality as a contributing factor; instead, it proposes that, at best, it can only partially explain the unrest. Therefore, the *full story* likely lies elsewhere, with alternative factors emerging as complementary or more probable causes of the discontent. The next section explores these possibilities. Before proceeding, however, a quick passage considering why the standard explanation gained such widespread acceptance despite its limitations is warranted.

5.4.3 Crafting of the Narrative

Why did the inequality-focused narrative gain so much traction in explaining Chile's social outburst in 2019 despite evidence that challenges its major claims? The answer to this question is crucial for understanding not only the rise of crisis but also the formation of consequent political and social debates. While the idea that inequality contributed to the unrest may be partially true, data imply that its role was exaggerated, and it was not the sole cause. The widespread acceptance of this explanation was likely as much a product of intellectual, political, and rhetorical efforts as it was a result of incorrect, or at the very least self-serving, data-driven analysis.

In the years before the unrest, prominent left-leaning intellectuals and political actors were increasingly advancing critiques of Chile's neoliberal model.[13] These critiques portrayed the economic system as fundamentally

Economics. Further evidence also points to the role of educational attainment in shaping mobility in urban Chile. See: Espinoza, O., L. E. González, and D. Uribe. 2009. "Movilidad social en Chile: El caso del gran Santiago urbano." *Revista de Ciencias Sociales* 15(4): 586–606.

[13] Readers may recall that through the early 2000s, much of the center-left intellectual elite continued to argue that the *Concertación* was delivering meaningful results. Concepts such as *reforma a las reformas* and *crecer con igualdad* served both to legitimize "the model" and to highlight its achievements, but this narrative began to lose force as indicators plateaued toward the end of Michelle Bachelet's first government, creating pressure for a new explanation ahead of elections. At this juncture, elites confronted what can be described as a "fork in the road": either attribute responsibility to the *Concertación* itself

flawed and emphasized persistent social inequity and structural exclusion. While these arguments often had their merits, they increasingly tended to attribute problems to "the system" rather than to issues that could be more plausibly explained by government incompetence.[14] When the social outburst occurred, critics were quick to frame it as the culmination of the systemic failures they had long been warning about and used the event as evidence to validate their claims.

Left-wing intellectuals and activists perceived and portrayed the crisis less as a surprising rupture and more as an inevitable reckoning. Many pointed to social and economic disparities as a sign of deep-seated systemic dysfunction for years. Articulated through books, essays, blogs, podcasts, and eclectic public commentaries, their critiques identified a receptive audience among Chileans who were seeking explanations for their frustrations. Highlighting real grievances such as increased household debt, perceived exclusion from economic opportunities, and dissatisfaction with privatized social services, they resonated with public sentiment, oversimplifying a complex issue by overwhelmingly attributing it to inequality.

or to the system as a whole. They chose the latter, thereby protecting their own political record while reframing the problem in structural terms. It is important to emphasize that this center-left elite was not an opposition force but the establishment, controlling the executive branch and a majority in Congress while facing no organized challenge to their left. As Chapter 4 noted, the far left did not gain formal entry into politics until the pactos de omisión in 2008 and did not secure representation in Congress through the Communist Party until 2009. This context helps explain why mainstream criticism of "the model" did not emerge until the *Concertación* itself opened the door—and why, when it did, its leaders perceived little political risk in doing so, assuming such criticism would help them win elections and retain power rather than destabilize the system.

[14] The tendency to deflect responsibility by blaming "the model" rather than specific administrations would naturally intensify after the fall of the *Concertación*, becoming a recurring rhetorical device for change during Michelle Bachelet's second government (see Chapter 8) and later serving as a justification for several failures under Gabriel Boric's government (see Chapter 15). In the latter case, it was common for government aligned sectors to criticize "the model" for shortcomings that could just as easily be attributed to the administration itself. One notable example was the security crisis that escalated after the social outburst and during the constitutional debates, where, despite clear evidence of operational and strategic shortcomings, public discourse often reframed the issue as a systemic flaw rather than an avoidable failure of leadership. See: Bunker, K. 2024. "La crisis de seguridad es culpa del modelo." *Ex Ante*. July 27. https://www.ex-ante.cl/la-crisis-de-seguridad-es-culpa-del-modelo-porkenneth-bunker/

The appeal of the narrative was intensified by its intellectual backing. Academics (i.e., sociologists, economists, and lawyers) played a key role in constructing a cohesive framework that blamed economic challenges in Chile on the excesses of neoliberalism. Using research papers, media appearances, and public lectures, they provided the theoretical foundation for the argument that inequality was the root of the unrest. While many of the claims were grounded in legitimate concerns, the framework mainly relied on selective data and, as such, inevitably overlooked evidence that contradicted their conclusions. For instance, as previously discussed, Chile's Gini coefficient steadily declined across decades, and the country achieved one of the highest rates of upward mobility among OECD nations. Challenging the notion of worsening inequality, these facts were frequently downplayed or outright ignored.

Moreover, the political landscape played a significant role in the narrative's dominance (this is discussed at length in Chapter 8). Left-leaning political elites quickly adopted and promoted the inequality argument, thereby framing it as the core justification for sweeping reforms. The social outburst presented these leaders with a unique opportunity to align policy proposals with public grievances, thus positioning themselves as champions of change. By associating the unrest with systemic inequality, they called for far-reaching reforms, including the subsequent constitutional process (see Chapter 10). While this framing clearly reduced a multifaceted crisis into a singular issue, it was politically effective and aligned with public sentiment, making it *well worth the while*.

At the same time, the inequality argument gained traction because it faced little opposition. The conservative right, which may have been expected to defend Chile's neoliberal model, found difficulty in presenting a compelling counternarrative. Conservatives mainly focused on macroeconomic stability and economic growth and failed to address the lived experiences of ordinary Chileans who felt excluded or left behind. This disconnect weakened their ability to challenge the inequality narrative, which in turn enabled critics to dominate the discourse. Furthermore, the majority of the right's support for the neoliberal model was pragmatic instead of ideological and focused on outcomes instead of values. This general scenario left them ill-equipped and out-of-step to engage in the type of value-driven rhetoric that resonated with the public.

Again, without a doubt, inequality was *a* factor in the social outburst. Real grievances related to wealth disparity, access to basic services, and perceptions of inequity fueled frustration among the public. However, the data complicate the argument that inequality was worsening, entrenched, or inherently associated with the unrest. As such, it is difficult if not impossible to argue that inequality was *the* factor in the outburst. As previously discussed, Chile made significant progress in reducing inequality and fostering upward mobility, and the economic model *was* delivering tangible improvements for Chileans. This indicates that other factors and perceptions *must have* been at play.

Ultimately, the inequality-focused narrative gained traction due to its explanatory power as well as its simplicity and political utility. It proffered a clear and emotionally resonant explanation for a multilevel crisis, which made its communication and mobilization easy. However, by overstating the role of inequality, this narrative overshadowed other important drivers of discontent and ultimately undermined the entire reformist effort itself (as described in Chapter 13 and, to a certain extent, again in Chapter 17).

5.5 Complex Theory

While income inequality remains a critical issue, as previously discussed, it could not have been the only—or even the primary—cause of the social unrest in Chile in 2019. If inequality had been truly the overriding factor, then the first constitutional proposal, which aimed to address many of these structural disparities, would have been approved. Instead, its rejection implies that other factors moderated the influence of inequality, or it was only one among other causes of the crisis.

With this in mind, it is important to lay out three plausible explanations that could serve as moderating factors amplifying the effects of inequality or directly as independent variables contributing to the unrest. These explanations—financial vulnerability, perceptions of systemic unfairness, and frustrations with perceived inequity in outcomes—help exemplify the multifaceted nature of the grievances that led to the outburst. They also highlight why the oversimplified narrative that "inequality was the root cause" falls short of fully explaining the unrest.

5.5.1 *Sense of Financial Vulnerability*

For instance, a critical factor in understanding Chile's 2019 social unrest, independent of economic inequality, is the pervasive sense of financial vulnerability. This reflects not just structural weaknesses but also a psychological dimension, encompassing individuals' concerns about their ability to sustain progress and withstand economic shocks. In Chile, this vulnerability was neither new nor isolated; it had been embedded in public consciousness for decades, shaped by a series of historical and structural conditions.

The 2007–2008 global financial crisis vividly exemplifies how financial vulnerability came to the forefront. Although Chile weathered the crisis better than many nations—due in part to Finance Minister Andrés Velasco's proactive countercyclical policies, including increased public spending and strategic use of sovereign wealth funds—the crisis nevertheless had a lasting impact on Chileans.[15] The sharp decline in global demand for copper, one of Chile's primary exports, resulted in GDP contraction, rising unemployment, and stagnating wages.[16] These disruptions directly affected households, forcing many Chileans to confront the fragility of their economic positions.

[15] Finance Minister Andrés Velasco's management of Chile's sovereign wealth funds during the 2007–2008 global financial crisis is widely regarded as a textbook example of countercyclical fiscal policy. By deploying accumulated surpluses to finance public spending during the downturn, Chile was able to cushion the economy and preserve macroeconomic stability. However, critics argued that while the strategy was effective at the macro level, it fell short in addressing immediate distributive concerns and public perceptions of vulnerability. See: *Diario Financiero*. 2009. "Velasco destacó política fiscal contra cíclica aplicada por el gobierno." January 20. https://www.df.cl/economia-y-politica/velasco-destaco-politica-fiscal-contraciclica-aplicada-por-el-gobierno/. It should also be noted that criticism regarding the fiscal prudence shown by Velasco and Bachelet up until the crisis shifted once it hit, as it became clear that Chile had been able to weather the downturn better than other countries precisely because of the specific economic policies adopted beforehand. Remarkably, Velasco rose to the top of the cabinet's popularity rankings—an achievement unmatched before or since. See: Long, G. 2009. "Innovative Leader of the Year: Andrés Velasco – Steward of Chile's Wealth." *LatinTrade*. http://latintrade.com/2009/10/innovative-leader-of-the-year-andres-velasco-steward-of-chile's-wealth/

[16] Chile's heavy reliance on copper exports—often accounting for nearly half of its total export revenues—has made the economy especially sensitive to fluctuations in global commodity prices. During the 2007–2008 financial crisis, the steep fall in copper demand contributed to a contraction in GDP, rising unemployment, and wage stagnation. These impacts exposed a structural vulnerability in Chile's growth model, highlighting how global shocks can quickly translate into household-level insecurity. For a comparative perspective on how Chile was affected by recent economic crises, see: Fierro, P. 2020. "¿Cuánto nos afectaron las últimas crisis?" *Diario Financiero*. June 5. https://www.df.cl/reportajes/cuanto-nos-afectaron-las-ultimas-crisis/

For families that had recently escaped poverty or joined the middle class, the crisis exposed how easily progress could be reversed. This sense of precariousness was not limited to the fallout from 2007–2008. Earlier crises, such as the 1998 Asian financial crisis, mentioned in Chapter 4, had also revealed the volatility of Chile's economy, which was heavily reliant on global commodity markets. In both cases, external shocks highlighted the limits of Chile's market-oriented model in insulating citizens from global economic instability.[17] It became evident that economic advancement in Chile was fragile, unevenly distributed, and vulnerable to forces beyond citizens' control.

Importantly, this sense of financial vulnerability does not only denote macroeconomic indicators such as GDP growth or unemployment rates. It is also shaped by daily experience and anxiety about maintaining standards of living. For example, households dependent on variable incomes (e.g., households with informal or precarious employment) felt disproportionately affected by economic downturns. Even workers in stable jobs were acutely aware of rising costs for essentials, such as healthcare and education, which strained family budgets and elevated feelings of insecurity. The perception of weak safety nets, which failed to provide adequate protection against shocks, compounded these pressures.

This perception of vulnerability provides a crucial distinction from the commonly held narrative that income inequality, as a byproduct of neoliberalism, was the sole driver of the unrest. In contrast to inequality, which emphasizes disparities in individuals that benefit the most from the

[17] As referenced in Chapter 4, by the turn of the century—and during the first five or so years of the 2000s—many of the most respected economists associated with the *Concertación* were offering a positive assessment of "the model's" performance. However, because the academic debate of the time was shaped by political incentives, the pivotal moment was set at 1989, with the model's benefits attributed to the return of democracy under the *Concertación* rather than to the earlier economic foundations. This was, among other, the position of Ricardo Ffrench-Davis, who, at least until 2005, continued to argue in favor of the Chilean economy's strengths. While the political dimension is examined in greater depth in other chapters, it is worth noting here that by then the 1998 Asian financial crisis was already being interpreted—or presented—as a factor capable of shifting Chilean public opinion. See Ffrench-Davis, R. 2002. "Entre el neoliberalismo y el crecimiento con equidad." *Revista de Economía Política* 22(4): 594–612; Ffrench-Davis, R. 2001. *Tres Décadas de Política Económica*. Santiago: Dolmen Ediciones; and Ffrench-Davis, R. 2005. *Economic Reforms in Chile: From Dictatorship to Democracy*, 4th ed. Ann Arbor, MI: University of Michigan Press.

system, financial vulnerability focuses on the broad failure of the system to ensure resilience and security for its citizens.

At the same time, financial vulnerability may function as a moderator that heightens the significance of inequality as a predictor of the unrest. Inequality alone cannot necessarily lead to widespread discontent unless it is paired with high levels of perceived vulnerability, in which citizens feel unprotected and insecure. Under such conditions, disparities in wealth and opportunity become increasingly pronounced, thus fueling grievance and resentment. In this manner, financial vulnerability magnifies the impact of inequality, thus making it a more potent driver of the unrest only when the perception of systemic fragility reaches critical levels. As such, this dual role positions vulnerability as an essential lens through which the dynamics of the social outburst in 2019 can be understood.

5.5.2 *Perception of Systemic Unfairness*

Another potential determinant of the 2019 social unrest, regardless of material inequality, is the pervasive perception of systemic unfairness, which local discourse denotes as *desigualdad de trato* or "inequality in treatment." In contrast to disparities in wealth or income, systemic unfairness mainly pertains to unequal access to opportunities, entrenched social hierarchies, and perceived favoritism in everyday life. It reflects frustration rooted in historical, cultural, and institutional dynamics, addressing the interpersonal and subjective dimensions of inequality that measurable economic metrics fail to measure.

This perception deeply resonates in Chilean society because it reflects structural patterns of exclusion rooted in the country's colonial past and its enduring ramifications.[18] Racial and cultural hierarchies, which were established during colonialism and reinforced by European immigration, historically privileged certain groups over others. These dynamics

[18] For a detailed analysis of the long-term persistence of social hierarchies and their impact on mobility in Latin American societies, see: Jaramillo-Echeverri, J., A. Álvarez, and N. Bro. 2021. *Surnames and social rank: Long-term traits of social mobility in Colombia and Chile*. Caracas, CAF—Development Bank of Latin America. This study uses historical surname data to trace elite family persistence over generations, revealing that patterns of entrenched privilege in Chile—similar to Colombia—are deeply rooted in colonial legacies. The findings provide empirical support for the notion of *desigualdad de trato* as a socially transmitted, institutionally reinforced phenomenon that extends beyond material inequality.

contributed to a sense of marginalization among indigenous populations, Afro-descendants, and other non-European groups. While evidence of upward mobility has been observed in these groups in recent years, the perception of exclusion from full participation in society remains a significant grievance.

Elite networks entrench systemic unfairness, as they focus on exclusive schools, family connections, and inherited social capital. These networks preserve cycles of privilege, thus ensuring that positions of power and influence remain concentrated within smaller, more insulated groups.[19] For many Chileans, these structures represented formidable barriers to upward mobility and reinforced the belief that opportunities were distributed based on privilege instead of merit. Despite certain exceptions, their persistence underscores the perception of systemic unfairness as a structural instead of an occasional phenomenon.

Similarly, entrenched hierarchies related to labor and occupation can perpetuate systemic unfairness in everyday life.[20] Domestic workers, janitors, and manual laborers typically face significant social devaluation and encounter limited opportunities for advancement, which can in turn reinforce perceptions of inequality in treatment. These occupational divisions

[19] Though numerically small, Chile's elite exerts disproportionate influence on the reproduction of privilege through mechanisms such as exclusive schooling, closed social networks, and intergenerational transmission of social capital. Economist Sergio Urzúa has discussed the role of elite endogamy in shaping inequality and limiting mobility, drawing on Rothkopf's evocative observation that "Chile is not a country, but a country club." These dynamics underscore how elite cohesion can amplify broader perceptions of systemic unfairness across society. See: Úrzua, S. 2024. "La élite endogámica de Chile: La desigualdad, pobreza y catástrofe social que impone la clase alta a través del sistema educacional." *El Ciudadano*. January 17. https://www.elciudadano.com/chile/elite-endogamica-chile-la-desigualdad-pobreza-y-catastrofe-social-que-impone-la-clase-alta-a-traves-del-sistema-educacional/01/17/

[20] Economic inequality alone does not fully capture the roots of social discontent in Chile. Research by Emmanuelle Barozet and Oscar Mac-Clure emphasizes that perceptions of injustice often arise from structural and symbolic dimensions of inequality—what they term inequality in treatment—which manifest in devaluation of labor roles, limited occupational mobility, and deep-seated social hierarchies. These factors contribute to a broader sense of exclusion and resentment that can persist even amid economic growth. See: Barozet, E., and O. Mac-Clure. 2015. "Tolerancia a la desigualdad y justicia social. Una agenda teórica de investigación." In *Desigualdades. Tolerancia, legitimación y conflicto en las sociedades latinoamericanas*, edited by M. Castillo and C. Maldonado, 151–182. Santiago: RIL Editores.

extend beyond economic issues, reflect profound societal attitudes toward the worth and roles of different groups.

The perception of systemic unfairness also manifests in interactions with institutions and governance. Bureaucratic inefficiency, perceived corruption, and favoritism in public agencies exacerbate feelings of alienation. Many Chileans have reported that their voices are ignored or deprioritized in decision-making processes, which likely fosters widespread mistrust in institutions. This alienation persists despite improvements in economic indicators, illustrating how systemic unfairness can remain a potent source of discontent regardless of material inequality.

Given these dynamics, systemic unfairness alone offers a compelling explanation for the 2019 social unrest in Chile. Its entrenched nature, rooted in the historical and societal structures, permeates every aspect of life—from interpersonal relationships to interactions with institutions—creating a pervasive sense of injustice. In contrast to income inequality, which can improve through targeted policies, addressing systemic unfairness is more difficult. This enduring perception of unequal treatment is sufficient to provoke widespread discontent because it undermines trust in the system and erodes the promise of equal opportunity.

At the same time, systemic unfairness can function as a critical moderating factor in the relationship between inequality and social unrest. While inequality alone may fail to incite large-scale discontent, it becomes increasingly impactful when paired with perceptions of unfair treatment. In these cases, disparities in wealth and opportunity are not merely perceived as economic grievances but also interpreted through the lens of systemic unfairness, amplifying their emotional weight. *Desigualdad de trato* transforms material inequality into a more deeply felt and urgent grievance, which renders inequality a significant predictor of unrest only when combined with high levels of perceived unfairness.

5.5.3 *Frustration with the Model's Fairness*

A third key factor that may have contributed to the social unrest in 2019, independent of economic inequality as above, was widespread frustration with the perceived fairness of the economic model adopted by Chile. In contrast to critiques that outrightly reject the neoliberal system, this frustration stems from tension between achievements due to the model and the growing aspirations it cultivated. Many Chileans recognized the capacity of the model to generate economic growth, reduce poverty, and extend access to goods and services. However, they were dissatisfied with the uneven distribution of these benefits and the incentives for higher expectations fostered by the system, which it ultimately failed to meet.

The economic model launched financial tools and programs that substantially improved access to diverse opportunities for many Chileans. For instance, government subsidies for homeownership enabled thousands of families to acquire their first homes, fostering a sense of security and progress. Similarly, supermarket credit cards and small bank loans provided households with a means to meet urgent needs and acquire goods that were previously out of reach. These financial innovations expanded participation in modern economic life, which showcases the system's ability to improve living standards and empower individuals to pursue long-term goals.

At the same time, the system's success in expanding access raised expectations that were not fully realized for many. Families faced with stagnant wages and rising living costs typically found difficulty in sustaining the opportunities introduced by the model. Frustration lay in the perceived inability of the model to deliver broader benefits to all instead of its core principles. For the majority of Chileans, readopting former state-centered economic systems was not a solution; they valued the market-based model but sought reforms to ensure receipt of a larger and fairer share of its rewards.

This frustration with fairness highlights how the model aroused aspirations for a better quality of life, which led people to desire not only access but also equity in the opportunities it introduced. The perception that financial rewards and opportunities were concentrated among elites, whereas ordinary citizens bore heavier burdens, encouraged resentment across socioeconomic groups. For middle-class Chileans with certain levels of upward mobility, this frustration frequently stemmed from the precariousness of their progress, as they struggled to maintain their quality of life amid economic uncertainty and mounting financial pressures.

Frustration with fairness thus provides a rival explanation for the unrest, which emphasizes how the system's successes paradoxically fueled discontent. It captures the sentiment of citizens who benefited from the model but still felt excluded from its rewards. By cultivating aspirations for increased participation and opportunity, the system raised expectations that were difficult to meet for large proportions of the population. These frustrations imply that the unrest was not necessarily a rejection of the model; instead, it was a demand for its broad and equitable delivery.

At the same time, frustration with fairness can also serve as a crucial moderating factor in the relationship between inequality and unrest.[21] Economic inequality may not always lead to discontent; however, it becomes a more potent source of grievance when paired with the perception that the system disproportionately benefits a small number of elites (which is not the same as believing the system is designed to hinder the majority, "systemically unfair"). When doubts about the uneven distribution of rewards and opportunities combine with dissatisfaction over income inequality, an emotionally charged concern can quickly escalate into a politically significant issue.

5.6 Conclusion

This chapter outlined Chile's extraordinary developmental achievements: sustained economic growth, dramatic poverty reduction, and significant improvement in social indicators such as life expectancy and access to clean water. These accomplishments placed Chile at the forefront of success stories in the region, illustrating the potential of "the model" in delivering broad-based progress. However, the 2019 social outburst presented a stark contradiction: despite decades of measurable advancements, a profound sense of public dissatisfaction erupted into one of the most significant social uprisings in the history of the nation. This paradox—the coexistence of progress with discontent—required an in-depth examination of the roots of Chileans' frustrations.

The standard explanation that emerged after the unrest was mainly focused on inequality and framed Chile's neoliberal model as the primary source of systemic failure. Advocates of this view argued that decades of market-driven policies concentrated wealth and opportunity among a privileged few, while leaving the majority feeling excluded. However, as demonstrated in this chapter, the data undermined this simplistic narrative. Income inequality steadily declined, upward mobility was low in comparison to advanced economies but still relevant in the internal context, and Chile balanced economic growth with improvement in

[21] Reader should note that all three alternative hypotheses, that are presented as mediators of the impact of income inequality, may also have moderating effects on each other. For example, Chileans that were doing well by the end of the 1990s, but were negatively impacted by the Asian crisis may have taken a more agressive stance against the economy for not being able to deliver on its promises later on.

equity. These findings suggest that the standard narrative failed to capture the actual complexity of social discontent in Chile.

The alternative explanations explored in this chapter offered a nuanced understanding of the unrest. These perspectives pointed out that public dissatisfaction was less on the outright rejection of the neoliberal model and more on side frustrations. A pervasive sense of financial vulnerability, which was deeply embedded in public consciousness, heightened anxieties about the precariousness of progress. This vulnerability stemmed from systemic exposure to economic volatility, such as reliance on commodity exports, and the lack of adequate safety nets to protect citizens from such instability.

Perceptions of unfair treatment—or *desigualdad de trato*—further amplified frustrations. Despite improvement in measurable inequality, many Chileans felt excluded through inefficiency and systemic inequity in accessing services such as healthcare, education, and housing. These perceptions reflected broad structural and institutional dynamics that left many with the perception that the system was not designed to work for them, regardless of their effort.

And dissatisfaction with the model's equity centered on its inability to deliver benefits quickly or equitably, instead of the outright rejection of its economic framework, also mattered. The system's success in improving access to opportunities and raising expectations paradoxically fueled discontent when progress was seemingly slow or disproportionate. For many citizens, frustrations originated from the perception that rewards and opportunities remained concentrated among elites, whereas ordinary citizens bore the heavy burden of economic precarity. This dissatisfaction highlighted a demand for reforms to address these inequities and deliver tangible, widespread benefits, and not a rejection of "the model."

These alternative theories suggest that the unrest was not simply a wholesale rejection of the neoliberal framework but a call to address its shortcomings. Many Chileans viewed "the model" as capable of producing wealth and progress, but were frustrated by its inability to distribute such benefits in a sufficiently quick or fair manner. This perspective alone challenges the standard narrative by reframing the unrest as a demand for an in-depth, more inclusive application of "the model" instead of its abandonment.

By presenting these contrasting theories, this chapter revealed the fragility of the oversold inequality narrative and underscored the need to focus on the structural and societal nuances that formed the unrest.

The frustration expressed in 2019 was inequality as well as fairness, inclusion, and the pace of progress. This realization reframes the discussion on Chile's social and political crisis and sets the stage for understanding the broad constitutional debates explored later in the book.

Part II: Rupture

CHAPTER 6

A Shifting Political System

6.1 Introduction

Up to this point, this book has explored how Chile's 1980 Constitution helped the country move from crisis and turmoil toward stability and development. Central to this success was the consolidation of Chile's political and economic model, which, although established under dictatorship, was deepened and widened in democracy, under four successive governments of the *Concertación* (1990 to 2010) and one of the *Alianza* (2010 to 2014). The results, partially described in Chapters 4 and 5, not only earned Chile international recognition, but also led to an invitation to join the OECD.

Far from accidental, this success was part of a design—particularly one rooted in the rules established by the 1980 Constitution, which provided the right incentives for the country to achieve stability and, from there, foster development. In particular, the stability resulted from a political system that balanced competition and coordination (see Chapter 2), with both major coalitions playing a central role in shaping public policy and governance, as well as insulating it from major disruptions. For two decades, Chile's political landscape remained predictable and resistant to fragmentation. However, as this chapter demonstrates, this foundation would begin to crack around 2010.

The cracks, however, would emerge from within, as suggested in Chapter 4. It was not the people demanding change, but political parties

K. Bunker, *Chile's Transformation Amidst Crisis*,
https://doi.org/10.1007/978-3-031-96463-3_6

that found it increasingly unable to coexist. The downfall of the two-party system was not a result of popular discontent, but rather the product of elite feuds and internal divisions. What had once provided stability began to unravel from the top, threatening to bring the whole established order with it.

The consequence was a series of institutional reforms that in turn led to a surge of new coalitions, parties, and candidates entering the political arena (see Figures A1, A2, and A3 in the Appendix). These newcomers not only challenged the long-standing dominance of the traditional coalitions but also boosted the critiques mentioned in Chapter 5 and generated momentum for sweeping changes to the existing political order.

This chapter traces how changes in the party system allowed these critiques to gain traction, ultimately contributing to a broader transformation of Chile's political landscape. By examining the historical development of the party system, it aims both to map its transformation over time and to identify the mechanisms that led to its fragmentation and polarization. In doing so, it provides a framework for understanding how the disintegration of the party system contributed to the political and institutional crisis of 2019.

6.2 Historical Eras Since the First Constitution

This section introduces the major political eras in Chile's history, providing a foundation for understanding the evolution of the country's political system. Readers familiar with Chile's political history may wish to skip ahead to Sect. 6.3, which focuses on the fifth political cycle (1990—forward). For those seeking additional context, this section summarizes Chile's democratic evolution and sets the stage for understanding the political transformations explored later in this chapter.

Table 6.1 outlines the great five political eras of Chile, spanning from the early Conservative Republic (1833–1861) to the contemporary Second Presidential Republic (since 1990). Generally marked by military interventions, each era represents a distinct phase of governance, political dynamics, and institutional structures—providing a critical framework for understanding both continuity and rupture in Chilean democracy, as well as the evolution of its party systems over time.

The earliest era, known as the Conservative Republic (1833–1861), marked Chile's initial consolidation into a nation-state. This period

Table 6.1 A general outline of political eras in Chile since 1833

Era	*Cycle*	*Year start*	*Year end*	*Number of presidents*	*Dominant coalitions/parties*
Conservative Republic	1	1833	1861	3	Conservative-Liberal
Liberal Republic	2	1861	1891	5	Liberal-Conservative
Parliamentary Republic	3	1891	1924	9	Liberal-Liberal Democratic
First Presidential Republic	4	1925	1973	11	Liberal-Radical-Socialist-Christian Democrat
Second Presidential Republic	5A	1990	2014	5	Concertación-Alianza
	5B	2014	–	–	Nueva Mayoría-Chile Vamos-Apruebo Dignidad

Note Military coups occurred in 1891, 1924, and 1932, each followed by a one-year dictatorship. The 1973 coup led to a 17-year military dictatorship. *Source* Author with data from Servel; Heise 1974; Cruz-Coke 1984; and Urzúa Valenzuela 1992[1]

followed the adoption of the 1833 Constitution, which established a highly centralized governance framework. Political power during this period was concentrated in the hands of the *Partido Conservador* (Conservative Party), which aligned closely with the Catholic Church and upheld traditionalist values. Three presidents—José Joaquín Prieto, Manuel Bulnes, and Manuel Montt—successively led the country, each serving for a decade. The Conservative Party's dominance was preserved through strategic alliances with the liberal elite, ensuring both stability and continuity. This era was characterized by limited political pluralism, with conservative and liberal factions operating within a narrow ideological spectrum. While the centralized nature of the system provided the stability essential for nation-building, it also restricted broader democratic participation.

This order was disrupted by the emergence of the Liberal Republic (1861–1891), which ushered in political and economic reforms. Power

[1] All data regarding post-transition elections are available in Servel. For data prior to 1989, see: Heise, J. 1974. *Historia de Chile: el período parlamentario, 1861–1925.* Santiago: Andrés Bello; Cruz-Coke, R. 1984. *Historia electoral de Chile 1925–1973.* Santiago: Jurídica de Chile; Urzúa Valenzuela, G. 1992. *Historia política de Chile y su evolución electoral: Desde 1810 a 1992.* Santiago: Jurídica de Chile.

shifted to the *Partido Liberal* (Liberal Party), which, although rooted in elite circles, championed modernization, secularization, and expanded civil liberties. Five presidents—José Joaquín Pérez, Federico Errázuriz, Aníbal Pinto, Domingo Santa María, and José Manuel Balmaceda—governed during these 30 years, each serving six-year terms. This era witnessed significant transformations, including efforts to separate church and state, introduce educational reforms, and expand infrastructure projects. However, tensions between liberal reformers and conservative factions persisted, especially concerning economic policy and regional governance. These tensions culminated in the 1891 civil war, which resulted in the defeat of President Balmaceda and marked the abrupt end of the Liberal Republic. Balmaceda's death, following his political downfall, symbolized the volatility of this period and paved the way for a new political order.

The third era, the Parliamentary Republic (1891–1924), represented a dramatic shift in the balance of power. Following Balmaceda's defeat, Chile transitioned to a system in which the legislature dominated the executive. This parliamentary model significantly weakened the presidency, concentrating decision-making authority in Congress. Nine presidents served during this period, including Jorge Montt, Federico Errázuriz, Aníbal Zañartu, Germán Riesco, and Arturo Alessandri. Most of these leaders were career politicians with strong associations with the legislature, and their presidencies were often marked by short-lived coalitions and political maneuvering. While this era allowed for greater pluralism within elite circles, it also experienced inefficiency and political stagnation. Frequent changes in government undermined stability, and the legislature's dominance often paralyzed the executive's ability to implement policies. Growing social unrest, driven by labor movements and urbanization, further intensified these tensions. By 1924, mounting dissatisfaction with the parliamentary system, combined with military discontent, culminated in a coup that marked the end of this era.

The next major shift occurred in 1925 with the adoption of Chile's first democratic constitution, which ushered in the First Presidential Republic (1925–1973). This era was intended to restore balance between the executive and legislative branches while expanding democratic participation. However, significant instability marked its early years. Between 1925 and 1932, Chile experienced eight presidencies, out of which only three were elected by the public. Figures such as Emiliano Figueroa, Carlos Ibáñez del Campo, and Juan Esteban Montero faced difficulty in navigating this turbulent period, while frequent coups and political crises undermined their efforts. Stability was restored in 1932 with the reelection of Arturo Alessandri, who had previously served as president during the Parliamentary Republic. Alessandri's second term laid the groundwork for a long-lasting political order.

Ideological diversity and new political actors characterized the subsequent decades of the First Presidential Republic. Presidents from Partido Radical, namely Pedro Aguirre Cerda, Juan Antonio Ríos, and Gabriel González Videla, dominated the political landscape from 1938 to 1952. Their administrations focused on industrialization, labor rights, and social reforms, and were frequently in alliance with leftist movements. At the same time, conservative and Christian Democratic leaders, including Jorge Alessandri and Eduardo Frei Montalva, counterbalanced radical policies.

The era culminated with the election of Salvador Allende in 1970, the first Marxist president elected through democratic means. Socialist policies purported by Allende, particularly his efforts to nationalize industries, polarized the country and amplified political divisions. These tensions ceased in 1973 due to a military coup that overthrew Allende and established a 17-year dictatorship under the command of General Augusto Pinochet.

The readoption of democracy in 1990 marked the beginning of the Second Presidential Republic (1990–present), the fifth and most recent era in Chile's political history. As described in Chapter 4, this era began with the 1988 plebiscite in which Chileans voted to end the military regime of Pinochet and restore democratic governance. The center-left *Concertación* coalition, which united Christian Democrats, socialists, and other progressive forces, shaped the early years. Also described at length previosuly, it was during this period that Chile underwent significant institutional and political stabilization.

This all changed in 2010 with the election of Sebastián Piñera, a member of the center-right *Alianza* coalition. Piñera's presidency marked the first conservative government since 1958 and signaled a broad transformation within Chile's political system. The effect of the defeat on the center-left, discussed in Chapter 4 and again in Chapter 8, exerted a significant impact on the coalition, which arguably marked the decline of a cycle.

6.3 The Fifth Political Era

An in-depth examination of Chile's fifth political era, the Second Presidential Republic, reveals the need to distinguish between two cycles: the relatively stable period that lasted up until about 2014 and the more fragmented phase that began thereafter. The first cycle (marked as 5A in Table 6.1), was characterized by the dominance of the *Concertación* and *Alianza* coalitions, and enabled predictable governance and a stable political system. These coalitions, which consolidated diverse ideological tendencies under their banners, fostered political stability and mitigated the risks of electoral fragmentation. During this period, the two-coalition system served as a bulwark against major disruptions, ensuring a level of political cohesion conducive to effective governance, as intended per the Constitution (readers may recall Chapter 2).

The second cycle (marked as 5B in Table 6.1) constitutes a turning point as new players entered the arena, reshaped the party system, and altered the balance of power. The long-term two-coalition structure began to erode and the party system became less cohesive. Electoral fragmentation gave way to profound changes in political dynamics, as the emergence of new actors upended the previously stable framework. The shift in power distributions introduced a political volatility into Chilean politics that had not been seen in almost four decades.

To better understand the degree and nature of these events, this chapter turns to the effective number of parties (ENP),[2] a measure of party system fragmentation that considers the distribution of votes and seats to derive the actually relevant number of parties in a given system. In contrast to taking the observed count of political parties, the ENP reflects overall electoral or legislative influence (weight). For example, while an ENP close to two indicates a closed system dominated by two large, and relatively equal parties or coalitions, a value of, say, 5, implies greater fragmentation as there are at least five different yet relatively equal parties. As such, the measure helps identify not only the number of parties that compete in elections but also the extent of their political influence.

[2] The concept of the Effective Number of Parties was developed by Laakso and Taagepera. For the original proposal, see: Laakso, M. and R. Taagepera. 1979. ""Effective" number of parties: a measure with application to West Europe." *Comparative Political Studies* 12(1): 3–27.

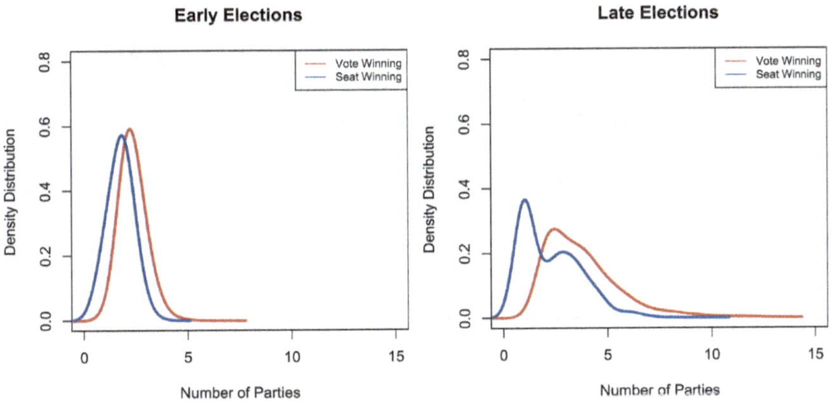

Fig. 6.1 Effective Number of Parties, 1989–2023 (*Note* Density distributions of the effective number of parties (electoral lists). Total sample size = 5,301, with each observation representing an individual electoral competition in any type of election held in Chile during the period covered (including Senate, Chamber of Deputies, Governors, Mayors, Regional Councilors, Local Councilors, and Constitutional assembly members). Left panel (1989–2008): sample size = 2,063; bandwidth = 0.5. Right panel (2008–2023): sample size = 3,238; bandwidth = 0.5. *Source* Author with data from Bunker 2025a[3])

[3] While it is clear that there are two distinct political eras within the Second Presidential Republic, as suggested in Table 6.1, based on traditional accounts that assess the rise and fall of the Concertación, dividing the period into equal parts allows us to test more systematically when meaningful shifts in the party system began to occur. When the data are split evenly, we observe a notable increase in the effective number of vote-winning parties (ENPv): from a mean of 2.36 (SD = 0.52, min = 1, max = 6.28) in the early period to 2.68 (SD = 0.82, min = 1, max = 7.30) in the late period. Using a 2014 cutoff—aligned with the end of the first part of the Second Presidential Republic—we see that ENPv rises only slightly, from 2.68 (SD = 0.82, min = 1, max = 7.30) in the 1990–2014 period to 2.78 (SD = 1.03, min = 1, max = 7.30) in the 2015–2023 period. This suggests that fragmentation was already underway well before the 2015 electoral reform. When isolating the analysis to lower chamber elections, where the impact of institutional change would be most direct, the pattern becomes even clearer. Under the equal split, ENPv increases from 2.34 (SD = 0.35, max = 3.65) to 3.10 (SD = 1.09, max = 7.01), and under the 2014 cutoff, it rises sharply from 2.38 (SD = 0.38, max = 4.14) to 4.39 (SD = 0.93, max = 7.01). These results indicate that while fragmentation began at some point towards the end of the 2000s, and that the 2015 reform did not cause the shift, but rather acted as a catalyst, amplifying existing trends and accelerating the breakdown of Chile's historically stable, two-party system.

Figure 6.1 shows the distribution of the ENP across every electoral contest in Chile since 1989.[4] It illustrates the ENP (measured in terms of vote-winning and seat-winning electoral lists) for two distinct periods: early elections on the left and late elections on the right. The differences in the shapes of the curves (in terms of height and length) highlight a clear contrast. In the earlier period, there were fewer parties, and the system was more stable, as reflected in the lower mean and standard deviation of the ENP compared to the later elections. These patterns illustrate the transition from a more consolidated and predictable party system to one increasingly fragmented and dynamic.

6.3.1 The Conventional Wisdom

Why is fragmentation higher in later elections? This is a key question, as it is obvious, at this point, that changes within the party system are connected to the broader social and political crisis of 2019. To address this, it is necessary to explore the factors that theoretically lead party systems to expand (fragment). Political science literature provides a well-established framework for understanding this phenomenon, emphasizing two main causes: changes in the structure of society and changes in the rules governing elections.

The first explanation argues that societies with more cleavages tend to have more political parties than those with fewer cleavages. Societies with numerous and deeper divisions—along lines such as class, religion, ethnicity, or region—are more likely to produce fragmented party systems, as distinct parties emerge to represent these diverse interests. In contrast, societies with fewer and less pronounced cleavages typically exhibit more consolidated party systems.[5]

[4] The data that underpin the figures in this Chapter are derived from an original dataset of 5,301 district-level electoral returns. For details on data, methods and applications, see: Bunker, K. 2025a. "Challenging Conventional Wisdom in New Democracies: Social Diversity, Electoral Rules, and Party System Fragmentation in Chile." *Election Law Journal: Rules, Politics, and Policy* (online first): 1–25; Bunker, K. 2025b. "Mapping party systems over time: A spatial distribution of ideological competition in Chile." *Journal of Political Ideologies* (online first): 1–18.

[5] The basic proposal is that large-scale social movements generate demand for new political parties, and as these parties consolidate, party systems transform. This theory originates in Lipset, S. M., and S. Rokkan. 1967. *Cleavage Structures, Party Systems, and Voter Alignments*. New York, NY: Free Press. Yet it has been refined and adopted

However, societal cleavages alone cannot fully account for variations in party system fragmentation. While they can generate the baseline demand for political representation, electoral rules must have a say in shaping the supply-side of parties by determining how easy it is to win. In this, it is clear that systems with high institutional barriers tend to restrict the number of viable parties more than those with permissive rules, that purposely create opportunities for smaller or emerging parties to enter the system.[6]

profusely since. See, for example, Deegan-Krause, K. 2007. "New Dimensions of Political Cleavage." In *The Oxford Handbook of Political Behavior*, edited by R. J. Dalton and H-D. Klingemann, 538–556. Oxford: Oxford University Press; Bartolini, S., and P. Mair. 1990. *Identity, Competition, and Electoral Availability: The Stabilization of European Electorates 1885–1985*. Cambridge: Cambridge University Press. The framework has also been applied substantially to the Latin American context, as visible in works such as Dix, R. H. 1989. "Cleavage Structures and Party Systems in Latin America." *Comparative Politics* 22(1): 23–37; Coppedge, M. 1998. "The Evolution of Latin American Party Systems." In *Politics, Society, and Democracy: Latin America*, edited by S. Mainwaring and A. Valenzuela, 172–206; Boulder: Westview Press; Roberts, K. M., and E. Wibbels. 1999. "Party Systems and Electoral Volatility in Latin America: A Test of Economic, Institutional, and Structural Explanations." *American Political Science Review* 93(3): 575–90. Mainwaring, S., and T. R. Scully, eds. 1995. *Building Democratic Institutions: Party Systems in Latin America*. Stanford, CA: Stanford University Press. The Chilean case has been examined in both the pre- and post-Pinochet eras. See: Gil, F. 1969. *El sistema político de Chile*. Santiago: Editorial Andrés Bello; Scully, T. R. 1992. Rethinking the Center: Party Politics in Nineteenth-and Twentieth-Century Chile. Stanford, CA: Stanford University Press. Gamboa, R., M. López, and J. Baeza. 2013. "La evolución programática de los partidos chilenos: 1970–2009: de la polarización al consenso." *Revista de Ciencia Política* 33(2): 443–67; Garretón, M. A. 1983. *El proceso político chileno*. Santiago: FLACSO; Valenzuela, J. S. 1995. "Orígenes y transformaciones del sistema de partidos en Chile." *Estudios Públicos* 58: 5–80; and Valenzuela, A., and J. S. Valenzuela. 1983. "Partidos de oposición bajo el régimen autoritario chileno." In Chile 1973–198?, edited by M. A. Garretón. Santiago: FLACSO. Chapter 11 of this book returns to the relevance of cleavages at the contextual level.

[6] The basic idea is that electoral rules shape the number of political parties according to their level of permissiveness—that is, the degree to which they lower or raise barriers to entry. This institutionalist line of literature can be traced back to Duverger, M. 1954. *Political Parties: Their Organization and Activity in the Modern State*. New York, NY: Wiley, where he famously argued that singlemember district systems tend to produce two-party competition—a proposition later known as Duverger's Law. The theory was further developed by Rae, D. 1968. The Political Consequences of Electoral Laws. New Haven, CT: Yale University Press; Riker, W. H. 1982. "The Two-Party System and Duverger's Law: An Essay on the History of Political Science." *American Political Science Review* 76(4): 753–66; and Lijphart, A. 1990. *Electoral Systems and Party Systems: A Study of Twenty- Seven Democracies, 1945–1990*. Oxford: Oxford University Press. In Latin America, this framework has been applied extensively across numerous case studies,

Crucially, these two explanations are interdependent. The extent of party system fragmentation depends on the interaction between societal cleavages and the permissiveness of electoral rules. Indeed, the conventional wisdom holds that in *more* diverse societies, *more* permissive rules will lead to a greater increase in the number of parties.[7]

including in broader comparative works such as Nohlen, D. 2005. Elections in the Americas. Oxford: Oxford University Press; Jones, M. P. 1995. "A Guide to the Electoral Systems of the Americas." *Electoral Studies* 14(1): 5–21. In Chile, a distinct tradition has developed that applies these theories to the country's unique institutional and political context. Key contributions include Siavelis, P. M. 2005. "Chile: The Unexpected (and Expected) Consequences of Electoral Engineering." In *The Politics of Electoral Systems*, edited by M. Gallagher and P. Mitchell, 433–452. Oxford: Oxford University Press; Rahat, G., and M. Sznajder. 1998. "Electoral Engineering in Chile: The Electoral System and Limited Democracy." *Electoral Studies* 17(4): 429–42; Gamboa, R., and A. Dockendorff. 2023. "Chilean Electoral System: A Moderate D'Hondt PR." In *Global Encyclopedia of Public Administration, Public Policy, and Governance*, edited by A. Farazmand. 1529–1534. Cham: Springer International Publishing; Angell, A. 2003. "Party Change in Chile in Comparative Perspective." Revista de Ciencia Política 23(2): 88–108; Magar, E., M. R. Rosenblum, and D. Samuels. 1998. "On the Absence of Centripetal Incentives in Double-Member Districts: The Case of Chile." *Comparative Political Studies* 31(6): 714–39; and Navia, P. D. 2003. *You Select the Rules of the Game and Lose? Advantages and Constraints When Choosing Electoral Rules: The Case of Chile*, (PhD Thesis). New York, NY: New York University.

7 A significant line of research explores the interactive relationship between social diversity—such as ethnic or ideological cleavages—and electoral systems. Rather than focusing exclusively on institutional design or social structures, this literature examines how these two dimensions jointly shape party system outcomes. Foundational contributions include Ordeshook, P. C., and O. V. Shvetsova. 1994. "Ethnic Heterogeneity, District Magnitude, and the Number of Parties." *American Journal of Political Science* 38: 100–123; Neto, O. A., and G. W. Cox. 1997. "Electoral Institutions, Cleavage Structures, and the Number of Parties." *American Journal of Political Science* 41(1): 149–74; Cox, G. W. 1997. *Making Votes Count: Strategic Coordination in the World's Electoral Systems*. Cambridge: Cambridge University Press; Clark, W. R., and M. Golder. 2006. "Rehabilitating Duverger's Theory: Testing the Mechanical and Strategic Modifying Effects of Electoral Laws." *Comparative Political Studies* 39(6): 679–708; and Teorell, J., and C. Lindstedt. 2010. "Measuring Electoral Systems." *Political Research Quarterly* 63(2): 434–448. In Latin America—and in other democratizing regions such as Eastern Europe—this interactive approach has gained considerable traction. See, for example, Bunker, K., and G. L. Negretto. 2024. "The Party System Effects of Unstable Electoral Rules in Latin America." *Party Politics* 30(6): 1126–1142; Crisp, B. F., S. Olivella, and J. D. Potter. 2012. "Electoral Contexts That Impede Voter Coordination." *Electoral Studies* 31(1): 143–158; Roussias, N. 2022. "The Evolution of New Party Systems: Voter Learning and Electoral Systems." *Political Studies Review* 20(3): 410–432; Tavits, M. 2005. "The Development of Stable Party Support: Electoral Dynamics in Post-Communist Europe." *American Journal of Political Science* 49(2): 283–298; Moser, R. G., and E.

How does this theory apply to Chile? Acknowledging that both variables are mutually dependent, it is also obvious that since Chile's social structure has remained relatively stable over the years observed, changes to electoral rules must be disproportionatly accounting for much of the increase in the number of parties. If this hypothesis were to be true, inductively, one would at least expect to see a significant increase in electoral reforms over time—and, as the next subsection shows, that is precisely the case.[8]

6.3.2 Institutional Reforms

The first significant reform to the electoral system after the 1990 transition came in 2004 when mayoral and local councilor elections were separated. Before this, elections were held jointly using a mixed-member system, in which the candidate with the most votes was elected mayor, while council seats were allocated through proportional representation. This reform likely provided incentives for independent candidates and smaller parties to seek visibility and gain political traction, possibly contributing to a more numerous and volatile party system at the local level.

A second notable reform was the 2005 abolition of *senadores designados* (lit. "designated senators"), which eliminated nonelected upper-chamber members who had been appointed to the Senate through constitutional requirements. As outlined in Chapter 2, this included former presidents, outgoing military generals, and former Supreme Court judges, among others. While limited in scope, this reform may have fostered a more open and competitive political system, as it created space for other parties to enter the debate.

Scheiner. 2009. "Strategic Voting in Established and New Democracies: Ticket Splitting in Mixed-Member Electoral Systems." *Electoral Studies* 28(1): 51–61; and Stoll, H. 2011. "Dimensionality and the Number of Parties in Legislative Elections." *Party Politics* 17(3): 405–429.

[8] Bunker (2025a) tests the conventional wisdom theory and finds support for the interactive model in the Chilean context, demonstrating that the relationship between social diversity and party system fragmentation holds even at the district level when local conditions are properly accounted for. However, the analysis also reveals that institutional features such as apparentment coalitions and the timing of second order elections mediate this relationship, contributing to observed variation in the number of effective parties.

A third important noteworthy reform was the introduction of voluntary voting in 2011, which replaced the mandatory voting scheme that had been in place since 1989. However, because its impact is presumably (theoretically) more related to voting behavior than party strategy, it is explored in greater detail in Chapter 7.

Continuing chronologically, a fourth reform that may have had an effect on the configuration of the party system was the introduction of direct elections for regional councilors in 2013, which aimed at decentralizing political competition. By allowing regional actors to contest elections directly, this reform may have empowered local or issue-based movements that were previously marginalized within the national framework.

A fifth and final reform, enacted just prior to the 2019 social unrest,[9] was the 2015 electoral reform that abolished the binomial system and took effect in the 2017 legislative elections. This reform increased the total number of seats in the assembly (for both senators and deputies) and raised the district magnitude across the board.[10] This "textbook" permissive reform almost certainly amplified fragmentation, weakening the dominance of traditional coalitions and increasing the complexity of governance at the first tier. It is also the most frequently cited reform in the literature as the key turning point for Chile's post-transition party system.[11]

[9] Other major electoral reforms conducted in the aftermath of the 2019 social outburst, and as such are not likely to have affected neither the event or its consequences, include the introduction of direct elections for Governors in 2021, and the return to mandatory voting in 2023–2024.

[10] District magnitude is a term commonly used in political science to refer to the number of representatives elected in a given electoral district. At its most basic level, it simply indicates how many seats are contested in that district. The concept can also be applied in aggregate terms—for instance, saying that the district magnitude was two under Chile's former binomial system means that on average two representatives were elected in each district (in this special case, the aggregate mean is identical to the individual magnitude, as the electoral systems designer set two as the number of seats available in both the Senate and Lower Chamber, across the board).

[11] Several studies look at the specific context and effects of the 2015 electoral reform. See, for example: Bunker, K. 2018. "La elección de 2017 y el fraccionamiento del sistema de partidos en Chile." *Revista Chilena de Derecho y Ciencia Política* 9(2): 204–229; Gamboa, Ricardo, and M. Morales. 2016. "Chile's 2015 electoral reform: changing the rules of the game." *Latin American Politics and Society* 58(4): 126–144; Scully, T. R. 2022. "A Fourth Critical Juncture?" *Critical Junctures and Historical Legacies: Insights*

6.4 Fragmentation, a Leftward Drift, and Party System Asymmetry

Given the abundance of reasons available to explain why more parties began to appear across the political specturm, the next question is when exactly did the party system begin to shift during the fifth political era, and how might this have influenced the political and social crisis of 2019? To explore this question, this chapter applies spatial theory to examine the fragmentation of the party system through the ideological classification of parties.[12] First, it situates party system fragmentation within a temporal framework, acknowledging that while it is evident that the party system fragmented over time, the precise starting point remains unclear. Second, it analyzes the ideological orientation of parties entering political competition during the fragmentation period, as new players likely introduced new elements into the political discourse. Finally, it evaluates the relative weight of these new parties to provide a nuanced understanding of their influence on the evolving political landscape.

6.4.1 Signs of Early Fragmentation

Figure 6.2 provides an overview of the evolving fragmentation in Chile's party system by illustrating ideological clustering among political parties over time.[13] It highlights areas of high political party density, indicating where electoral competition has been most concentrated.[14] Notably, the

and Methods for Comparative Social Science 351; Toro Maureira, S., and M. Valenzuela Beltrán. 2018. "Chile 2017: ambiciones, estrategias y expectativas en el estreno de las nuevas reglas electorales." *Revista de Ciencia Política* 38(2): 207–232; Jofré, H., and J. M. Cabezas. 2025. "Los Efectos de la Reforma Electoral de 2015 sobre el Sistema de Partidos Chileno." *Dados* 68(3): e20221091.

[12] This section draws heavily on Bunker (2025a; 2025b). See the Appendix for guides regarding ideological positioning of many of the coalitions, parties, and presidential candidates mentioned in this chapter and throughout the book.

[13] The figures in the Appendix summarize the evolution of post-transition Chile through spatial maps based on data from this chapter. Figure A1 shows the general area of influence of political coalitions; Figure A2, political parties; and Figure A3, presidential candidates. All three maps include a background layer showing the general area of influence of broader political sectors.

[14] It excludes independents to focus solely on party competition patterns. The full list of independents that have competed in Chilean elections is available on the author's website.

figure shows an increase in the number of parties participating in the political system around 2009.

This finding is significant for two reasons. First, it marks the departure from the stable two-coalition system that had dominated earlier

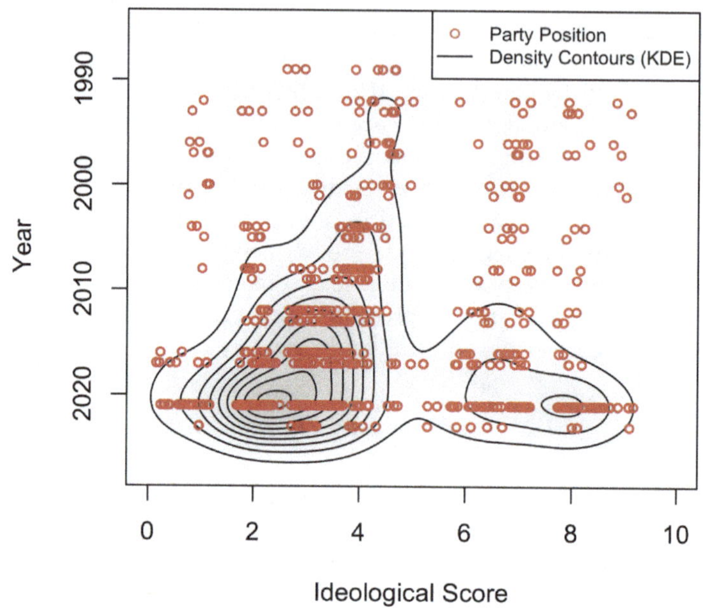

Fig. 6.2 Ideological distribution of the Chilean party landscape, 1989–2023 (*Note* Two-dimensional kernel density estimate of party ideological positions over time. Each red circle represents a party's ideological score in a given election year, based on a total of *n* observations. The vertical axis shows time from 1989 (top) to 2025 (bottom), while the horizontal axis represents ideological positioning from left (0) to right (10). The gray shading indicates the estimated density of party positions, with darker areas reflecting higher concentrations. Contour lines outline regions of similar density. *Source* Author with data from Bunker 2025b[15])

[15] The original work shows a scatterplot with highest-density regions (HDR) to visualize the distribution of party positions across elections. This figure extends that approach by applying a two-dimensional kernel density estimation to highlight broader structural patterns in ideological competition over time. The dataset includes 779 party-year observations from 184 unique parties, covering 17 national elections held between 1989 and 2023. Ideological scores range from 0.15 to 9.17 (mean = 4.02, SD = 2.15).

decades. While the parties of the *Concertación* and *Alianza* coalitions remained dominant in 2010 and 2014, it is clear that they were losing ground by this point. This trend aligns view the idea of a zero-sum game in Chile's political system following the division of the center-left before and after the 2009/2010 election, as departing party members did not exit the party system but instead formed or joined new parties. For example, the two former members of the Socialist Party mentioned in Chapter 4 founded new political parties—Enríquez-Ominami established the *Partido Progresista* (Progressive Party), while Navarro founded PAIS. Others gravitated toward recently formed parties such as the *Partido Regionalista Independiente* (PRI), a faction of the Christian Democrats, or *Chile Primero* (CH1), a vehicle for shifting ideological interests.[16]

The second important conclusion is that this departure point occurred significantly earlier than is commonly acknowledged. While most scholars identify the 2015 reform as the major breaking point (see references in the previous section), this analysis suggests that fragmentation began much earlier.[17] This underscores that the transformation of the party system was not sudden in 2017 or 2019 but had been underway for

[16] Themes of party switching are explored in more detail in Chapter 7, yet it is relevant to briefly summarize the trajectories of these two parties, as they serve as early examples of a party system in motion—both being subject to ideological takeovers that led them to shift sides of the political aisle. The PRI, on the one hand, was the product of several mergers of minor and unsuccessful parties, and only gained prominence in 2007 when Senator Adolfo Zaldívar joined along with five legislators—Jaime Mulet (District 6), Pedro Araya (District 4), Carlos Olivares (District 18), Alejandra Sepúlveda (District 34), and Eduardo Díaz (District 51)—following a split from the Christian Democrats. Though initially centrist, the party gradually moved to the right, ultimately supporting Sebastián Piñera in the 2017 election, before dissolving. Chile Primero, on the other hand, was born as a right-leaning project but quickly became a transient platform, passing through the hands of ideologically diverse figures such as Senator Fernando Flores, Jorge Schaulsohn, Vlado Mirosevic, Esteban Valenzuela, and Tomás Jocelyn-Holt. It was eventually rebranded as the Liberal Party and, in a reversal of its original position, went on to support Gabriel Boric in the 2021 election.

[17] Most studies that identified the 2015 electoral reform as the primary trigger for party system fragmentation in Chile relied on national-level aggregate data, which often obscured subnational variation and earlier shifts in electoral dynamics. However, newly available district-level data (e.g., Bunker, 2025a; 2025b) offers a more granular view of electoral competition, precisely indicating that fragmentation had begun well before the reform, particularly in lower-profile contests and peripheral districts. This challenges the conventional timeline and highlights the value of disaggregated data in understanding the evolution of Chile's party system. It also points to a hitherto unexplored potential bottom-up, inverse cascade effect.

nearly a decade, implying that either social structures were moving undetected, that the reforms of 2004, 2005, and 2013 were having an effect much greater than what was expected, or both forces were impacting the party system landscape together, as conventional wisdom holds. It also supports the view that Chile's political system was more unstable than previously assumed (this idea is further explored in Chapter 7).

6.4.2 *A Drift Toward the Left*

Given that it is clear that fragmentation was rapidly increasing over time, the next question is whether this trend favored one specific political sector over another? To address this, Fig. 6.3 shows a best-fit line through a plot with time as the explanatory variable and the ideological position of parties as the response variable. The data reveal that, over time, left-of-center parties drifted further to the left than right-of-center parties drifted to the right. In fact, considering the entire period from 1990 to 2023 and all measured parties, it can be argued that the party system generally tended to drift to the left.

This dynamic is significant as it highlights the changing nature of the party system, particularly the center-left's struggle to maintain power following the loss of the 2009/2010 election. Notably, if the same line were fitted only to left-of-center for the period following Piñera's victory over Frei Ruiz-Tagle in the second round, the leftward drift would become even more pronounced. This reflects both the entry of new parties and the strategic repositioning of existing ones to capture niche voter bases.

At the same time, the pattern underscores the growing influence of leftist discourse. As new and established parties populated the political spectrum, competition intensified alongside the diversity of ideas being promoted. This helps explain why the progressive narrative gained strength during this period. In contrast, right-leaning parties exhibited no significant ideological drift, as the regression analysis for these parties produced a nearly flat slope. This stability highlights the ideological cohesion within the right, which maintained its traditional positioning over time.

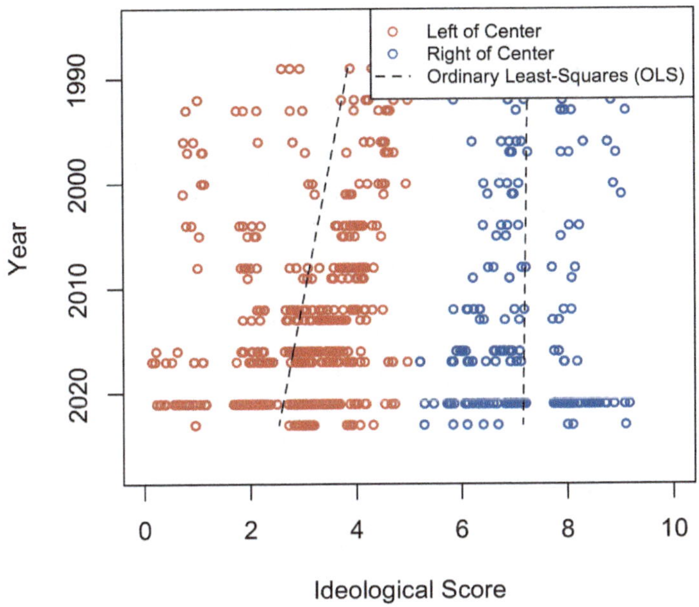

Fig. 6.3 Ideological shifts in the Chilean party landscape, 1989–2023 (*Note* Each point represents a party's ideological position in a given election year, with left-of-center parties shown in red and right-of-center parties in blue. The vertical axis shows time from 1989 (top) to 2025 (bottom), while the horizontal axis represents ideological positioning from left (0) to right (10). Dashed black lines indicate ordinary least-squares (OLS) regression trends for each group, illustrating gradual shifts in ideological positioning over time. *Source* Author with data from Bunker 2025b[18])

18 Ordinary Least Squares (OLS) regression results reveal a statistically significant downward trend in the ideological positioning of left-of-center parties over time. For left-wing parties (n = 573), the estimated slope is –0.039 (SE = 0.0048, $p<0.001$), indicating a modest but consistent leftward shift between 1990 and 2023. The model explains approximately 10% of the variation in party scores ($R^2 = 0.10$). In contrast, no significant temporal trend is observed for right-of-center parties (n = 206), where the slope is –0.0033 (SE = 0.0060, p = 0.58) and the explained variance is negligible ($R^2 \approx 0$). These results drive the idea that suggests that while left-wing parties in Chile have moved further left over time, right-wing parties have remained ideologically stable.

6.4.3 An Asymmetrical and Opposite Evolution

Building on the two inferences above, the only remaining question concerns the leverage each party had on the political debate within the fragmenting, leftward-drifting party system. To explore this, Fig. 6.4 examines the ideological evolution of the party system by weighing political parties according to their vote shares. The data reveal an asymmetrical and opposite-party system: an expanding left with more but smaller parties and a contracting right with fewer but larger parties.

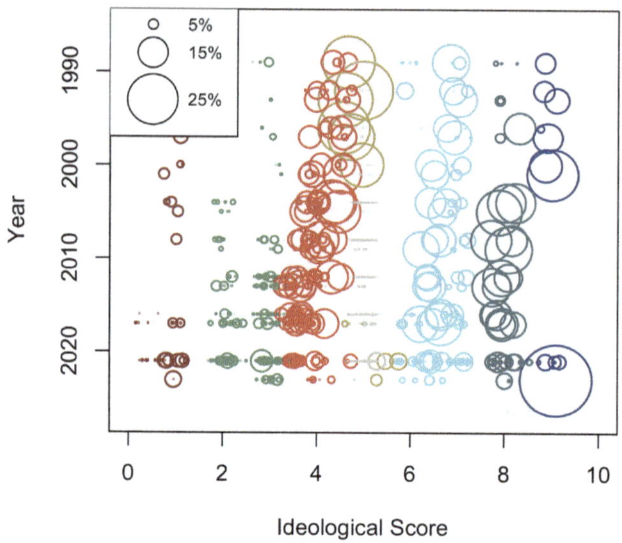

Fig. 6.4 Electoral and ideological presence in the Chilean party landscape, 1989–2023 (*Note* Each circle represents a party's ideological position in a given election year. Circle size is proportional to the party's share of the national vote (%), and colors reflect party family classification. The vertical axis shows time from 1989 (top) to 2025 (bottom), while the horizontal axis represents ideological positioning from left (0) to right (10). Minor jitter is applied on the x-axis to reduce overlap. *Source* Author with data from Bunker 2025b[19])

[19] The figure displays 4,157 party-year observations across 17 national elections from 1989 to 2023, covering 185 unique parties. Circle sizes correspond to each party's national vote share, which ranges from 0% to 35.4%. Most parties captured in the data received small vote shares and limited representation. The majority of observations are

This pattern aligns with a political system characterized by multiple left-leaning parties and movements capable of dominating the political discourse, with limited counteraction from the right.

For the left, increased competition likely diluted political support across various entities, making it difficult to consolidate power within a unified coalition. This fragmentation may explain why independents and outsiders later emerged to challenge the mainstream establishments during the first constitutional process. For the right, by contrast, larger and more dominant parties continued to occupy the ideological space over time, demonstrating a lower susceptibility to fragmentation. However, this did not prevent the emergence of the Republican Party at the outset of the second constitutional process.

6.5 Conclusion

This chapter examined the dramatic transformation that reshaped Chile's political system during the fifth political era, focusing on how fragmentation, ideological drift, and asymmetry in party competition redefined the political landscape in the second cycle. These changes not only affected the immediate electoral arena but also had profound implications for governance, political stability, and Chile's broader democratic framework. By tracing these transformations back to the mid 2000s, the chapter revealed that the fragmentation of Chile's political system was neither a sudden development nor solely the result of the 2015 electoral reform. Instead, it reflected a longer-term process shaped by deeper structural changes within the party system.

The analysis demonstrated that party system fragmentation began to emerge as early as 2009, disrupting the stable two-coalition framework that had dominated Chilean politics since the return to democracy in 1990. This shift was driven by a combination of factors, including the emergence of new political actors, structural reforms to the electoral system, and evolving voter demands. While the 2015 reform amplified fragmentation by lowering institutional barriers to representation, earlier changes—such as the abolition of designated senators, the separation of mayoral elections, and the introduction of direct elections for

classified as "Independent" (n = 3,378), followed by Left (n = 315), Center-Left (n = 201), Center-Right (n = 118), Right (n = 69), Far Left (n = 47), Center (n = 16), and Far Right (n = 13).

regional councilors—had already begun to reshape the political landscape. These incremental reforms fostered an environment in which new parties and movements could gain traction at the subnational level, ultimately diluting the dominance of traditional coalitions "from below."

Another key finding of this chapter is that the fragmentation of the party system was not uniform but characterized by ideological asymmetry. On the left, the proliferation of smaller parties and movements led to increased competition within the ideological spectrum, creating a dynamic but fragmented political space. This fragmentation complicated efforts to build cohesive coalitions and govern effectively, even as it expanded the range of political ideas and representation. By contrast, the right remained more cohesive, with fewer but larger and more dominant parties maintaining their ideological positioning over time. This asymmetry in fragmentation and cohesion had significant implications for electoral competition, coalition-building, and governance.

Yet a third key finding is that the party system was drifting leftward over time. As new parties entered the political arena, they tended to introduced demands for more progressive policies, many of them in favor of rejecting the established neoliberal framework. This ideological repositioning was not mirrored on the right, where parties maintained a relatively stable and traditional stance. The resulting imbalance led to an increasingly polarized and assymetrical political system, primed to give rise to ideas of structural overhaul.

CHAPTER 7

The Erosion of Voter–Party Linkages and Representation Backsliding

7.1 Introduction

This chapter investigates the erosion of voter–party linkages in Chile, exploring its far-reaching consequences for the country's democratic stability. It addresses how declining voter turnout, a collapse in trust toward political parties, and the emergence of "ghost" parties and "zombie" party members uncovered a deepening disconnect between citizens and the political system. Moving the focus from political parties to the electorate's disengagement, this chapter builds on the previous chapter's analysis and offers a more comprehensive understanding of the factors destabilizing Chilean democracy.

As the title suggests, the center of the discussion is the disconnection between voters and political parties, a gradual but transformative shift with profound consequences for the representational system. As disillusionment with the political process grew, citizens began withdrawing from active participation, including voting and membership in political parties. This withdrawal weakened the previously robust democratic foundation that had connected citizens to their representatives, leaving the system increasingly fragile and unresponsive to societal demands.

The 2011 electoral reform, which introduced voluntary voting, marked a pivotal moment in this transformation. By removing the legal compulsion to vote, the reform laid bare the frayed nature of a party system that had once seemed stable. It exposed the extent of voter disengagement,

K. Bunker, *Chile's Transformation Amidst Crisis*,
https://doi.org/10.1007/978-3-031-96463-3_7

accelerating a trend that had already taken root. Historically, moderate and centrist voters, who had provided a stabilizing influence on the political system, were among the first to withdraw, leaving the political landscape increasingly dominated by extreme, activist factions.

This chapter delves into how these dynamics led to the hollowing out of Chile's democracy, where political institutions and parties continued to function formally but became increasingly disconnected from the electorate. The rise of "ghost" parties and "zombie" party members exemplified this trend, as the political system became increasingly dominated by elites. In this way, the erosion of voter–party linkages intensified public disillusionment, setting the stage for the upheaval that would follow.

Lastly, this chapter introduces the concept of "representation backsliding," which refers to the breakdown of the critical relationship between voters and their representatives, in the context of party system fragmentation. As presented here, representation backsliding reflects how diminished voter engagement weakened democratic legitimacy and institutional trust, in a party system incapable of addressing mainstream societal needs. By placing this concept within the broader historical and political context, the chapter provides key insight into the governance crises and challenges to representation that emerged in the 2010s.

7.2 From Entrenched Stability to Sudden Change

As mentioned in Chapter 6, Chile began transitioning from a two-party system to a multiparty one sometime in the late 2000s. This shift gradually redistributed political power from a few dominant coalitions to several small parties. However, at the time, there were few indications that such a transformation was underway. Even as early signs of fragmentation emerged, there was little warning that it could carry such significant negative consequences.

One reason this shift was initially overlooked is that fragmentation was not viewed as inherently problematic. On the contrary, many, particularly those on the left, welcomed it as a correction to the perceived artificiality of the two-party system within the broader Chilean political landscape. When fragmentation eventually became more visible, it was celebrated as a victory for representative democracy, especially by those gaining political power for the first time. For them, the rise of third parties signaled the restoration of voter–party linkages and a more inclusive political system.

However, this optimism masked deeper structural weaknesses. Far from strengthening voter–party linkages, the proliferation of parties concealed a growing disconnect between political institutions and the electorate. This misalignment explains, in part, why the erosion of democratic stability accelerated: it was not immediately recognized. Political attention remained fixated on the increasing number of parties, rather than the weakening connection between those parties and the public. This disconnect not only deepened the effects of fragmentation but also ensured that its destabilizing consequences could no longer be ignored as the political system became increasingly fragile.

7.2.1 Entrenched Stability

As detailed in Chapter 4, the *Concertación* coalition dominated the political landscape during the first two decades of democracy, winning four consecutive presidential elections before Sebastián Piñera and the *Alianza* coalition ended their streak in 2010. Chapter 5 further quantified this dominance, showing how the two main coalitions maintained an unchallenged incidence in Chilean politics for twenty years, despite the gradual rise of alternatives.

Table 7.1 illustrates the electoral outcomes for the lower chamber of Congress between 1989 and 2017, underscoring the extent to which this dominance marginalized third parties. The two main coalitions consistently secured over 95% of the seats in every election until 2013. While third parties occasionally attracted substantial voter support—amassing just less than one million votes combined in several elections—it rarely translated into meaningful political representation. Between 1989 and 2013, third parties managed to secure only 18 seats in the Lower Chamber, effectively relegating them to the political periphery.[1]

[1] Of the 18 seats, half were independents. Their names can be found in the footnote references of Chapter 10. The 9 winners awarded seats after campaigning on third-party tickets are: Juan Pablo Letelier (PAIS, 1989); Juan Martínez (PAIS, 1989); Alejandro García-Huidobro (UCC, 1997); María Victoria Ovalle (UCC, 1997); Marta Eliana Isasi (PAR, 2005); Pedro Araya (PRI, 2009); Luis Lemus (PRI, 2009); Alejandra Sepúlveda (PRI, 2009); and Vlado Mirosevic (PL, 2013).

Table 7.1 Results for Lower Chamber elections in Chile, 1989–2021

	Number of votes			*Number of seats*		
Election	Alianza	Concertación	*Others*	Alianza	Concertación	*Others*
1989	2,323,581	3,499,713	973,828	48	69	3
1993	2,471,789	3,733,276	533,794	50	70	0
1997	2,101,392	2,927,692	766,689	47	69	4
2001	2,720,195	2,942,989	480,849	57	62	1
2005	2,556,386	3,417,207	627,804	54	65	1
2009	2,874,674	2,934,378	806,804	57	58	5
2013	2,253,781	2,967,896	998,545	48	68	4
2017	2,318,719	2,082,808	1,485,723	72	57	26
2021	1,609,482	1,085,978	3,632,536	53	37	65

Note The names of the coalitions changed over time, as have the parties within them.[2] The categories follow votes for the main parties in each alliance, making as few exceptions as possible. In 2013 and 2017, the *Concertación* was joined by the Communist Party. In 2021, the Communist Party switched to *Apruebo Dignidad* (in partnership with the *Frente Amplio*). In 2013, the Christian Democrats competed on their own, but their votes were counted here as part of the *Concertación*.
Source Author with data from Servel

The binomial electoral system (described in Chapters 2) played a crucial role in sustaining this duopoly. Designed to encourage consensus and minimize polarization, the system created high thresholds for smaller parties to gain representation. Even when voters showed interest in alternatives, structural barriers prevented these votes from converting into

[2] For simplicity, this table uses the labels *Alianza* and *Concertación* to refer to Chile's main political coalitions, though both the names and the composition of these blocs have changed multiple times over the years. For example, the centre-right coalition debuted in 1989 as *Democracia y Progreso*, evolving through several names—*Participación y Progreso, Unión por Chile, Alianza por Chile, Alianza, Coalición por el Cambio,* and *Coalición*—before consolidating as *Chile Vamos* in 2015. It later ran as *Vamos por Chile* in the 2021 constitutional convention and as *Chile Seguro* in the 2023 council elections, while using similar labels in legislative and municipal contests. The centre-left, by contrast, began in 1988 as the *Concertación de Partidos por el No*, soon renamed *Concertación de Partidos por la Democracia*, and then simply *Concertación* until around 2010, when it rebranded as *Nueva Mayoría* in 2013. It competed in the constitutional process as *Lista del Apruebo* (2021) and *Todo por Chile* (2023), and has adopted varying names in municipal elections, such as *Unidad Constituyente*, *Contigo Chile Mejor*, and other local configurations. Other relevant coalitions include *Juntos Podemos Más* (2000s), *Frente Amplio* (since 2017), *Apruebo Dignidad* (2021), and *Republicanos* (since 2021), all of which have also changed names and composition over time. The figures in the Appendix show the graphical evolution of these major coalitions across the years.

political influence. Consequently, the dominance of the *Concertación* and *Alianza* created a highly predictable and stable political environment, reinforcing the binary nature of Chile's democracy.

The 2015 electoral reform, which replaced the binomial system with a fully proportional framework, allowed latent dynamics, as explained in Chapter 6, to emerge at the forefront of the political arena. As the final reform in the sequence, it fundamentally reshaped Chile's political landscape. For the first time, smaller parties could organize strategically and seek votes and seats without knowing their fate beforehand. By replacing the binomial system, elites removed long-standing structural barriers and created opportunities for smaller parties to gain representation. Whether intentionally or not, this change brought to light the fragmentation that had been quietly unfolding at the subnational level for years.

Indeed, it was only after the implementation of this new electoral system that third parties would surpass the one-million-vote threshold in a legislative election for the first time. In 2017, they secured 26 seats—eight more than the total number of seats that had gone to them in the previous seven elections combined.

Figure 7.1 further illustrates the magnitude of the change, showing the sharp rise in both the share of votes and seats secured by third parties once the 2015 reform took effect. The shift was particularly noticeable on the left, where, after just two elections, new parties were able to match the sectorial establishment. Following a strong showing in the 2017 election, the *Frente Amplio* tied with the sum of the ex-*Concertación* parties in the number of seats in 2021, each securing 37 seats—the remaining seats went to the *Frente Social Cristiano* (15), the PDG (6), *Dignidad Ahora* (3), PEV (2), *Independientes Unidos* (1), and a single independent (Carlos Bianchi).

7.2.2 A Sudden Change

Following the discussion on the conventional wisdom theory used to explain the fragmentation of the Chilean party system over time in Chapter 6, it becomes evident that the rise of third parties cannot be explained without considering the series of permissive reforms passed through Congress over the years. Without these interventions, it is unlikely the party system would have fragmented as it did.

While this theory neatly accounts for the rise of new parties, it does not explain the decline of traditional ones. This presents a particularly

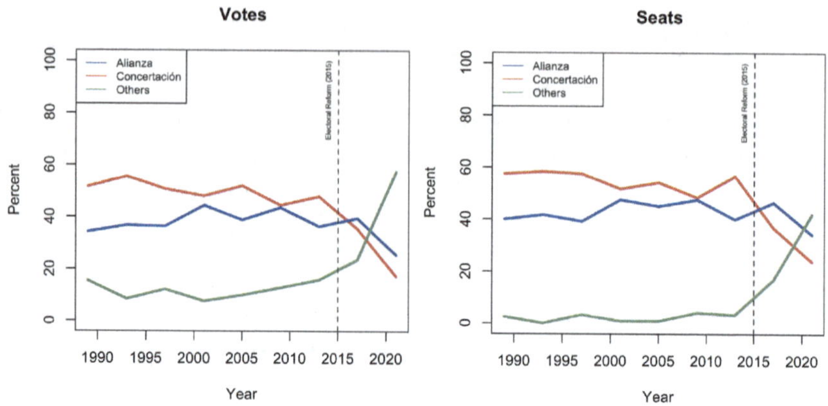

Fig. 7.1 Percentage of votes and seats in the Lower Chamber, 1989–2021 (*Note* The red line represents the percentage of votes for *Concertación* parties in Deputy elections. The blue line represents the percentage of votes for *Alianza* parties in Deputy elections. The green line represents the percentage of votes for third parties and independent candidates. In 2017 and 2021, this last category includes the Communist Party and the *Frente Amplio*. *Source* Author with data from Servel)

relevant puzzle—not only because there is no comprehensive account of why voters abandoned traditional parties, but also because of its relevance in the greater debate: it is obvious that the weakening of traditional parties directly contributed to the social outburst and the constitutional process that followed, in one way or another.

The next section proposes that the answer to why voters shifted from old parties to new ones lies in a deep-seated disillusionment with the political system that had been brewing for years. Perhaps frustrated by the rigidity of the system and its inability to respond to their needs (as outlined in the latter part of Chapter 5), voters were eager for alternatives. Even though many of the smaller parties lacked strong grassroots foundations, they offered an outlet for voters to express their dissatisfaction with the status quo.

This situation, which reflects the erosion of voter–party linkages, is evident in three key trends that were unfolding behind the scenes in the years leading up to the social outburst: declining voter turnout, increasing dissatisfaction with political parties, and the emergence of "ghost" parties.

7.3 The Erosion of Voter–Party Linkages

To understand the erosion of voter–party linkages, it is essential to examine the impact of the 2011 electoral reform. This reform exposed a brewing problem beneath the surface of the stability projected during the two decades of the *Alianza–Concertación* era.

During the years of mandatory voting (1989–2011), voter turnout among registered voters remained relatively high, as abstention was penalized with fines. However, the electorate began to shrink over time as younger generations increasingly opted not to register. Despite this scenario, the mandatory voting system still ensured that centrist and moderate voters—whose ideological preferences are typically normally distributed—constituted a significant portion of the electorate.

The reform in 2011 fundamentally altered this status quo. Once voting became voluntary, centrist and moderate voters were the first to disengage from the electoral process, which left voter rolls increasingly at the mercy of more mobilized and more extreme political and ideological segments.

But Chileans were not only withdrawing from the electoral process, they were disengaging from the democratic process as a whole. Available evidence suggests that while fragmentation was increasing and new parties were emerging, the overall "health" of the system—measured in terms of party membership numbers and organizational stability—was in clear decline. These themes are each explored in turn.

7.3.1 Declining Electoral Turnout Rates

The first and most obvious effect of the 2011 reform was that it exposed the true level of voter engagement. Under the original arrangement, voting was mandatory, but voter registration had been declining over time. While it was clear that fewer people were voting, it was not evident how many were actively engaging in politics more broadly, as the reasons for not registering to vote were never thoroughly studied at the time.[3]

[3] This is distinct to the issue regarding voter profiles, which has always been at the center of electoral studies in Chile. One exception that did look at the decline in turnout from a system-level perspective before the 2011 electoral reform is: Carlin, R. E. 2006. "The decline of citizen participation in electoral politics in post-authoritarian Chile." *Democratization* 13(4): 632–651. After 2011, research began to focus on the effect of the mandatory-to-voluntary switch. For example: Brieba, D., and K. Bunker. 2019. "Voter equalization and turnout bias after electoral reform: Evidence from

Figure 7.2 shows the sharp divergence between reported voter turnout and actual voter turnout. It clearly illustrates that while official reports suggested a healthy democracy with a highly engaged electorate, the percentage of people voting was, in fact, falling at an alarming rate. This trend became evident in the 2012 local elections, which marked the debut of the new voluntary voting regime.

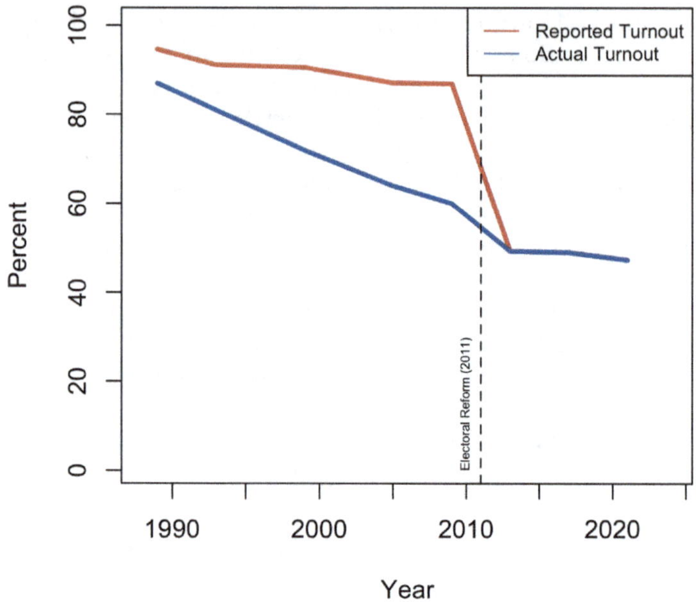

Fig. 7.2 Electoral turnout in first-round presidential elections, 1989–2021 (*Note* The red line represents the reported number of voters over the total number of registered voters. The blue line represents the number of voters over the total number of eligible voters. *Source* Author with data from Servel)

Chile's voluntary voting law." *Latin American Politics and Society* 61(4): 23–46; Contreras, G., A. Joignant, and M. Morales. 2016. "The return of censitary suffrage? The effects of automatic voter registration and voluntary voting in Chile." *Democratization* 23(3): 520–544; Cox, L., and R. González. 2022. "Fewer but younger: Changes in turnout after voluntary voting and automatic registration in Chile." *Political Behavior* 44(4): 1911–1932.

In this way, the introduction of voluntary voting had two implications. First, it exposed the extent of voter disengagement, as described above. And second, it weakened the political center. Previously, campaigns could rely on a relatively stable base of registered voters who were legally compelled to vote. With this guarantee removed, parties were forced to recalibrate their strategies, shifting their focus toward mobilizing already engaged voters rather than seeking new ones—an effort that would have required significant campaign funds.

For the dominant coalitions, this adjustment was especially challenging, as their traditional voter base had already disengaged, and their funding levels were lower than ever before. However, for smaller parties and political movements, the new arrangement presented an opportunity to appeal to their bases, expand their electorates, and make a push for power.

7.3.2 Increasing Disengagement of Voters

Voter disengagement from the political process is also evident in the growing distrust toward political parties. Over time, Chileans began to lose faith in parties to the extent that Chile's party system became one of the weakest in Latin America.

Figure 7.3 plots the decline in trust in political parties over time, using data from the *Latinobarómetro* poll. The trend is striking: the share of people expressing little or no trust in political parties rose from 64% in 1995 to 81% in 2011 and nearly 89% by 2023. This suggests that people were not only withdrawing from public life in general but also feeling increasingly disconnected from political parties in particular.

To contextualize this trend, Figure 7.4 illustrates how Chile ranked last among Latin Americans in terms of political party sympathy in 2014, based on data from the *Latin American Public Opinion Poll* (LAPOP). Compared with other democratic frontrunners in the region, the contrast is striking. While all three nations consistently rank high in democracy indexes,[4] Costa Rica and Uruguay benefited from strong public support for political parties, whereas Chile lacked this organic connection. This evidence supports previous research characterizing Chile's party system

[4] Including democracy ratings such as those offered by *Freedom House*, *V-DEM*, and *The Economist Intelligence Unit Democracy Index*.

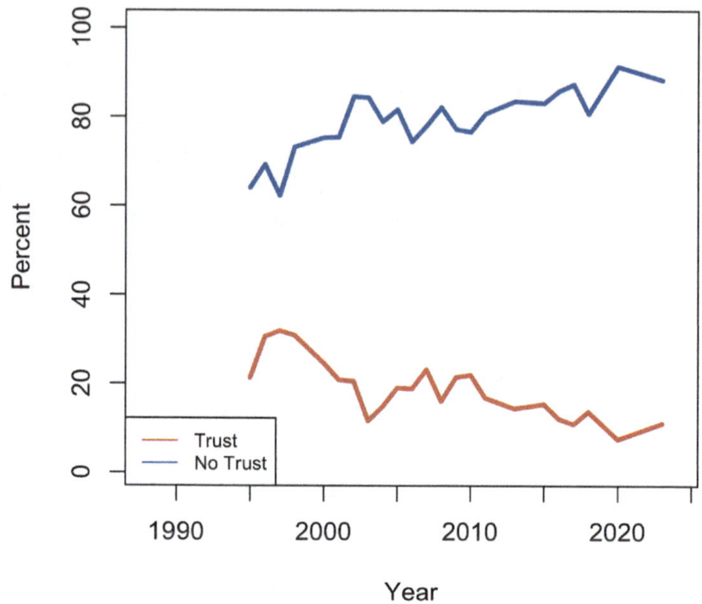

Fig. 7.3 Trust in political parties, 1995–2023 (*Note* The question is regarding how much people trust political parties. The blue line represents the sum of answers "A lot" and "Somewhat." The red line represents the sum of answers "Nothing" and "A little." *Source* Author with data from Latinobarometro)

as strong but uprooted—functionally stable, but lacking genuine public support.[5]

[5] This original argument put forward by Juan Pablo Luna and David Altman was that the Chilean party system was not homogenously institutionalized (as conventionally argued) but instead simultaneously frozen at the elite level and increasingly disconnected from civil society. See: Luna, J. P., and D. Altman. 2011. "Uprooted but stable: Chilean parties and the concept of party system institutionalization." *Latin American Politics and Society* 53(2): 1–28. That study, in turn, stems from a line of literature that was, at the time, challenging research stemming from the 1990s looking at Party System Institutionalization (PSI). One account describes the Brazilian democracy as a *hydroponic* party system, "as some proto-roots exist, but are not fixed to anything solid." See: Zucco, C. 2010. "Stability Without Roots: Party System Institutionalization in Brazil." *Social Science Research Network, SSRN*. https://ssrn.com/abstract=2002359. The original PSI work, however, would later be updated to account for emerging patterns. See: Mainwaring, S., and T. Scully (eds.). 1995. *Building Democratic Institutions*. Stanford: Stanford University

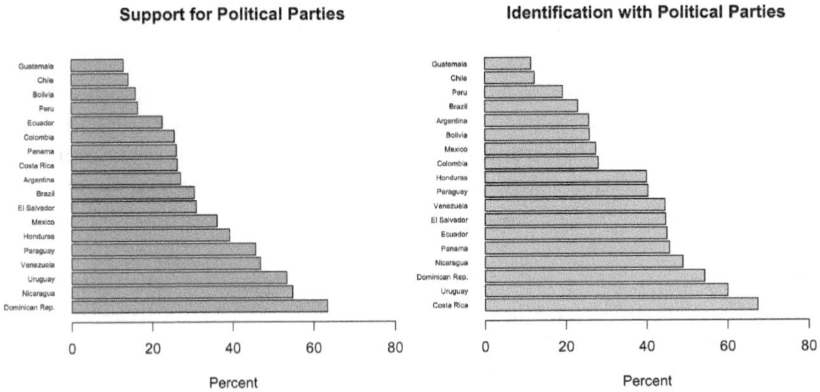

Fig. 7.4 Support and identification of political parties in Latin America, 2014 (*Source* Author with data from Latin American Public Opinion Poll, 2014)

7.3.3 *The Rise of "Ghost" Parties*

Despite the growing disillusionment with political parties, the extent of the problem remained unclear until a major turning point in 2016, when a new law required political parties to re-register their members,[6] mandating that parties maintain accurate membership records and have active members reaffirm their affiliations. The result revealed the true scale of the problem.[7]

Press; Mainwaring, S (eds.). 2018. *Party Systems in Latin America: Institutionalization, Decay, and Collapse*. New York, NY: Cambridge University Press.

[6] This was regulated by laws 18.603, 20.900 and 20.915. It was one of the first reforms to directly regulate the entry of political parties, rather than relying on electoral system incentives. The law required "traditional parties" (those formed before May 5, 2015) to re-register all their members by April 14, and "new parties" (formed after that date) to do so by April 15. It also retained the original provision that only parties established in either three contiguous regions or eight regions overall could register presidential and legislative candidates. See: *Servel*. 2017. "Culmina el proceso de reinscripción a partidos políticos." April 15. https://www.servel.cl/2017/04/15/culmina-el-proceso-de-reinscripcion-a-partidos-politicos/

[7] Errors in the registrar had been adverted at least through 2013, but by 2016 still not corrected. See: Ramos, N. 2013. "Servel afirma que siguen figurando votantes muertos en este proceso electoral." *La Tercera*. November 11. https://www.latercera.com/diario-impreso/servel-afirma-que-siguen-figurando-votantes-muertos-en-este-proceso-electoral/

Membership numbers, which had reportedly hovered above 800,000 in a country of 18 million, plummeted to about 500,000 after the first round of re-registrations was published in late 2017.[8] Subsequent reviews would reduce this figure even further, as parties would be dismantled for failing to meet legal thresholds in elections. The decline in party membership over time reflected not only growing disillusionment with political parties but also systemic issues within the registrar process. The sharp drop highlighted the existence of "zombie" party members—individuals who remained in party rolls despite being disengaged or even deceased. These phantom memberships had likely inflated party figures for years, masking the extent of the hollowing-out process.[9]

Traditional parties were the most affected by the clean up. Indeed, some of them ended up with more members suspended for inactivity than back in their rolls. This was certainly the case with ex *Concertación* parties. For example, the Socialist Party had 87,578 members suspended, and just 37,017 members re-register. The Christian Democrats had 81,783 members removed from their rolls, and just 31,369 members re-enroll. The PPD saw 83,393 members go, and just 35,595 come in. It was not better for the *Alianza*. While the UDI lost 63,324 members and gained 40,582, *Renovación Nacional* lost 78,787 and kept just 31,744.

When the "zombies" were removed from the registrar, "ghost" parties emerged.

[8] Prior to the implementation of Laws 20.900 and 20.915, Chilean political parties reported 884,561 registered militants. Following the April 2017 deadline for re-registration, 549,197 affiliates remained active, 40,396 formally resigned, and 720,629 were suspended for failing to re-register. This means that over 81% of the original base either took no action or formally exited the system, leaving only 163,932 individuals (less than one in five) who actively reaffirmed or updated their party affiliation. The gap between the pre-reform rolls and those who revalidated reflects the depth of organizational decay prior to the legal cleanup. See: Servel. 2018. "Con 549 mil afiliados concluyen 2017 los partidos políticos vigentes." January 11. https://www.servel.cl/2018/01/11/con-549-mil-afiliados-concluyen-2017-los-partidos-politicos-vigentes/

[9] Part of the issue was that political parties managed their own membership records until the 2016–2017 legal reforms. Because it was in their interest to maintain high, visibly healthy membership numbers, they routinely reported new affiliations while omitting unenrollments—whether due to resignation, death, or legal disqualification. This practice resembled the phenomenon of inflated electoral turnout figures, which similarly obscured the underlying weaknesses of Chile's democratic participation. See: *Tele 13*. 2016. "Los fallidos intentos para evitar los "papelones" en el padrón electoral." October 5. https://www.t13.cl/noticia/politica/Los-fallidos-intentos-para-evitar-los-papelones-en-el-padron-electoral/

This phenomenon aligns with patterns observed in other countries experiencing party system fragmentation, where the proliferation of parties was not only a consequence of external incentives such as permissive electoral rules but also of internal elite behavior, including party switching, legislative ambitions, and strategic takeovers.[10] Taken together, these dynamics suggest that the political system was being destabilized not only from the outside but also from within, through endogenous processes that undermined the coherence and institutionalization of the party system.

7.4 Representation Backsliding

If anything should be clear by this point, it is that the simultaneous fragmentation of the party system and the erosion of voter–party linkages did not occur in isolation from each other. These two forces developed alongside one another, with their effects becoming intertwined and self-reinforcing over time. The increasing number of political parties, driven by structural reforms and public dissatisfaction, deepened the disconnection between citizens and political institutions. At the same time, the weakening of voter–party linkages created the conditions for further fragmentation, as disengaged voters opened space for new actors to emerge. Together, these dynamics formed a feedback loop, where each factor amplified the other, destabilizing Chile's democratic system.

[10] Evidence from Brazil shows that the party system was able to expand without shift in social structures or significant electoral reform, due to elite takeover of small parties. See: Cheibub, J. A., T. Moreira, G. Sin, and K. Tanabe. 2022. "Dynamic party system fragmentation." *Electoral Studies* 76, 102440. Examples of this phenomenon are abundant in Chile and are most evident in the high rate of party switching that began in the mid-2000s. Several legislators changed parties as many as four times (one remarkable case is that of Eduardo Díaz del Río, who in and out of congress passed through at least five parties: SUR, UDI, DC, PRI and *Amplitud*). See: Bunker, K. 2024. "El aumento de los "party switchers" en el Congreso Nacional de Chile, 1990–2024." *Ideas: Laboratorio Democracia y Gobierno USS* 1(18): 1–5. The numbers are even higher among politicians outside of Congress. One notable case is Jaime Mulet, who began his career as a center-left Christian Democrat in 1980, joined the right-leaning *Partido Regionalista Independiente* in 2008, registered a regionalist and populist movement (literally *Frente Regional y Popular*) in 2015, and ultimately took over several smaller, struggling parties and movements to form the *Frente Regionalista Verde Social* in 2017 when his previous effort faltered.

This process can be best understood as "representation backsliding": the combined effect of increasing party system fragmentation amidst an ongoing erosion of voter–party linkages.[11] If nothing else, representation backsliding undermines a democracy's capacity to effectively connect citizens with their representatives, eroding trust in institutions and weakening governance. In Chile, this phenomenon became a defining feature of the political system after 2014, leaving it increasingly fragile and unable to address the needs of its citizens, while still appearing functional.

The fragmentation of the party system, discussed in Chapter 6, significantly contributed to this situation both directly and in combination with the erosion of voter–party linkages. The introduction of permissive electoral rules enabled more parties to enter the political arena, but because these parties lacked deep societal roots or coherent policy platforms quickly they made the problem worse. Although voters were presented with an array of choices, the options they were presented with were either disconnected from real societal needs or focused on narrow ideological goals. The proliferation of parties diluted representation and contributed to legislative instability, in which changing coalitions and frequent policy gridlock further alienated voters from the political system.

At the same time, the erosion of voter–party linkages accelerated the fragmentation of the party system. With the decline in voter turnout and collapse of trust in traditional parties, the electorate became increasingly disengaged. This disconnection opened opportunities for the emergence of new parties and movements, which were frequently driven by figures

[11] A growing body of scholarship has recently turned its attention to the phenomenon of *democratic backsliding*—the gradual erosion of democratic institutions and norms from within, rather than their sudden breakdown (see Tom Ginsburg and Aziz Huq, *How to Save a Constitutional Democracy*, 2018, University of Chicago Press; Adam Przeworski, *Crises of Democracy*, 2019, Cambridge University Press; Kurt Weyland and Raúl Madrid, *When Democracy Trumps Populism*, 2019, Cambridge University Press; Pippa Norris and Ronald Inglehart, *Cultural Backlash*, 2019, Cambridge University Press; Stephan Haggard and Robert R. Kaufman, *Backsliding: Democratic Regress in the Contemporary World*, 2021, Cambridge University Press). This should be distinguished from *representation backsliding*, which refers more narrowly to the erosion of voter–party linkages, in the context of increasing party system fragmentation. The Chilean case illustrates the distinction: even as the country was climbing in major democracy indices (such as *The Economist Intelligence Unit Democracy Index* and *Freedom House*), its party system was expanding in size and losing its rootedness in society. Focusing exclusively on democracy index scores would thus be misleading, as it obscures important declines in the quality of political representation.

that endeavored to capitalize on the dissatisfaction of the public with established coalitions. However, because new parties lacked the institutional capacity or broad support required to foster meaningful representation, they made the problem worse. The disengagement of moderate and centrist voters—who historically stabilized the system—left a void that was increasingly filled by ideologically extreme or narrowly focused parties, further fragmenting a political landscape that was already in decline.

As a result, the interplay between these two forces formed a feedback loop that fundamentally weakened Chile's representative democracy. The fragmentation of the party system overwhelmed voters with choices that failed to reflect their interests, while the weakening of voter–party linkages provided a fertile ground for the growth of new, ambitious and unpredictable political actors. Adapting to these changes was impossible for traditional parties, which had long been the foundation of Chile's democratic stability; as a result, the system was left without the anchors that normally help keep political volatility at bay.

7.5 Conclusion

This chapter explored the erosion of voter–party linkages in Chile and its profound implications on the stability and functionality of the country's democracy. By examining the declining voter turnout, the collapsing trust in traditional political parties, and the emergence of "ghost" parties and "zombie" party members, all in the context of a gradually fragmenting party system, the analysis highlighted how Chile's representative system became weakened.

The electoral reform of 2011 marked a decisive moment in this trajectory. By introducing voluntary voting, the reform exposed the uprooted nature of a party system that had long been perceived as stable but was disconnected from society in reality. However, the reform also aggravated existing problems. The withdrawal of mandatory voting disproportionately disengaged moderate and centrist voters, which led to the rise of ideologically extreme and activist groups. This shift amplified polarization and weakened the capacity of political parties to serve as effective mediators between citizens and the state, which in turn accelerated the onset of a crisis.

Fragmentation and the erosion of voter–party linkages evolved in parallel, and their effects became increasingly intertwined. Electoral reforms lowered the barriers of entry, while disengagement from the overall political process allowed parties that would have never been successful under other circumstances to rise amidst the confusion. Over time, this reciprocal relationship destabilized the political system, undermining its capacity to respond to the increasingly diverse needs of Chilean society.

In this way, the process of "representation backsliding" left behind a fragmented, polarized, and increasingly unresponsive political system—one ill-equipped to confront the growing challenges facing the country. The following chapter explores how the coalitions, parties, and leaders that rose to power in this context would go on to play a central role not only in the system's collapse during the social outburst, but also in the eventual failure of the constitutional process that followed.

CHAPTER 8

Emergence of a Rupturist Discourse

8.1 Introduction

This chapter explores the rise of a transformative and rupturist discourse that took place in Chilean politics between 2010 and 2018. This is a crucial moment as it was during this period, that the two-party system began to give way, and the calls for systemic change that had failed to resonante with voters previously, finally began to gain traction in the public debate that would fundamentally restructure the political landscape of the country.

The rise of the disruptive discourse unfolded sequentially across three interconnected developments. First, the deep ideological divisions and power struggles within the *Concertación* began to take their toll. The fragmentation of the once succesful coalition weakened its ability to play a moderating role in what was happening, and forced it to take a seat on the sideline. Second, the rise of a younger generation of leaders opened up a window into what replacement would look like. Their roles in the 2006 and 2011 movements demonstrated not only the potency of direct action in challenging status-quo, but also that bold, unapologetic discourse could lead to change if sustained long enough. Finally, Michelle Bachelet's second government (2014–2018) reinforced the momentum through structural reforms that highlighted the feasibility of such transformations. Through ambitious policies in education, taxation, and the

K. Bunker, *Chile's Transformation Amidst Crisis*,
https://doi.org/10.1007/978-3-031-96463-3_8

electoral system, her administration expanded the boundaries of political possibilities and raised expectations for meaningful reform, decisively deviating from Chile's long-standing tradition of gradualism.

This chapter individually analyzes these developments and situates them within the broader process of "representation backsliding" the country was going through (as discussed in Chapters 6 and 7).

8.2 Cracks Within

As discussed at length in Chapters 4 and 6, the *Concertación* was one of the most successful and significant political alliances in Chile's history, as it governed the country for two decades after the country's return to democracy. Rooted in pragmatism, consensus, and gradual reform, its approach delivered unparalleled stability, poverty reduction, and economic growth (see Chapter 5). However, by the mid-2000s, the strengths that initially defined its success also revealed its limitations. The internal fractures of the coalition, which had been building for years, ultimately laid the groundwork for its downfall and exposed the limits of its incrementalist approach to governance.

As introduced in Sect. 4.5, two competing visions for Chile's future underlined the divide.[1] The first was held by the *autocomplacientes*, who celebrated the coalition's achievements and defended its pragmatic governance. For them, gradual reforms implemented under successive *Concertación* administrations demonstrated its ability to strike a balance between stability and progress. They viewed moderation as an essential component for maintaining economic growth and political consensus and argued that Chile's success was based on the avoidance of polarization and fragmentation.

The second vision was held by the *autoflagelantes* who purported that the compromises of the coalition came at a very high cost. While recognizing the coalition's achievements, they argued that its incrementalism had reached its limits. They concluded that persistent inequality and unresolved structural issues highlighted the need for in-depth transformative reforms. They believed that the *Concertación*'s cautious approach

[1] While much of this matter is discussed earlier in the book, it is worth reiterating some of the main ideas that led to the division of the *Concertación* here. Readers already familiar with the internal feuds may wish to skip ahead to next section.

had prevented it from addressing the roots of Chile's socioeconomic divisions, which in turn had left a large number of Chileans excluded from the progress the country had made.

By the late 2000s, with the 2009/2010 elections fast approaching and clear signs of fatigue setting in, rifts intensified. While the *autocomplacientes* continued to emphasize the perks of continuity and stability, and the *autoflagelantes* began openly pushing for a new direction—one that could tackle the structural injustices that they believed incremental reforms had failed to resolve. What began as an internal difference was turning into an increasingly obvious public fracture,[2] weakening the coalition's unity and undermining its legitimacy.

The 2009/2010 presidential election, also described in Chapter 4, marked the breaking point. Unable to reconcile differences, the *Concertación* failed to maintain the internal cohesion that was once its hallmark, and splintered, as key figures from parties within the coalition began launching their own independent campaigns.[3]

[2] A particularly revealing episode underscoring the internal tensions within the *Concertación* coalition occurred during the 2009 presidential race, when José Antonio Gómez of the *Partido Radical* publicly confronted Camilo Escalona of the Socialist Party at the official proclamation of Eduardo Frei Ruiz-Tagle's candidacy. Gómez, who had lost to Frei Ruiz-Tagle in an odd primary (where the rule was that the candidate who first won by 20% in a series of regional contests would win the overall nomination— meaning the process could end early if that margin was reached, as it did after the first and only primary, held in Maule and O'Higgins), openly questioned the legitimacy and transparency of the selection process. The resulting argument between Gómez and Escalona, described in the press as "very unpleasant," exposed the fraying sense of unity and growing mistrust between coalition members. While the exchange was not explicitly ideological, it reflected a deeper fragmentation within the coalition, suggesting that the spirit of cooperation and cohesion that had once defined the *Concertación* was rapidly eroding. See: *La Tercera*. 2009. "Gómez por impasse con Escalona: 'Fue muy desagradable'." April 6. https://www.latercera.com/noticia/gomez-por-impasse-con-escalona-fue-muy-desagradable/.

[3] The fragmentation of the *Concertación* was dramatically illustrated by the emergence of multiple breakaway presidential candidacies from within its own ranks. Marco Enríquez-Ominami, a young and charismatic former deputy of the Socialist Party, broke away to run as an independent, casting himself as a modern, untainted alternative to the traditional political establishment. His campaign drew considerable attention, particularly among younger voters disillusioned with the established order. Simultaneously, veteran figures Jorge Arrate and Alejandro Navarro—both longtime members of the Socialist Party—launched their own presidential bids, further signaling discontent with the coalition's direction. Although Navarro eventually withdrew from the race, the proliferation of dissident candidacies and the public airing of internal disputes sent a clear message: the *Concertación* was no longer able to contain the ideological and generational tensions that

The official candidate of the *Concertación* that year, Eduardo Frei Ruiz-Tagle, struggled to overcome the division. As a former president and a symbol of the pragmatic past of the coalition, Frei Ruiz-Tagle embodied the essence of gradualism that the *autoflagelantes* were rejecting. As a result, his campaign failed to inspire a unified coalition, underscoring the challenges faced by the *Concertación*, which could by this point no longer present a coherent vision that addressed demands for continuity and increasing calls for transformative change at the same time.

Faced with mounting internal tensions, Frei Ruiz-Tagle acknowledged the pressing need for change. In an effort to counter the *autoflagelantes*' position without alienating the *autocomplacientes* in the first round, he focused on signaling generational renewal rather than proposing any real shift in the direction of policy. This led him to appoint Sebastián Bowen, a like-minded but younger independent, as head of his campaign in the first round. However reasonable it may have seemed, the strategy, meant to appeal to younger voters and reassure the alienated segment, clearly failed, as the candidate fell short of a third of the vote and obtained the lowest result for any *Concertación* candidate since the return of democracy.

In an attempt to correct course in the second round, Frei Ruiz-Tagle replaced Bowen with three emerging figures from the *Concertación*: Carolina Tohá, Claudio Orrego, and Ricardo Lagos Weber. Yet rather than signal a substantive shift, the move only reinforced the limits of what was possible by this point. He did not pivot left or embrace Enríquez-Ominami's momentum. Instead, he did what he could and doubled down on compromise, which was obviously less than what was needed to save the ship from sinking.[4]

once coexisted under its broad umbrella. These events underscored the coalition's waning ability to present a unified front, foreshadowing its eventual decline and fall.

[4] The trio tapped to replace Sebastián Bowen as the public face of Frei's runoff campaign represented a younger, more dynamic, and more political, generation within the *Concertación*. Carolina Tohá, a prominent member of the Party for Democracy (PPD), had served as President Bachelet's government spokesperson and was widely seen as a progressive voice with strong communication skills and urban appeal. Claudio Orrego, a Christian Democrat and former mayor of Peñalolén , was known for his focus on social equity and participatory governance, cultivating a reputation for community-based leadership. Ricardo Lagos Weber, son of former President Ricardo Lagos (Escobar), brought political pedigree and technocratic credentials, having served as Minister Secretary General of Government and as a key figure in trade negotiations. Other renewal figures included in the campaign's second-round push were Felipe Harboe, a security-focused former Undersecretary of the Interior, and Fulvio Rossi, a reform-minded senator from the Socialist

Unsurprisingly, this led to Sebastián Piñera's victory in the second round, which is why the election is often remembered more as an example of electoral discoordination than of ideological turnover. It was the center-left coalition's failure to resolve its internal divides and adapt to a changing political context that made Piñera's win possible more than anything else. He was simply there to capitalize on the opening and position himself as a viable alternative.[5]

Ultimately, the decline of the *Concertación* can be understood through its internal tensions. The gradualist approach of the coalition, which was previously a source of strength, became a liability in the face of increasing demands for change. At the same time, failure to accommodate the demands of more ambitious factions within the coalition laid the groundwork for the emergence of new actors and movements who perceived value in the rejection of incrementalism.

In this context, the fall of the *Concertación* did not merely signal the end of the coalition. It also announced the imminent rise of a new political

Party. While their inclusion was intended to signal generational change and fresh thinking, the effort ultimately appeared superficial to many voters, especially when contrasted with the outsider momentum building around Marco Enríquez-Ominami. In the years that followed, several of these figures would remain influential in Chilean politics (Tohá would become Minister of the Interior under President Boric; Orrego would be elected Governor of the Metropolitan Region; Lagos Weber would serve as a Senator and head the Senate's Finance Committee; Harboe would become a Senator and 2021-2022 constitutional delegate; and Rossi would continue as a key legislative actor in health and education policy). See: *Cooperativa*. 2010. "Frei prometió 'renovación política' en el regreso de la franja televisiva." January 3. https://cooperativa.cl/noticias/pais/politica/presidenciales/frei-prometio-renovacion-politica-en-el-regreso-de-la-franja/2010-01-03/215104.html/.

[5] For a discussion on the break-up of the *Concertación* and how it allowed for the victory of Piñera, see: Bunker, K. 2010. *The 2009 Presidential Election in Chile*, (MA Thesis). San Diego, CA: San Diego State University. The main argument is that the division of the left into three like-minded candidacies divided the electorate to the point of no return. Indeed, the votes for Frei Ruiz-Tagle (2,065,061 votes), Enríquez-Ominami (1,405,124 votes), and Arrate (433,195 votes), added up to 55,9% of the vote in the first round, and even though voting was mandatory at the time, Sebastián Piñera was still able to reverse the result in the second round, securing 51.6% for himself. Remarkably, this discoordination, of sorts, was not unprecedented. In 2005/2006 the same situation had occurred on the opposite side of the fold. In that election, the division of the right into two candidacies paved the way for Michelle Bachelet's second-round victory. In the first round, the sum of votes between Piñera (1,763,694 votes) and Joaquín Lavín (1,612,608 votes) surpassed that of Bachelet (3,190,691 votes). Yet the destructive campaign within the conservative sector divided the electorate to the point of no return, allowing Bachelet to win with 53.5% of the vote.

order. With the failure of social democracy to find its way, a new configuration was emerging, shaped by the implicit triumph of the *autoflagelantes* and the consolidation of the conservative right in power. In the void that followed, new political forces began to stake their claims in an effort to redefine the direction of the country.

8.3 Rise of a New Generation

In parallel with the ideological debate taking place within the *Concertación*, a growing national conversation was emerging regarding the role of social services. Dissatisfied with the incrementalism that had long defined Chilean politics, a younger generation of student leaders had found an entry point in the educational system on which to push for concrete improvements. Although these efforts unfolded alongside the *Concertación*'s internal struggles, the student leaders brought fresh energy, ideas, and ambition to the political arena. Their rise marked a cultural and generational shift and introduced a new wave of leaders who were determined to challenge the status quo.

The first major sign of this generational awakening was observed in 2006 through the *Revolución Pingüina* ("Penguin Revolution").[6] High school students across Chile organized an unprecedented wave of protests to directly challenge the inequalities entrenched in the education system, which was implemented during the Pinochet dictatorship (see Chapter 3). At its peak, the movement mobilized approximately 600,000 students nationwide, and occupied about 400 schools.[7] Their demands focused on

[6] The name *Revolución Pingüina* ("Penguin Revolution") refers to the black-and-white school uniforms worn by Chilean high school students, resembling penguins. The term became a symbol of youth-led activism, as students organized walkouts, school occupations, and marches to demand education reform. Such characterizations of protest movements through symbolic imagery were not uncommon; for example, *La marcha de los paraguas* (lit. "the Umbrella March") in 2011 became emblematic of that year's student movement, as thousands showed up to march through Santiago in the rain.

[7] One of the most emblematic centers of student mobilization was the *Instituto Nacional*, Chile's oldest and most prestigious public high school, historically known for producing generations of political and intellectual leaders. By the late 2000s and into the 2010s, however, it had become a focal point of escalating tensions. What began as peaceful student protests gradually gave way to more radicalized tactics, including the use of Molotov cocktails, arson attempts, and violent clashes with police on school grounds. These developments reflected not only a breakdown in school governance but also growing frustration with the perceived stagnation of educational reform. Some observers,

concrete reforms to address what they argued was deep-seated inequity in Chile's privatized education system and particularly targeted the *Ley Orgánica Constitucional de Enseñanza* (lit. "Organic Constitutional Law of Education," a special category of law with constitutional standing in Chile)—widely understood to be a key factor in the institutionalization of the "market-driven model" of education (see Chapter 2 for more on the origin and fate of LOCs).

This shift in political culture during Michelle Bachelet's first administration established an important precedent, forcing the government to take action when the students mobilized. To calm protests, the government established the *Consejo Asesor Presidencial para la Calidad de la Educación* ("Presidential Advisory Council on Education") and introduced reforms to address the most visible grievances. However, these measures were ultimately criticized as superficial. While addressing demands put forward by the movement, they primarily laid the groundwork for large-scale mobilization in the future.

If protests in 2006 marked the emergence of youth activism, then mobilizations in 2011 demonstrated its maturity and transformative potential. The earlier movement focused on improving the quality of elementary and high school education, which was driven by an immediate and narrowly defined set of grievances. In contrast, the protests in 2011, led by university students, expanded the scope of critique, targeting what they argued were "structural inequalities in Chile's neoliberal model." At the core, they demanded free, high-quality public education and challenged a system in which families bore 75% of the costs for higher education while the state contributed a mere 25%.[8] Building on the

including former student leader and later Minister of National Assets Julio Isamit, would later describe this wave of school-based violence—particularly during 2019—as a prelude to the broader social unrest that erupted in October of that year. See: Escalona, F. 2021. "Ministro y exlíder pingüino Isamit: 'La violencia en los colegios en 2019 fue el preámbulo al 18 de octubre.'" *El Líbero*. May 13. https://ellibero.cl/actualidad/la-violencia-en-los-colegios-en-2019-fue-el-preambulo-al-18-de-octubre/.

[8] Beyond the cost burden, students also protested the widespread reliance on private institutions and the profit-driven nature of the system. Approximately 70% of Chilean students depended on loans, often entering the workforce already indebted, with repayments beginning from their first job. Many of the poorest students, having attended under-resourced municipal schools, were funneled into lower-tier private universities with high tuition fees—typically between US$300 and US$1,200—further entrenching inequality. Analysts described the model as one that reproduced, rather than reduced, socioeconomic disparities. See: Smink, V. 2011. "Las razones de las protestas estudiantiles

momentum of the protests in 2006, those in 2011 endeavored to address what their predecessors had left unfinished, pushing for systemic change.

The 2011 protests not only galvanized a transformative movement but also elevated new leaders who would prove to be nearly as influential as the mobilization. Among the most prominent were Camila Vallejo and Giorgio Jackson.

Vallejo was the leader of the *Federación de Estudiantes de la Universidad de Chile* (FECH) and a member of the Communist Party. She became a central figure and leveraged organizational skills and media presence to link the demands of the movement to broad critiques of Chile's political and economic systems. President of the *Federación de Estudiantes de la Universidad Católica de Chile* (FEUC), Jackson offered a centrist and reformist, yet still ambitious perspective. Together, they personified a generational shift in Chilean politics—rejecting gradualism and championing a narrative seeking a bold, new Chile.[9]

en Chile." *BBC Mundo*. August 10. https://www.bbc.com/mundo/noticias/2011/08/110809_chile_estudiantes_2_vs/.

[9] The 2011 movement launched its leaders—Camila Vallejo and Giorgio Jackson—into global prominence. In October of that year, they traveled to Europe to internationalize the Chilean student cause, meeting with representatives from the European Parliament, UNESCO, the OECD, and the UN Human Rights Council. They participated in a demonstration at the *Sorbonne* in Paris, gave a conference in Geneva, and met with Stéphane Hessel, author of *Indignez-vous!* and co-drafter of the *Universal Declaration of Human Rights*. See: *El Mundo*. 2011. "La gira europea de los estudiantes chilenos." October 13. https://www.elmundo.es/america/2011/10/13/noticias/1318525610.html. Vallejo, a member of the Communist Party and president of the FECH, quickly became a symbol of youth-led protest. In December 2011, *TIME* magazine included her among its "People Who Mattered" (see: Padgett, T. 2011. "Chile's Student Protesters." *TIME*. December 14. https://content.time.com/time/specials/packages/article/0,28804,2101745_2102130_2102585,00.html), and in early 2012, *The Guardian* named her "Person of the Year" (see: Franklin, J. 2012. "Camila Vallejo: Chile's Student Leader Heralds a New Era of Protest." *The Guardian*. January 13. https://www.theguardian.com/world/2012/jan/13/protesters-camila-vallejo-chile-students/). A few months later, *The New York Times* profiled her as "the world's most glamorous revolutionary." See: Murphy, A. 2012. "Camila Vallejo, the World's Most Glamorous Revolutionary." *The New York Times Magazine*. April 8. https://www.nytimes.com/2012/04/08/magazine/camila-vallejo-the-worlds-most-glamorous-revolutionary.html. Jackson, representing a more centrist and reformist line as president of the FEUC, went on to found *Revolución Democrática*, lead the *Marca AC/Marca tu Voto* campaign for constitutional change, and later serve as a minister in Gabriel Boric's government (first Presidency, then Social Development). Vallejo would also become a minister under Boric, serving as Secretary General. (Francisco Figueroa, who was vice president of the FECH under Vallejo in

In contrast to politicians from the *Concertación*, who worked within the constraints of the 1980 constitution, these leaders rejected previous compromises (such as comfort with the legitimacy of origin and rigidity critiques, laid out in Chapter 2) and articulated a vision of transformative change. Their success lay not only in mobilizing large numbers of people but also in framing their demands as part of a broad critique of the neoliberal system in Chile. Their independence from the political establishment rendered them especially effective because they were not obliged to uphold the decisions of previous governments or their reluctance to pursue bold and extensive reforms.

Enríquez-Ominami, who could have occupied this space, never truly gained traction after resigning from the Socialist Party in 2009, for the inverse reason.[10] While his departure signaled a willingness to pursue a more expansive agenda, his rise lacked the grassroots connection that defined the new generation of leaders. Perhaps if he had aligned himself with student grievances during the mass mobilizations of 2006—instead of inheriting a position as a Socialist deputy in his senator stepfather's

2011, and also took part in the European tour, would later serve as Minister of National Assets under President Boric.)

[10] Marco Enríquez-Ominami is the biological son of Miguel Enríquez, founder and General Secretary of the *Movimiento de Izquierda Revolucionaria* (MIR), a Marxist-Leninist guerrilla movement active during the Allende and Pinochet years. He was later adopted by Carlos Ominami, a prominent Socialist Party politician who served as Minister of Economy under Patricio Aylwin and as senator for the Valparaíso region until 2010. Enríquez-Ominami entered national politics as a Socialist Party deputy (elected under the binomial system in District 10 to serve 2006—2010) but broke with the party in 2009 to run as an independent presidential candidate. Years later he would found and launch the *Partido Progresista* (PRO). While he contributed to public debate, particularly around political renewal and anti-establishment critique, he failed to build lasting grassroots support or translate his media profile into institutional power. He ran in four consecutive presidential elections, earning 20.14% of the vote in 2009, 10.99% in 2013, 5.71% in 2017, and 7.61% in 2021—reflecting a clear decline in support over time, despite a modest recovery in his final attempt.

district—his trajectory might have been different.[11] However, his association with the political elite shaped a public perception that he would never really be able to shake off.

In contrast, the leaders who emerged from the student movements of 2006 and 2011 began with a strong foundation of grassroots support. These leaders were not defined by elite quarrels but by their ability to channel public discontent into a vision for systemic reform. In 2013, Camila Vallejo and Giorgio Jackson successfully transitioned from leading student protests to securing seats in the Chamber of Deputies. Their election marked a decisive deviation from the traditional political class, and their legitimacy was rooted in the mass mobilizations they spearheaded. In contrast to Enríquez-Ominami's rise, which was personalist and based on specific issues, Vallejo and Jackson embodied a collective movement for structural change.

In 2014, political momentum further expanded through Gabriel Boric, another prominent figure of the 2011 mobilizations. As president of the FECH (after Vallejo), Boric played a key role in broadening the movement's critique of the neoliberal system in Chile. Entering mainstream politics in 2013, he deliberately avoided established parties, giving himself the freedom to challenge both the right and the *Concertación*. Taken together, Boric, Vallejo, and Jackson represented a new force in Chilean politics, one that, while still shaped by elite ambitions, could at this early point present itself as acting on behalf of the people.

[11] In retrospect, Enríquez-Ominami had the makings of a generational figure—someone who, under different circumstances, might have embodied elements of what Camila Vallejo, Giorgio Jackson, and Gabriel Boric would later come to represent. With roots in exile, a family legacy of resistance, and fluency in the language of political renewal, he could have positioned himself as an authentic voice of post-dictatorship discontent. Yet, as mentioned above, rather than building grassroots credibility, he opted for the path of least resistance: running for a congressional seat in his adoptive father's stronghold—under the Socialist Party banner. This early decision reinforced the perception that he was an insider operating within the political establishment, rather than a break from it. His public image further complicated matters: he married a well-known television presenter and cultivated a dandy-like persona tied to the world of film, celebrity, and the cultural elite. While this helped raise his media profile, it distanced him from the activist credibility that defined the new generation of left leaders. Moreover, his party, the PRO, appeared to many as more of a personal electoral platform than a genuine political organization, lacking strong voter-party linkages and institutional depth, as discussed in Chapter 6.

By the end of this period, Chile's political landscape was clearly undergoing a generational realignment.[12] The emergence of these new leaders signaled a break from the past. Fueled by student protests and the fragmentation of the traditional centerleft, they were laying the foundation that would not only serve to replace the old, fatigued *Concertación*, but also to make a constitutional push possible.

8.4 Shifting the Fence

Michelle Bachelet's return to the presidency in 2014 denoted a decisive and final shift in the post-*Concertación* era. Her second government introduced a bold and unapologetic program that departed extremely from the incrementalism of her first term in power.[13] With a clear mandate for transformative reforms, Bachelet's plan was both a signal of

[12] By 2017, Chile's political landscape reflected not only ideological fragmentation but also a clear generational realignment. New parties had emerged on both the left and right, often led by the literal sons and daughters of the political elite from the transition era. On the left, *Revolución Democrática* and other *Frente Amplio* formations were populated by figures with deep ties to the *Concertación*. For example, Miguel Crispi (RD Lower Chamber deputy, and later Undersecretary) is the son of Claudia Serrano, who served as Minister of Labor under Michelle Bachelet (first term); Nicolás Grau (Minister of Economy under Boric) is the son of Paulina Veloso, Secretary General of the Presidency under Bachelet (first term); and several others such as Camilo Riffo and Javiera Parada also emerged from families linked to the Socialist or PPD traditions. On the right, *Evopoli* represented a parallel generational phenomenon within the former *Alianza*: Felipe Kast and Pablo Kast are sons of Miguel Kast, Minister of Planning (Social Development) and later Central Bank President under Pinochet; Hernán Larraín Matte is the son of UDI Senator Hernán Larraín Fernández and Magdalena Matte, Minister of Housing under Sebastián Piñera (first term). While these parties styled themselves as forces of renewal, they were also rooted in the same elite networks that shaped post-authoritarian Chile. See: Bellolio, C. 2019. "Juego de generaciones: las claves del recambio político en Chile." *Estudios Públicos* 154: 201–229; Bunker, K. 2021. "The Age Cleavage: Cultural Backlash in Chile." *América Latina Hoy* 87: 3–28.

[13] The 2013 election marked a pivotal moment in Chile's political trajectory, not only because of Bachelet's return but due to the stark contrast between her campaign and the disarray on the right. The center-right alliance, then operating as the *Alianza*, cycled chaotically through a series of presidential candidates including Laurence Golborne, Andrés Allamand, Pablo Longueira, and finally Evelyn Matthei, in a primary and post-primary process that exposed internal division and strategic confusion. In contrast, Bachelet's candidacy was defined by clarity and cohesion. She ran on a bold and comprehensive platform that openly broke with the gradual reformism of previous *Concertación* governments. Her program promised structural changes in education, tax policy, and the constitution, marking a decisive change in both tone and direction. For an overview of the election's

victory for the *autoflagelantes*, who had drafted her presidential manifesto, and a sign of definitive defeat for the *autocomplacientes*, who had failed to defend the socialdemocratic legacy of the *Concertación*.

The three major reforms promised in Bachelet's manifesto were regarding taxation, education, and electoral reform. These initiatives were framed as a response to elevated public discontent, which was, according to her campaign, clearly visible in the social movements of 2006 and 2011. While education reform resonated with grassroots activists, the other measures, taxation and the overhaul of the electoral system, reflected more of the elite's will than that of the people.

Once in power, she delivered swiftly. Her first major achievement came during her first year, as she was able to pass legislation that aimed to significantly increase tax revenue.[14] To do so, she specifically targeted long-term loopholes that primarily benefited the wealthiest Chileans. Although framed as a necessary step in addressing socioeconomic disparities in Chile, the reform was also presented as a break with the neoliberal policies that had molded the country since Pinochet.

Education reform was the second reform to pass through Congress. It was perhaps the most prominent item on Bachelet's agenda, which in contrast to the other two reforms, directly responded to grassroots demands and a broad critique of neoliberalism and the existing model. Building on the momentum of the student protests in 2006 and 2011, she openly sought to dismantle and restructure the privatized education system, which was by this point viewed by many as a source of debt and inequality. Approved by Congress in early 2015, measures included free tuition for low-income students, strict regulations on for-profit educational institutions, and efforts to strengthen public education.[15] Citizens

cleavages and institutional context, see: Bunker, K. 2013. "The 2013 Presidential and Legislative Election in Chile." *Electoral Studies* 33(4): 346–348.

[14] Bachelet's 2014 tax reform aimed to increase state revenue by approximately 3 percent of GDP in order to finance social policies such as education reform. The legislation closed major loopholes used by large firms and high-income individuals, gradually raised corporate tax rates, and reduced incentives for profit reinvestment that had long favored business elites. It was one of the most ambitious fiscal overhauls since the return to democracy. See: *BBC Mundo*. 2014. "Bachelet promulga reforma tributaria en Chile." September 26. https://www.bbc.com/mundo/ultimas_noticias/2014/09/140926_chile_aprueba_reforma_tributaria_ac/.

[15] The education reform approved in early 2015 aimed to address longstanding demands from the student movements and correct inequalities entrenched since the

generally perceived these changes as fulfillment of promises that earlier *Concertación* governments had failed to deliver. Student leaders, who pushed education reform to the forefront of national politics, not only monitored the process but also guided its direction.[16]

The third major reform during Bachelet's presidency was the overhaul of the electoral system. In contrast to education reform, this initiative was driven by the elite's perceptions of systemic shortcomings and not public outcry.[17] A legacy of the Pinochet era, the binomial electoral system has long been criticized for artificially favoring two dominant coalitions and stifling political diversity (see Chapters 2 and 6). In early

Pinochet-era privatization of education. Among its central pillars were the provision of free university tuition for low-income students, stronger oversight of educational quality, and a reassertion of the state's role in public education. One of its most celebrated and controversial components was the ban on profit in publicly funded schools, which had long allowed private providers to extract surpluses while receiving state subsidies. See: *Deutsche Welle*. 2015. "Senado chileno aprueba reforma educativa." January 22. https://www.dw.com/es/senado-chileno-aprueba-reforma-educativa/a-18210199/

[16] Though formally advanced by Bachelet's administration, the reform was largely conceptualized, drafted, and pushed forward by younger policy teams linked to *Revolución Democrática*. Key architects included Gonzalo Muñoz, a policy expert with a background in educational research, and Miguel Crispi, a founding member of RD and former student leader. Both served within the Ministry of Education as crucial intermediaries between the government and the *Frente Amplio*-aligned generation. Once the core components of the reform were passed in Congress, Muñoz and Crispi resigned in May 2016. Crispi would later be elected deputy (2018–2022) and go on to serve as Undersecretary and a key political strategist in Gabriel Boric's government. See: *El Desconcierto*. 2016. "RD oficializa salida de Miguel Crispi y Gonzalo Muñoz del Ministerio de Educación." May 23. https://eldesconcierto.cl/2016/05/23/rd-oficializa-salida-de-miguel-crispi-y-gonzalo-munoz-del-ministerio-de-educacion/.

[17] Unlike the tax and education reforms—which were largely responses to grassroots mobilization—Chile's electoral reform was a top-down initiative led by political elites. While the binomial system had long been criticized by experts and some sectors of civil society for favoring bipartisan dominance and distorting representation, it had never been the subject of widespread public pressure. The reform was framed as a necessary correction to a system inherited from the Pinochet dictatorship rather than as a direct demand from the citizenry. Approved by Congress in early 2015, the new law replaced the binomial system with a proportional representation model, expanded the number of deputies from 120 to 155, and redrew electoral districts to increase district magnitude—that is, the number of representatives per district. These changes aimed to foster political pluralism by opening space for smaller parties and independent actors, particularly benefiting younger parties and leaders emerging from outside the traditional coalition structures. See: Montes, R. 2015. "Chile reforma el sistema electoral heredado de Pinochet." *El País*. January 21. https://elpais.com/internacional/2015/01/21/actualidad/1421808746_668476.html/.

2015, Congress approved a new proportional system, overtly attempting to increase pluralism in the political system. While the reform opened the door for new and small parties, as intended (see Chapter 6), it particularly benefited the movements of theleaders who had emerged from the student protests. By this point, they were ready to shift gears and formalize as political parties in an effort to directly challenge, and perhaps even replace, the dominance of the traditional political class.

Bachelet's government culminated in its most ambitious gesture: a proposal for a new constitution. Announced in late 2015, she framed the constitutional process in a speech in response to Chile's systemic challenges, which she attributed to the 1980 Constitution and the entrenched neoliberal model.[18] While reforms in taxation, education, and the electoral system targeted specific issues, the objective of the constitutional proposal was to rewrite the foundations of the nation.[19] This initiative signaled a definitive rejection of the gradualist legacy of the *autocomplacientes*, demonstrated her commitment to systemic change, and aligned the government with the demands of the younger generation.

[18] In October 2015, President Bachelet formally announced the launch of a constituent process in a nationally televised address, framing it as a response to widespread "citizen discontent" and the structural constraints "imposed" by the 1980 Constitution. The roadmap she presented included a series of civic education campaigns, *diálogos ciudadanos* (lit. "citizen dialogues"), and consultations across the country, culminating in a constituent assembly or body tasked with drafting a new constitution. The process was planned to unfold in phases over several years, with an emphasis on citizen participation and transparency. See: *BBC Mundo*. 2015. "Bachelet anuncia el inicio de un largo proceso constituyente en Chile." October 15. https://www.bbc.com/mundo/noticias/2015/10/151014_chile_consitucion_bachelet_az/

[19] On March 5, 2018—just six days before the end of her second presidency—Bachelet submitted a draft constitutional proposal to Congress. The proposed text sought to strengthen social rights, guarantee gender equality, expand indigenous recognition, and redefine the state's role in education, health, and welfare. It also introduced checks on presidential power and reforms to the judiciary, reflecting a clear departure from the subsidiary model embedded in the 1980 Constitution. See: Sánchez, V. 2018. "Chile: a días de terminar su mandato, Michelle Bachelet propone reformar la Constitución." *France 24*. March 7. https://www.france24.com/es/20180307-reforma-constitucion-chile-bachelet-propuesta/. [This document, *Bases Ciudadanas para la Nueva Constitución (boletín 11.617-08)*, is available on the author's website.]

Although the constitutional proposal did not come to fruition during Bachelet's presidency, its symbolic importance was immense.[20] It demonstrated that Chile's political boundaries were no longer fixed, and that the *fence* of what was possible could be moved. It emphasized transformation, lowering the bar for future changes, and establishing guidelines for what had to be done.

8.5 The Emergence of a Rupturist Discourse

In sum, between 2010 and 2018, Chilean politics witnessed the convergence of ambition, generational urgency, and the precedent of structural reform—three forces that together created fertile ground for the emergence of a rupturist discourse. These developments were distinct yet intertwined, reinforcing one another to cultivate a climate where change seemed both necessary and inevitable.

At the center of this process was, a sense of debt weighed heavily on the center-left. The *autoflagelantes* within the *Concertación*, long critical of the coalition's gradualist approach, were determined to prove they could do more—more ambitious, more transformative, and more attuned to growing dissatisfaction. For years, they had argued that Chile's incremental reforms had failed to address structural inequalities and that a deeper reckoning with the country's economic and political model was overdue. Their ascendance within the *Nueva Mayoría* coalition under Michelle Bachelet's leadership marked a moment of vindication but also set expectations dangerously high. The desire to settle this political "debt" pushed the center-left to adopt a rhetoric of structural change that risked exceeding the bounds of both institutional capacity and public consensus.

Simultaneously, a new generation of leaders emerged with a persistent determination to replace their predecessors. Shaped by the *Revolución Pingüina* in 2006 and the student protests in 2011, figures such as

[20] Despite its symbolic weight, Bachelet's constitutional initiative failed to materialize into binding institutional change. Several factors contributed to its collapse: the shifting political and social context during her second term, a flawed institutional design that lacked enforceable steps toward ratification, the exclusion of established political parties from meaningful participation in the process, and the absence of elite consensus across party lines. These four interrelated dynamics ultimately limited the initiative's legitimacy and viability. See: Henríquez Viñas, M., and J. F. García. 2023. "Bachelet's Constitution-Making Process in Chile (2015–2018): Reasons for a (Foreseeable) Failure." *International Journal of Constitutional Law* 21(5): 1496–1516.

Vallejo, Jackson, and Boric rejected the policies of the *Concertación* as well as the norms and compromises that characterized its leadership. For these leaders, coming to power was not only an aspiration but also a necessity, as they approached politics with the urgency of those who believed that change could no longer wait. Their resolve to deviate from the past drove them to express bold demands for systemic change, but also revealed a willingness to prioritize disruption over pragmatism. In their bid to replace the old order, the new generation added to the accumulating atmosphere of rupture, thus positioning themselves as challengers and inheritors of the leftist tradition.

Finally, the structural reforms implemented during Michelle Bachelet's second presidency proved that significant change was, in fact, achievable. Reforms in taxation, education, and electoral laws symbolized a decisive break from the cautious incrementalism of the *Concertación* and challenged the limits of aspects that Chilean politics considered possible. Whether their implementation was successful or not, these reforms carried symbolic weight, as they planted the idea that in-depth transformation could be achieved through political will. By the end of Bachelet's term, the spirit of change was palpable in the air.

The next chapter turns to look at the impact that the second election of Piñera had on a political class and a party system that was gearing up for structural overhaul.

8.6 Conclusion

This chapter examined the emergence of the transformative and rupturist discourse that appeared in Chilean politics between 2010 and 2018. By looking at some of the major political happenings that took place across these eight years, it traced the evolution of the divisive political narrative to the internal fractures within the *Concertación*, the rise of a bold younger generation, and the ambitious reforms during the second presidency of Michelle Bachelet. Together, these issues indirectly set the stage for the greatest political crisis in post-Pinochet Chile.

In any case, it should be noted that the relevance behind the emergence ofthis discourse can only be fully understood within the broader political context. As discussed in Chapters 6 and 7, the years studied in this chapter were unlike any that had come before. They were marked by a quiet yet growing fragmentation of the party system and erosion of voter–party linkages. This structural instability served both as a cause of the rise of the narrative and as a catalyst for its amplification. Perhaps, in the absence of "representation backsliding", such rupturist discourse would have been quelled from the outset.

By 2018, however, it was too late. The convergence of these factors—ambition within the center-left, the rise of a younger generation, the precedent of structural reforms, and the weakening of established political structures—had already fundamentally shifted the political landscape in Chile. The boundaries of possibilities were redefined, thus raising the minimum bar for future changes. This period not only foreshadowed the dramatic events of 2019, but it also laid the ideological and structural groundwork that rendered such a crisis inevitable.

CHAPTER 9

October 18, 2019

9.1 Introduction

The social outburst of October 2019 in Chile was not an isolated event but the culmination of a greater, invisible political process. As explored in previous chapters, long-term structural factors—including the fragmentation of the party system, the erosion of voter–party linkages, and the rise of new generational narratives advocating systemic change—created fertile ground for an explosion of public discontent. Against this backdrop, a modest Metro fare hike in October 2019 became the spark that ignited the fire, rapidly transforming a peaceful protest into full-blown mayhem.

This chapter begins with Sebastián Piñera's return to power in 2018, a moment that highlighted both his political skill and the emerging divisions within the left. It then traces how a seemingly minor transport policy triggered public frustration, sparking a wave of small, disorganized protests that quickly grew in size and coordination. These mobilizations escalated into a broader social and political crisis. Finally, the chapter examines how the opposition leveraged the dual character of the protests, both peaceful and violent, to delegitimize the government and transform a specific grievance into a broader call for systemic change.

K. Bunker, *Chile's Transformation Amidst Crisis*,
https://doi.org/10.1007/978-3-031-96463-3_9

9.2 The Return of Piñera

Sebastián Piñera's return to the presidency in 2018 reflected his ability to position himself as a stable, experienced leader. Campaigning on economic growth and pragmatic governance, he capitalized on dissatisfaction with Michelle Bachelet's administration, which struggled with declining public trust after a major scandal in early 2015.[1] A divided opposition aided in Piñera's victory. In the 2017 presidential election, Alejandro Guillier, a center-left senator for Antofagasta with limited political experience, emerged as a major rival. However, Guillier failed to unify the left, which was fractured by the unexpected rise of the *Frente Amplio*. Led by Beatriz Sánchez, this newly formed leftist coalition (tied to both Giorgio Jackson and Gabriel Boric) secured a surprising 20% of votes in the first round, which signaled a definitive shift in Chilean politics but also left the broader political sector fragmented and Piñera's path to victory clear.

After taking office, Piñera aimed to replicate the technocratic, market-oriented governance of his first term by appointing a Cabinet that brought together experienced figures from his earlier administration with independent experts. His team was intended to project competence and continuity, reflecting Piñera's belief that his administration could focus on stability and incremental progress. However, these decisions revived familiar tensions. By reappointing several figures from his first term, Piñera reinforced the perception among critics that his presidency represented a return to the status quo. This was further compounded by his decision to shelve Bachelet's 2015 constitutional reform project—a move that was interpreted as a signal of his unwillingness to address broader policy changes.[2]

[1] A little less than a year into her second term, the investigative journal *Qué Pasa* uncovered an irregular financial scheme tied to Bachelet's son, Sebastián Dávalos. Acting as part of the real estate firm *Caval*, co-owned by his wife, Natalia Compagnon he allegedly used political connections to secure a multi-million-dollar loan for land speculation, triggering a national scandal and his resignation from the Sociocultural Directorate of the Presidential Office. See: Salaberry, J. P. 2015. "Un negocio Caval."*Qué Pasa*. February 5. http://www.quepasa.cl/articulo/actualidad/2015/02/1-16218-9-un-negocio-caval.shtml/

[2] Just five days after his inauguration, Piñera shelved Bachelet's constitutional reform, arguing it was unnecessary. See: *Página 12*. 2018. "Piñera frenó la reforma constitucional." March 16. https://www.pagina12.com.ar/101842-pinera-freno-la-reforma-constitucional/

While Piñera may have expected pushback from the left, he underestimated the evolving political landscape. The emergence of a more assertive *Frente Amplio*, along with the increasing presence of younger political actors, fostered challenges for which his administration was simply unprepared. Piñera's confidence in his pragmatic, technocratic approach not only made him vulnerable to criticism from the outset, but also foreshadowed the serious unrest that would soon erupt.

Although Piñera returned to power with a decisive mandate, garnering 54.6% of the vote in the second round, a mismatch between expectations and the realities of a changing opposition quickly defined his tenure. The political landscape was shifting underneath, citizens were increasingly detaching from the political class, and the new left was growing bolder by the minute.

9.3 A Hike to the Metro Fare

Approximately one and a half years into the second Piñera administration, the *Panel de Expertos de Transporte Público* ("Panel of Experts on Public Transportation") announced a fare increase for the Metro system on October 1, 2019, which affected the Province of Santiago and the communes of San Bernardo and Puente Alto. Specifically, the fare for buses within the Metropolitan Mobility Network increased by 10 pesos (approximately $0.01 USD), while the Metro fare during peak hours increased by 30 pesos (approximately $0.03 USD).[3] Amounting to an increase of less than 4%, this hike was justified through a legally mandated rate index of variables such as fuel price, labor cost, inflation, and currency exchange rates for the US dollar and Euro.

For context, at the time, a commuter in Santiago spent approximately 13.8% of the minimum wage on Metro transportation per month in

[3] On September 25, 2019, the Panel Public Transport Experts approved a fare hike based on projections for *Transantiago*'s financial viability. On October 1, Minister of Transportation Gloria Hutt signed Resolution No. 42.470, formalizing the increase (that had been originally determined in resolution number 2 of the Panel). It was publicly announced on October 4, published in the *Diario Oficial* the next day, and scheduled to take effect at midnight on Sunday, October 6. See: Espinoza, C. 2020. "La primera chispa: El alza del pasaje que detonó el estallido social." *The Clinic*. October 1. https://www.theclinic.cl/2020/10/01/la-primera-chispa-el-alza-del-pasaje-que-detonó-el-estallido-social/. [This document, *Ley 42.470 (resolución n. 2)*, is available on the author's website.]

2019,[4] an amount similar to that of Medellin (12.6%), higher than those of Buenos Aires (5.7%), Lima (8.2%), and Mexico City (8%), but lower than that of the Sao Paulo Metro, where costs amounted to approximately 20% of the minimum monthly income.

While some argued that specific decisions made by the Piñera government played a role in prompting this increase,[5] it is clear that this is not the case, as similar hikes had occurred not only during the previous administration but also in the subsequent one.[6]

Anyway, as soon as the fare hike came into effect on October 6, high school students began to organize. They coordinated efforts to evade the fare, leaping over turnstiles to avoid paying. By October 14, the movement had gained momentum, growing from dozens of students to hundreds of passengers. Soon after, the fare evasion escalated into station occupation, and then into clashes with the *Carabineros* (the Chilean police).

The government's response was widely read as both delayed and out of touch. On the day the fare hike took effect, Economy Minister Juan Andrés Fontaine remarked that "those who start their commute earlier

[4] This question captured the interest of several media outlets at the time. See, for example: Cádiz, P. 2019. "¿El Metro más caro de Sudamérica? Esto gastan los chilenos en transporte (y qué pasa en el mundo)." *Tele 13*. October 18. https://www.t13.cl/amp/noticia/nacional/evasion-masiva-metro-valor-pasaje-chile-mundo-sueldo-minimo/

[5] Ex minister of Transportation of the Bachelet government, Paola Tapia, argued that the hike was due to decisions made by the Piñera administration. *Cooperativa*. 2019. "Ex ministra de Transportes: Alza de pasajes es consecuencia directa de las decisiones del Gobierno." October 6. https://cooperativa.cl/noticias/pais/transportes/transantiago/ex-ministra-de-transportes-alza-de-pasajes-es-consecuencia-directa-de/2019-10-16/175705.html/

[6] Several fare hikes were conducted under the presidency of Gabriel Boric, showing that these sort of adjustments were not unique to any one administration. See: *Cooperativa*. 2024. "Panel de Expertos anuncia alza de 20 pesos en el transporte público de la capital." February 1. https://cooperativa.cl/noticias/pais/transportes/transantiago/panel-de-expertos-anuncia-alza-de-20-pesos-en-el-transporte-publico-de/2024-02-02/161032.html/; Olivares Nieto, B. 2024. "Transporte público vuelve a subir: Panel de expertos aplica alza de $10 para buses y Metro en Santiago." *Emol*. November 8. https://www.emol.com/noticias/Nacional/2024/11/08/1147955/nueva-alza-transporte-publico.html/; Carvajal, S. 2025. "A tres meses del último aumento: Panel de Expertos determina nueva alza en pasajes de buses y metro." *La Tercera*. February 7. https://www.latercera.com/nacional/noticia/a-tres-meses-del-ultimo-aumento-panel-de-expertos-determina-alza-en-pasajes-de-buses-y-metro/J6ZT4IDZVJB3XFT5Y5BZRHEBL4/

would benefit from relatively lower prices." [7] When the protests intensified, the president of the Panel of Experts, Juan Enrique Coeymans, commented that "people don't protest when the price of tomatoes or bread rises." [8] As the situation worsened and the damage surpassed the cost of the fare hike itself, former Metro president Clemente Pérez labeled the protests as "unjustified" and "stupid," urging students to return home as their efforts to reverse the fare hike had "failed."[9]

A few days later, the situation deteriorated further. On October 18, 2019, Metro authorities announced the partial closure of stations on Lines 1 and 2 due to attacks on drivers and guards, and a general lack of security for operators and users.[10] In response, the entire Metro network was shut down, stranding hundreds of thousands of commuters who were seen walking *en masse* toward the southern and southeastern neighborhoods of Santiago. Peaceful protests that had started earlier in the day began to turn violent, shifting from chants and dances to rock-throwing and Molotov launching.

[7] The statement was made on October 7. See: *CNN Chile*. 2019. "Ministro de Economía y nueva tarifa del Metro: "Quien madrugue puede ser ayudado a través de una tarifa más baja"." October 7. https://edition.cnn.com/lodijeron encnn/entrevista-ministro-economia-tarifa-metro_20191007/. He would later roll back on his words. See: Jara, A. 2019. "Fontaine y su llamado a "madrugar" para ahorrar en el metro: "Preferiría haberlo dicho de una manera distinta"." *La Tercera*. October 18. https://www.latercera.com/politica/noticia/fontaine-llamado-mad rugar-ahorrar-metro-preferiria-haberlo-dicho-una-manera-distinta/866433/

[8] Juan Enrique Coeymans, president of the Panel of Public Transport Experts, dismissed student fare-evasion protests by observing that even when the price of staples like tomatoes or bread rises, there are no comparable protests. He characterized the fare-evasion movement as politically managed, arguing that students were protesting despite no fare increase, unlike interurban passengers who remained silent despite larger hikes. See: Chechilnitzky, A. 2019. "Presidente del Panel de Expertos del Transporte Público por evasiones: "Cuando suben los tomates, el pan, todas las cosas, no hacen ninguna protesta"." *La Tercera*. October 17. https://www.latercera.com/nacional/noticia/presidente-del-panel-expertos-del-transporte-publico-evasiones-creo-manejo-politico/864440/

[9] See: *24 Horas*. 2019. "Clemente Pérez por evasiones masivas en el Metro: "Es una protesta más bien tonta y poco justificada"." October 16. https://www.24horas.cl/programas/entrevistas/clemente-perez-por-evasiones-masivas-en-el-metro-es-una-protesta-mas-bien-tonta-y-poco-justificada-3663318/

[10] By this point, *Carabineros* had deployed 90% of its personnel to guard various Metro stations. See: *El Mostrador*. 2019. "Múltiples puntos de evasión masiva en el Metro marcan la quinta jornada de protesta." October 18. https://www.elmostrador.cl/noticias/multimedia/2019/10/18/multiples-puntos-de-evasion-en-el-metro-marcan-la-quinta-jornada-de-protesta/

A bus set ablaze in central Santiago marked a turning point and prompted the government to respond, announcing a press conference at 7 p.m. From *La Moneda*, Interior Minister Andrés Chadwick invoked the *Ley de Seguridad del Estado* (lit. "State Security Law"), expanding procedures to address crimes deemed threats to internal security.[11] Meanwhile, Transportation Minister Gloria Hutt confirmed that the Metro system would remain closed indefinitely and that the 30-peso fare increase would stand.

A photograph of President Piñera dining at a pizzeria that evening sparked criticism from the political opposition,[12] who accused the government of failing to address the escalating crisis. From that point onward, violence only intensified. Barricades emerged along major avenues in Santiago, disrupting movement throughout the city. The corporate offices of energy giant *Enel* would be set on fire, and Metro stations were increasingly targeted, with a total of seven stations set ablaze before midnight.[13]

In an extraordinary national broadcast just after midnight on October 19 (1:13 a.m.), Piñera declared *Estado de Emergencia* (lit. "State of Emergency") in Santiago, calling on the military to intervene. This decision, like others taken throughout the unrest, was seen as incendiary by part of the organizing opposition, which by this point was looking to gain a foothold in the protests.

By the morning of October 19, the unrest had spread to cities across Chile, with violence from the previous night advancing both north and south of Santiago. Cities that had previously remained unaffected

[11] By this point in time, videos depicting the situation were flooding social media. The government called to "unite against the violence." See: *CNN Chile*. 2019. Gobierno invoca Ley de Seguridad del Estado y hace llamado a los chilenos a "unirnos contra la violencia." October 18. https://www.cnnchile.com/pais/gobierno-invoca-ley-seguridad-estado-evasion-metro_20191018/

[12] The image would circle the world. See: *Corriere della Sera*. 2019. "Il Cile brucia e lui mangia la pizza»: bufera contro il presidente Piñera." October 19. https://www.corriere.it/esteri/19_ottobre_20/cile-brucia-lui-mangia-pizza-bufera-contro-presidente-pinera-27111afe-f32a-11e9-ad64-4488d500d2a2.shtml/

[13] By the end of the protests, 25 Metro stations had been destroyed. See: *Deutsche Welle*. 2020. "Todas las estaciones del metro de Santiago operativas a casi un año del estallido social." September 25. https://www.dw.com/es/todas-las-estaciones-del-metro-de-santiago-operativas-a-casi-un-a%C3%B1o-del-estallido-social/a-55054542/

were now drawn into the escalating crisis. In response, the government imposed curfews under the already-declared *Ley de Seguridad del Estado* and *Estado de Emergencia*, signaling a shift toward more forceful control measures. That evening, President Piñera addressed the nation again, announcing plans to reverse the Metro fare hike but controversially declaring that "the country [was] at war with a powerful enemy."[14]

This statement, coupled with his earlier declaration of a state of emergency, became a critical flashpoint. For many Chileans, the invocation of curfews and Piñera's rhetoric evoked memories of military rule during the 1973–1990 dictatorship. Curfews, unused since 1987, carried heavy historical connotations that resonated deeply among those still scarred by the authoritarian past. These measures, intended to restore order, instead exacerbated tensions. Until this point, protests had been fragmented and largely unorganized, reflecting diffuse grievances rather than unified demands. However, the government's heavy-handed response began to unite disparate groups. What was incoherent now became a bridge between citizens on the streets and the political opposition in rejecting the government's actions.

This growing like-mindedness set the stage for the events that followed. The government's efforts to assert control were met with defiance. Military machinery had replaced the police, and politicians had taken the place of the first protesters on the ground. As tanks rolled down *Avenida Providencia* toward *Plaza Baquedano*, political figures, including Lower Chamber lawmaker Gabriel Boric, were preparing to meet them. The whole ordeal added a new layer to the protests, transforming a spontaneous expression of discontent into a moment of significant political consequence.

From this point onward, *Plaza Baquedano* would become the focal point of the unrest, increasingly symbolizing resistance and defiance and reflecting the convergence of citizen frustration and political critique. This marked an important transition in the movement, as protests gained both broader visibility and ideological cohesion.

[14] *Presidencia de la República*. 2019. Presidente Piñera: "Estoy seguro de que, con la unidad de todos los chilenos, vamos a derrotar a los violentistas y vamos a recuperar el país en paz y el país con libertad que todos queremos." October 20. https://prensa.presidencia.cl/comunicado.aspx?id=103689/

Violence would intensify and expand, as protesters began targeting both public infrastructure and private property. Looting would become widespread, with chain supermarkets across the country targeted and transformed into battlegrounds between military forces and citizen looters. Media would capture scenes of chaos and destruction, showing cars and buses being set ablaze nationwide. Disorganized groups of protesters roamed the streets, contributing to an atmosphere of uncertainty and fear.

The unrest turned deadly on October 20. In Santiago's Renca district, a warehouse fire killed five people, including three children, after the building was looted. On the same day, in the northern region of Coquimbo, two protesters were killed and one was gravely injured by the military. These incidents underscored the escalating severity of the crisis.

9.4 The Dual Faces of Protest

In the weeks and months that followed, the unrest would persist, though with a stark contrast between day and night. During the day, the protests were a vivid display of inclusivity and collective organization. Participants from all generations and ages filled the streets, creating a diverse cross-section of Chilean society. Families marched alongside students, workers, and pensioners, transforming public spaces into arenas of civic expression. These daytime demonstrations reflected an organized and deliberate effort to articulate a wide range of grievances, with banners and placards addressing systemic issues such as the rising costs of living and dissatisfaction with services like healthcare, education, and pensions.

Daytime protests would often carry a hopeful and symbolic tone. Protesters waved Chilean and Mapuche flags, each representing distinct but interconnected struggles. The Chilean flag would frequently bear messages like "*Dignidad*" ("Dignity") or "*No estamos en guerra*" ("We Are Not at War"), rejecting President Piñera's earlier rhetoric. Meanwhile, the Mapuche flag, a symbol of Indigenous resistance, underscored the long-standing marginalization of Indigenous communities. Chants, music, and speeches accompanied the marches, fostering a sense of unity and purpose. Some slogans like "*No son treinta pesos, son treinta años*"

("It's not 30 pesos, it's 30 years") encapsulated dissatisfaction with neoliberal policies.

As night fell, however, the inclusivity and organization of the daytime protests gave way to a far narrower and more chaotic dynamic. Unlike the daytime demonstrations, which drew people from all walks of life, the nighttime unrest was predominantly led by younger segments. Disorganized groups took to the streets, clashing with security forces and engaging in destructive acts that would contrast sharply with the peaceful displays held earlier in the day. Fires lit up the urban skylines as barricades would block streets, and Metro stations, buses, and other public infrastructure became targets of arson and vandalism.

While the daytime protests were characterized by visible solidarity, the nighttime violence often deepened divisions. Looting became even more widespread, targeting supermarkets (like *Jumbo* or *Líder*) and retail chains (like *Falabella* or *Ripley*) that symbolized corporate power.

The human cost of the nighttime violence was stark. The deaths mentioned earlier highlighted the darker side of the unrest, as the violence escalated beyond the government's ability to maintain order. The security forces, already stretched thin, struggled to distinguish between peaceful demonstrators and those engaging in destruction, leading to heavy-handed responses that further inflamed tensions.

While the daytime protests would offer a sense of hope and collective purpose, the nighttime violence inflicted significant losses—both in human life and in the movement's public image. Media coverage focused heavily on scenes of chaos, with images of burning buses, looted supermarkets, and clashes with the military dominating headlines. Comparisons to the 1992 Los Angeles riots reflected the scale and intensity of the unrest, portraying the nighttime actions as destructive and directionless.

9.5 Government Crisis Sets In

The government faced significant challenges in responding to the rapidly escalating crisis. The dual nature of the protests—peaceful and organized during the day, but chaotic and violent at night—created a situation that complicated the development of a coherent and consistent response. Each attempted response seemed either excessive or insufficient, deepening public frustration and eroding the government's legitimacy.

One of the key difficulties was the absence of explicit demands during the first days of the unrest. What began as protests over a modest Metro fare hike quickly transformed into an expression of discontent without an articulated agenda. This lack of focus left the government with little to address. Neither a single policy could be resolved nor specific reforms could be proposed, which made de-escalating the situation through negotiation or concession nearly impossible.

At the same time, confusion on the streets led to difficulty in distinguishing between peaceful protesters and those engaged in nighttime violence. The deployment of the military, which was intended to contain the destruction, was met with widespread criticism when soldiers were witnessed patrolling streets during peaceful daytime demonstrations. As previously mentioned, for many Chileans, certainly not all, the sight of armed personnel evoked memories of the dictatorship, thus undermining any endeavor to portray the government as a stabilizing force. This further alienated the mobilized public and fueled perceptions of an administration that overlooked the people's frustration.

Curfews and states of emergency added to the increasing sense of discontent (readers should note that at this point, COVID-19-related "lock-ups" were still to come). While such measures were arguably necessary to address nighttime violence, they were widely perceived as heavy-handed when applied to peaceful gatherings. The inability of the government to tailor responses to the dual dynamics of the protests—repression at night and dialogue during the day—contributed to the perception of a government that was struggling to comprehend the crisis it faced.

Together, these events severely impacted Piñera's approval ratings (see Fig. 9.1). While stable before the crisis, his popularity plummeted to less than 20% in the aftermath, and rejection rates increased to unprecedented levels. The shift in sentiment marked a critical turning point for an administration that would never really recover.

9.6 Push for Constitutional Change

In the power vacuum, the opposition intervened to give meaning to an otherwise incoherent situation. While massive and powerful, the protests initially lacked a unifying demand. They reflected diverse frustrations with inequality, the private sector, and institutional detachment, but the lack of focus made channeling grievances into actionable outcomes difficult. Against this background, the opposition, particularly from the more

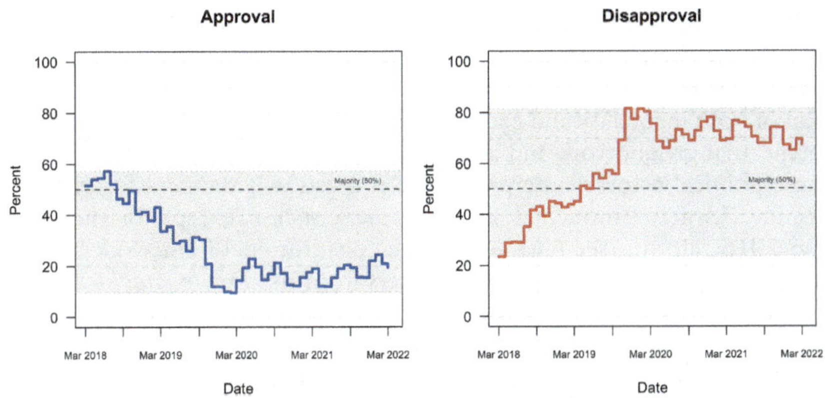

Fig. 9.1 Presidential popularity of Sebastián Piñera (2018–2022) (*Note* The panel on the left displays the monthly average of presidential approval, while the panel on the right shows the monthly average of disapproval. In both panels, the staircase line represents the average for each month based on available survey data. The shaded gray area indicates the full range (minimum to maximum) of monthly averages observed during the term. Horizontal dotted lines mark this range, and the dashed horizontal line at 50% serves as a reference point for majority approval or disapproval. *Source* Author with data from Tresquintos)

extreme left, seized the moment to reshape the narrative and direct the energy on the streets toward a clear political project.[15]

[15] While anti-neoliberalism was a central ideological pillar, it increasingly served as a vehicle for a broader strategy aimed at destabilizing the existing order. Opposition actors used emotionally charged symbols and narratives to erode public trust in institutions and justify radical change. The projection of *Hambre* (lit. "Hunger") onto the *Telefónica* Tower, for instance, was used to pressure the government into approving early pension withdrawals, despite Chile ranking among the highest in Latin America in nutrition and health indicators. The slogan *Nos están matando* (lit. "They are killing us") framed the state as criminally negligent during the pandemic—though Chile would later be recognized as one of the most effective countries in managing COVID-19. The adoption of *Perro Matapacos* (lit. "Cop-Killer Dog") promoted an anti-police narrative that resonated with protestors, even as the country slid into increasing disorder. Similarly, chants like *El que no baila no pasa* (lit. "If you don't dance, you don't pass") blended festive energy with coercion, illustrating how performative rituals during the protests could simultaneously include and exclude, frame some as complicit and others as righteous, thereby deepening divisions and legitimizing confrontation

The opposition's framing of the protests introduced a sharp critique of Chile's neoliberal model and the 1980 Constitution, which had by this point long been viewed by progressive elites as the institutional foundation of both inequality and exclusion (see Chapter 2). Drawing on years of intellectual groundwork and activism (see the second part of Chapter 5), these political actors reinterpreted the protests as a demand for systemic change. Largely untouched since the dictatorship (except for the 2005 and 2015 reforms, see Chapter 4), the constitutional framework became the focal point of their narrative. Leaders from the *Frente Amplio* and the Communist Party emphasized that only a new constitution could address the structural injustice that drove people to the streets.

This reframing proved highly effective. By aligning the movement with a call for constitutional change, the opposition provided a focal point for mobilization that was previously diffuse. An increasing critique among intellectual and activist circles, anti-neoliberalism became a rallying cry. Messages that highlighted the failure of privatized utilities, pensions, and education systems gained traction, and protests coalesced with the rejection of the existing political and economic order.

Symbolically, the opposition positioned itself as an interpreter of the people's grievances, thus translating public outrage into concrete political demands. Changes were most evident in events such as *La Marcha Más Grande* on October 25, when more than one million Chileans took to the streets. Again, although the protesters did not initially call for a new constitution, the ability of the opposition to shape the discourse ensured that constitutional change would become the only possible answer for the question at hand.

If nothing else, this strategy enabled the new left to consolidate its influence by leveraging the symbolic power of the protests to advance its long-term political agenda.[16] By November 2019, political negotiations

[16] Some time later intellectual leaders of the *Frente Amplio* would acknowledge that the violence was necessary to open the constitutional process. See, for example: *El Dinamo*. 2021. "El polémico argumento de Fernando Atria: justifica violencia como impulsora de "proceso constituyente"." July 9. https://www.eldinamo.cl/politica/2021/07/09/las-polemicas-declaraciones-fernando-atria-justifica-violencia-como-impulsora-de-proceso-constituyente/. Five years after the social outburst, many would still minimize the gravity of the situation and its social consequences. Lower Chamber deputy, and 2025 (losing) primary presidential candidate of the *Frente Amplio*, Gonzalo Winter, would suggest that the violence was marginal. See. *Ex-Ante*. 2024. "Gonzalo Winter y sus cuestionados dichos sobre el daño "marginal" de

culminated in a proposal for a constitutional plebiscite (see Chapter 10), which marked a decisive shift in Chile's political trajectory. Although imposed instead of organic, the process successfully transformed the protests into a movement for systemic change.

9.7 Conclusion

This chapter analyzed the immediate triggers and extensive consequences of the social outburst of October 18, 2019, thus highlighting how the protest became a pivotal moment in Chile's political and social trajectories. Although it began as a response to a modest fare hike in Santiago's Metro system, it quickly transformed into a nationwide movement that expressed a wide range of grievances. Protesters voiced frustrations over issues related to quality of life, such as cost of living, access to education, healthcare, and pensions, along with demands for dignity and equity. While these demands were broad and typically disconnected, they reflected a shared sense of dissatisfaction with the status quo instead of an explicit critique of the political or economic model.

Duality defined these events. Daytime protests demonstrated remarkable inclusivity and organization, which drew citizens from various generations and backgrounds to take to the streets. Families, workers, and students marched together and raised banners that articulated diverse and mainly overlapping frustrations. These peaceful mobilizations promoted the visibility and legitimacy of the movement, highlighting shared struggles without any association with a singular, unifying demand. In contrast, the nighttime unrest exposed raw anger simmering beneath the surface. Arson, looting, and violent clashes with security forces underscored the opportunism of the underworld and added layers of complexity to the interpretation of the movement.

For the Piñera administration, the crisis exposed its inability to navigate these multifaceted dynamics. The government's approach was reactive in an effort to address peaceful mobilization and disperse violence at the same time. Unavoidable decisions, such as deploying the military and invoking curfews, exacerbated public distrust and evoked memories of authoritarianism. Without a clear demand to address, the government appeared detached and incapable of providing meaningful solutions.

las revueltas del 18-O." August 22. https://www.ex-ante.cl/perfil-lo-que-hay-que-saber-de-gonzalo-winter-y-su-batalla-ideologica-reivindicando-el-18-o/

In this context, the opposition decisively moved to reframe the unrest. While the protests were not explicitly against the model or the Constitution, political actors—particularly from the new left—transformed such grievances into a broad critique of Chile's neoliberal framework and the 1980 Constitution. By proposing a constitutional plebiscite as a solution, they afforded an otherwise fragmented movement with coherence. This strategic move positioned the opposition as interpreters of the crisis, aligning themselves with protesters and redirecting the energy on the streets toward reform. This would undoubtedly give them the upper hand in the negotiations that would shape the path out of the crisis.

CHAPTER 10

The Constitutional Design

10.1 Introduction

The social outburst that erupted in October 2019 launched Chile into the global spotlight. International media, human rights organizations, and foreign observers all descended on *Arturo Merino Benítez* International Airport (SCL) in Santiago to document the unrest and uncertainty gripping the country. Simultaneously, Chile's political class faced the daunting task of navigating a path forward, attempting to channel the escalating turmoil into an institutional resolution. This chapter explores the critical period in which the nation's leaders wrestled with competing visions for Chile's future and the negotiations that ultimately shaped its historic constitutional process.

The stakes during those tumultuous days could not have been higher. Fears of President Piñera's potential resignation and a resulting power vacuum divided the political landscape into two camps. On one side stood the institutionalists, comprising the government coalition and the ex-*Concertación* center-left bloc. These actors viewed democratic traditions as paramount and were determined to uphold them even amid chaos. Their commitment to institutional resolution was evident in the joint statement issued on October 20 by Piñera, Senate President Jaime Quintana, Chamber of Deputies President Iván Flores, and Supreme Court

K. Bunker, *Chile's Transformation Amidst Crisis*,
https://doi.org/10.1007/978-3-031-96463-3_10

President Haroldo Brito, urging Chile's political class to take collective responsibility and seek a solution.[1]

Opposing them were the Communist Party and other far-left groups, which withheld support for pragmatic resolution, viewing the crisis as a unique opportunity to disrupt the *status quo* and ascend to power. Their stance was starkly illustrated when the long-standing president of the Communist Party announced that they would be impeaching President Piñera as soon as possible.[2]

Caught between these opposing forces were newer political actors, like the *Frente Amplio*, whose rise to prominence was both recent and fragile (see Chapter 8). As a coalition seeking institutional legitimacy, the *Frente Amplio* positioned itself as a traditional player in Chile's political arena while simultaneously recognizing that transformative change was necessary to transcend entrenched barriers to power. Their generational perspective (as described in Chapter 8) would eventually prove crucial, influencing the course of the constitutional process and the broader balance of power.

This chapter focuses on the interplay of these opposing forces and the eventual resolution of their contradictions. It examines the high-stakes negotiations that set the rules of Chile's constitutional process, leading to the 2020 plebiscite and the 2021 election of Constitutional Convention members. The chapter argues that while the balance of power initially tilted in favor of the anti-institutionalists in alliance with newcomers like the *Frente Amplio*, the full implications of the

[1] Quintana was a long-standing member and former president of the *Partido por la Democracia*. Flores was a career Christian Democrat and would be elected to the Senate for the Los Ríos region in 2021. See: Jara, A., and R. Gallardo. 2019. "Tras reunión con Piñera, presidentes del Senado y Cámara llaman a una "autocrítica de la clase política."" *La Tercera*. October 20. https://www.latercera.com/nacional/noticia/tras-reunion-pinera-presidentes-del-senado-camara-llaman-una-autocritica-la-clase-politica/870204/

[2] Less than a week after the social outburst, the President of the Communist Party, Guillermo Teillier, was blaming the economic model for the unrest and stating that it was a moral duty to impeach President Piñera. See: Cáceres, F. 2019. "Guillermo Teillier, presidente del Partido Comunista: "No tengo que pedir perdón a la gente." *La Tercera*. October 25. https://www.latercera.com/politica/noticia/guillermo-teillier-presidente-del-partido-comunista-no-pedir-perdon-la-gente/877056/. In the months that followed, the Communist Party would go on to support every impeachment effort against Piñera and his government, cementing a pattern of persistent constitutional accusations that shaped the political climate after October 2019 (see Chapter 15).

shift would only became evident as the process drew to a close in the 2022 referendum (see Chapter 12).

10.2 Early Negotiations

Before delving into the core of the negotiations that took place, it is important to step back and recall that this moment had been preceded by a three-year constitutional process, which ended abruptly when President Bachelet left office in 2018. This context is relevant, as it helps to explain why, during the 2019 negotiations, Bachelet's proposal remained fresh in the minds of many at the table seeking a solution. Indeed, the *Bases Ciudadanas para la Nueva Constitución* (lit. "Citizen Bases for a New Constitution"), which had been submitted to Congress as a bill, was already seen by many as a convenient starting point—or even a potential shortcut—when the crisis unfolded.[3]

However, as discussed in Chapter 9, when Sebastián Piñera took office, he promptly dismissed the initiative and declared that his administration did not prioritize constitutional reform.[4] This position remained consistent throughout his first year and a half in office, as there was little legislative interest in advancing the proposal independently. Even after the outbreak of the social outburst in October 2019—and despite escalating protests and violence across Santiago and other cities—Piñera continued to resist constitutional change.

[3] President Bachelet's constitutional initiative was designed as a participatory and symbolic effort to lay the groundwork for replacing the 1980 Constitution. The process included local self-convened meetings (*encuentros autoconvocados*), regional dialogues, and a digital platform for public input, ultimately leading to the *Bases Ciudadanas para una Nueva Constitución*, a synthesis of collective citizen priorities. While Bachelet presented the draft to Congress in March 2018, just before leaving office, the plan stipulated that any new constitution would still require approval through Congress and a national plebiscite before entering into force. See Jara, A., and L. Ayala. 2018. "Nueva Constitución impulsada por Bachelet deberá ser aprobada en plebiscito." *La Tercera*. March 6. https://www.latercera.com/politica/noticia/nueva-constitucion-impulsada-bachelet-debera-aprobada-plebiscito/88880/. [This document, *Bases Ciudadanas para una Nueva Constitución (boletín 11.617-07)*, is available on the author's website].

[4] In an early interviews, Piñera dismissed Bachelet's constitutional reform proposal and criticized the left for behaving as though it were "the only one with legitimacy to govern Chile." See: Montes, R. 2018. "La izquierda piensa que es la única con legitimidad para gobernar Chile." *El País*. March 11. https://elpais.com/internacional/2018/03/11/actualidad/1520730340_914044.html/

When he finally did present a proposal, it was far removed from Bachelet's. On October 22, after four days of intense unrest, President Piñera addressed the nation to acknowledge the crisis and recognize the legitimacy of citizens' demands. However, rather than proposing structural change, he focused on a package of short-term measures aimed at easing public discontent. In his address, he introduced a document titled *Nueva Agenda Social* (lit. "New Social Agenda"), which outlined a series of reforms intended to provide immediate and medium-term relief.[5] These included a 20% increase in pensions, higher taxes on top earners, stabilization of electricity prices, an immediate increase in the minimum wage, and expanded healthcare coverage under state insurance.

While members of the government coalition viewed the plan as a potential solution, the opposition rejected it as superficial. From centrist Christian Democrats to the Communist Party, center-left and left-leaning parties collectively denounced *Nueva Agenda Social* as insufficient for

[5] Beyond increases to pensions and the minimum wage, the *Nueva Agenda Social* included a broad array of social and institutional reforms. In health, it proposed urgent discussion of a law to create a public insurance for catastrophic illnesses, a new subsidy for families' out-of-pocket spending on medications not covered by existing programs (such as *Garantías Explícitas de Salud*, GES, or *Ley Ricarte Soto*), and an expanded agreement between FONASA and private pharmacies to reduce medicine prices—expected to benefit over 12 million people. It introduced a *Ingreso Mínimo Garantizado* of CLP $350,000 for full-time workers, with proportional benefits for workers under 18 or over 65. To address cost-of-living concerns, it established a tariff stabilization mechanism to roll back a recent 9.2% increase in electricity prices. On tax policy, it created a new 40% bracket for monthly incomes above CLP $8 million. The agenda also addressed institutional reforms: it proposed cutting parliamentary salaries and high public-sector wages, reducing the number of legislators, limiting re-election, and boosting the *Fondo Común Municipal* to strengthen equity between rich and poor communes. Additional initiatives included a new *Defensoría de las Víctimas* to support crime victims; the acceleration of bills on child protection (replacing the *Servicio Nacional de Menores*, SENAME), catastrophic health insurance, universal daycare access, and reduced property taxes for vulnerable elderly; and a national reconstruction plan following the recent unrest, budgeted at over USD $350 million. See: *Presidencia de la República*. "Presidente Piñera anuncia Agenda Social con mayores pensiones, aumento del ingreso mínimo, freno al costo de la electricidad, beneficios en salud, nuevos impuestos para altas rentas y defensoría para víctimas de delitos." October 23. https://prensa.presidencia.cl/comunicado.aspx?id=123766. [This document, *Nueva Agenda Social (comunicado 123766)*, is available on the author's website.]

addressing what they considered were the systemic issues underlying the unrest.[6]

The rejection intensified the protests, culminating in large-scale demonstrations such as the *La Marcha Más Grande* (described in Chapter 9). Internal chaos in the government also deepened, as Piñera requested the resignation of his entire cabinet; ultimately, however, only eight ministers would be replaced.[7]

Another turning point occurred on November 7, when the *Asociación de Municipalidades* ("Association of Municipalities") announced plans to hold a national referendum on whether a new Constitution should be

[6] Communist deputy Daniel Nuñez (elected senator for Coquimbo in 2021) called the proposals "cosmetic" and insufficient to end the protests, while Carmen Hertz described them as "crumbs" that failed to challenge the "wage appropriation model." Frente Amplio deputy Gael Yeomans criticized the plan as "the same as usual" and just another path to a "corrected neoliberalism" that fell short of public demands. See: Márquez, Y. 2019. "Los dardos de la oposición a la "Agenda Social" con la que Piñera busca poner fin a la crisis." *Biobio Chile*. October 22. https://www.biobiochile.cl/noticias/nacional/chile/2019/10/22/oposicion-cuestionan-agenda-social-con-que-pinera-intenta-salir-de-la-crisis.shtml/

[7] President Sebastián Piñera's request for the resignation of his entire cabinet on October 26, 2019—just after *La Marcha Más Grande*—was framed as a dramatic response to public outrage, though only eight ministers were ultimately replaced. Departing officials included: Andrés Chadwick (UDI, Interior), Felipe Larraín (RN, Treasury), Gonzalo Blumel (*Evópoli*, Presidency), Cecilia Pérez (RN, Secretary General), Juan Andrés Fontaine (RN, Economy), Nicolás Monckeberg (RN, Labor), Felipe Ward (UDI, National Assets), and Pauline Kantor (*Evópoli*, Sports). Their successors, respectively, were: Gonzalo Blumel (*Evopoli*, moved to Interior), Ignacio Briones (*Evópoli*, Treasury), Felipe Ward (UDI, shifted to Presidency), Karla Rubilar (RN, Secretary General), Lucas Palacios (UDI, Economy), María José Zaldívar (DC-friendly, Labor), Julio Isamit (UDI, National Assets), and Cecilia Pérez (RN, returned as Minister of Sports). The reshuffle marked an attempt to signal renewal, though it largely preserved coalition balance. See: *El Desconcierto*. 2019. "Piñera cede a la presión tras "la marcha más grande de la historia" y pide la renuncia a todos sus ministros." October 27. https://www.eldesconcierto.cl/nacional/2019/10/26/sebastian-pinera-pide-renuncia-a-todos-sus-ministros-y-prepara-cambio-de-gabinete.html/. Remarkably, it was not the first time a Chilean president had asked their entire cabinet to resign. Michelle Bachelet did the same in May 2015 in response to a sustained political and credibility crisis following a series of corruption scandals that had affected both her administration and her family. See: *BBC* Mundo. 2015. "Bachelet pide la renuncia de todos sus ministros." May 7. https://www.bbc.com/mundo/noticias/2015/05/150507_chile_bachelet_renuncia_gabinete_aw/

drafted.[8] Spearheaded by Communist Party mayor Daniel Jadue (Recoleta) and *Renovación Nacional* mayor Germán Codina (Puente Alto), the bipartisan initiative gained support across diverse political sectors. The proposal resonated with protesters and the broad political class, who at this point viewed constitutional overhaul as the only viable solution to address the unrest that engulfed all major cities in the nation.

In response, the government attempted to regain control of the narrative. On November 11, Interior Minister Gonzalo Blumel of *Evopoli* announced the constitutional proposal of the administration, which envisioned the existing Congress drafting amendments to the current Constitution.[9] However, opposition parties swiftly rejected this plan and demanded an independent constitutional process led by a fully elected, sovereign assembly.[10] At this point, the Piñera administration lost its grip on the political agenda. The induced inability of the government to contain violence on the streets or present an institutionally credible path forward left Piñera isolated, with plummeting approval ratings and diminishing political support.

[8] The informal plebiscite was held on December 15, 2019, though some municipalities opened voting as early as December 9 and others, like Osorno, extended it into January. A total of 225 municipalities participated, allowing citizens aged 14 and older to vote via in-person, digital, or mixed methods. More than 2.3 million people voted on the constitutional questions: 92.2% supported drafting a new Constitution, and 73.1% favored a fully elected Constitutional Convention over a mixed one. While non-binding and criticized for weak digital security and voter ID verification, the vote signaled strong public demand for structural reforms and directly anticipated the binding plebiscite of 2020. [This dataset, *Resultados Comunales del Plebiscito Constitucional de 2019*, is available on the author's website.]

[9] See a first hand account of the then Gonzalo Blumel, who at this point was a presidential advisor, but would soon become Minister of Interior: Blumel, G. 2023. *La vuelta larga: Crónica personal de la Crisis de Octubre*. Santiago: Ediciones UC.

[10] The petition was signed by fourteen parties, including the Communist Party, the Socialist Party, Christian Democrats, *Revolución Democrática*, *Partido por la Democracia*, *Ecologista Verde*, *Partido Radical*, *Igualdad*, *País Progresista*, *Federación Regionalista Verde Social*, *Comunes*, *Partido Liberal*, *Convergencia Social*, and the *Partido Humanista*. In their joint declaration they demanded a plebiscite and the creation of a *Constitutional Assembly*. This stood in direct contrast to the government's proposal of a *Constitutional Congress*, which implied reform within the existing institutional framework. See: *Mega*. 2019. "Desde la DC hasta el FA: Oposición pide Plebiscito, Asamblea Constituyente y Nueva Constitución." November 12. https://www.meganoticias.cl/nacional/281859-oposicion-asamblea-constituyente-plebiscito-declaracion-publica.html/

Between October 19 and November 12, Piñera's political status rapidly deteriorated due to his failure to establish coalitions with other political actors or secure consensus on his proposals. This was both induced by and beneficial to his opposition. By mid-November, however, all parties perceived that the resolution to the social outburst was comprehensive constitutional reform. The remaining question was not *if* but *when* and *how* this process would commence.

10.3 La Moneda Meetings

Major negotiations to address the constitutional question began on November 13, 2019. The first point of contention was the composition and selection process of the body assigned to draft the new constitution. The government and right-wing parties favored an assembly primarily composed of sitting legislators, arguing that it would ensure control over the direction of reforms and prevent unpredictable outcomes. Conversely, the opposition—comprising various left-leaning and centrist parties—advocated a fully elected body of ordinary citizens. They emphasized that this approach would confer legitimacy on the process and resultant text.

Proposals emerged to bridge the divide, such as a mixed body with 20% sitting legislators and 80% newly elected members; however, these compromises received limited enthusiasm from both sides.

The second point of contention was related to the procedural rules of the drafting process. The key debate focused on the quorum required to pass articles for the new constitution. Would a simple majority be sufficient, or would higher thresholds, such as two-thirds or three-fifths of the majority, be required? These procedural rules were considered crucial determinants of the final content of the Constitution. The opposition and leftist parties leaned toward lower quorums to facilitate substantive changes. In comparison, the government and its allies advocated higher quorums to safeguard their interests as potential veto players.

These disagreements underscored extensive ideological and strategic divisions within the political landscape. Traditional parties, including those in the opposition, pragmatically approached the negotiations in an effort to mitigate the chaos in the streets and avert institutional collapse. In contrast, other radical actors, such as the Communist Party, adopted a confrontational stance, as they openly supported the protests and called for President Piñera to resign. These diverse approaches reflected earlier historical cleavages, such as those observed during the transition from Pinochet's dictatorship during the mid-1980s, when certain groups worked toward a negotiated democratic transition, whereas others sought to undermine it.[11]

Amid the tension, negotiations moved forward and alternated between the Congress in Valparaíso and *La Moneda* in Santiago. After a few days of intense deliberation, an agreement was reached on November 15, as encapsulated in the *Acuerdo por la Paz Social y la Nueva Constitución* ("Agreement for Social Peace and the New Constitution").[12] The document outlined 12 key points, the most significant of which was the call for a national plebiscite.[13] Citizens would answer two questions: whether they wanted a new constitution, and whether the drafting body should be composed entirely of newly elected members or a combination of sitting legislators and elected members. The other significant point was the decision to require two-thirds of the majority to approve articles in the process, a rule that would apply regardless of whether the assembly was fully elected or mixed.

[11] The Communist Party's confrontational posture during the 2019 crisis echoed a long-standing tradition of positioning itself as an extrainstitutional force. Throughout the democratic period, the party often described itself as part of the *izquierda extra-parlamentaria* (lit. "extra-parliamentary left"), opposing successive constitutional reform efforts—including those under Lagos and Bachelet—and initially refusing to endorse Gabriel Boric in the 2021 primaries, instead fielding their own candidate, Daniel Jadue (see Chapter 11). Yet despite its anti-systemic rhetoric, the Communist Party consistently integrated itself into institutional politics when opportunities for influence arose. It played prominent roles in all constituent processes after 2019 and held key positions within Boric's administration, including the Secretary General's cabinet, as well as the Ministries of Education, Justice, Labor, and Science. This tension between rejectionist discourse and strategic institutional engagement is not new. In the 1980s, during Chile's transition from dictatorship, the Communist Party rejected the negotiated approach taken by the *Concertación* and instead pursued a strategy of *rebelión popular de masas* ("popular mass rebellion"). See: Venegas Valdebenito, H. 2009. "Trayectoria del partido comunista de Chile. De la crisis de la unidad popular a la política de rebelión popular de masas." *Universum* 24(2): 262–293.

[12] This document, *Acuerdo por la Paz y una Nueva Constitución*, is available on the author's website.

[13] *Diario Constitucional*. 2019. "Firman acuerdo por la paz social y nueva Constitución." November 15. https://www.diarioconstitucional.cl/2019/11/15/firman-acuerdo-por-la-paz-social-y-nueva-constitucion/.

The compromise reflects the balance of power in the negotiations.[14] While the decision to move forward with a plebiscite satisfied opposition parties by effectively signaling (or so they thought) the end of the Pinochet-era constitution, the two-thirds quorum reassured parties aligned with the government that they would be able to have veto power (or so they thought) over the drafting process. Both sides considered it a fair tradeoff at the time, although later developments would challenge both their assumptions (see Chapter 12).

In addition, the agreement addressed logistical and procedural considerations. Elections for the constitutional body would follow the rules of lower chamber congressional elections (see Chapter 6), and a special multiparty committee would be tasked with drafting the regulations that would govern these elections. Furthermore, a closing referendum would enable citizens to approve or reject the final constitutional proposal. Ten political parties across the ideological spectrum, along with one independent Lower Chamber legislator, Gabriel Boric, signed the two-page agreement.[15]

What is perhaps most interesting from a political perspective is what was missing from the document. Not all legally registered political parties endorsed the agreement. This was the case of the *Frente Amplio*, which had competed as a six-party coalition in the 2017 legislative election and had remained largely intact until this point. The decision to sign the agreement by three presidents of the coalition—Catalina Pérez (*Revolución Democrática*), Luis Felipe Ramos (*Partido Liberal*), and Javiera Toro

[14] The events that unfolded between October 18 and November 15, 2019, would create a temporal and symbolic cleavage in Chilean political culture—separating chaos from order, uprising from negotiation, and violence from institutional restraint. *The Acuerdo por la Paz y una Nueva Constitución*, signed on November 15, marked not only a turning point in tone and method from the events that had upended Chile since the social outburst on October 18, but also gave rise to a lasting conceptual division: between the so-called *octubristas*, who saw the revolt as a legitimate refounding moment, and the *noviembristas*, who believed in channeling change through institutional consensus. This dichotomy, widely referenced in political commentary, encapsulates a deeper rift over the very nature of democratic transformation. See: Bunker, K. 2021. "Octubre contra Noviembre." *Las Últimas Noticias*, October 20.

[15] See: *Cooperativa*. 2019. "Histórico: Los chilenos definirán, en Plebiscito, si hay nueva Constitución y su mecanismo." November 15. https://cooperativa.cl/noticias/pais/manifestaciones/historico-los-chilenos-definiran-en-plebiscito-si-hay-nueva/2019-11-15/012059.html/

(*Partido Comunes*)—along with one leader of a growing movement, Gabriel Boric (*Convergencia Social*), created a significant internal fracture.

Indeed, as a response, three parties,[16] and several leading figures of *Convergencia Social*[17] who had vocally opposed the agreement, resigned from the political alliance. For them, it was a *historical error*, and those who had signed it had committed a fatal and inexcusable mistake.

Now, while the document did help to curb the chaos on the streets, as mentioned in Chapter 9, it was just the beginning for politicians who had participated in the negotiations in Valparaíso and *La Moneda* and been forced to make concessions to the other side. For those in the Piñera government, it signified the end of an era—as they were almost certain that they had effectively signed the *death certificate* for their own constitution. For those in the opposition, it marked the beginning of a new age in which they would finally be able to replace the authoritarian constitution with their own. For both sides, however, it represented more than anything else a path out of the crisis.

From that moment on, political blocs moved swiftly to shape the regulations surrounding the elections in ways that would both benefit their political standing and secure popular legitimacy. The technical committee established by the agreement, composed of an equal number of government and opposition members, was convened to finalize the agreement's details. By December 7, the committee had drafted a bill outlining the timeline and procedures for the upcoming elections, including the plebiscite. The bill was submitted to both chambers of Congress, where it passed overwhelmingly, with 127 votes in favor and 18 against in the

[16] The three parties that existed were the *Partido Ecologista Verde*, *Partido Humanista*, and *Igualdad*. Green Ecologist Party president Félix González criticized the deal as having been made "behind the people's backs" and highlighted internal tensions over the coalition's hesitance to back the constitutional accusation against Piñera. See: *Biobio Chile*. 2019. "Se agudiza división en Frente Amplio tras acuerdo político: dos partidos dejarían bloque". November 19. https://www.biobiochile.cl/noticias/nacional/chile/2019/11/19/se-agudiza-division-en-frente-amplio-tras-acuerdo-politico-dos-partidos-dejarian-bloque.shtml/

[17] Among them was Mayor Jorge Sharp of Valparaíso, who denounced the deal as excluding "*el Chile que despertó*" (lit. "the Chile that woke up") and accused the party of prioritizing institutional negotiation over grassroots demands. *El Desconcierto*. 2019. "Jorge Sharp renuncia a Convergencia Social tras diferencias internas por acuerdo constituyente." November 19. https://www.eldesconcierto.cl/nacional/2019/11/15/jorge-sharp-renuncia-a-convergencia-social-tras-diferencias-internas-por-acuerdo-constituyente.html/

Chamber of Deputies (out of 155 total), and 38 votes in favor and three against in the Senate.[18]

The roadmap was officially enacted on December 24, setting the stage for the constitutional process. Notably, it included a modified proportional representation system to accomodate the 17 seats that would be allocated directly to Indigenous groups based on their demographic presence.[19] However, the bill notably omitted two key aspects on which both sides had agreed in principle but not in detail: gender quotas and the inclusion of independents. Thus, negotiations continued among politicians and technical committee members to settle on a formula that would satisfy both sides.

A few weeks later, a final agreement was reached.[20] Regarding the gender quota, all registered lists would be required to present an equal number of women and men as candidates, with their names interlaced

[18] The reform was backed by nearly all major parties across the political spectrum. In the Chamber of Deputies, support included members of *Chile Vamos*, the Socialist Party, the PPD, and the Christian Democrats, as well as segments of the *Frente Amplio*. The eighteen votes against came primarily from the Communist Party and left-leaning deputies that were critical of the agreement's institutional framing. The following deputies voted against the proposal: Florcita Alarcón (PH), René Alinco (Independent), Boris Barrera (PC), Karol Cariola (PC), Félix González (PEV), Hugo Gutiérrez (PC), Carmen Hertz (PC), Tomás Hirsch (PH), Pamela Jiles (PH), Amaro Labra (PC), Jaime Mulet (FRVS), Daniel Núñez (PC), Marisela Santibáñez (PC), Alejandra Sepúlveda (FRVS), Guillermo Teillier (PC), Ignacio Urrutia (UDI), Camila Vallejo (PC), and Esteban Velázquez (FRVS). In the Senate, the three dissenting votes were also associated with sectors skeptical of the pact's legitimacy or scope. The following senators voted against the proposal: Alejandro Guillier, Alejandro Navarro, and Kenneth Pugh. See: Caro, I., and F. Cáceres. 2019. "Senado despacha a ley reforma que habilita plebiscito de abril y proceso constituyente." *La Tercera*. December 19. https://www.latercera.com/politica/noticia/senado-despacha-ley-reforma-habilita-plebiscito-abril-proceso-constituyente/946433/

[19] The Electoral Service (*Servel*) confirmed the allocation of 17 reserved seats for Indigenous peoples based on self-identification in the national registry. These included: 7 seats for the Mapuche, 2 for the Aymara, and 1 each for the Rapa Nui, Quechua, Atacameño, Diaguita, Colla, Kawésqar, Yagán, and Chango peoples. See: *CNN*. 2019. "Convención Constitucional: Servel distribuyó los escaños reservados para pueblos originarios." December 26. https://edition.cnn.com/pais/convencion-constitucional-servel-escanos-reservados-pueblos-originarios_20201226/

[20] See: *El Mostrador*. 2020. "Por unanimidad: Senado aprueba en general legislar proyecto de independientes y paridad de género." January 21. https://www.elmostrador.cl/braga/2020/01/21/por-unanimidad-senado-aprueba-en-general-legislar-proyecto-de-paridad-de-genero/

on the ballot by gender.[21] In the case of a mixed convention, this requirement would apply only to the elected half. Additionally, a corrective mechanism was introduced to ensure that if seats were distributed disproportionately between genders, the underrepresented gender would receive compensatory adjustments.

The bill also established guidelines to ensure that independents would be able to participate in the process. The goal was to level the playing field, as (it was argued) the existing electoral system favored party lists. Under the final electoral rule, independents who could collect a pre-specified number of endorsement signatures in their districts could form lists with other qualifying independents and compete directly against party lists. This measure was unprecedented, as proportional representation systems typically seek to strengthen established political institutions rather than empower independent candidates.

10.4 The 2020 Plebiscite

Following the establishment of the procedural and regulatory framework, the next milestone was the national plebiscite, originally scheduled for April 26, 2020. However, the emergence of the COVID-19 pandemic led to the plebiscite being postponed by six months to October 25. As the plebiscite approached, political parties and social organizations campaigned vigorously for their preferred options. Among the major parties, the *Unión Demócrata Independiente* (UDI) fully supported the *Rechazo* ("Reject") option, while *Renovación Nacional* (RN) was internally divided between *Apruebo* ("Approve") and *Rechazo.* Initially, *Evopoli* supported *Apruebo* but later adopted a neutral stance. Meanwhile, all other significant parties—including those in the *Nueva Mayoría* center-left coalition, the Communist Party, and the *Frente Amplio*—advocated for *Apruebo.* A similar pattern emerged regarding the second question, with most parties supporting the Fully Elected Constitutional Convention.

Public opinion polls consistently showed strong support for *Apruebo* and, to a lesser extent, for the Fully Elected Constitutional

[21] See: *Tele 13.* 2020. "Así votaron los senadores la aprobación de paridad de género para el órgano constituyente". March 4. https://www.t13.cl/noticia/plebiscito-2020/politica/asi-votaron-senadores-aprobacion-paridad-genero-organo-constituyente/

Convention.[22] However, as election laws prohibited the publication of polls in the 15 days leading up to the vote, some uncertainty prevailed. On election day, these predictions were validated—*Apruebo* and the Fully Elected Convention won decisively, each securing nearly 80% of the vote. The results (shown in Table 10.1) seemed to signal the end of the Pinochet-era constitution and the beginning of a new chapter in Chile's democratic history.

Perhaps the most striking result of the plebiscite was the overwhelming support for the *Apruebo* option. The high level of consensus naturally drew comparisons to the 1989 referendum, when 91.2 percent of Chileans approved the constitutional reforms proposed by the outgoing Pinochet regime. While the 1989 reforms were significant in their own right, they still built upon an existing framework. The 2020 plebiscite, however, pointed to a completely new one. For many, this is what made the event the most politically significant in forty years.

Table 10.1 Results of the 2020 Plebiscite

First question: Do you want a new Constitution?			*Second question: What kind of body should write the new constitution?*		
	Number of votes	*Percent of votes*		*Number of votes*	*Percent of votes*
Approve (*Apruebo*)	5,899,683	78.31	Fully elected (*Convención Constitucional*)	5,673,793	79.18
Reject (*Rechazo*)	1,634,506	21.69	Half elected (*Convención Mixta*)	1,492,260	20.82
Valid votes	**7,534,189**	**99.48**	**Valid votes**	**7,166,053**	**94.62**
Null votes	**27,381**	**0.36**	**Null votes**	**283,794**	**3.75**
Blank votes	**12,344**	**0.16**	**Blank votes**	**123,277**	**1.62**
Total	**7,573,914**	**100**	**Total votes**	**7,573,124**	**100**

Note Voting was voluntary. Registered voters: 14,855,719. Estimated turnout: 50.98%. *Source* Author with data from Servel

22 See a comparison of all pollsters that fielded vote intention polls, in: Bunker, K. 2022. "Forecasting Two-Horse Races in New Democracies." *Revista Latinoamericana de Opinión Publica* 11(1): 81–108.

10.5 The 2021 Constitutional Convention Elections

Intense coalition negotiations followed the period subsequent to the October 2020 plebiscite, as political parties strategized to secure as many as possible of the 138 open seats that would be available in the Constitutional Convention (recall that 17 of the 155 seats would be reserved for Indigenous groups). The primary focus of all parties was the two-thirds rule, which was the quorum set to approve articles.

For the right, which was represented by *Chile Vamos* (renamed *Vamos por Chile*), the goal was to secure at least 52 seats. This threshold would provide veto power, thus enabling them to block legislation in the worst of cases and influence the overall direction of the constitutional process in the best of them. Meanwhile, the objective of the opposition, which included various left-wing and center-left coalitions, was the opposite—to surpass the 103-seat mark to enable them to legislate without relying on the right. To better understand how these goals played out, it is essential to examine the evolving party system that shaped the electoral competition.

In the 2017 election, the political landscape had been divided among four major coalitions, namely, *Chile Vamos* (right-wing), *Nueva Mayoría* (center-left), *Convergencia Democrática* (led by the Christian Democrats), and the nascent left-wing *Frente Amplio*. While the four-coalition setup remained in place, transfers of parties between them marked the 2021 process. Not only had the social outburst and its ripples transformed the context, but the effects of the electoral system were also incentivizing new alignments.

One of the most significant changes was the departure of the Communist Party from the center-left Nueva Mayoría coalition. The social outburst gave the party new incentives to break away from its former allies, whom it now viewed as part of the problem rather than the solution. In a bold yet natural move, they aligned with the *Frente Amplio* to form *Apruebo Dignidad*. This new left-wing coalition comprised six parties, including the PC, *Revolución Democrática*, *Federeación Regionalista Verde Social*, *Partido Igualdad*, *Comunes*, and *Convergencia Social*. Prominent figures, such as Mayor Jadue and legislators Giorgio Jackson (*Revolución Democrática*) and Gabriel Boric (*Convergencia Social*), led the coalition.

In contrast, the Christian Democrats rejoined the center-left ex *Concertación* coalition, now rebranded as *La Lista del Apruebo.* Two factors explain this decision. First, electoral support for the Christian Democrats was declining, as evidenced by their poor performance in 2017, in which they achieved the lowest records of vote and seat share in their history. And second, the departure of the Communist Party rendered the coalition more favorable, as they had previously expressed discomfort with the leftward shift by *Nueva Mayoría*. The reconstituted *La Lista del Apruebo* included seven parties, including Christian Democrats, the Socialist Party, *Partido por la Democracia*, *Partido Radical*, *Partido Liberal*, *Partido Progresista*, and *Ciudadanos.*

In any case, the big novelty was the emergence of independent lists—an unprecedented development in both Chile and elsewhere. Of the more than 60 lists that registered to compete, more than 50 of them were comprised solely of independents. These lists represented a broad spectrum of interests, from anti-establishment movements to localized grassroots organizations. Among them, three stood out due to their national presence, namely, *Independientes No Neutrales*, *La Lista del Pueblo*, and *Asamblea Popular.* While the former aligned with the center-left, the two other lists embraced anti-system and anti-elite rhetoric. However, because of their novelty, the poor track record of independents in previous elections (see Chapter 6), and the inability to track voter preferences at the district level, they were dismissed as a relevant force before the election.

The majority of analysts expected three major coalitions to dominate the election, namely, *Vamos por Chile*, *Apruebo Dignidad*, and *La Lista del Apruebo*. Public opinion polls supported this expectation, as major coalitions garnered the bulk of campaign finance and dominated television advertisements prior to the election. The primary questions was whether progressive forces combined (*Apruebo Dignidad* and *La Lista del Apruebo*) would be able to surpass the two-thirds threshold, enabling them to direct the process, or whether *Vamos por Chile* would be able to secure the 52 seats required to exert veto power.

However, as votes were tallied on May 16, the most unexpected of all scenarios emerged. Not only had *Vamos por Chile* fallen short of the 52-seat mark, but institutional leftist parties had also significantly underpreforemed. In their place, independents had achieved remarkable success, garnering seats across almost all districts. By the end of the night, it was clear that a major political earthquake had hit the country.

Vamos por Chile secured only 37 seats, which was obviously less than the target. Similarly, *Apruebo Dignidad* and *La Lista del Apruebo* won only 28 and 25 seats, respectively. In contrast, *La Lista del Pueblo*, a previously non-existent coalition, captured 26 seats and ranked third overall. Independents collectively won 65 out of 155 seats (41.94%), which emphasized a historic departure from Chile's electoral pattern. For comparison, only 9 independents had been able to get elected to the Lower Chamber in all elections between 1989 and 2017.[23] Tables 10.2 and 10.3 summarize the results for regular and reserved seats, respectively.

The 2021 Constitutional Convention election defied expectations, highlighting the strength of anti-establishment sentiment and the desire for systemic change. The success of *La Lista del Pueblo*, along with the large number of elected independents, underscored a rejection of traditional political parties. By capturing 82 seats (52% of the 155 seats in the Convention), independents and Indigenous groups became a formidable force over night, reshaping not only the party system, but also all expectations of what would come.[24]

[23] The list of Lower Chamber deputies that were able to win elections as independents are the following: in 1989, Hosain Sabag (District 42); in 1997, Samuel Venegas (District 15), and Rosa González (District 1); in 2001, Iván Paredes (District 1); in 2009, Pedro Velásquez (District 8), and Miodrag Marinovic (District 60); and in 2013: Giorgio Jackson (District 22), Alejandra Sepúlveda (District 34), and Gabriel Boric (District 60). Remarkably, the numbers have remained low under the new electoral system. In the first two elections in place, only two independents were elected: in 2017, René Saffirio (District 23); in 2021: Carlos Bianchi (District 28). Independents have fared equally poorly in Senatorial elections. Only four non-party endorsed candidates were able to win a seat between 1989 and 2021: Notably, Carlos Bianchi won twice (2005 and 2013) before "passing" his district (Magallanes) to his son Karim Bianchi, who also won as an independent (in 2021). The only other independent to win a senate seat in this time frame was Fabiola Campillai (also in 2021). For a historical account of independents in post transition legislative elections, see: Bunker, K. 2017. *Nota Electoral: Independientes* (Notas Electorales: Programa Electoral). Santiago: UCEN. The list of winning third-party candidates is available in the footnote references of Chapter 7.

[24] Daniel Stingo, an independent leftist and the most-voted member of the Constitutional Convention, captured the post-election mood on the left when he stated bluntly on national television: "We are going to set the major themes. We're going to write the rules of the game. The right didn't win here." The remark, made on TVN (*Televisión Nacional de Chile*) and widely shared, was seen by critics as confirmation that the left intended to dominate the constitutional process without compromise. See: *El Mostrador.* 2019. "Daniel Stingo, el constituyente más votado: 'Nosotros vamos a poner los grandes temas, vamos a escribir las reglas del juego. Aquí no ganó la derecha.'" May

Table 10.2 Results of the 2021 Constitutional Convention, regular member election

Coalition/List	*Number of votes*	*Percent of votes*	*Number of seats*	*Percent of seats*
Vamos por Chile	1,175,166	20.57	37	23.87
Apruebo Dignidad	1,071,654	18.76	28	18.06
Lista del Pueblo	926,602	16.22	26	16.77
Lista del Apruebo	825,688	14.45	25	16.13
Independientes No Neutrales	504,145	8.82	11	7.10
Other independents	854,923	14.96	28	18.06
Other parties	355,680	6.22	0	0
Valid votes	**5,713,858**	**92.30**		
Null votes	**187,819**	**3.03**		
Blank votes	**288,771**	**4.66**		
Total	**6,190,448**	**100**	**138**	**100**

Note Voting was voluntary. Registered voters: 14,900,089. Estimated turnout: 43.41%. Also note that both *Lista del Pueblo* and *Independientes No Neutrales* competed nationally, yet using different list names in different districts. Their total votes and seats are the estimated sum of their district-level results. The category "Other independents" includes all independent lists other than *Lista del Pueblo* and *Independientes No Neturales*, plus full independents (known as *Independientes Fuera de Pacto* in Chile). The category "Other parties" includes: *Partido Ecologista Verde*, *Partido de Trabajadores Revolucionarios*, *Unión Patriótica*, *Partido Conservador Cristiano*, *Partido Nacional Cristiano*, and *Partido Humanista*. The percentage of votes is computed from the total number of votes cast in the regular member election. The percentage of seats is computed from the total number of seats available (155). *Source* Author with data from Servel.

10.6 The Aftermath

The election of the Constitutional Convention in May 2021 introduced profound changes to the political landscape in Chile; however, several critical observations must be considered. Foremost among them was the immediate and direct effect of the results on the political balance of power. With *Vamos por Chile* failing to secure one-third of the seats, the right-wing coalition effectively lost its veto power. This scenario left them unable to block or significantly influence the drafting process of the new constitution. For the first time since the return to democracy, the right found itself entirely sidelined in a key institutional process. Whether as

21. https://www.elmostrador.cl/dia/2021/05/24/daniel-stingo-el-constituyente-mas-votado-nosotros-vamos-a-poner-los-grandes-temas-aqui-no-gano-la-derecha/

Table 10.3 Results of the 2021 Constitutional Convention, reserved seats election

Indigenous group	*Number of votes*	*Percent of votes*	*Number of seats*	*Percent of seats*
Mapuche	218,444	83.06	7	4.52
Aimara	19,255	7.32	2	1.29
Diaguita	11,231	4.27	1	0.65
Atacameño (or Lican Antay)	6,780	2.58	1	0.65
Colla	2,136	0.81	1	0.65
Quechua	2,072	0.79	1	0.65
Rapa Nui	1,870	0.71	1	0.65
Chango	900	0.34	1	0.65
Kaweshkar	248	0.09	1	0.65
Yagan (or Yámana)	55	0.02	1	0.65
Valid votes	**262,991**	**93.06**		
Null votes	**5,134**	**1.82**		
Blank votes	**14,484**	**5.13**		
Total	**282,609**	**100**	**17**	**100**

Note Voting was voluntary. Registered voters: 1,231,276. Estimated turnout: 21.36%. The percentage of votes is computed from the total number of votes cast in the reserved seats election. The percentage of seats is computed from the total number of seats available (155). *Source* Author with data from Servel.

a veto player (1990–2010, 2014–2018) or as a formateur (2010–2014, 2018–2022), the right had played a crucial role in shaping the political agenda. The loss of this role indicated a dramatic shift in their influence. Despite the magnitude of the defeat, the coalition failed to issue a joint statement acknowledging the setback, which signaled its unwillingness to recalibrate its strategy in the immediate aftermath.

A second significant observation pertains to the effective number of political parties. The fragmentation of representation sharply increased compared with that of prior elections, which signaled a departure from traditional patterns of political competition. While the deviation can be largely attributed to the unique electoral rules that governed the Constitutional Convention election, it also reflected a trend toward pluralism in the Chilean electorate. The election demonstrated that Chilean voters were willing to embrace diversity in representation when presented with a wider array of choices. This phenomenon challenged the narrative of in-depth polarization that characterized the binomial system years

(1989–2013) and persisted to a certain extent even after the adoption of proportional representation in 2017. However, as discussed in Chapter 11, the fragmentation observed in the Constitutional Convention election was only partially transmitted to the legislative election in November 2021, which implies that its impact was context-dependent despite its significance. Nevertheless, the results served as a clear warning sign of a shifting political landscape.

In summary, the aftermath of the May 2021 Constitutional Convention election revealed a political system in flux. The sidelining experienced by the right wing highlighted a dramatic redistribution of power, while the increased fragmentation signaled the electorate's desire for increased representation and diversity. Furthermore, the election marked a pivotal moment in Chile's ongoing political evolution, which laid the groundwork for a redefined party system and ushered in subsequent electoral contests. As the country moved toward the drafting of its new constitution, these developments underscored the profound and long-term impacts the social outburst would have on everyday politics moving forward.

10.7 Conclusion

This chapter argued that two pivotal, unexpected happenings defined the period that followed the social outburst, namely, the overwhelming public consensus in favor of the drafting of a new constitution and the dramatic electoral shift that followed the selection of members of the Constitutional Convention. It explored how a combination of institutional negotiations, societal demands, and unexpected electoral outcomes fundamentally overturned Chile's political landscape, which had long been dominated by an entrenched two-party system.

Sharp divisions within the political class marked the initial phase. Encompassing the government coalition and the traditional center-left, institutionalists prioritized a democratic solution to stabilize the country amid escalating protests. However, radical factions, such as the Communist Party and anti-establishment groups, who rejected incremental reforms seeking to disrupt the status quo, opposed them. An eventual compromise, the *Acuerdo Por la Paz Social y la Nueva Constitución*, created a path forward by establishing rules for constitutional reform while securing a certain extent of institutional stability. This agreement balanced competing interests, such as the inclusion of a fully elected

Constitutional Convention favored by the opposition and the two-thirds majority rule that (apparently) provided the government factions with a form of veto power.

The first major outcome of these negotiations was the plebiscite held in October 2020, in which nearly 80% of voters supported the drafting of a new constitution through a fully elected body. The scale of the support was remarkable and was read at the time as widespread public dissatisfaction with the existing political and economic systems. In contrast to previous critical moments in Chilean history, a broad consensus for change defined a way forward.

The second unexpected scenario emerged during the May 2021 election of members of the Constitutional Convention. While traditional coalitions, such as *Vamos por Chile*, *Apruebo Dignidad*, and *La Lista del Apruebo*, were expected to dominate the process, the results brought a surprise. Independents, including anti-establishment groups (e.g., *La Lista del Pueblo*), won an unprecedented share of seats. Combined with Indigenous representatives, these groups accounted for more than half of the 155 members of the Convention. This dramatic fragmentation reflected not only the influence of the ad-hoc electoral system but also the electorate's disillusionment with established political parties and their desire for new voices in the constitutional process. The right-wing coalition, *Vamos por Chile*, fared particularly poorly as it secured only 37 seats, which was less than the threshold required to exert veto power. This result left them sidelined for the first time since the transition to democracy.

Part 3: Replacement

CHAPTER 11

The Rise of Gabriel Boric

11.1 Introduction

In the aftermath of the October 2020 plebiscite and the May 2021 election of members of the Constitutional Convention, Chileans entered a period of anticipation for the inaugural session of the newly elected assembly on July 4, 2021. Chapter 12 presents this event in detail. However, prior to looking at the inner workings and themes of the Constitutional Convention, addressing another pivotal moment that followed in the constitutional process is crucial: the 2021 presidential election, which was held on November 21. The two events, namely, the election of Convention members and the presidential race, are deeply intertwined, as it is clear that the triumph of the *Apruebo* in the plebiscite, the rise of the left and independents in the Convention election, and the eventual presidential outcome all stemmed from the same political and social phenomenon.

Similar to the majority of presidential contests in Chile, the 2021 election was shaped by a central political cleavage—a divide that organizes voter choices and political competition. While these cleavages typically reflect structural realities, they also emerge from pressing contemporary issues.[1] In 2021, the defining divide was the social outburst that had

[1] Cleavages are generally understood as major social fault lines that divide significant portions of the population and generate demand for the emergence of new political parties.

K. Bunker, *Chile's Transformation Amidst Crisis*,
https://doi.org/10.1007/978-3-031-96463-3_11

recently shaken the country to its foundations. The election was not merely a contest between ideologies or party platforms, but a confrontation between the positions candidates had taken—and were perceived to have taken—regarding the causes and consequences of the upheaval. In this way, the 2021 presidential election represented a departure from earlier contests, which typically revolved around change versus continuity within an established political framework. It marked a broader reckoning that included everything from the legacy of the 1980 Constitution to the violence associated with the outburst.

This chapter examines the inseparable nature of the constitutional process and the 2021 presidential election and considers the historical implications of its outcome. It also provides insight into Gabriel Boric, a relatively unknown congressman who would ascend to the presidency as

As Seymour M. Lipset and Stein Rokkan argue in *Cleavage Structures, Party Systems, and Voting Alignments* (New York, NY: Free Press, 1967), once such parties achieve electoral success, they tend to "freeze" into the party system—until shifting societal dynamics prompt realignment. While this dynamic, interactive relationship is further explored in Chapter 6, it is important to highlight that the study of cleavages in Chile is particularly noteworthy. One of the most prominent debates centers on the post-dictatorship Sí/No cleavage that emerged from the 1988 plebiscite and continued to influence political behavior into the 1990s (see: Tironi, E. and F. Agüero. 1999. "¿Sobrevivirá el nuevo paisaje político chileno?" *Estudios Públicos* 74; Valenzuela, J. S. 1999. "Respuesta a Eugenio Tironi y Felipe Agüero: Reflexiones sobre el presente y futuro del paisaje político chileno a la luz de su pasado," *Estudios Públicos* 75; Engel, E. and A. Hernando. 2003. "Chile: ¿dos o más bloques?" *Perspectivas en Política, Economía y Gestión* 6: 219–230). A broader body of literature has examined the persistence and transformation of cleavages in the Chilean party system, exploring long-term sociopolitical alignments, electoral behavior, and institutional shifts (see Tironi, E., F. Agüero, and J. S. Valenzuela. 2001. "Clivajes políticos en Chile: Perfil sociológico de los electores de Lagos y Lavín." *Revista Perspectivas* 5(1): 73–87; Ortega Frei, E. 2003. "Los partidos políticos chilenos: Cambio y estabilidad en el comportamiento electoral 1990–2000," *Revista de Ciencia Política* 23(2): 109–147; Montes, J. E., S. Mainwaring, and E. Ortega. 2000. "Rethinking the Chilean Party Systems." *Journal of Latin American Studies* 32(3): 795–824; Aubry, M., and A. Dockendorff. 2014. "Cuarenta años no son nada: ¿La reposición del clivaje autoritarismo-democracia en el sistema de partidos chileno?" *Revista de Sociología* 29: 9–36; Bonilla, C. A., R. E. Carlin, G. J. Love, and E. Silva Méndez. 2011. "Social or Political Cleavages? A Spatial Analysis of the Party System in Post-Authoritarian Chile." *Public Choice* 146(1): 9–21; Álvarez, R. M., and G. Katz. 2009. "Structural Cleavages, Electoral Competition and Partisan Divide: A Bayesian Multinomial Probit Analysis of Chile's 2005 Election." *Electoral Studies* 28(2): 177–189). Although not all elections produce systemic change, many are shaped by contingent or issue-specific cleavages that help explain why certain presidential candidates align more closely with the political and social mood of a particular moment (see a historical application of this in Eugenio Tironi's *Radiografía de una derrota*; Santiago: Uqbar Editores, 2010).

the youngest leader in the world at the time of his inauguration. Boric's election marked not only a rupture in the political landscape after the Pinochet administration but also a reflection of the transformation of the era. As a figure of the left and a leader of a newly established political party, his rise complemented the elite realignment initiated in 2017.

The 2021 election presented Chileans with a pivotal choice: to embrace the radical change ignited by the social outburst, the *Apruebo*, and the leftist gains in the Constitutional Convention or to return to the path laid out by the *Concertación* and the first of the Piñera administrations. Ultimately, the nation opted for the former. This chapter examines the factors that led to that choice, explores its timing and impact, and sheds light on how it reshaped not only the presidency and the party system but also the evolving constitutional process.

11.2 Four Big Names and Three Independents

Six months after the Constitutional Convention election, Chileans prepared to return to the polls. Having already voted for Constitutional Convention members in May—alongside governors, mayors, and local councilors—and then again in primary elections in July, they faced yet another round of voting in November: for president, senators, deputies, and regional councilors. The year 2021 was truly unprecedented in this sense, with no prior instance in Chilean history of so many elections taking place within a single calendar year. Yet among all these contests, the presidential election still stood out as the most significant in the eyes of the public. Unlike the other votes, the presidential race was viewed as a direct opportunity to bring about change, even though what that change meant varied widely depending on whom was asked. For the right, it was a chance to restore order and halt what they saw as the excesses unleashed by the social outburst. For the left, it was an opportunity to deepen the transformation and secure a decisive break from the old order.

A key feature of the 2021 presidential elections was the return to "normal" electoral rules. Unlike the exceptional mechanisms used in the Constitutional Convention election—which had lowered barriers for independents and facilitated a strong showing by third-party and nontraditional candidates—this round followed the standard rules last used in

2017.[2] In institutional terms, the process reverted to the usual framework, benefiting by default many of the parties that had been disadvantaged by the rules used in the Constitutional Convention process. When the dust settled, the major political sectors, including all those that had gained legislative representation in 2017, were once again back in competition. The remainder of this section examines how these sectors prepared for the elections; readers may wish to consult Figure A3 in the Appendix for a graphical overview of presidential competition that year.

11.2.1 Disarray in the Center-Left

The center-left coalition, *Nuevo Pacto Social* (formerly named the *Concertación* and later *Nueva Mayoría*), faced particularly acute challenges. Its inability to respond effectively to the slogan "*No son treinta pesos, son treinta años*" (lit. "It's not thirty pesos, it's thirty years"; see Chapter 9 for more on the origin and context of this phrase) underscored its struggle. Despite being the main legislative opposition to the Piñera government (2018–2022), the center-left still encountered substantial difficulty in influencing the course of the agenda.

At the time, Chilean law allowed for only one formal primary election per coalition. To navigate this, *Nuevo Pacto Social* allowed its constituent parties to hold informal internal primaries prior to participation in the formal coalition primary. For example, *Partido por la Democracia* held an internal primary among Heraldo Muñoz, Francisco Vidal, and Jorge Tarud, while the Christian Democrats held their primary between Senator Ximena Rincón and Alberto Undurraga. Muñoz decisively won with

[2] While the 2021 presidential election was conducted under the same runoff rules used since 1989 and held concurrently with legislative elections for both chambers of Congress, it marked the second time the reformed proportional electoral system—introduced in 2015—was fully implemented. Voters elected 155 deputies (up from 120 prior to the reform) and 27 of the 50 senators, completing the staggered renewal of the Senate (50 seats total).

54% of votes,[3] and Rincón with 62%.[4] Meanwhile, the Socialist Party and *Partido Radical* nominated Paula Narváez and Carlos Maldonado, respectively.

Despite this slate of candidates, the Constitutional Convention election in May 2021 upended the strategy of the coalition. The dramatic results rendered their approach obsolete, which led to a cascade of withdrawals. Rincón[5] and Muñoz[6] stepped down, and attempts to align Narváez with

[3] Muñoz won the PPD primary with 7,130 votes (54%), ahead of Vidal's 5,781 (43%) and Tarud's 336 (3%). Beyond the numerical margin, his victory underscored the party's endorsement of a candidate with diplomatic experience and centrist credentials amid a fragmented political landscape. See: *Biobio Chile*. 2021. "Heraldo Muñoz se impone en primaria del PPD y será el abanderado presidencial de su partido." January 31. https://www.biobiochile.cl/noticias/nacional/chile/2021/01/31/primer-conteo-de-votos-en-primarias-internas-del-ppd-dan-por-ganador-a-heraldo-munoz.shtml/

[4] Rincón secured the DC nomination with 62% of approximately 27,000 votes, defeating Undurraga in what was widely seen as an unexpected outcome. The result highlighted her political resilience and underscored internal party shifts, as the Christian Democrats sought to reposition themselves. See: *El Mostrador*. 2021. "Primarias DC: contra todo pronóstico Ximena Rincón gana a Undurraga y se impone como candidata presidencial del partido." January 24. https://www.elmostrador.cl/destacado/2021/01/24/la-dc-zanja-su-candidata-presidencial-senadora-ximena-rincon-gana-primarias-a-alberto-undurraga/

[5] Rincón announced her withdrawal from the DC presidential candidacy during a National Council meeting, stating that the political context had changed and emphasizing the need for unity within the center-left to confront upcoming electoral challenges. See: *La Tercera*. 2021. "Rincón también se baja: senadora anunció en Junta Nacional que renuncia a candidatura presidencial de la DC." May 19. https://www.latercera.com/politica/noticia/rincon-tambien-se-baja-senadora-anunciara-en-junta-nacional-que-renuncia-a-candidatura-presidencial-de-la-dc/JFGWIUAKO5FNBNW2YNR5TKO74E/

[6] Muñoz stepped down from his presidential candidacy expressing his support for Narváez and calling for the formation of "the broadest possible primary" to strengthen the center-left's prospects in the upcoming election. See: *La Tercera*. 2021. "Heraldo Muñoz depone candidatura presidencial y anuncia apoyo a Narváez "en la primaria más amplia posible"." May 19. https://www.latercera.com/politica/noticia/heraldo-munoz-depone-candidatura-presidencial-y-anuncia-apoyo-a-narvaez-en-la-primaria-mas-amplia-posible/ITZZC53SAVDMVKP2ZE5WUTKENM/

Apruebo Dignidad[7] were rebuffed.[8] Ultimately, Yasna Provoste, a left-leaning Christian Democratic senator, emerged as a fallback candidate and won an informal coalition primary in August with 60.8% of votes. However, the lowest turnout in decades, a mere 150,000 participants,[9] highlighted the coalition's weakening relevance. Provoste's campaign failed to resonate with the political climate shaped by the social outburst, which left the center-left increasingly out of step with the moment.

11.2.2 The Momentum of the New Left

In stark contrast, *Apruebo Dignidad* was gaining momentum. The coalition had performed strongly in the May 2021 Constitutional Convention elections (considering it had just formed) and enjoyed increased support in public opinion polls. Daniel Jadue, the mayor of Recoleta and a

[7] Nárvaez sought to compete in a primary election with the far left until the last moment. See: *La Tercera*. 2021. "PS descarta competir sólo con Unidad Constituyente y Narváez llama "a inscribir primaria amplia con todos los sectores de la oposición"." May 19. https://www.latercera.com/politica/noticia/ps-descarta-ir-a-primaria-presidencial-con-unidad-constituyente/QGY23YMPLNFW3II7D3BDQTY6NM/

[8] The proposed presidential primary between the Socialist Party, *Frente Amplio*, and Communist Party collapsed just hours before the registration deadline due to internal vetoes. Disagreements arose over the inclusion of the PPD and the Liberal Party, with *Unir*, segments of the PC, and *Convergencia Social* opposing their participation. As a result, the pact was withdrawn, prompting Narváez to issue a public statement blaming the PC and *Frente Amplio* for the failure. See: *El Mostrador*. 2021. "Vetos hacen caer pacto de primarias del FA, PC y PS: Narváez golpea la mesa y dice que "ellos se han farreado esta oportunidad y no dan garantías de gobernabilidad"." May 19. https://www.elmostrador.cl/noticias/multimedia/2021/05/19/vetos-hacen-caer-pacto-de-primarias-del-fa-pc-y-ps-narvaez-golpea-la-mesa-y-dice-que-se-han-farreado-esta-oportunidad-y-no-dan-garantias-de-gobernabilidad/. Something similar would ocurr four years later, in the 2025 primaries, when the President of the Socialist Party, Paulina Vodanovic, and the President of the Christian Democrats, Alberto Undurraga, would be forced to forego their presidential candidacies against their will, in favor of government-aligned frontrunners: Carolina Tohá (of the PPD) and Jeannette Jara (of the Communist Party).

[9] Despite the victory of the Christian Democratic Party (DC), the result reflected the party's long-term decline. By 2021, the DC had lost much of its congressional strength, holding fewer deputies than in previous legislatures, and had secured only a single seat in the 155-member Constitutional Convention. These numbers underscored the party's eroding influence in a political landscape increasingly dominated by new coalitions and outsider figures. See: *La Tercera*. 2021. "Con escasa participación, Provoste (DC) se convierte en la abanderada de Unidad Constituyente." August 21. https://www.latercera.com/la-tercera-domingo/noticia/con-escasa-participacion-provoste-dc-se-convierte-en-la-abanderada-de-unidad-constituyente/I4CHJ6BPIRCLVL7BTM5WN2SYI4/

prominent member of the Communist Party, led voter intention polls for two years and was mainly expected to advance to the presidential runoff. Jadue's visibility and the Communist Party's prominent role in the aftermath of the social outburst made him a formidable contender.

However, the *Frente Amplio* had yet to join with a candidate. Several names were considered (among them, Karina Oliva, Marcelo Díaz, Beatriz Sánchez, and Juan Ignacio Latorre). However, none gained traction until Gabriel Boric, a congressman from *Convergencia Social*, entered the scene. Logistical hurdles initially complicated Boric's candidacy because *Convergencia Social* had not achieved national party registration at the time. A rapid signature-gathering campaign was used to resolve this issue, which succeeded on May 17, 2021, only a few days before the registration deadline. With Boric officially in the race, the *Apruebo Dignidad* primary became a head-to-head contest between him and Jadue. Remarkably and surprisingly, Boric defeated Jadue with 60.4% of the vote, becoming the only candidate of the newly formed leftwing coalition.[10]

11.2.3 Division of the Right

The right faced its own challenges in the 2021 election. Joaquín Lavín, a longtime frontrunner, entered the *Vamos por Chile* primary along with Sebastián Sichel, Ignacio Briones, and Mario Desbordes. While Lavín was initially favored, Sichel emerged as a surprise winner and narrowly defeated Lavín with 49.3% of the vote. This outcome was notable not only because Sichel defied poll predictions, but also because he came from a political background distinct from traditional right-wing party structures, having built his career largely outside the core of Chile's conservative establishment.[11]

[10] A career politician within the Communist Party, Jadue first ran for public office in the early 2000s, losing bids for deputy in 2001 (District 19) and 2005 (District 10), as well as for mayor of Recoleta in 2004 and 2008, before finally being elected in 2012. He gained national attention for pioneering the "Farmacia Popular," a municipal initiative to lower drug prices. After losing the 2021 *Apruebo Dignidad* presidential primary to Gabriel Boric, Jadue became the subject of multiple legal investigations, including allegations of corruption and financial misconduct during his time as mayor.

[11] Sichel began his political career on the center-left, originally as a member of the Christian Democratic Party. He ran unsuccessfully for deputy twice: first in 2009 (District 24) and again in 2013 (District 23), both times backed by the DC. He later resigned

Table 11.1 displays the results of the only two official primary elections held that year. Notably, *Apruebo Dignidad* outperformed *Vamos por Chile* in overall primary turnout, receiving 57% of the total number of votes cast. This was widely interpreted as a sign that the new left was gaining momentum. Within the coalition, Gabriel Boric's unexpected victory over Daniel Jadue marked a turning point. The win gave Boric immediate national visibility and allowed him to quickly expand his support beyond his original base. Combined with *Apruebo Dignidad*'s strong overall performance in the primaries, his candidacy helped establish the coalition as a leading force in the presidential race—causing quiet unease among more conservative sectors.[12]

11.2.4 The Far Right

The candidacy of José Antonio Kast, founder of the far-right Republican Party, added an additional layer of complexity to the election. Kast was a former congressman and UDI member who had previously run as an independent in the 2017 presidential election. He positioned himself as a conservative alternative to *Vamos por Chile*. Similar to Boric, Kast's party was newly formed, and he entered the race with a full slate of legislative candidates, which further highlighted the growing fragmentation within the right (described in Chapter 6). His campaign resonated with a subset of voters who were drawn to his hardline stance on law and order (which was by this point in time becoming a major theme).[13]

from the DC and joined centrist movement Fuerza Pública, which later became the party *Ciudadanos*. After breaking with *Ciudadanos*, Sichel supported Sebastián Piñera's 2017 presidential campaign and later joined his second administration. He served as Executive Vice President of CORFO (2018–2019), Minister of Social Development and Family (2019–2020), and President of *BancoEstado* (2020).

[12] Remarkably, Boric was already being framed as the more moderate or palatable option—even by market standards. Following his victory over Jadue, Chilean stocks surged and the peso strengthened, reflecting relief among investors wary of Jadue's more radical platform. See: Fuentes, V. and M. Malinowski. 2021. "Chile Stocks Surge as Communist Knocked Out of Presidential Race." *Bloomberg*. July 18. https://www.bloomberg.com/news/articles/2021-07-18/chile-stocks-surge-as-communist-knocked-out-of-presidentialrace

[13] Kast's emergence as a serious contender, with a platform rooted in nationalism, conservatism, and tough-on-crime rhetoric, contributed significantly to framing the 2021 election as the most polarized in Chile in decades. Alongside Boric's progressive platform,

Table 11.1 Results of the 2021 presidential primary election

Apruebo Dignidad			Vamos por Chile		
Candidate	*Number of votes*	*Percent of votes*	*Candidate*	*Number of votes*	*Percent of votes*
Gabriel Boric	1,059,060	60.42	Sebastián Sichel	660,250	49.26
Daniel Jadue	693,862	39.58	Joaquín Lavín	416,604	31.08
			Ignacio Briones	131,996	9.85
			Mario Desbordes	131,622	9.82
Valid votes	**1,752,922**	**97.33**		**1,340,472**	**96.54**
Null votes	**41,930**	**1.33**		**41,930**	**1.33**
Blank votes	**6,080**	**0.19**		**6,080**	**0.19**
Total	**1,800,932**	**100**		**1,388,482**	**100**

Note Null and Blank votes are shared in primary elections, as voters can only choose one ballot. Party members are only eligible to vote in their own parties' primaries, while independent voters can choose. Voting was voluntary. Registered voters: 14,693,433. Estimated turnout: 21.71%. Estimated *Apruebo Dianidad* turnout (of total, not considering party member restrictions): 12.26%; Estimated *Vamos por Chile* turnout (of total, not considering party member restrictions): 9.45%. *Source* Author with data from Servel

11.2.5 Other Candidates

Three other candidates entered the race, each representing distinct ideological niches, all of which had competed in presidential elections before. An academic-turned-politician, Franco Parisi ran under the banner of his own *Partido de la Gente*. Notably, Parisi conducted his entire campaign from the United States, never visiting Chile during the election period. His populist rhetoric, anti-establishment appeal, and ability to avoid being categorized along the traditional political spectrum posed him as a wildcard in the race. Yet, because he had received 10.1% of the vote in 2013, he could not be discarded as a minor threat.

Kast's candidacy reinforced sharp ideological divisions, leading both domestic and international observers—including financial markets and media outlets—to anticipate a deeply contentious political outcome. See: *Nasdaq*. 2021. "Chile Is Set for Its Most Polarized Election in Decades." November 18. https://www.nasdaq.com/articles/explainer-chile-is-set-for-its-mostpolarized-election-in-decades

Marco Enríquez-Ominami also entered the race representing the *Partido Progresista*. After running in previous elections with diminishing returns—20.1%, 10.9%, and 5.7% of the vote in 2009, 2013, and 2017, respectively—his candidacy in 2021 was mainly viewed as symbolic. Nevertheless, it underscored the persistence of alternative center-left voices.

Finally, Eduardo Artés, a representative of the *Unión Patriótica* party, campaigned from the extreme left. A staunch admirer of the North Korean regime,[14] Artés advocated policies that aligned with his ideologies, although his support base remained minimal. In 2017, he garnered a mere 0.5% of the vote, and his 2021 campaign, while unlikely to alter the election dynamics, depicted the broad ideological spectrum of the race.

11.3 The Crux of the 2021 Presidential Campaign

With the registration of the candidates, the campaign period of the election officially began on August 23, 2021. Historically, presidential candidates positioned themselves along a traditional left-to-right spectrum. While the left typically represented a combination of anti-dictatorship sentiment, progressive values, and a call for a larger government, the right leaned on pro-Pinochet nostalgia (which increasingly subsided over time), conservative values, and advocacy for minimal government intervention. Between 1989 and 2017, this framework made the categorization of candidates relatively straightforward. However, the crisis in 2019 fundamentally altered this dynamic. While the left–right axis persisted, the social outburst, including its causes and consequences, introduced new dimensions that candidates could not overlook.

[14] In a 2021 interview, Artés defended North Korea's government structure and criticized the influence of South Korean pop culture, reflecting the ideological consistency of his platform beyond typical political discourse. See: Quiroz, N. 2021. "Eduardo Artés realizó llamativas declaraciones sobre Corea del Norte y el K-pop." *ADN Radio*. October 22. https://www.adnradio.cl/politica/2021/10/22/eduardo-artes-realizo-llamativas-declaraciones-sobre-corea-del-norte-y-el-k-pop.html/. In 2025, as he collected signatures to register for another presidential race, he once again upheld his opinion in favor of North Korea. See: González, A. 2025. "Eduardo Artés afirma que en Corea del Norte "tienen una democracia" que responde a su propio contexto"."*Biobio Chile*. July 11. https://www.biobiochile.cl/noticias/nacional/chile/2025/07/11/eduardo-artes-afirma-que-en-corea-del-norte-tienen-una-democracia-que-responde-a-su-propio-contexto.shtml/

In this context, the social upheaval and its institutional counterpart, the constitutional process, constituted a distinct cleavage. The positions of candidates could now be mapped onto a two-dimensional space: one axis representing the *elite–people* continuum, reflecting interpretations of the causes of the social outburst; and a second axis denoting the *chaos–order* continuum, addressing the societal fallout of the unrest. The former can be thought of as a direct reaction to the protests in 2019, which were mainly perceived as a grassroots uprising against the entrenched upper class. The latter, instead, can be considered an implicit judgment of its aftermath in terms of whether the disruptions were justified byproduct of inequality or a sign of dangerous precarity.

These dimensions additionally offer practical insights into the stances of the candidates. For example, the term *elite* signaled a defense of traditional politics and successes attributed to the post-1990 model, while *people* reflected a preference for grassroots-driven politics, which was frequently critical of Chile's post-transition status quo. Similarly, *chaos* could be interpreted as a justification of the instability triggered by the social outburst, while *order* represented the drive to re-establish rule of law, even if it required hardline measures.[15]

Figure 11.1 illustrates this conceptual idea and partitions candidates into the four quadrants. Conservative candidates Kast and Sichel were aligned in quadrant 2 as they defended traditional institutions and advocated the restoration of stability. Meanwhile, left-of-center candidates, including Boric and Provoste, were positioned in quadrant 3, attempting to align with the transformative energy of grassroots movements. Parisi, in turn, fits best in quadrant 4, on the side of the people, while Enríquez-Ominami, distinguished representative of the Chilean political elite, fell

[15] Importantly, aligning with "chaos" does not necessarily mean that the candidates would support violence, just that they were not willing or able to condemn it outright—a strategic choice that was used and abused throughout the social outburst for clear political purposes. Lucy Oporto documents how the chaos ended up serving those who did not condem it. See for example: Gómez, A. 2024. "Lucy Oporto, filósofa: "La veleidad y travestismo de Boric es parte de un plan y una forma de manipulación"." *La Tercera*. May 19. https://www.latercera.com/la-terceradomingo/noticia/lucy-oporto-filosofa-la-veleidad-y-travestismo-de-boric-es-parte-de-un-plan-y-una-forma-demanipulacion/Q55ODJ4ONJFAFBZZ62MWJULEFI/. Pablo Ortúzar *(Instituto de Estudios de la Sociedad, IES)* also has several articles and interviews describing how the chaos of the social outburst served only the purposes of the Frente Amplio. See, for example: "No eran sus votitos." *La Tercera*. September 5, 2022.

naturally in quadrant 1. For reasons outlined above, Artés did not clearly fit in any of the quadrants.

In any case, quadrant 3 was expected to enjoy significant favor in 2021, because the public mood strongly leaned toward change. However, the dynamics shifted with the progress of the campaign. Discomforted with Sichel's past as a former Christian Democrat, conservative voters rallied

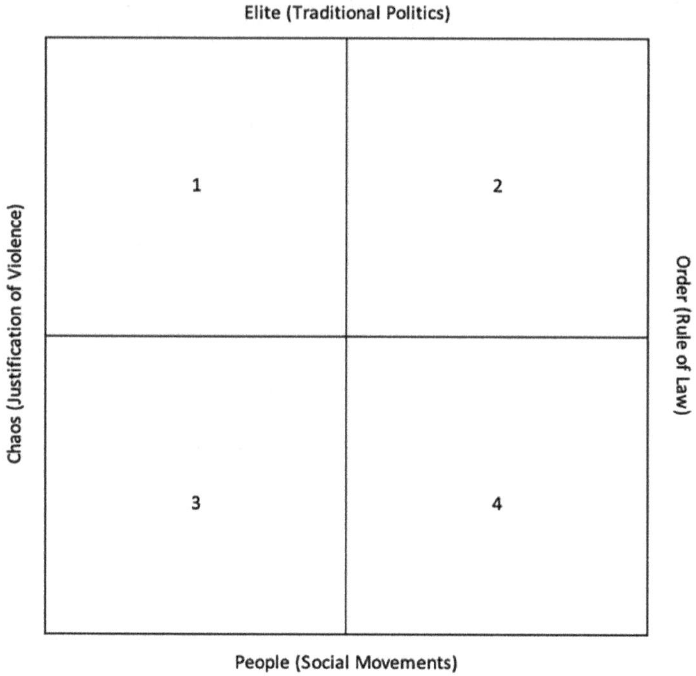

Fig. 11.1 The 2021 first-round presidential election cleavage (*Source* Author based on Bunker 2021)[16]

[16] For the origin of this thesis, see: Bunker, K. 2021. "Orden versus Violencia y Elite versus Pueblo: Los ejes cardinales de la elección presidencial." *Ex-Ante*. October 23. https://www.ex-ante.cl/orden-versus-violencia-y-elite-versus-pueblo-los-ejes-cardinales-de-la-eleccion-presidencial-por-kenneth-bunker/. Also see: Zúñiga, D. 2021. "Elecciones presidenciales en Chile: ¿orden o cambio?" *Deutsche Welle*. November 11. https://www.dw.com/es/elecciones-presidenciales-en-chile-orden-o-cambio/a-59869427/

behind Kast, whose hardline stances gained momentum through debates held in September and October. Sichel's support eroded as Kast surged. Meanwhile, Boric retained his position as the favorite, with the majority of surveys predicting a first-round victory for him and Kast securing second place. Late in the campaign, a number of polls indicated that Kast had high chances of winning the first round, although a runoff was always anticipated.

Table 11.2 presents the first round outcome, which generated several unexpected results. The most striking was Kast's first-place finish, ahead of Boric. Regardless of poll predicitions, the outcome contradicted popular sentiment that held that voters would align with a candidate that favored the constitutional process more than one opposed to it.

Another equally surprising result was the underwhelming vote count for Boric. Despite his position as the frontrunner, he secured only 25.8% of the vote, which barely exceeded the number of votes cast in the *Apruebo Dignidad* primary (around 1.8 million). This alone suggests that the quadrant-3 position must have alienated centrist voters and limited his appeal to the electorate.

The results prompted strategic recalibration. For Kast, the outcome validated his focus on law and order, which demonstrates that Chileans

Table 11.2 Results of the 2021 presidential election

	First round		*Second round*	
Candidates	*Number of votes*	*Percent of votes*	*Number of votes*	*Percent of votes*
José Antonio Kast	1,961,779	27.91	3,650,662	44.13
Gabriel Boric	1,815,024	25.82	4,621,231	55.87
Franco Parisi	900,064	12.81		
Sebastián Sichel	898,635	12.79		
Yasna Provoste	815,563	11.60		
Marco Enríquez-Ominami	534,383	7.60		
Eduardo Artés	102,897	1.46		
Valid votes	**7,028,345**	**98.79**	**8,271,893**	**98.89**
Null votes	**55,480**	**0.78**	**68,616**	**0.82**
Blank votes	**30,493**	**0.43**	**23,972**	**0.29**
Total	**7,114,318**	**100**	**8,364,481**	**100**

Note Voting was voluntary. Registered voters: 15,030,974. Estimated first round turnout: 47.33%. Estimated second round turnout: 55.64%. *Source* Author with data from Servel

desired change but were wary of the chaos that accompanied it. The takeaway for Boric, instead, was more complex. His leniency toward protest-related violence and staunchly leftist stance, in stark contrast to Provoste's more centrist approach, failed to resonate with a rapidly shifting electorate. To prepare for the December runoff, Boric pivoted toward the center and softened many of his radical proposals. Meanwhile, Kast strengthened his first-round messaging.

Center-right *Vamos por Chile* endorsed Kast, while center-left *Nuevo Pacto Social* rallied behind Boric.

The runoff, held one month later, in December 2021, produced its own share of surprises. For starters, it set a record for voter turnout, with over 8 million ballots cast, making it the election with the highest turnout in Chilean history. Boric's victory also broke another record: he received the highest number of votes any Chilean presidential candidate had ever received up until that point, with more than 4.6 million votes. This reversed his rather modest showing in the first round. Kast also performed strongly in the second round, nearing the standing record set by Sebastián Piñera in 2017. Ultimately, Boric's decisive win, capturing 55.9% of the vote, marked a generational and political shift.[17] His victory ended three decades of shared center-left and center-right rule, bringing in a new era of governance by the left.

11.4 Gabriel Boric Rises

Gabriel Boric was sworn into office on March 11, 2022. At just 36 years old, he became not only the youngest president in Chile's history but also the youngest serving president in the world at that time. This instantly turned him into a symbol for the regional left, much like Pablo Iglesias of *Podemos* in Spain and Alexis Tsipras of *Syriza* in Greece had been in

[17] It should be noted, however, that while Boric secured victory in the second round of the presidential election, a significant portion of his support came from so-called borrowed votes. The 2.7 million votes he gained were largely second-choice preferences from voters who perceived José Antonio Kast as the greater threat. For many, Boric represented the lesser of two evils—or simply the candidate they disliked the least. Although the moment was dominated by the celebratory immediacy of his win, it was evident that such a conditional mandate would have implications for his ability to govern. His support, while sufficient for victory, was ultimately fragile. See: Galindo, J. 2021. La victoria condicionada de Gabriel Boric. *El País*. December 20. https://elpais.com/internacional/2021-12-20/la-victoria-condicionada-de-gabriel-boric.html

Europe. Boric embodied the promise of a progressive, open, and ambitious new left, distinctly different from his predecessors. Although his *Frente Amplio* coalition committed to sharing power with the Communist Party, a traditional workers' party, Boric's government represented a significant departure from the frameworks of the *Concertación* and *Nueva Mayoría* coalitions. His administration began with a pledge to address long-standing inequalities, and although he had shifted toward the center during the runoff, he did not shy away from his intent of generating structural change in his inaugural speech.[18]

Boric's rise to prominence began in 2012 when he was elected president of the University of Chile Student Federation (FECH) following his involvement in the transformative 2011 student protests (see Chapter 8). Led by high-profile figures such as Camila Vallejo and Giorgio Jackson, these protests placed Boric under the spotlight. After departing from his hometown of Punta Arenas—the southernmost city in Chile, located 3,500 km from Santiago, to study law, Boric found his *true calling* in politics. Similar to many federation presidents before him, his leadership role propelled him into national recognition. Within one year, Boric became a central figure in the consolidation of the left-wing *Izquierda Autónoma* movement, which signaled his transition from student activism to mainstream politics.[19]

[18] In his first speech as president from the balcony of *La Moneda*, Gabriel Boric explicitly invoked the historical memory of Salvador Allende, quoting his famous phrase: "Estamos de nuevo, compatriotas, abriendo las grandes alamedas por donde pase el hombre y la mujer libre." This symbolic gesture was widely interpreted as a deliberate signal to the historic Chilean left and a reaffirmation of Boric's ideological lineage. While the speech was moderate in tone and careful to emphasize unity—naming figures across the political spectrum such as Patricio Aylwin and Michelle Bachelet—it nonetheless anchored his administration within the broader struggle for social justice and structural transformation. Boric also highlighted themes of redistribution, social rights, constitutional change, and historical reckoning, underscoring his commitment to a progressive agenda. See: Rivas Molina, F. 2022. "Gabriel Boric rescata la épica de Salvador Allende en su primer discurso como presidente." *El País*. March 12. https://elpais.com/internacional/2022-03-12/gabriel-boric-rescata-la-epica-de-salvador-allende-en-su-primer-discurso-como-presidente.html/. [This document, *Primer discurso de S.E. el Presidente de la República, Gabriel Boric Font, desde el Palacio de La Moneda*, is available on the author's website.]

[19] Like Izquierda Autónoma, the other political movements Boric participated in were the result of fusions, splits, and ideological reconfigurations. Rather than a single coherent trajectory, his political path reflects the broader pattern of mutation and realignment that has characterized the Chilean left since 2011—particularly within the *Frente Amplio*. See:

In 2013, Boric formalized his political career by running for a seat in the national Congress as an independent candidate. Without a law degree and competing under the binomial system (introduced in Chapter 2 and explained in Chapter 6), which mainly favored established parties, Boric defied the odds and was elected. The win made him one of nine independents that would manage to be elected to Congress as independents in the seven elections that were held using the binomial system (see the footnote references in Chapter 10 for the full list).

Notably, the binomial system was abolished under Bachelet's second government, and during his first term (2014–2018), which paved the way for several new left-wing initiatives, including the one spearheaded by Giorgio Jackson, who founded the left-leaning social democratic party *Revolución Democrática* in 2016. While invited, Boric decided in favor of a different path and positioned himself further left of Jackson. His movement, *Izquierda Autónoma*, however, would experience significant internal discord and eventually implode. As a result, Boric deviated from the group and founded *Movimiento Autonomista*, which became a platform for other emerging political figures such as Jorge Sharp and Gonzalo Winter.

Despite this upheaval, Boric would retain his congressional seat in 2017 (this time backed by the *Partido Humanista*), securing reelection for the 2018–2022 term. This both reaffirmed his popularity among constituents and established him as a key player in national debates.

As Sebastián Piñera assumed office for a second term on March 11, 2018, Boric entered his second term as a deputy. Early on, he distinguished himself by exhibiting a willingness to engage with the conservative president. In stark contrast to many left-leaning peers, Boric participated in discussions on prevalent national issues, demonstrating a commitment to constructive dialogue. However, this phase of cooperation was short-lived. The social outburst in October 2019 marked a turning point for Boric and elevated him from just another legislator to a defining figure.

His presence was first recognized during the crisis by opposing Piñera's decision to deploy the military to disperse protests. Captured by the

Nogué, A., and E. Barozet. 2023. "Dio de una crisis del sistema político: la trayectoria del Frente Amplio chileno y sus limitaciones (2011–2022)." *Revista de Ciencia Política* 61(1): 7–35.

media as he called on "soldiers to return to their barracks,"[20] Boric became a vocal critic of the President's management of the unrest. However, his influence extended beyond public displays. Behind the scenes, Boric played a significant role in negotiating a political solution to the crisis. While many on the left, including the Communist Party, opted out of engagement with Piñera, Boric joined the discussion, thus contributing to the agreement established on November 15, 2019.

The decision to participate in the negotiations was controversial within Boric's movement (as described in Chapter 10). A few days before the agreement, opposition parties insisted on a Constitutional Assembly as a precondition for talks. This stance was supported by most members of *Convergencia Social*, Boric's party. When compromise became clearly inevitable, Boric worked to shape the terms of the agreement.[21] This move alienated a significant faction of his party, which led to an exodus of members, including Jorge Sharp, the mayor of Valparaíso. In total, 73 high-ranking members deserted *Convergencia Social*.[22] Boric's signature on the agreement was notably unaffiliated with a party, which underscored the (predictable) fractures within his base.

[20] During a tense moment at *Plaza Baquedano*, Boric was filmed confronting armed soldiers—a scene that quickly circulated in national media. See: *El Desconcierto*. 2019. "Video: Tienen armas de guerra. Gabriel Boric increpa a militares en Plaza Italia." October 19. https://eldesconcierto.cl/2019/10/19/video-tienen-armas-de-guerra-gabriel-boric-increpa-a-militares-en-plaza-italia/.

[21] Gabriel Boric's decision to sign the *Acuerdo por la Paz Social y la Nueva Constitución* in November 2019 caused immediate tension within his party, *Convergencia Social*. While Boric viewed participation as a necessary step to shape the terms of Chile's constitutional process, most of his party's leadership had pushed for a fully sovereign Constituent Assembly and viewed the negotiated agreement as politically insufficient. The party released a public statement criticizing the pact for its lack of "social legitimacy" and for failing to guarantee meaningful public participation in the drafting of a new constitution. Boric's unilateral signature triggered significant internal backlash and exposed a broader generational and strategic divide within the *Frente Amplio*. See: *Cooperativa*. 2019. "Partido de Boric: Acuerdo por la Paz Social y Nueva Constitución es aún insuficiente." November 19. https://cooperativa.cl/noticias/pais/politica/frente-amplio/partido-de-boric-acuerdo-por-la-paz-social-y-nueva-constitucion-es-aun/2019-11-19/172430.html/.

[22] Almost half of those that resigned would be later be hired by Mayor Sharp in the municipality of Valparaíso. *El Libero*. 2019. "Casi la mitad de los 73 militantes que renunciaron a Convergencia Social fueron contratados en Valparaíso por Jorge Sharp." November 21. https://ellibero.cl/actualidad/casi-la-mitad-de-los-73-militantes-que-renunciaron-a-convergencia-social-fueron-contratados-en-valparaiso-por-jorge-sharp/

Between December 2019 and March 2020, *Convergencia Social* was built under the leadership of figures such as Gael Yeomans, a deputy in the Lower Chamber. Initially registered only as a regional political entity, the party shortly gained momentum. By October, Alondra Arellano, a 22-year-old, was elected as its president and became the youngest leader of a political party in Chile's history. *Convergencia Social* formally achieved national status in May 2021, as mentioned above. Within this period, it remained critical of Piñera but also refrained from outright condemnation of ongoing violence. This stance was calculated to align with public sentiment (recall quadrant 3).

The coalition primary in July 2021 highlighted the strategic dilemmas faced by Boric and his allies. While the Communist Party adopted a radical approach, Boric's *Convergencia Social* attempted to balance its alignment with grassroots movements with its ambitions for broader appeal. This tension became increasingly pronounced in the first round of the presidential election, where Boric's position was both a strength and a liability. Recognizing these contradictions early, he adjusted his strategy after his lackluster first-round performance. In the second round, Boric downplayed his leniency toward protest-related violence and shifted toward centrist proposals, which enabled him to gain support from undecided voters while maintaining credibility among his base.

Despite these adjustments, Boric's participation in the November 15 agreement remained a cornerstone of his campaign narrative. It allowed him to claim a moderate stance, thus bridging the divide between grassroots activism and institutional reform. This dual approach proved instrumental in his eventual victory, which cemented his reputation as a leader capable of navigating complex political landscapes.

11.5 A Shift to the Left

As Gabriel Boric took office, inevitable comparisons with Salvador Allende surfaced. For the first time since 1970, a self-identified left-wing leader assumed control of *La Moneda*. Boric's election was significant not only at the electoral level but also at the symbolic level, representing the culmination of a dispute between the left and center-left across a decade. This victory firmly swung the political pendulum toward the former camp. While this outcome was unsurprising given the results of the plebiscite and the election of Constitutional Convention members (see Chapter 10),

Boric's ascent to the presidency underscored Chile's dramatic political shift on the global stage.

From a domestic political perspective, Boric seized full control of the narrative of the moment. By March 2022, he was unquestionably the most popular politician in Chile, as the right and conservative parties were in disarray. After losing not only in the constitutional plebiscite and subsequent elections but also control of the presidency, the conservative bloc clung to its distribution of senate seats as a weak bulwark against irrelevance. However, the Boric administration acted as if these parties were fully sidelined from mainstream discourse. Elected with a record-breaking number of votes, Boric approached his presidency with confidence and anticipated a prolonged honeymoon period that would culminate in the successful conclusion of the constitutional process. He aimed to shepherd the new constitutional proposal through its final stages (see Chapter 15 for more on this), secure approval from Chileans, and thereby mark the definitive end of the transitional era.

With the momentum of the constitutional process, Boric promptly assembled his cabinet. He appointed 23 ministers, which signaled a decisive shift toward the left. The majority were firmly aligned with progressive ideologies, reflecting his intent to make a clean break from the political establishment. At the core of his administration, Boric placed three of his closest allies in key positions. A polarizing figure who connected with low-income communities during the campaign, Izkia Siches was named Minister of the Interior; Camila Vallejo, who represented the Communist Party, was appointed as government spokesperson; and Giorgio Jackson of *Revolución Democrática* was assigned as the primary liaison to Congress (Presidency). These appointments not only underscored a strong ideological shift but also marked a significant generational departure from Chile's political past.

The traditional center-left, represented by Yasna Provoste during the first round of the 2021 presidential election, was left with minimal representation in Boric's administration, despite their support in the runoff against Kast. Among a few notable exceptions were Mario Marcel (appointed to the Treasury) and Carlos Montes (assigned to Housing). Both were members of the Socialist Party. Their appointments were seemingly designed to placate the ex-*Concertación*, signaling fiscal prudence and commitment to long-term planning. However, these gestures were isolated ones within an otherwise left-dominated administration.

This administration was not a coalition government in any traditional sense. The Boric administration was unequivocally a government *of the left, by the left,* and *for the left*. In its first six months, the center-left and the right were conspicuously excluded from notable decision-making processes. This exclusion was a deliberate statement that emphasized the irrevocable change in the political landscape. It was a brief but decisive period, which left little doubt among Chile's political class about who now held the reins of power.[23]

11.6 Conclusion

The 2021 presidential election and the constitutional process were milestones that redefined the political and social trajectories of Chile. These events were not isolated occurrences but deeply interconnected reflections of a society at a crossroads. The choice faced by Chileans was emblematic of a broad political moment: whether to embrace the radical

[23] While the book now shifts focus and turns to examine the constitutional process in more detail, readers should note that the inauguration of Boric also symbolized the unequivocal end of social democracy as understood by the *Concertación*. This event, however, was neither unannounced nor unexpected. The *Concertación* had already begun to disassemble following its 2010 electoral defeat (recall Chapter 4), and was later reborn—albeit in a different form—as the *Nueva Mayoría* (see Chapter 8). Although arguments could still be made that the coalition embodied social democracy during the 2014–2018 period—given that the same parties remained in power (DC, PPD, PR, PS)—this was certainly no longer the case after 2018, by which point most of these parties had lost much of their political weight (recall Chapters 6 and 7). While they managed to retain some presence in the Senate, their overall influence had deteriorated significantly compared to what it once was. The DC, for example, fell from securing 25.9% of the vote and 38 out of 120 seats (31.6%) in the Lower Chamber in 1989 to just 4.2% of the vote and 8 out of 155 seats (5.2%) in 2021. The PPD dropped from 11.5% of the vote and 16 seats (13.3%) in 1989 to 3.8% and 7 seats (4.5%) in 2021. Similarly, the PRSD declined from 3.8% of the vote and 5 seats (4.2%) to 1.7% and 4 seats (2.6%). Their waning influence was also evident in the constitutional process. In the first Constitutional Convention, the DC won just two seats (Fuad Chahín and independent Christian Viera), the PPD three (Felipe Harboe, Eduardo Castillo, and independent Luis Barceló), and the PRSD only one (independent Renato Garín). In the second constitutional process, the PS secured just one seat (along with five independents), while the PPD, DC, and PR were excluded from the plenary altogether. While the Socialist Party (PS) generally fared better over time, losing fewer votes and seats than the others, it was still relegated to a secondary role in the Boric government and, by 2025, was politically incapable of fielding its own presidential candidate. The loss of political territory once occupied by these parties in the Chilean system is strikingly visible in the figures provided in the Appendix.

change catalyzed by the social outburst or to opt for stability and continuity, which had characterized the nation's governance for decades. At the fork in the road, Chile chose the former—a radical path that endorsed generational change and a decisive shift toward the far left.

The election was a referendum on the nation's future. The triumph of Gabriel Boric—a young, progressive candidate who represented a new generation of leadership—was more than a political victory. It symbolized a demand for a change. The momentum of grassroots activism and the promise of a government that could address the structural inequity exposed by the social outburst fueled Boric's rise. His victory also reflected the declining relevance of traditional political forces, particularly the center-left coalition that dominated Chilean politics for three decades but failed to adapt to the demands of the evolving electorate.

Boric's government, which overlooked traditional power structures in favor of a younger, ideologically cohesive cabinet, mirrored this generational shift. The symbolism of this move was clear: the left not only won at the ballot box but also claimed the narrative of the moment. For the first time since 1970, the presidency in Chile represented a self-identified left-wing vision of governance that was unapologetically rooted in social justice and equality. This marked a definitive rupture in the political cycles of the past, which were characterized by gradualism and compromise between center-left and center-right coalitions.

In electing Boric and the transformative agenda he represented, Chileans reaffirmed their commitment to change. The election was not only presented as a rejection of the past but also as a declaration of generational renewal, far-left ideals, and the promise of in-depth institutional change. This moment, defined by its bold departure from continuity, cemented itself as yet another turning point in Chile's political history that would ripple beyond the constitutional process and reshape the nation dramatically over the years to come.

CHAPTER 12

The (First) Constitutional Convention

12.1 Introduction

The 2021–2022 Chilean Constitutional Convention was a historic effort to address the crisis that emerged from the social outburst in 2019. With a mandate to replace the 1980 Constitution, it was propelled by a strong political swing to the left. For the progessive elites that designed and were poised to lead it, the process represented a chance to address historical grievances and fundamentally reshape Chile's political and social framework. However, tensions would gradually emerge between the bold ambitions of the convention members and the more cautious priorities of the broader electorate. The sidelining of moderates and conservatives would ultimately prove a decisive error, not only deepening divisions in an already polarized political landscape but also setting the stage for an outcome that few could have anticipated.

This chapter begings by recounting the events that marked the Constitutional Convention's first day on July 4, 2021, a moment full of symbolism and chaos. Indeed, it was from the outset that it became clear the diverse and nontraditional membership of the Convention, which in many ways mirrored the 2019 protests, would introduce significant challenges to the legislative process. In fact, on day one, the left-leaning majority quickly consolidated its power by designing internal rules that would streamline the process in their favor, even though these were arguably at odds with the 12-point agreement. In doing so—by

K. Bunker, *Chile's Transformation Amidst Crisis*,
https://doi.org/10.1007/978-3-031-96463-3_12

acting in such a decisive manner—they not only alienated the right-aligned minority within the Convention, but also many in moderate segments of general Chilean society.

The chapter then turns to examines the ideological dynamics of the Convention via analysis of its member positions and coalition alignments. By mapping ideological leanings and voting patterns, the analysis reveals the influence of the dominance of left-leaning forces on the legislative process and content of the constitutional draft. Despite their numerical strength, progressives typically encountered internal divisions with disagreements over strategy and policy direction. Conversely, the conservative bloc, which was fragmented and marginalized, struggled to exert a meaningful influence on the decisions of the assembly. This polarization underscored the challenges of obtaining consensus within a partisan body tasked with drafting a document meant to foster unity.

Attention then shifts to the content of the proposed constitution, which reflected not only the progressive orientation of the plenary, but also that of the thematic commissions from which legislation originated. The key provisions of the finished proposal included plurinational recognition, expansive social and environmental rights, and a *de facto* unicameral system that aimed to redefine Chilean governance. While these elements may have resonated with the base of the left, they also risked alienating moderate voters who, while supportive of reform, were not necessarily willing to support just anything presented to them.

Finally, the chapter considers the public sentiment that led to the September 2022 plebiscite in which the proposed constitution was overwhelmingly rejected. Polling data revealed increasing skepticism among voters. By tracing the trajectory of the Convention from its inception to its ultimate failure, this chapter highlights the risks of ideological overreach and proffers a cautionary lesson on the importance of striking a balance between transformative goals and broader public support.

12.2 Day One: Symbolism and Chaos

In the 49 days that passed between the May 2021 election and the official inauguration of the Constitutional Convention, the government undertook extensive preparations to lay the groundwork for the process. One of the key decisions was to designate the former National Congress in Santiago and the nearby *Palacio Pereira* as the primary legislative venues. These locations were chosen to symbolize a connection to Chile's historical institutions while paving the way for transformative change.

To ensure the Convention's operations ran smoothly, the government allocated 22 billion pesos (approximately $26 million). This budget was used to provide essential resources, including personnel, computers, cameras, stationery, and an online platform to broadcast the legislative sessions to the public, thereby ensuring transparency and accessibility. Additionally, a supplementary budget was allocated specifically to facilitate the participation of Indigenous community members, reflecting the Convention's commitment to inclusivity. All funding decisions were overseen and managed directly by the elected directive and, under its authority, by the budget committee.

On July 4, 2021, the Convention officially convened, marking its transition to full autonomy with the election of its directive.[1] Carmen Gloria Valledares, a staff member from the electoral service (Servel), officiated as a temporary formateur, tasked solely with guiding the members through the election of their first president. From that moment on, the only limitations placed on the assembly were those outlined in the November 15 agreement (see Chapter 10), rendering even the *Contraloría* (National Comptroller), Chile's independent legal regulatory authority, unable to intervene.

As members arrived at the former National Congress for the opening session, the atmosphere was charged with both anticipation and tension. Outside the venue, large crowds gathered, chanting and protesting as the 155 members prepared to assume their roles. Inside, the opening ceremony commenced with a children's orchestra playing the Chilean national anthem. However, the performance was abruptly interrupted when several elected members loudly objected, refusing to recognize the anthem as a legitimate symbol for the assembly. The disruption caused chaos, lasting 15 minutes before order was restored.

After the resumption of proceedings, Valledares invited members to vote for the assembly's president via an open ballot, which required an

[1] From the outset, it was decided that there would be two leadership directives (boards), each composed of a president and a vice president. Each board would serve for six months: the first elected in July 2021, and the second in February 2022.

absolute majority for victory. The first round of voting ended inconclusively, as no candidate surpassed the required fifty-percent-plus-one threshold. During a break, negotiations unfolded behind the scenes. The left, independents, and indigenous representatives consolidated support for Elisa Loncon, who received 37 votes in the initial round. Meanwhile, the right rallied behind Harry Jürgensen, who secured 36 votes. In the second round, Loncon emerged victorious, securing 96 votes (61.9%) over 33 votes (21.3%) for Jürgensen. Two other candidates, namely, Isabel Godoy (far left) and Patricia Politzer (center-left), garnered 5 and 18 votes, respectively.

Following Loncon's election, the session was temporarily halted as members celebrated her historic victory. For many, it was a defining moment in history. A largely unknown activist and teacher with strong ties to the Mapuche community, for many Loncon became a powerful symbol of Chile's departure from its colonialist legacy. Set to last six months (ending in February 2022), her presidency was deemed pivotal from the outset. This earned her international recognition, including a feature on the cover of *TIME* magazine as one of the world's most influential women.

When the session reconvened, again, Loncon took her seat at the head of the table and presided over the remaining 154 members. Attention now diverged to the election of the vice president. Governed by the same absolute majority rule, this election emphasized a shift from symbolic celebration to a strategic political maneuver. The left intended to elect a vice president who could complement Loncon's symbolic leadership with legal expertise and political acumen. After discreet negotiations and three rounds of voting, Jaime Bassa was elected vice president with 84 votes (54.2%).

A lawyer and academic from the Valparaíso region, Bassa was affiliated with Gabriel Boric's *Convergencia Social*. Although relatively unknown to the general public, he was recognized within some academic and political circles as an emerging intellectual voice in constitutional debates. During his campaign, Bassa was an outspoken critic of the existing constitution. His legal expertise and academic background made him an appealing choice for drafting a progressive legal framework. Together, Loncon and Bassa formed a leadership team well-suited to guide the Convention through its transformative purpose.

For supporters of the 2019 social uprising, the election of Loncon and Bassa represented a realization of their aspirations—a clear signal of the commitment of the Convention to the production of a groundbreaking and progressive document. For the rest, however, it signaled the marginalization of conservatives. Having suffered a significant electoral defeat, it was already clear that the right lacked the one-third quorum necessary to block legislation. The election of Loncon and Bassa further ensured that they would be excluded from the process, as they would have no say in the formulation of the internal rules of the Convention, which, as suspected, would end up being repeatedly amended by the left-leaning directive to favor themselves.

The leadership of Loncon and Bassa was presented as a mandate to fulfill the demands of the protests on October 18, 2019. Their rise quickly exhibited a nearly mythic quality. An edited photograph of the pair, which depicted them standing in front of *Plaza Baquedano* (renamed *Plaza Dignidad* by protesters), surrounded by symbols of the social movement, widely circulated on social media. Bassa shared the image on his *X* (then *Twitter*) account, while Loncon endorsed it with a like. The photograph became an iconic representation of their leadership and was shared numerous times as a testament to their symbolic rise.[2]

12.3 Establishing New Rules of the Game

The early days of the Constitutional Convention's sessions were marked by the missteps expected from such a diverse group. Some members arrived in elaborate costumes, while others wore traditional attire. Some engaged in singing and chanting, while others argued and shouted. From the outset, the highly politicized nature of the process became evident, when just two days into the sessions a document, authored by members of the Communist Party, the Socialist Party, and the *Frente Amplio*, called for the release of the *presos del estallido* ("prisoners of the social outburst"). The directive soon instructed the assembly to vote on the document as one of its first orders of business. While only a simple majority of 78 votes was required for approval, the document comfortably

[2] A *Vamos por Chile* convention member, Bernardo Fontaine, shared the image in critical fashion, pointing out that there leadership was underpinned by the violence of the circumstances surrounding the social outburst: (https://x.com/berfontaine/status/1582531326636236800).

exceeded the two-thirds threshold of 104, with 105 members endorsing it, 34 voting against it, and 10 abstaining.

The vote foreshadowed the dynamics that would shape the months ahead. Congress had established a two-thirds quorum requirement for passing legislation in the Constitutional Convention. However, the directive led by Elisa Loncon and Jaime Bassa quickly reinterpreted this rule, asserting that the two-thirds requirement would only be applied to the plenary, while all other votes would pass with a simple majority.[3]

The strategic adjustment lowered the voting threshold to a level that the left and independents alone could reach. For instance, by requiring only a simple majority in committees (commissions), the left could ensure that the first-tier proposals advanced more easily to the floor. Conversely, had the original two-thirds rule been applied across all levels, conservatives would have had greater leverage to veto left-leaning proposals in committees, reducing their chances of reaching the plenary.

The next priority for Loncon and Bassa was organizing members into permanent and temporary committees. The distribution of seats in these committees reflected the overall composition of the assembly, favoring the left and independents while disadvantaging the conservative right. The temporary committees focused on designing the legal framework envisioned by the directive, while the permanent, or thematic, committees were responsible for drafting articles to be submitted to the plenary for approval or rejection.

In the second session, held on July 7, 2021, the first three committees—Regulation, Budget, and Ethics—were established. Over the following months, more than 10 additional committees were formed. Among the temporary committees, one stood out for its explicitly political nature: the *Comisión de Derechos Humanos de la Convención Constitucional* ("Human Rights Commission of the Constitutional Convention"). This committee aimed to assess and document the political events leading up to the Convention. Its subcommittee, the *Subcomisión de Verdad Histórica, Reparación Integral y Garantías de No Repetición* ("Subcommission on Historical Truth, Comprehensive Reparations and Guarantees

[3] This issue bacame a major turning point, as it further weakened the ability of any opposition—beyond just the conservative sector—to organize. See: Sánchez, J. 2021. "El primer round por el quorum de 2/3 y los vacíos en las normas de la Convención Constitucional." *Ex-Ante*. July 6. https://www.ex-ante.cl/el-primer-round-por-el-quorum-de-2-3-y-los-vacios-en-las-normas-de-la-convencion-constitucional/

of Non-Repetition"), produced a comprehensive report condemning "human rights violations" during the social outburst and advocating for reparations. Published in December 2021, this document became one of the most politically significant outputs of the entire process.[4]

On July 15, 2021, during the Convention's eighth session, five additional temporary committees were formed.[5] Collectively, these committees established many of the procedural rules and determined the structure and responsibilities of the permanent committees. However, the permanent, or thematic, committees were not officially constituted until late September 2021. These seven committees were responsible for drafting the new constitutional proposal and were named as follows: (1) Political System, Government, Legislative Power, and Electoral System; (2) Constitutional Principles and Democracy; (3) Form of State and Territorial Justice; (4) Fundamental Rights; (5) Environment and Economic Model; (6) Justice Systems, Autonomous Bodies of Control, and Constitutional Reform; and (7) Knowledge Systems, Science and Technology, Culture, Art, and Heritage.

Before examining the Convention's substantive work, it is crucial to consider the role of the directives in scheduling and organization. For example, one significant decision was to limit the first directive's term to six months, necessitating new elections in February (this is why Loncon was due to step down). This decision proved pivotal, as the second directive's tenure began just as commission votes ended and plenary votes commenced. Another important decision involved dissolving all committees after the voting process was completed. The directive established that,

[4] See: "Informe final: Verdad histórica, reparación integral y garantías de no repetición: Resultado de proyecto de sistematización de audiencias de la Comisión de Derechos Humanos de la Convención Constitucional, Subcomisión de Verdad Histórica, Reparación". [This document, *Informe Final: Verdad Histórica, Reparación Integral y Garantías de No Repetición*, is available on the author's website.]

[5] The six temporary commissions were: *Derechos Humanos, Verdad Histórica y Bases para la Justicia, Reparación y Garantías de No Repetición*; *Comunicaciones, Información y Transparencia*; *Participación y Consulta Indígena*; *Participación Popular y Equidad Territorial*; *Descentralización, Equidad y Justicia Territorial*; *Participación Ciudadana* (although this last commission, while initially approved, was dissolved before it could be inaugurated).

once the voting concluded, members would be reassigned to three new committees responsible for finalizing the draft for public presentation.[6]

Finally, it is worth noting that one member of the Convention, Rodrigo Rojas Vade (of the leftist *Lista del Pueblo*), was expelled early in the process, reducing the total number of members to 154. While this initially seemed inconsequential in terms of the Convention's ideological balance, it would later resurface as a significant issue in the plebiscite campaign.

12.4 A Left-Leaning Assembly

To fully understand the outcomes of the Constitutional Convention, it is necessary to examine the political and ideological forces that shaped its operations. While earlier sections explored the historical foundation and structural framework of the Convention, this section reveals its internal dynamics. Specifically, it focuses on coalition formation and voting patterns to uncover how decisions were made and how the authorship of the constitutional proposal was shaped. This analysis highlights the strategic efforts of various factions to consolidate power, overcome opposition, and advance their agendas within the assembly.

To assess the ideological leanings of members and the coalitions they formed, this section draws on research previously conducted,[7] which applied spatial voting models to map ideological alignments and coalition dynamics.[8] Using the W-NOMINATE method, a well-known scaling

[6] The Harmonization Committee would be responsible for rewriting the final draft into a clear, readable format. The Preamble Committee would draft the text's introduction. The Transitory Norms Committee would design the process for transitioning from the current constitution to the new one, should the latter be approved in the exit referendum.

[7] See: Bunker, K. 2023a. "¿Cuál fue el nivel de acuerdo en el pleno de la convención constitucional de 2021?" *Ideas: Laboratorio Democracia y Gobierno USS* 1(6): 1–4; Bunker, K. 2023b. "¿Cuál fue el nivel de acuerdo en las comisiones de la convención constitucional de 2021?" *Ideas: Laboratorio Democracia y Gobierno USS* 1(5): 1–4.

[8] See theoretical foundations of spatial models: Hinich, M. J., and M. C. Munger, M. C. 1992. "A Spatial Theory of Ideology." *Journal of Theoretical Politics* 4(1): 5–30; McFadden, D. 1973. "Conditional Logit Analysis of Qualitative Choice Behavior." In *Frontiers of Econometrics*, edited by P. Zarembka, 105–142. New York, NY: Academic Press.

technique, members' ideological positions were mapped along two dimensions: the first measuring ideological placement from far left (−1) to far right (+1), and the second assessing value orientations, ranging from liberal or progressive (−1) to conservative or authoritarian (+1).[9] Based on these maps, the area of influence of different coalitions was determined.

12.4.1 *Ideological and Value Positions of Coalitions and Parties*

Figure 12.1 illustrates the placement of Convention members along the first dimension, with progressive members clustered on the left and conservative members on the right. The dashed line indicates the key threshold of two thirds (103 members) required to pass constitutional articles in the plenary.

[9] Bunker (2023a; 2023b) applies the "W-NOMINATE" method developed by Poole and Rosenthal (1984) to the Constitutional Convention. This method estimates legislators' ideological positions based on roll-call voting patterns, mapping them along two dimensions. While the axes do not have fixed, objective meanings, they are conventionally interpreted as follows: the first dimension orders members from left (−1) to right (+1), and the second from liberal or progressive (−1) to authoritarian or conservative (+1). These interpretations are inherently subjective and context-dependent. Nevertheless, the method offers a much more fine-grained and empirically grounded approach to understanding ideological alignments than simply assuming a member's position based on their electoral affiliation or campaign rhetoric.

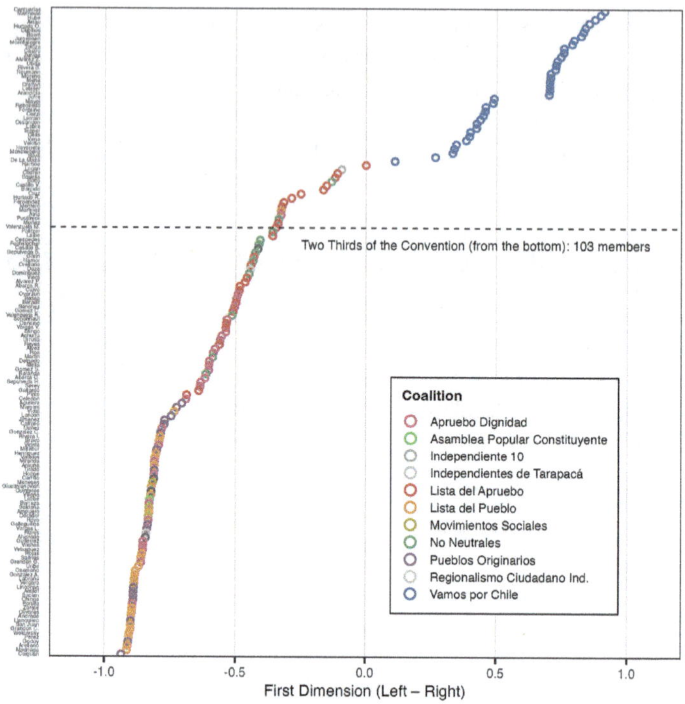

Fig. 12.1 One-dimensional ideological placement of Constitutional Convention members in the plenary (*Note* Each point represents a member, colored by coalition affiliation and positioned along a left–right scale from –1 (left) to 1 (right), with 0 at the center. Members are ordered vertically from highest to lowest on this scale. The dashed horizontal line marks the position of the 103rd member (two-thirds of the Convention), counted from the bottom up.[10]) *Source* Author with data from Bunker 2023a)

[10] In total, 4,377 votes were cast in the plenary of the Constitutional Convention. Of this total, 1,581 (36.1%) passed with more than two-thirds. [This dataset, *Roll-call votes inof the Plenary of the Constitutional Convention of Chile, 2021-2022*, is available on the author's website.]

The figure underscores the Convention's strong ideological skew toward the left. More than 50% of members scored below − 0.5 on the ideological scale, and over two-thirds were positioned left-of-center.[11] This imbalance enabled the leftist leadership, under Loncon and Bassa, to secure majorities with relative ease. Their ideological dominance ensured that most articles passed in plenary sessions with minimal resistance, reflecting the left's control over the legislative process.

In contrast, the conservative bloc was fragmented into at least two factions: one leaning closer to the center and another further to the right. This division weakened the political sector's ability to effectively challenge the progressive majority. It would also deepen what until this point was a small crack in the conservative sector, and have significant political repercussions in the future (see Chapter 16).

Figure 12.2 introduces a second dimension to the analysis by incorporating both ideology and value orientations. Members are grouped into rectangles representing their respective coalitions or parties, with smaller rectangles indicating higher internal party discipline. This two-dimensional visualization reveals stark polarization within the assembly, as parties are clustered on opposite ends of the ideological spectrum.

[11] Specifically, 85 members (54.8%) scored between -1 and -0.5; 33 members (21.3%) scored between -0.5 and 0; 16 members (10.3%) scored between 0 and 0.5; and 21 members (13.6%) scored between 0.5 and 1. For reference, the most extreme members on the left were Alexis Caiguan and Tania Madriaga, while the most extreme on the right were Teresa Marinovic and Rocío Cantuarias. The 103rd voter (from the bottom-up) was César Valenzuela of the Socialist Party (ironically, the leader of the 10 Scatter plot showing data points distributed along the x-axis labeled "First Dimension (Left–Right)" ranging from -1.0 to 1.0. The y-axis is not labeled. Data points are primarily clustered around the center, with labels such as "Cheon," "Harbor," and "De La Maza" visible. Horizontal dashed lines mark sections labeled "Two Thirds: 103 Members," "NMPF/Un. Obs: 76 Members," and "Two Thirds: 20 Ortho/Hy sites." A vertical red dashed line is at the center of the x-axis.A horizontal dot plot displays the ideological positions of all members of Chile's 2021–2022 Constitutional Convention along a one dimensional left–right scale ranging from –1 (far left) to 1 (far right). Each dot represents one member and is colored according to their political coalition. Members are arranged vertically from the most right-leaning at the top to the most left leaning at the bottom. A dashed horizontal line crosses the plot at the position of the 103rd member from the bottom, indicating the two-thirds threshold required to approve articles in the Convention. Coalition labels and a legend are included on the right-hand side. The x-axis is labeled "First Dimension (Left–Right)" and features tick marks at –1.0, –0.5, 0.0, 0.5, and 1.0. Image Alt Text (Alternative text) 2006 student protests). The most centrists voters (closest to 0) of each sector, were Felipe Harboe and Bernardo de la Maza

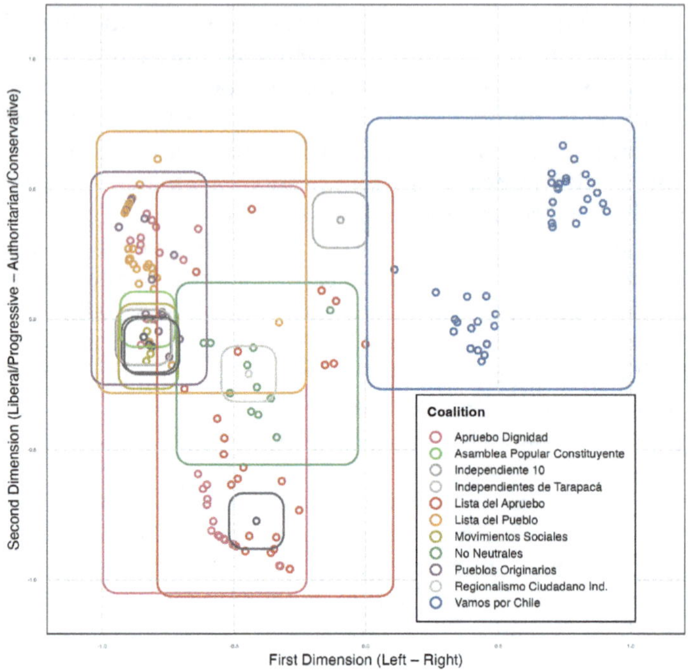

Fig. 12.2 Two-dimensional placement of Constitutional Convention members in the plenary (*Note* Each point represents a member of the 2021–2022 Constitutional Convention, positioned in a two-dimensional ideological space derived from roll-call voting patterns. The horizontal axis reflects a left–right dimension, while the vertical axis captures a liberal/progressive versus authoritarian/conservative orientation. Points are color-coded by coalition, and rectangular outlines indicate clusters of members belonging to the same coalition. *Source* Author with data from Bunker 2023a)

On the left, the figure shows a clear dominance of progressive forces, with most members clustered near the far left (−1). However, significant internal divisions also emerged within the sector. The upper-left quadrant represents the authoritarian or conservative left, composed mainly of independents, the Communist Party, and indigenous representatives. In contrast, the lower-left quadrant includes the more progressive *Frente Amplio*, Socialist Party, and former *Concertación* independents. These ideological divisions within the left often influenced internal debates, making intra-left conflicts key battlegrounds in shaping the constitutional proposal.

On the right, the two groups mentioned above emerged. While parties such as *Renovación Nacional* and *Evopoli* positioned themselves closer to the center, UDI members were more aligned with the far right, indicating that the coalition aligned with both liberal and conservative values. This internal polarization left little room for cross-party collaboration, with most members operating within their ideological silos. This dynamic illustrates not only how the numerical strength of the left and independents allowed them to neutralize and bypass their opposition, but also how this took a toll on the greater unity of the conservative sector.

Although Figures 12.1 and 12.2 illustrate ideological alignments in plenary sessions, it is equally important to examine decision-making at the commission level. Figure 12.3 focuses on the composition of the eight thematic commissions, where articles were drafted before being submitted to the plenary. The plots reveal not only the broader left-right ideological split, but also key differences in internal cohesion, polarization, and strategic alignment within and across political sectors. Readers may find use in this guide to interpret the ultimate composition of the proposal, which is presented in the next section.

Several commissions—most notably Commission 5 (Environment and Economic Model) and Commission 6 (Justice Systems, Oversight Bodies, and Constitutional Reform)—stand out for their intense polarization. In Commission 5, the left was strongly concentrated on the far left of the ideological space, while the right appeared highly cohesive, positioned in direct opposition. This produced a stark, binary structure with minimal overlap. Similarly, Commission 6 reveals a sharply divided field, though here the right appeared more fragmented. The left, by contrast, was tightly clustered, signaling coordinated efforts on institutional transformation. One independent (Rodrigo Logan) acted unpredictably, and did not really align with any side.

Another pattern emerges in commissions where the right displayed internal polarization, splitting into two relatively cohesive but ideologically distinct groups. This is visible in both Commission 1 (Political System, Government, Legislative Power, and Electoral System) and Commission 4 (Fundamental Rights). In these cases, while the right maintained group identity, its internal differences—visible especially along the vertical axis—point to divergent priorities or strategies. The left, meanwhile, was consistently located on the left of the spectrum, but showed broader dispersion. In Commission 1, this variation was especially notable among members of *Lista del Apruebo*, who ranged widely vertically. In Commission 4, this group leaned toward a social democratic, or even (relatively) centrist-right (in the case of Felipe Harboe, PPD), voting record, suggesting moderation within a generally progressive bloc.

In committees like Commission 2 (Constitutional Principles and Democracy) and Commission 3 (Form of the State and Territorial Justice), the right was again divided, particularly on the vertical (value) axis, indicating clear differences over institutional design or foundational principles between RN and the UDI. The left in both commissions remained firmly on the left, though with some internal variation. In both cases, one *Lista del Apruebo* member (Agustín Squella in Commission 2, and Eduardo Castillo en Commission 3) stood apart from the broader left cluster, signaling internal ideological differentiation even among allies.

Commission 7 (Knowledge Systems, Science and Technology, Culture, Art, and Heritage) presented a slightly different configuration. Here, there was one member of *Independientes No Neutrales* (Miguel Ángel Botto, former Christian Democrat) occupying a centrist-conservative position, while the rest of the commission was polarized. The right showed additional internal polarization, with members spread afar across the second dimension (Bernardo de la Maza, of *Evopoli*, is the member with the more liberal values in this commission). The left, by contrast, appeared relatively cohesive, maintaining a consistent orientation around cultural and educational policy.

Finally, Commission 8 (Rights of Indigenous Peoples and Plurinationality), though not a permanent commission, represented a distinct case. Its ideological layout did not conform to the typical left-right structure observed in the others. Here, members from the Indigenous groups (*Pueblos Originarios*) operated on a logic separate from conventional partisan politics, with distinct priorities and alliances. As a result, ideological positioning in this commission reflected a unique issue-based dynamic, rather than a standard ideological spectrum. It is shown here precisely to show the consistency of dimension labels in other commissions.

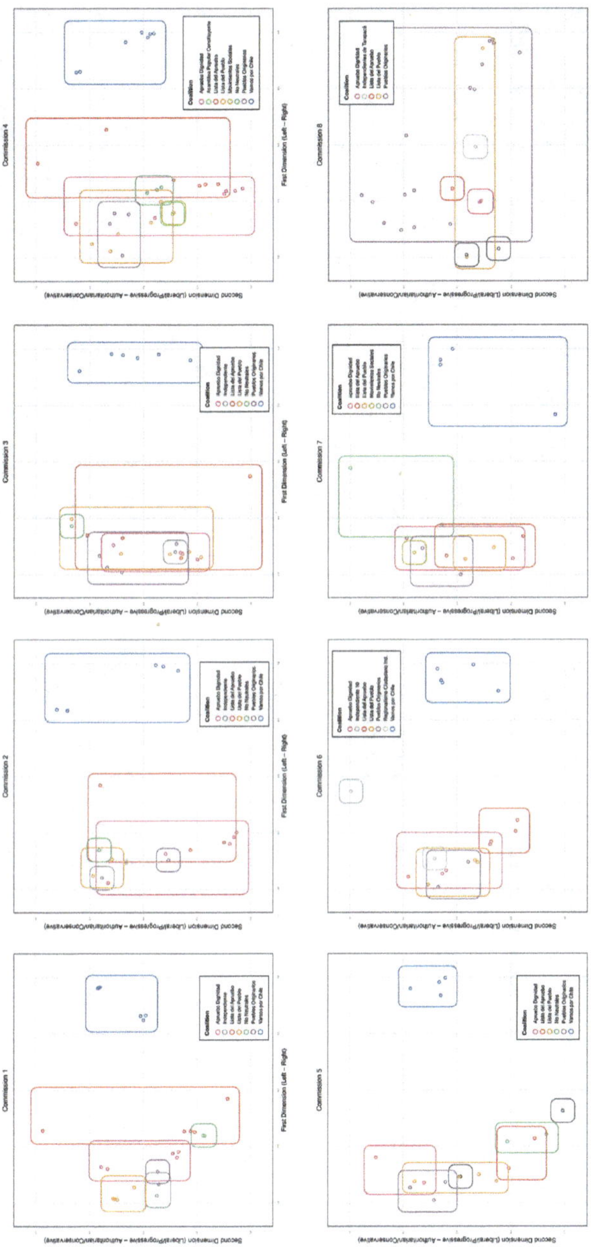

◀**Fig. 12.3** Two-dimensional placement of Constitutional Convention members in their respective commissions (*Note* Each circle represents a member of the 2021–2022 Constitutional Convention, positioned in a two-dimensional ideological space derived from roll-call voting patterns. The horizontal axis reflects a left–right dimension, while the vertical axis captures a liberal/progressive versus authoritarian/conservative orientation. Points are color-coded by coalition, and rectangular outlines indicate clusters of members belonging to the same coalition. The full names of the commissions are as follows: Commission 1 was *Sistema Político, Gobierno, Poder Legislativo y Sistema Electoral* ("Political System, Government, Legislative Power, and Electoral System"). Commission 2 was *Principios Constitucionales y Democracia* ("Constitutional Principles and Democracy"). Commission 3 was *Forma de Estado y Justicia Territorial* ("Form of the State and Territorial Justice"). Commission 4 was *Derechos Fundamentales* ("Fundamental Rights"). Commission 5 was *Medioambiente y Modelo Económico* ("Environment and Economic Model"). Commission 6 was *Sistemas de Justicia, Órganos Autónomos de Control y Reforma Constitucional* ("Justice Systems, Autonomous Oversight Bodies, and Constitutional Reform"). Commission 7 was *Sistemas de Conocimiento, Ciencia y Tecnología, Cultura, Arte y Patrimonio* ("Systems of Knowledge, Science and Technology, Culture, Art, and Heritage"). Commission 8 was *Derechos de los Pueblos Indígenas y Plurinacionalidad* ("Rights of Indigenous Peoples and Plurinationality"), which, although not a permanent commission, was nonetheless highly relevant to the constitutional process. *Source* Author with data from Bunker 2023b[12])

12 Across the commissions of the Constitutional Convention, approval rates varied significantly. In Commission 1, on the political system, 1,188 votes were cast, of which 406 passed with more than 50 percent, amounting to 34.2%. Commission 2, focused on constitutional principles, saw 1,250 votes, with 454 passing, or 36.3%. Commission 3, addressing the form of the state, had 1,032 votes, with a much higher approval rate—651 votes, or 63.1%. In Commission 4, on fundamental rights, 651 of 2,045 proposals passed, representing 31.8%. Commission 5, dealing with environmental issues, recorded 1,076 votes, of which 523 passed, or 48.6%. In Commission 6, on the justice system, 744 of 1,186 votes passed, totaling 62.7%. Commission 7, on knowledge systems, saw 419 of 739 votes pass, a rate of 56.7%. Finally, in Commission 8, which focused on Indigenous rights, 76 of 133 votes passed, resulting in an approval rate of 57.1%. [This dataset, *Roll-call votes in the Commissions of the Constitutional Convention of Chile, 2021-2022*, is available on the author's website.]

12.4.2 *An Unbalanced Combination*

All in all, voting patterns reveal a deeply polarized assembly dominated by the left and independents. Their electoral strength, combined with procedural control at both the plenary and commission levels, enabled them to consolidate power and shape the constitutional proposal with minimal opposition. The right's weak and polarized opposition lacked the votes to influence legislation with a simple majority in thematic committees or to block the progressive agenda with a one-third threshold in the plenary.

Given the left's overwhelming numerical advantage, the structural and procedural setup of the Convention, and the ideological leanings of its members, it is unsurprising that the resulting constitutional proposal reflected a strong bias toward progressive and left-leaning ideals.

12.5 The First Proposal Ssummary

The final draft of the new constitution was unveiled on July 4, 2022. Comprising 11 chapters, 383 articles, and 52,824 words, the document outlined an ambitious and sweeping redefinition of governance in Chile.[13] Its cover featured a purple background with the Chilean flag broken down into bits and pieces—visually reflecting the proposal's emphasis on plurinationalism and the fragmentation of traditional national identity.[14]

Chapter 1 (pp. 5–8), titled General Principles and Provisions, articulated the founding values of the new state. In sixteen Articles, it sought to clarify the state's role, responsibilities toward its people, and restructured the territorial framework. A striking divergence from the subsidiary model written into the 1980 Constitution was the formal recognition of Chile as a social and democratic State, as well as a pluricultural, intercultural, regional and ecological one–signifying its inclusive shift, yet left room for

[13] As a reference, the 1980 constitution had 25,299 words upon its ratification in 1980, 25,360 words upon its debut in 1990, 25,649 words after it was reformed in 2005, and 25,821 words at the time of the social outburst in 2019, the year the constitutional process began. In comparison, the 2018 Bachelet proposal had 28,119 words, the 2023 constitutional council proposal had 49,882 words, and the 2023 Experts preproposal had 40,329 words.

[14] This document, *Propuesta de Nueva Constitución (2022)*, is available on the author's website.

debate about practical implementation and national unity. Article 5, for example, mentioned that at least 11 tribes would be recognized as nations of their own, yet did not resolve what this would mean in practice.

Chapter 2 (pp. 9–45), on Fundamental Rights and Guarantees, was the lengthiest and arguably most ambitious, spanning Articles 17 to 126. It expanded the state's obligations to ensure a dignified life and environmental equilibrium, extending rights not only to people but to nature itself. The chapter introduced sweeping protections for marginalized groups, including migrants, sexual minorities, and indigenous peoples, while also mandating the dismantling of systemic barriers, such as Article 61, which explicitly recognized the unrestricted right to abortion and other sexual and reproductive rights, free from interference or limitation. The chapter further established the right of indigenous peoples to be consulted in any policy that could affect them (Art. 66), impeded deportation (Art. 71), and allowed expropriation if the price was "fair" (Art. 78). While noble in scope, the chapter's breadth also invited concern over enforceability.

Chapter 3 (pp. 45–51), titled Nature and Environment, encompassed Articles 127 to 150 and embedded environmentalism deeply into constitutional law. It granted legal rights to nature, penalized ecological harm, and advocated sustainable practices in the management of land, water, and biodiversity. Additionally, animals were recognized as sentient beings (Art. 131), a noteworthy development. A new institution, the Defense of Nature, was tasked with upholding these novel mandates (Art. 148–150). While symbolically powerful, as with the previous chapter, it raised questions about its applicability to the existing legal structure.

Chapter 4 (pp. 52–56), titled Democratic Participation and comprising Articles 151 to 164, proposed a reimagined democracy built on direct and participatory engagement. Provisions included compulsory voting for adults, referendums, and a popular initiative mechanism triggered by 3% of the electorate (Art. 157). The chapter also introduced parity mandates (Art. 161) and reserved seats for indigenous communities (Art. 162), hallmarks of the convention's inclusive ethos. It also granted migrants living in the country for five years the right to vote (Art. 160, n. 5). However, it was also evident that the absence of rigorous thresholds or safeguards in citizenship legislation could potentially complicate governance.

Chapter 5 (pp. 57–63), on Good Government and Public Function, outlined in Articles 165 to 186, set out to establish integrity and transparency at the heart of public administration. It created a Transparency

Council (Art. 169) to monitor corruption and offered protections for whistleblowers. The chapter expanded its scope to include fiscal policy and governance of public enterprises, all under the banner of sustainable development, in harmony with nature (Art. 184).

Chapter 6 (pp. 64–84), Regional State and Territorial Organization, detailed in Articles 187 to 250, introduced a framework of decentralized governance. It empowered communes, provinces, and regions with legal and financial independence. This move toward federal-like autonomy marked a stark shift from the highly centralized tradition of Chilean governance. The creation of communal assemblies (Art. 209) and regional assemblies (Art. 222), as well as autonomous indigenous territories (Art. 234–235), was especially innovative. This fragmentation of authority marked a clear breaking point from the order outlined in the 1980 constitution.

Chapter 7 (pp. 85–100), on Legislative Power, and spanning Articles 251 to 278, outlined a dramatic restructuring of Congress. The traditional Senate was abolished and replaced by a newly formed Chamber of the Regions (Art. 245–255), which notably held weaker legislative power. Most lawmaking authority was consolidated in the Congress of Deputies, resulting in a de facto unicameral system, arguably one of the most consequential departures from the past. Supporters viewed it as a way to streamline decision-making, while detractors warned it risked centralizing power and undermining checks and balances.

Chapter 8 (pp. 101–113), titled Executive Power, covered in Articles 279 to 306, reaffirmed Chile's presidential system, including the absolute majority, two-round election system. The President would be eligible to be elected as of the age of 30 (Art. 280, lowered from 35), and would be able to serve a four-year term with one immediate re-election. The chapter regulated the terms of the Secretaries of State, as well as all the powers of the president. Remarkably, it also regulated the armed forces and police, stipulating that they should operate from a gender perspective (Art. 297; Art. 299).

Chapter 9 (pp. 114–125), Systems of Justice, in Articles 307 to 349, proposed a significant break from the unitary judicial model. It recognized multiple legal systems, including those of indigenous peoples (Art. 309), to operate alongside a national judiciary. Article 311 sentenced that justice would be imposed from an intersectional perspective and Article 312 held that it would be guided by gender parity and perspective. New institutions, such as neighborhood courts (Art. 334) and a revised Supreme Court (Art. 328–329), were introduced. A Council of Justice (Art. 342–349), tasked with judicial oversight, was presented as autonomous. However, the coexistence of parallel legal systems raised apprehensions about coherence, equal access, political influence, and long-term consistency in the rule of law.

Chapter 10 (pp. 126–138), Autonomous Constitutional Bodies, spanned Articles 350 to 382 and created six independent institutions to safeguard democratic functions. These included the General Comptroller (Art. 351–356), Central Bank (Art. 357–364), Public Ministry (Art. 365–372), Public Criminal Defense Office (Art. 373–375), National Data Protection Agency (Art. 376), and Constitutional Court (Art. 377–382). Each was required to have gender-balanced leadership. While these reforms appeared to strengthen institutional independence, concerns were raised about the actual autonomy of these bodies within the broader political environment.

Chapter 11 (pp. 139–141), Constitutional Replacement and Reform, concluding the document in Articles 383 to 388, set forth avenues for future constitutional change. Whole replacement could only be done via a constituent assembly (Art. 386, n. 1), which could be initiated via popular initiative, presidential proposal, or legislative agreement. Deliberations would require a minimum of 18 months and would have to adhere to gender parity and inclusivity standards. Though the process seemed innovative, it also opened questions regarding how frequent revisions and political volatility would become.

In summary, the proposed constitution presented a sweeping and transformative vision of the Chilean state. Its emphasis on inclusion, rights, and sustainability was clear, yet its structural overhauls, including unicameralism and legal pluralism, left a mixed impression. Whether this ambitious proposal could achieve the balance between principle and practice remained the central question as the nation prepared to vote.

12.6 Vanishing Approval and a Surprise Rejection

Figure 12.4 provides a visual representation of shifts in public sentiment toward the Constitutional Convention process from February 2022 to September 2022, based on polling data. The figure illustrates the proportion of valid responses to open-ended voting intention questions,

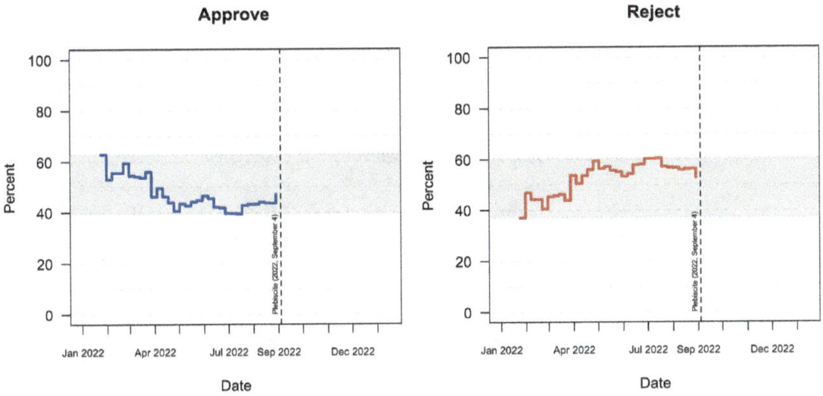

Fig. 12.4 Voting intention trends for the 2022 constitutional plebiscite (*Note* The panel on the left displays the weekly average of support for the Approve option, while the panel on the right shows the weekly average of support for the Reject option, in the lead-up to Chile's 2022 constitutional plebiscite. In both panels, the staircase line represents the average for each week based on available survey data. Percentages are calculated using only the responses for Approve and Reject, excluding undecided or other responses. The shaded gray area indicates the full range (minimum to maximum) of weekly averages observed during the period. Horizontal dotted lines mark this range, and the vertical dashed line marks the date of the plebiscite (September 4, 2022). Note that, by law, polls could not be published during the final two weeks before the vote, and this is reflected in the absence of data during that period. *Source* Author with data from Tresquintos)

distinguishing between approval and rejection of the proposed constitution. A crucial shift in public opinion became evident as rejection gained momentum in the months leading up to the referendum. Initially, support for the process remained relatively stable, reflecting optimism following the inauguration of the Convention. However, as skepticism grew, rejection began to outpace approval, signaling increasing public disillusionment.[15]

[15] Although few polls tracked voting intentions prior to 2022, it became increasingly clear that public support for the constitutional process was steadily eroding. This stood in stark contrast to the nearly 80% who had voted in favor of drafting a new constitution in the October 2020 plebiscite. By April 2022, the deterioration of the Constitutional Convention's credibility had become a topic of international concern. Analysts pointed

Table 12.1 Results of the 2022 constitutional plebiscite

Question: Do you approve the proposal drafted by the 2021–2022 constitutional convention?		
	Number of votes	*Percent of votes*
Approve (*Apruebo*)	4,859,103	38.11
Reject (*Rechazo*)	7,891,415	61.89
Valid votes	**12,750,518**	**97.86**
Null votes	**200,881**	**1.54**
Blank votes	**77,340**	**0.59**
Total	**13,028,739**	**100**

Note Voting was mandatory. Registered voters: 15,173,929. Estimated turnout: 85.86%. *Source* Author with data from Servel

On September 4, 2022, coinciding with the fifty-third anniversary of President Salvador Allende's inauguration, the referendum was held. The proposal was not just defeated—it was overwhelmingly rejected (see Table 12.1). Nearly 8 million votes were cast against it, marking the largest majority for any electoral option in Chilean history (to that point in time). The final tally—62% voting against the *Apruebo*—came from almost 12.8 million mandatory votes, making the outcome unequivocal. The shock reverberated across the political spectrum. The proposal's architects were left blindsided. They had operated under the shared assumption that constitutional change was not only necessary but inevitable. Drafted by a democratically elected body, the constitutional proposal was widely expected to pass. Instead, the result served as an unanticipated and sobering reality check.[16]

to at least three key factors behind the decline: the absence of broad-based consensus, deepening ideological polarization, and persistent issues with communication and disinformation. See: Paul, F. 2022. Convención Constituyente: 3 razones que explican la caída en el apoyo al organismo que trabaja en la nueva Constitución de Chile. *BBC Mundo*, April 8. https://www.bbc.com/mundo/noticias-america-latina-61015040.

[16] Analysts widely described the September 4 plebiscite as the most severe political and ideological defeat for the left since Chile's transition to democracy in 1990, noting the scale and breadth of the rejection across the electorate. See: Tralma, D. 2022. "Por qué el plebiscito del 4-S se transformó en la mayor derrota de la izquierda desde 1990, según los analistas." *Ex-Ante*. September 19. https://www.ex-ante.cl/por-que-el-plebiscito-del-4-s-se-transformo-en-la-mayor-derrota-de-la-izquierda-desde-1990-segun-los-analistas/

12.7 Conclusion

The Constitutional Convention of 2021–2022 represents a pivotal chapter in Chile's political history, marked by ambitious aims and profound challenges. Emerging from the demands of the 2019 social uprising, the Convention symbolized hope for a new, inclusive constitution that would address long-standing grievances. The election of Elisa Loncon—a *Mapuche* woman—as president set a transformative tone, embodying grassroots change. However, tensions between the progressive ambitions of its majority and the need to align with a moderate electorate ultimately defined the process.

From the outset, the dominance of left-leaning and independent representatives heavily influenced the Convention's internal dynamics. The majority swiftly established procedural rules that expedited the advancement of progressive proposals while sidelining moderates and conservatives. While these decisions facilitated efficient drafting, they also deepened divisions and reinforced perceptions of imbalance. The lack of meaningful engagement with dissenting voices curtailed opportunities for compromise, ultimately undermining the Convention's ability to craft a constitution with broad public appeal.

The analysis of ideological positions and coalition dynamics in this chapter reveals the complexities of consensus-building in such a context. The left's numerical dominance enabled the inclusion of ambitious provisions, such as plurinational recognition, environmental protections, and institutional reform. However, these transformative elements also likely alienated moderate and centrist voters, who perceived the draft as overly radical and disconnected from their priorities.

Public sentiment evolved as the details of the draft constitution came under scrutiny. While initial optimism surrounded the Convention's work, skepticism steadily grew in the months leading up to the September 2022 plebiscite. The overwhelming rejection of the proposal underscores the consequences of overreach and the disconnect between the Convention's ambitions and public expectations. If nothing else, this highlights the risk of neglecting the median voter in the push for change.

CHAPTER 13

Understanding Rejection: Why the First Constitutional Process Failed

13.1 Introduction

The rejection of Chile's proposed constitution in the 2022 plebiscite marked a historic change in the political trajectory of the nation. With 62% of voters rejecting the draft, the plebiscite represented the most significant electoral defeat for a single proposal in Chile's history. This outcome is particularly notable given the overwhelming mandate for reform that was expressed only two years earlier. In the September 2020 (entry) plebiscite, nearly 80% of voters supported the drafting of a new constitution, which reflected widespread optimism and the collective desire for transformative change after the social unrest in 2019. However, by 2022, public sentiment dramatically shifted, thus raising a fundamental question: why did the electorate overwhelmingly abandon a process that it initially endorsed?

A key point of the reversal was the ideological misalignment between the vision of the Constitutional Convention and the priorities of the electorate. The proposed constitution was ambitious in terms of scope, as it prioritized transformative provisions such as plurinationality, expansive social guarantees, and environmental rights. While these proposals aligned with progressive ideals, they were disconnected from the larger concerns of the electorate. In a search for practical solutions to their problems, Chileans perceived the draft as extremely radical, impractical,

K. Bunker, *Chile's Transformation Amidst Crisis*,
https://doi.org/10.1007/978-3-031-96463-3_13

and detached from their daily reality.[1] This notion decreased trust in the process, which left voters skeptical of the relevance of the draft.

However, ideological misalignment alone only partially explains the rejection of the proposal. A series of contextual challenges further alienated voters, deepening their skepticism about the feasibility and viability of the draft. Changes in leadership within the Constitutional Convention disrupted continuity and weakened symbolic resonance, while the transition to substantive deliberation in plenary sessions exposed ideological divisions and attracted heightened public scrutiny. Perceived disorganization within the assembly, which was compounded by the media's portrayal of theatrical behavior, further undermined its credibility. Increasing crime rates and economic instability added to the public's anxiety, which created a sense of insecurity and financial hardship that led to the perception that the ambitious provisions of the draft were seemingly disconnected from the immediate needs of the electorate. Finally, the association between the process and Gabriel Boric's administration—which was struggling to address escalating economic and security crises—amplified doubt among voters.

This chapter argues that a fundamental misdiagnosis influenced this outcome. Political leaders and intellectual elites interpreted the widespread social discontent of 2019 as a call for a radical structural transformation, linking demands for a better quality of life to the wholesale dismantling of the neoliberal model (readers may wish to revisit the discussion in the second part of Chapter 5). However, this narrative underestimated and overlooked the pragmatic concerns of the electorate and its preferences for stability, incremental progress, and tangible improvement in daily life. By prioritizing ambitious ideological goals instead of addressing the practical needs of the electorate, the designers of the proposal widened the gap between their vision and the expectations of the public, ultimately undermining the credibility of the proposal.

[1] The proposed 2022 constitution was widely labeled as woke in both domestic and international media, a term used to capture its strong emphasis on progressive values such as gender parity, Indigenous autonomy, environmental protections, and social rights. The label reflected not only the document's content but also the generational and ideological shift it represented. See: Bartlett, J., and S. Schmidt. 2022. "Chile Writes a Woke Constitution. Are Chileans Ready for It?" *The Washington Post.*, July 5. https://www.washingtonpost.com/world/2022/07/05/chile-constitution-draft-boric/

13.2 Ideological Misalignment: The (Forgotten) Average Voter

The primary reason for the rejection of the 2022 constitutional proposal was the mismatch between the objectives of the Constitutional Convention and the priorities of the electorate. While the 2020 plebiscite demonstrated overwhelming public support for constitutional reform—nearly 80% of voters endorsed the drafting of a new constitution—this enthusiasm did not reflect a demand for extensive structural change. Instead, it revealed a desire for practical and targeted reforms to address long-standing social challenges. However, because the proposed constitution emphasized transformative institutional changes, it failed to resonate with the electorate.

The provisions of the draft emphasized extensive reforms, such as plurinational recognition, expansive social guarantees, and transformative environmental protection. While these elements reflected progressive ideals and were supported by certain sectors, they alienated a significant portion of the electorate. The proposal seemingly did not align with the voters' immediate concerns, who expected pragmatic solutions and not a document that focused on abstract and far-reaching ideologically-oriented goals. This incongruity between the priorities of the document and the expectations of the public weakened trust in the process.

In an effort to foster a constitution perceived as visionary and morally just, members of the Constitutional Convention left the average voter behind. The members of the Convention prioritized their own political goals and extensive changes instead of aligning themselves with the practical concerns of the electorate. This scenario promoted the perception that a group of elites who were disconnected from the daily reality of ordinary Chileans was driving the process. By focusing on what *they* considered appropriate for the country, those in charge failed to adequately address the preferences of the majority, thus increasing the wide gap between the document and its intended audience.

Ultimately, the Convention's focus on drafting a document they deemed to reflect the right path forward, instead of one that aligned with public priorities, amplified the notion of ideological overreach. By overlooking the average voter and prioritizing ideological goals, the Convention lost public trust in the constitutional process. This failure to effectively engage with the electorate and address its expectations was the critical factor in the rejection of the draft during the 2022 plebiscite.

13.3 Moderating Variables

The overwhelming rejection of Chile's 2022 constitutional proposal cannot be understood without considering the moderating factors that formed public attitudes throughout the process.[2] Apart from ideological misalignment, the interaction among a range of influences (e.g., leadership transition, shift to substantive deliberation, and increased perception of disorder), contextual pressure (e.g., increasing crime rates and economic instability), and the role of the Boric administration—increased skepticism and decreased trust. Distinct from one another, each element played a complementary role in undermining the Convention's efforts and contributed to the outcome.

13.3.1 Leadership Transition and Process Shift

The transition in leadership within the Constitutional Convention and the shift from administrative to substantive deliberation were pivotal in shaping the public perception of the process. As described in Chapter 12, during its early stages, the Convention was led by figures such as Elisa Loncon and Jaime Bassa, whose style symbolized the transformative aspirations that surfaced during the social outburst in 2019. Specifically, Loncon represented diversity and inclusion, thus embodying the hope of a new beginning for Chile. This early leadership bolstered trust and optimism and linked the Convention with the societal hope for progress.

However, in February 2022, the replacement of Loncon and Bassa with María Elisa Quinteros and Gaspar Domínguez, respectively, marked a significant shift. While the new leaders were reasonably capable, they found difficulty in maintaining the same symbolic resonance with the public. This leadership transition occurred at a crucial juncture, when the Convention faced increased scrutiny and tighter deadlines, which

[2] While the main issue may have stemmed from the content of the proposal, the drafting process itself was also a significant factor. The constituent assembly was not representative of Chilean society, and instances of misconduct and misinformation further eroded public trust. Additionally, the broader context was unfavorable: inflation had reached a 28-year high, the peso was at an all-time low, violent crime was rising, and President Boric's approval rating had dropped to 38%. The overall sentiment was that everything was going wrong. See: Barry, E. 2022. Why Chileans Rejected a New, Progressive Constitution. *TIME.*, September 5. https://time.com/6210924/chile-rejects-new-constitution-referendum/

made projecting the stability and competence required to reassure voters increasingly challenging.

At the same time, the work of the Convention transitioned from procedural tasks by committees to deliberations on substantive constitutional provisions by the plenary. Early administrative efforts, such as rule-setting and committee organization, gained limited public attention. However, media coverage intensified, and public engagement significantly grew when substantive debates reached the plenary. Key issues such as indigenous autonomy, environmental protection, and institutional reform became topics for criticism, with voters paying closer attention to the contents of the proposals as they came to the forefront.

With the progress in deliberations, media narratives increasingly reported on the process as polarized and mismatched with mainstream concerns. The highly publicized plenary debates provided a clear view of the drafters' intentions, which in turn enabled the electorate to form strong opinions. As voters became more informed, they began to view the draft with greater skepticism, as polling suggests (see voting intention trends in Chapter 12). In this way, the transition in leadership, together with the start of plenary voting, boosted public viewership but also heightened suspicion.

13.3.2 Theatrics and Perception of Disorder

The unconventional behavior displayed by several assembly members contributed to the mounting perception of disorder, which became a defining characteristic of the Constitutional Convention in the mind of the public. Early on, the involvement of grassroots figures such as Giovanna Grandón (also known as "Aunt Pikachu," *Tía Pikachu*) and Cristóbal Andrade (nicknamed "The Blue Dinosaur," *El Dinosaurio Azul*) was celebrated as a testament to the inclusivity of the process. Their presence symbolized the deviation from traditional political norms and the empowerment of regular citizens in shaping Chile's future. Similarly, the visible enthusiasm of crowds that chanted and danced outside the Convention initially added to the perception of a democratic and participatory spirit.

However, as the process unfolded, these moments of unconventional behavior overshadowed the severity of the task. Prominent controversies, such as an admission by Rodrigo Rojas Vade (also known as *Pelado Vade*) of falsifying his cancer diagnosis, further damaged public trust in the assembly.[3] Beginning as a celebration of diversity and renewal, the Convention ultimately became associated with scandal and deception. Instances of members singing, chanting, and dancing within the chambers, combined with media coverage of moments such as playing guitar during deliberations, or parties while on tour, produced an image of frivolity that undermined the gravitas of the Convention.[4]

Reports of members remotely casting votes from casual or inappropriate settings, such as beach houses or the shower, added to the mounting sense that the Convention was disorganized and lacked decorum.[5] Media outlets that were eager to highlight sensationalist moments amplified these incidents, which, in turn, fueled disillusionment.

[3] Rojas Vade emerged as one of the most emblematic figures to rise from the resistance movements associated with the 2019 social outburst, securing his seat in the Constitutional Convention largely on the strength of that symbolic status. He gained notoriety for appearing at protests with a shaved head, medical equipment visibly attached to his body, and claiming to be undergoing intensive cancer treatment—projecting an image of personal sacrifice that resonated with many. However, that carefully constructed persona would soon unravel. After admitting to having fabricated his illness, he was forced to resign from the Convention. In 2023, he was sentenced to 61 days in prison and fined 850 dollars for fraud. See: Laborde, A. 2023. "Condenado por estafa Rodrigo Rojas Vade, el exconstituyente chileno que inventó padecer cáncer." *El País*. February 13. https://elpais.com/chile/2023-02-13/condenado-por-estafa-rodrigo-rojas-vade-el-exconstituyente-chileno-que-invento-padecer-cancer.html

[4] Among the earliest scandals to taint the reputation of the Constitutional Convention was a party held by a group of delegates at the *Hotel Pettra* in *Concepción* during an official tour. Although the Convention initially attempted to downplay or deny the incident, it was later confirmed by former constituent Jorge Baradit, a member of the Socialist Collective, in his book *La Constituyente*. Baradit recounted that the party involved unauthorized access to the hotel's closed pool area, and that at least one delegate—whom he identified as a fellow Socialist—admitted to having swum at night as part of the festivities. Despite early denials, Baradit's confirmation aligned with earlier investigative reporting thatcited multiple eyewitnesses and detailed the presence of alcohol, noise, and other inappropriate behavior. The *Colegio de Periodistas* (Chilean Association of Journalists), which had initially condemned the reporting as false, later issued a public apology. See: Parra Tapia, N., C. Suazo, and F. Díaz Montero. 2022. "Baradit confirma veracidad de carrete constituyente en hotel de Concepción." *BioBio Chile*. September 12. https://www.biobiochile.cl/especial/bbcl-investiga/noticias/depasillo/2025/08/03/universidad-la-republica-al-borde-de-la-quiebra-por-deuda-de-mas-de-650-millones-contrabajadores.shtml

[5] Constitutional Convention member Nicolás Núñez (FRVS) voted, while on camera, during a session of the Environmental Commission. While the assembly dismissed the incident as an insignificant gaffe, it would prove to be a more influential event in the broader course of the process. See: *El Mostrador*. 2022. Convencional Nicolás Núñez realizó votación en la Comisión de Medio Ambiente mientras se tomaba una ducha. May

For many Chileans, these theatrics reinforced the impression that the assembly lacked discipline and focus.

The cumulative effect of these behaviors, combined with heightened scrutiny from the media and the electorate, diminished public confidence in the ability of the Convention to produce a coherent and credible document. This perception of disorder was not only a distraction—it became emblematic of broad concerns about the process. The unconventional spirit that initially inspired hope was now alienating voters who expected professionalism and rigor in the crafting of a document with such national significance.

13.3.3 Contextual Pressures

The broad societal and economic contexts in which the constitutional process also influenced voter attitudes (readers may wish to skip ahead to Chapter 15 for a detailed account of the social and economic issues described in what follows). Elevated crime rate emerged as one of the most pressing concerns for Chileans by 2022. High-profile incidents, including cases of kidnapping, homicide, and organized crime, dominated headlines and fostered a pervasive sense of insecurity. Perceptions of government inaction and leniency, particularly regarding undocumented immigration, which was linked to the worsened safety crisis, further increased public anxiety. Against this background, the emphasis of the draft on social and cultural rights seemingly mismatched with the immediate priorities of citizens, such as public safety and law enforcement.

Economic instability further compounded skepticism among the public. The economic fallout of early pension withdrawals, which were initially framed as a relief measure, led to rising inflation and financial insecurity for many households.[6] By the time of the plebiscite, Chileans were faced with skyrocketing prices, declining purchasing power, and a

3. https://www.elmostrador.cl/noticias/multimedia/2022/05/03/convencionalnicolas-nunez-realizo-votacion-en-la-comision-de-medio-ambiente-mientras-se-tomaba-una-ducha/

[6] Inflation in Chile surged to 13% in 2022, marking the highest level since 1991 and fueling widespread public frustration. This sharp rise in the cost of living, partly driven by early pension withdrawals and broader global pressures, significantly eroded household purchasing power and deepened skepticism toward the government's economic management, and by extension to the policy of the constitutional process it was endorsing. See: Ramos Miranda, N. 2023. "Crime, Inflation Hammer Support for Chile's Boric in

pervasive sense of economic uncertainty. The ambitious promises of the draft, such as expansive social guarantees and environmental protection, failed to fit in with the harsh reality of the day-to-day. For many, the draft appeared to prioritize long-term ideological goals more than the daily struggles of citizens.

In the same vein, the memory of the 2019 social outburst also played a crucial role in the formation of public perceptions. While the protests initially inspired hope for transformative change, their aftermath—marked by violence, destruction, and prolonged unrest—tarnished their legacy.[7] Scenes of burned churches, looted businesses, and violent clashes were converted into enduring images that overshadowed the aspirations that fueled the movement. Leaders associated with the protests were increasingly considered enablers of chaos instead of agents of constructive reform. This fractured memory cast a shadow over the constitutional process, which made viewing the draft as a solution to the challenges in the country difficult for voters.

13.3.4 Role of the Boric Administration

Finally, the Boric administration also played a significant and, ultimately, compounding role in the constitutional process. As a vocal supporter of reform and a key political ally of the Convention, Boric's government initially intended to position itself as a champion of transformative change. This alignment bound the success of the constitutional process to the broad agenda of the administration, thus posing opportunities and risks.

However, as the Boric administration faced mounting criticism for its failure to address urgent issues, such as inflation, crime, and immigration, it became a liability. The failure of the government to manage immediate

Tough First Year." *Reuters*. January 23. https://www.reuters.com/world/americas/crimeinflation-hammer-support-chiles-boric-tough-first-year-2023-0123/

[7] Public anxiety over worsening crime significantly shaped perceptions in the wake of the 2019 protests. Although Chile has historically had lower crime rates than its regional neighbors, the years following the social unrest saw sharp increases in violent offenses, including kidnappings and gun-related homicides. The government acknowledged rising insecurity but struggled to convey effective control, deepening public unease and contributing to declining support for the administration. See: Ramos Miranda, N. 2023. "A punto de cumplir tumultuoso primer año, crimen e inflación golpean respaldo a Boric en Chile." *Euronews/Reuters*. January 23. https://es.euronews.com/2023/01/23/politica-chile-boric

concerns undermined public confidence not only in its leadership but also in the constitutional draft. Additionally, the administration encountered difficulty in exerting a stabilizing influence on the Convention. Because the government appeared to mirror the shortcomings of the Convention it ended up reinforcing doubt about the process's credibility instead of projecting competence and order.[8] By the time of the plebiscite, public frustration with the Boric administration was transmitted into perceptions of the constitutional draft. For many Chileans, voting against the proposal became a means for expressing dissatisfaction with the performance of the government. Although Chapter 15 explores Boric's role in detail, it should already be obvious that the struggles of his administration amplified the challenges faced by the Convention and, in its own way, contributed to the rejection of the draft.

13.4 The Misdiagnosis

The mismatch between the constitutional proposal and the electorate stemmed from a fundamental misdiagnosis of the ideals of Chileans in terms of constitutional reform. For many years, intellectuals, activists, and political leaders deemed that the widespread social discontent, which culminated in the protests of 2019, was a clear demand for radical change (as described in Sect.5.3). They interpreted the dissatisfaction as a collective call for extensive reforms to undo the Pinochet legacy, rather than an honest demand for a better quality of life regardless of the origin or characteristics of the constitution at hand.

The roots of the misdiagnosis can be traced back to the 1980s when the Pinochet-era constitution was criticized as an authoritarian artifact incompatible with democracy (see the discussion in Chapter 2). Critics argued that its neoliberal underpinnings were designed to perpetuate inequality and limit state intervention in addressing social grievances. This

[8] Even after the defeat in the 2022 plebiscite and amid mounting political difficulties, President Boric remained notably disconnected. In his 2023 address to Congress, he delivered a message filled with optimism and rhetorical appeals, portraying Chile as a country steadily moving forward. This narrative stood in sharp contrast to widespread concerns over inflation, crime, and governance, further reinforcing the perception of a government out of touch with everyday realities. See: Soto, M. 2023. "Kenneth Bunker y discurso del Presidente: 'El optimismo de Boric contrasta con un país que está en crisis.'" *Ex-Ante*. June 1. https://www.ex-ante.cl/kenneth-bunker-y-discurso-del-presidente-el-optimismo-de-boric-contrasta-con-un-pais-que-estaen-crisis/

critique emerged even before the results of the system could undergo a fair evaluation. Inequality and social stratification were framed as inevitable products of the Constitution's design, even when the document had not yet been put to the test.

As Chile experienced sustained economic growth, reduction in poverty, and substantial social mobility (as described in the early parts of Chapter 5), the critiques did not dominate public discourse. Instead, they only rose circa 2010, when dissatisfaction with political representation began to increase, and the emergence of rupturist discourses prompted a reevaluation of the Constitution's legacy. Emboldened by their willingness to embrace radical change to ascend to power, the younger generation of political actors (first introduced in Chapter 8) purported the view that the Constitution was not only outdated but was also the primary obstacle to justice and equality. They framed constitutional replacement and the eradication of neoliberalism as inseparable goals, thus reinforcing the notion that restructuring the old order was the only way forward.

The 2019 social outburst further solidified this narrative, elevating it to the status of conventional wisdom among left-leaning intellectual and political elites in Chile. The protests were (erroneous and misleadingly) interpreted as an extensive rejection of the neoliberal model and an urgent demand for structural transformation. This interpretation was widely embraced, however, sidelining alternative explanations that emphasized the pragmatic concerns of the electorate. In essence, the protests were used to validate a preexisting critique of the 1980 Constitution and frame the constitutional process as an inevitable and singular solution to existing challenges.

If the diagnosis would have been accurate, then the democratic origins of the proposed constitution alone should have ensured its approval. If the legitimacy of the origin argument would have held any weight, then voters would have supported the proposal simply because it had been drafted in democracy. Similarly, if neoliberalism would have *truly* been the concern, then voters would have overwhelmingly supported the proposal, even if it featured flaws or seemed impractical. However, none of this occurred. The rejection of the draft exposed the limits of these assumptions and revealed that the priorities of the electorate were more nuanced than those implied by the dominant narrative.[9]

The fact that this misdiagnosis became self-reinforcing after the social outburst compounded the problem. The public was *informed* that the constitutional process was not *a solution* but *the solution*. The political and intellectual establishment also amplified this narrative, neutralizing critics and deplatforming dissenting voices. Trusting in the promise of reform, many citizens supported the process as best as they could. However, as the draft materialized, its ambitious scope and ideological framing clashed with their pragmatic expectations. In the end, the proposal demanded tradeoffs that voters were ultimately unwilling to make.

Of course, the rejection of the proposal cannot be solely attributed to the misdiagnosis. External factors, which were difficult to forecast, including the political missteps, legislative ambition, and the broader social and economic context mentioned earlier in this chapter, played significant roles in the formation of public attitudes. But it is also true that it is almost impossible to imagine the whole ordeal would have gone so far if the initial diagnosis had been made with greater fairness or at least based on performance rather than origin.

13.5 Conclusion

The rejection of the proposed constitution in the 2022 plebiscite was a defining moment in Chile's political trajectory and leaves behind profound lessons on the challenges of pursuing meaningful constitutional reform. Despite the strong calls for change after the 2019 social outburst and the overwhelming support for the drafting of a new constitution in the 2020 plebiscite, the final proposal failed to bridge the gap between transformative ambition and societal expectation.

This chapter highlighted that the rejection was rooted in a combination of ideological overreach and contextual misstep. The Convention

[9] One of the most recognized intellectuals of the left, Fernando Atria, who was also a member of the 2021–2022 Constitutional Convention, would later dismiss any responsibility in the failure of the proposal. See: Martínez, R. 2022. "Exconvencional Atria por derrota del *Apruebo*: "No creo haber sido el artífice"." *La Tercera*. September 5. https://www.latercera.com/politica/noticia/exconvencional-atria-por-derrota-del-apruebo-no-creo-haber-sido-el-artifice/7R4SVKCTKJFM5LLIN6EHEPQX6A/

members envisioned a constitution that would restructure the neoliberal framework and replace it with a model that would emphasize justice, inclusion, and sustainability. However, this sweeping vision clashed with the priorities of a public that valued stability and incremental progress more than they did radical transformation. For many, the perceived detachment of the draft constitution from their lived reality, especially its focus on plurinationality, environmental rights, and expansive social guarantees, eroded trust and reinforced skepticism.

Contextual challenges, including economic instability, elevated crime rate, and an environment of institutional distrust, compounded this ideological misalignment. The public's experience of worsening daily conditions under the new Boric administration directly undermined the lofty promises of reform. Changes in leadership, the portrayal of the media of disorganization within the Constitutional Convention, and the association of the process with a fumbling, clumsy government further alienated voters, who eventually viewed the draft as part of a broader ideological project that failed to address their immediate concerns.

Ultimately, the chapter suggests that, at the very least, the rejection of the 2022 constitutional proposal can be interpreted as a backlash against a misdiagnosis. While Chileans might have desired change, they were not seeking a complete constitutional overhaul—certainly not at any cost. This stark finding serves as a cautionary lesson for any nation that is contemplating major overhauls based on principle and not performance.

CHAPTER 14

Constitutional Resurrection

14.1 Introduction

The rejection of Chile's 2022 constitutional proposal was a defining moment in the nation's political trajectory, which left the Boric administration and its allies at a crossroads. With 62% of voters rejecting the draft, this overwhelming defeat underscored a profound mismatch between the transformative ambitions of the Constitutional Convention and the pragmatic priorities of the electorate. For the government, this setback necessitated a rapid reassessment of its approach. The question, however, was not *whether* to proceed with constitutional reform, but *how* to do so under circumstances that now required compromise, humility, and strategic recalibration.

The rejection forced the Boric administration to go into damage control mode, as it sought to address the fallout and salvage the reform process. The official diagnosis of the draft's failure pointed to its ideological overreach and lack of resonance with median voters (generally in line with the ideas presented here in Chapter 13). However, the administration maintained that entirely abandoning the process was not an option. Two imperatives underlay this decision: the enduring democratic mandate expressed in the 2020 plebiscite (in which nearly 80% of voters supported the drafting of a new constitution) and the political cost of appearing to endorse the 1980 Constitution by default. For the left, continuing the

K. Bunker, *Chile's Transformation Amidst Crisis*,
https://doi.org/10.1007/978-3-031-96463-3_14

constitutional process was essential to retaining credibility at its core, even if it would require relinquishing control of the terms.

Meanwhile, the right entered negotiations with a renewed sense of purpose. While conservatives initially supported constitutional reform as a response to the social outburst of 2019, the weakened position of the left after the rejection opened an opportunity for them to now assert influence. This shift was evident in the structural and procedural changes negotiated for the second process, including the exclusion of independent candidates, a smaller and more disciplined Constitutional Council, and the establishment of expert committees to guide the drafting process. These measures reflected a deliberate effort to disassociate the second attempt from the perceived chaos of the first.

Ultimately, the decision to pursue a second constitutional process was an issue of pragmatism as well as principle. This chapter examines the political dynamics, strategic compromises, and structural adjustments that defined Chile's renewed constitutional journey. Additionally, it looks at the results of the 2023 Constitutional Council election, in which an emboldened right cemented its dominance, and analyzes the political realignment and its implications for the ongoing efforts of the country to reach a balance between constitutional transformation and public expectations.

14.2 Back to the Drawing Board

Without a doubt, the rejection of the 2022 proposal delivered a profound impact to the Boric administration, forcing the government into a defensive position of damage control. Despite the magnitude of the rejection, the administration clearly stated that abandoning the constitutional process was not an option. The official diagnosis attributed the failure of the proposal to its excessive bias and lack of connection with median voters. However, a conviction persisted that a new constitution was both necessary and achievable. This belief quickly coalesced into a decision: a second constitutional process would be held.[1]

[1] Just one day after the defeat, President Boric announced a second constitutional process. See: Rivas Molina, F., and R. Montes. 2022. "Gabriel Boric prepara un nuevo proceso constituyente para Chile." *El País*. September 5. https://elpais.com/chile/2022-09-05/gabriel-boric-prepara-un-nuevo-proceso-constituyente-para-chile.html/

The administration justified this move by referring to the 2020 plebiscite, during which an overwhelming majority of Chileans voted in favor of the drafting of a new constitution. For them, the result represented an enduring mandate from the public that had to be honored. They contended that ending the process would not only betray the democratic mandate but also risk being interpreted as a tacit acceptance of the 1980 Constitution, which at this point in time would have been politically untenable for the left. The administration was very aware that its core base of support—the voters that pushed the hardest for constitutional reform—would consider the cessation of efforts as an unforgivable abandonment of their cause.

Another equally pressing issue for the administration was the need to move forward swiftly. Prolonging the fallout from the plebiscite would have only increased public scrutiny of the government's role in the failed campaign. The overt involvement of the administration in advocating the *Apruebo* option had drawn formal warnings from the National Comptroller, Jorge Bermúdez, which underscored the perception that the government bore a significant responsibility for the debacle.[2] To avoid worsening its political liabilities, the administration intended to reframe the narrative, pivoting decisively toward a new institutional process while still signaling its ongoing commitment to reform.

The dynamics were more complex for the right. In contrast to the left, the conservative sector never really viewed the 1980 Constitution as a problem.[3] However, after initially supporting the move toward constitutional reform—mainly in response to the social upheaval of 2019—the right could not afford to reverse course entirely. After all, the Piñera administration initiated the constitutional process, such that outright

[2] The Comptroller's warning was widely interpreted as a formal rebuke of the executive's campaigning role—deepening the perception of political overreach. See: Durán, V. H. 2022. "Intervencionismo electoral: El mensaje del contralor Bermúdez que encendió todas las alarmas en La Moneda." *Ex-Ante*. July 27. https://www.ex-ante.cl/intervencion-electoral-el-mensaje-de-bermudez-que-encendio-todas-las-alarmas-en-la-moneda/

[3] An exception to this general posture was *Evópoli*, the newest permanent party to join the coalition. Unlike most of the right, it was openly critical of the Pinochet regime and more willing to question the legacy of the 1980 Constitution—a stance that only more recently began to surface within the broader conservative sector.

rejecting its continuation would have been politically inconsistent.[4] Moreover, many within the conservative bloc identified an opportunity in the rejection of the first proposal. With the left weakened by its failure, the conservatives believed they could exert greater influence over the second process and ultimately shape the outcome in their favor.

Nonetheless, internal divisions emerged within conservative ranks. While mainstream factions of the right determined a strategic value in continuing the constitutional process, a few hardliners viewed it as unnecessary and illegitimate. These dissenters argued that the initial mandate for constitutional change, derived from the first plebiscite, effectively expired with the rejection of the proposal. Without a new plebiscite to reaffirm public support for a new constitution draft, they contended that the process lacked legitimacy. Although these objections did not derail the conservative consensus, they underscored the contentious nature of the decision to proceed.

Ultimately, this impasse was resolved through informal negotiations between the government (led by the *Frente Amplio*, the Communist Party, and the Socialist Party) and the traditional right (represented by *Unión Demócrata Independiente*, *Renovación Nacional*, and *Evopoli*). The two sides agreed that launching a new constitutional process was the best path forward, although the terms of this agreement reflected the diminished leverage of the left. In a weaker position, it was forced to accept significant concessions demanded by the right, which marked the tone for a dramatically different constitutional effort.

[4] While the traditional right initially signed the foundational agreements and actively participated in designing the first constitutional process, it quickly turned to campaigning for *Rechazo* once the Constitutional Convention began to drift away from a moderate consensus. However, knowing that asking the electoral to return to the 1980 Constitution would be politically unviable (at that point in time), right-wing leaders strategically framed rejection not as the end of constitutional change, but as a way to restart the process under more institutionally grounded and politically balanced terms. This approach offered moderates a justification to oppose the draft without abandoning the broader goal of reform. As Javier Macaya, president of the UDI, put it shortly before the plebiscite: "The Chilean right has a commitment to the continuity of the constitutional process." See: Montes, R. 2022. "Javier Macaya: "La derecha chilena tiene un compromiso con la continuidad del proceso constituyente"." *El País*. September 2. https://elpais.com/chile/2022-09-02/javier-macaya-la-derecha-chilena-tiene-un-compromiso-con-la-continuidad-del-proceso-constituyente.html/

14.3 New Rules

After an informal agreement to undergo a new constitutional process was reached, the focus shifted to the negotiation of the rules of the game. As discussed in Chapter 10, the election and assembly rules for the first Constitutional Convention were devised under the pressure of crisis and were heavily influenced by the left, which had the upper hand in driving popular demand. At this point in time, however, the right controlled the terms of the debate, leveraging the momentum gained after the overwhelming rejection of the previous proposal. This reversal was immediately evident in the manner in which electoral and legislative rules were redefined.

In negotiations, a straightforward diagnosis emerged: the major issue in the previous convention was the presence of too many unpredictable, independent members.[5] The idea was that these members lacked discipline and acted impulsively, erratically aligning with the dominant left, a chaos that upended the entire process. As such, the right proposed to bar independents from running for election. Instead, only candidates from established political parties would be allowed to participate. The reasons were clear—traditional parties, rooted in society, possessed structured organizations and were able to produce predictable legislators (at least in theory, an idea that is qualified in Chapter 7). The hope (at least) was that this would make the legislative process more efficient. Unable to defend the role of independents after witnessing the failure of the first process, the left accepted the condition without much resistance.

Another major flaw diagnosed at the time was the sheer size of the previous convention. The original body consisted of 138 regular members and 17 reserved seats for indigenous groups, for a total of 155 members. With proportional representation and high district magnitudes ranging from three to eight, the arrangement promoted excessive fragmentation. Many members were elected with small vote percentages, which diminished their legitimacy and enabled erratic behavior. To address the concern, the right demanded a drastic reduction in the size of the council.

[5] One view put forth was that the first convention failed because it was made by amateurs who didn't understand the political code, reinforcing the idea that independents had undermined the process. See: Rivas, C. 2023. "Kenneth Bunker: En el primer proceso se pecó en hacer una Constitución por amateurs que no entendían el código político." *Diario Financiero*. February 10. https://www.df.cl/df-constitucional/kenneth-bunker-en-el-primer-proceso-se-peco-en-hacer-una-constitucion/

The total number of members was set to 50 elected representatives and one reserved indigenous seat. District magnitudes were also decreased to a lower, more moderate range of two to five. This shift was intended to ensure that the elected members represented a large share of their constituencies. Once again, the left agreed to the changes due to its diminished leverage.

To disassociate the new process from the chaotic image of the first convention, its name was changed from "Constitutional Convention" to "Constitutional Council." This rebranding was more than symbolic—it reflected the desire for a more structured and traditional approach.[6] To ensure the integrity of the process, a three-tiered system was established. First, a Technical Committee was established to oversee the process and act as a safeguard. Composed of experts nominated by Congress, this body was tasked to ensure adherence to constitutional norms and the agreed framework in all proceedings. Second, an Experts Committee, also appointed by Congress, was introduced to draft an initial proposal. Consisting of 24 members, this group would create a foundational draft based on extensive legal and constitutional research. Finally, the Constitutional Council itself would review, amend, and finalize the proposal within the guidelines set by the Technical Committee.

A further point of negotiation was the voting threshold for approving constitutional articles. During the first process, the two-thirds quorum proved to be a double-edged sword, as it fostered broad consensus but also enabled blockage (though this never materialized, as the results of

[6] Generally speaking, many of the terms and concepts associated with the first constitutional process were symbolically and politically charged. For instance, the nature and naming of the first convention sparked significant debate. The political left had long favored the term asamblea constituyente, which aligned with a tradition of rupture from institutional politics and emphasized constituent power "from below." Notably, this was also the name of the political movement founded by Giorgio Jackson, which debuted in the 2013 elections with the campaign *Marca tu voto/Marca AC* (see Chapter 8). The final compromise led to the term *Convención Constitucional*, blending left and right preferences. In contrast, the second process—controlled from the outset by the political right—adopted the name *Consejo Constitucional*, signaling a more measured and institutional approach. This rebranding extended to the design of the plebiscite itself: whereas the first offered the options *Apruebo* and *Rechazo* (echoing the binary choices of the 1989 plebiscite), the second used *A Favor* and *En Contra*—a deliberate attempt to avoid the historically loaded *Sí/No* framework seen in the 1978, 1980, and 1988 referendums, and to align more closely with the terminology used in the National Congress when voting to approve or reject laws.

the election were so lopsided). This time, the quorum was lowered to three-fifths. The left championed this adjustment in the hopes that it would grant them sufficient room to influence the decisions of the council despite its diminished strength.

Finally, with these agreements in place, an official timeline was established. Congress was tasked with appointing members to the Technical and Experts Committees, who would begin their work on March 6, 2023. Elections for the Constitutional Council were scheduled for May 2023 (initially discussed for April), with the inaugural session of the council set for June (postponed from May). The council was given three months to refine the draft provided by the Experts Committee and deliver a final proposal by October 2023. A national referendum would then be held in December (initially planned for November), giving Chileans a second opportunity to approve or reject a proposed new constitution.

All of the elements described above—the institutional design, procedural safeguards, composition of the various committees, voting thresholds, and timeline—were consolidated into a formal political agreement known as the *Acuerdo por Chile* (lit. "Agreement for Chile"). Signed on December 12, 2022, by most of the parties represented in the National Congress—including both government and opposition sectors—the agreement established the legal and political foundation for the second constitutional process. It laid out not only the structure and responsibilities of the Experts Committee, Technical Admissibility Committee, and Constitutional Council, but also codified the twelve guiding principles that would serve as non-negotiable boundaries for the drafting of the new constitution. Unlike the 2019 *Acuerdo por la Paz Social y la Nueva Constitución*, which was negotiated under pressure during mass protests, *Acuerdo por Chile* was shaped from a position of political stability and right-wing ascendancy, marking a shift from reactive reform to controlled institutional engineering.

14.4 The 2023 Constitutional Council Election

The results of the 2023 Constitutional Council election signaled a significant and unexpected victory for right-wing parties, particularly the Republican Party and *Chile Vamos* (UDI, RN, and *Evopoli*, now called

Chile Seguro).[7] Together, they secured more than 56% of the total votes, which translated into 34 out of 50 regular election seats available on the Council. The landslide performance was unexpected given the subsequent political climate of the social unrest in 2019 and the constitutional process that followed. In prior electoral cycles, left-wing and center-left parties consistently gained ground, leveraging public demand for reform. However, the results of the 2023 election indicated a dramatic and unanticipated shift in voter sentiment.

Several factors likely contributed to this outcome, beginning with the increased disillusionment with the direction of the previous constitutional process (discussed in Chapter 13). Many voters perceived the 2021–2022 Convention as excessively radical and disconnected from the concerns of the population. The rejection of its resultant constitutional proposal denoted not only dissatisfaction with its content but also mistrust of the left-leaning forces that dominated its creation.

Additionally, right-wing parties skillfully capitalized on increased public anxiety about stability, security, and economic challenges (described in Chapter 15). By presenting themselves as the more competent alternative to address these pressing issues, the Republican Party and *Chile Seguro* resonated with a large proportion of the electorate. Their message emphasized pragmatism and stability, which came in sharp contrast to the idealism and perceived impracticality imbued by the left's earlier proposals. As such, the election reflected a significant realignment in Chilean politics, as voters gravitated toward conservative and stability-based solutions in response to the turbulence of recent years.

The magnitude of the right's victory also underscored the failure of the left to retain its influence. Representing the progressive and center-left bloc, *Unidad para Chile* (an umbrella coalition for Apruebo Dignidad plus the Socialist Party and the PL) managed to secure only 32% of the votes or 16 seats, which was far less than expected. *Todo por Chile* (composed of the remaining parties of the *Concertación*, DC, PPD, and

[7] Remarkably, the Republican Party was one of only two parties with legislative representation that did not sign the *Acuerdo por Chile* agreement (the other being the *Partido de la Gente*). Ironically, this mirrored the outcome of the first process, in which the Communist Party had not signed the *Acuerdo por la Paz Social y Nueva Constitución* but went on to play a dominant role in the constitutional process that followed.

PR) and *Partido de la Gente*, in turn, failed to secure any representation whatsoever, thus highlighting their inability to adapt to the shifting political landscape.

The election results presented in Table 14.1 illustrate the scale of the political shift. The Republican Party emerged as the single largest party, securing 23 seats with more than 35% of the vote. The coalition of more traditional conservative forces, *Chile Seguro*, followed with 11 seats. Taken together, these blocs formed a powerful majority, which effectively sidelined left-wing and centrist coalitions. Despite its relatively strong presence, *Unidad para Chile* (traditional center-left) was left in a position of limited influence and unable to counterbalance the consolidated right. Its association with an increasingly unpopular government, as well as its previous effort to overhaul the sitting constitution, clearly did not benefit them.

Table 14.1 Results of the 2023 Constitutional Council election

Coalition/party	*Votes*		*Seats*	
	Number	*Percentage*	*Number*	*Percentage*
Partido Republicano	3,476,333	35.43	23	46
Unidad para Chile	2,806,330	28.60	16	32
Chile Seguro	2,066,681	21.06	11	22
Todo por Chile	877,824	8.95	0	0
Partido de la Gente	537,424	5.48	0	0
Independents	48,620	0.50	0	0
Valid votes	**9,813,212**	**78.46**		
Null votes	**2,124,906**	**16.99**		
Blank votes	**568,555**	**4.55**		
Total	**12,506,673**	**100**	**50**	**100**

Note One member was elected in a parallel reserved seat election, in which only two candidates competed (a total of 306,823 votes were validly cast, out of which the elected member received 160,870 votes). Voting was mandatory. Regular election registered voters: 15,150,572. Estimated regular election turnout: 84.87%. Reserved seats registered voters: 1.318.212. Estimated reserved seat election turnout: 21.83%. *Source* Author with data from Servel

14.5 The Aftermath

The 2023 Constitutional Council election marked a pivotal moment in Chilean politics, not only determining the immediate balance of power in the constitutional process but also revealing deeper shifts within the country's party system.

For the right, the election results represented a clear vindication of their strategy to present themselves as defenders of pragmatism, stability, and public security. The Republican Party emerged as the largest single political force, capitalizing on widespread dissatisfaction with the left's handling of the previous constitutional process. Alongside them, *Chile Seguro*, representing the more traditional and institutional right, played a critical role in consolidating support among centrist and moderate conservative voters. Their emphasis on experience, discipline, and technocratic governance contrasted with the Republican Party's sharper tone but complemented it strategically. In contrast, the left, now unified under *Unidad para Chile*, suffered a major defeat. With just 32% of the vote and only 16 seats, the progressive bloc was left in a weakened and defensive posture, unable to meaningfully counterbalance the momentum of the right.

More consequential than the immediate result, perhaps, was the broader political realignment that the election triggered. The three main blocs (each in turn composed of several parties) that succeeded in this election would go on to shape the political landscape. On the right, the division between the new Republican Party and the traditional *Chile Vamos* coalition became entrenched, forming two distinct but electorally compatible wings of the conservative field. Meanwhile, on the left, the outcome marked the complete collapse of the once-dominant *Concertación* coalition. *Apruebo Dignidad*, which had previously operated on the fringes of the institutional left, emerged as its new core. The Socialist Party, once a pillar of the social democratic center-left, aligned itself with both the *Frente Amplio* and the Communist Party, leaving its former allies without any meaningful hope. The realignment became fully visible in the subsequent electoral cycle, in which the left's presidential candidate and the bulk of its legislative slate came from the newer progressive camp (see Figures in the Appendix).

For the Boric administration, in turn, the results of the election represented both good and bad news. On the one hand, the administration had lost the battle but won the war: while it had ceded control of the process, its broader political sector had effectively taken over what remained of the *Concertación*. This marked the consolidation of *Apruebo Dignidad* as the dominant force on the left, absorbing key figures and parties from the old center-left coalition and redefining the progressive camp's institutional base. On the other hand, this was achieved on unfavorable terms, with diminished political power and limited room to maneuver within a process now firmly steered by a right-leaning majority. The government was soon to face the difficult task of navigating a political landscape that had shifted abruptly to opposition control, while still attempting to preserve the reformist vision that had originally motivated the constitutional effort, all in the context of mounting social and economic decline (a situation serious enough to merit a closer look in the next chapter).

14.6 Conclusion

This chapter examined the aftermath of the rejection of the 2022 constitutional proposal with a focus on the recalibration of the reform process, ensuing political negotiations, and outcomes of the 2023 Constitutional Council election. The primary objective was to analyze the responses of the government and main political actors to the overwhelming defeat, how the lessons from the first convention informed the redesign of the second process, and how these adjustments reshaped the political landscape. By addressing these dynamics, the chapter elucidated the interplay among institutional design, public sentiment, and political strategy in significant efforts toward reform.

A notable outcome of the recalibration was a deliberate rewriting of the rules for the second constitutional process to address the shortcomings of the first one. Structural changes, such as the exclusion of independents, reduction in assembly size, and introduction of expert committees, were intended to enhance discipline and predictability in the drafting process. These measures were viewed as a direct response to the perceived chaos and ideological overreach associated with the earlier effort. They also reflected a rebalancing of power in favor of traditional political actors, particularly on the right, and signaled a significant shift in the governance approach to the reform.

The results of the 2023 Constitutional Council election further underscored this shift, with right-wing parties achieving a decisive victory. The new procedural framework and widespread public dissatisfaction with the first convention enabled their success. The Republican Party and

Chile Seguro effectively positioned themselves as advocates of stability and pragmatism, in contrast to the perceived excesses of their counterparts. Together with the relative success of *Unidad para Chile*, these developments marked a broader realignment of the party system, reshaping the balance of power across Chile's political landscape.

In sum, Chile's second constitutional attempt underscores the critical role of strategic institutional design in mitigating the risks of political ambition. The revised rules were intended to ensure that the elected representatives would be more aligned with public priorities and less prone to ideological excess, and that was, at least initially, the outcome reflected in the election. This alone provides a compelling case study of the effects of designing electoral systems in unstable contexts. Yet, as the broader process revealed, institutional design alone does not guarantee success.

CHAPTER 15

From Instability to Realignment

15.1 Introduction

The failure of Chile's first constitutional process and the subsequent ascent of the right in the second were deeply influenced by the political and social environment in which they unfolded. While previous chapters explore some elements of this context, the deeper origins of the instability—and their consequences—require further examination. This chapter looks at how political ambition, governance failures, and a growing disconnect between leadership and public priorities shaped the period surrounding Chile's constitutional process.

It begins by revisiting the period immediately following the social outburst in Sebastián Piñera's second administration, when political disruption was embraced as a strategy rather than a risk. It argues that in an effort to position itself as a force of transformation, Piñera's opposition contributed to an atmosphere of institutional erosion and economic unpredictability that would later constrain its own capacity to govern. Once in power, the Boric administration inherited the instability that it helped bring about. And rather than containing the crisis, it ignored or exacerbated it through a series of miscalculations or ideologically driven decisions that ended up widening the gap between the government and public priorities.

This not only had severe consequences on both the first and second constitutional processes, but also on the greater trajectory of Chile's

K. Bunker, *Chile's Transformation Amidst Crisis*,
https://doi.org/10.1007/978-3-031-96463-3_15

society, economy, and political system. This chapter captures the critical moment in which a country already in crisis was led deeper into uncertainty. While some of these trends are explicitly referenced in Chapters 13 and 17, the context and analysis of the inter-constitutional period are well worth examining in their own light.

15.2 The Left as Opposed to Piñera

During Sebastián Piñera's second term (2018–2022), the political left—then in opposition—played a central role in shaping one of the most unstable periods in recent Chilean history. While the country faced genuine shocks, such as social unrest and the COVID-19 pandemic, opposition forces actively worked to amplify crisis conditions, not just to criticize the government, but to delegitimize it entirely and position themselves as the harbingers of transformative change (see Chapter 9). Rather than seeking national unity or institutional resilience, the left's strategy centered on destabilizing the existing order, regardless of the long-term consequences.[1]

An institutional expression of this approach was the weaponization of institutional mechanisms such as impeachment and interpellation. Historically used sparingly and reserved for serious misconduct, these tools became routine instruments of political theater under opposition control. As shown in Figure 15.1, the frequency of impeachment attempts and interpellations during this period surpassed that of any administration since Chile's return to democracy.[2] Piñera himself was impeached

[1] The reader may recall the earlier discussion (in Chapters 8 and 9) on how symbolic acts and emotionally charged rhetoric became central tools of the protest movement. These tactics were not merely expressions of dissent but were strategically deployed to delegitimize institutions and justify radical shifts in the political order. One example is the slogan "*Nos están matando*" ("They are killing us"), which framed state violence in existential terms, heightening moral urgency. As these symbols and practices circulated widely, they contributed to the construction of a discursive framework in which the state was portrayed as inherently oppressive—making moderate reform appear insufficient or even complicit.

[2] Among those impeached during Sebastián Piñera's second administration (2018–2022) were former Minister of the Interior Andrés Chadwick, who was found guilty in 2019 and barred from holding public office for five years; Minister of Health Emilio Santelices (2018) and President Sebastián Piñera himself (2019 and 2021), whose cases were dismissed on procedural grounds or not admitted; as well as Minister of Education Marcela Cubillos (2019), Minister of the Interior Víctor Pérez (2020), Minister of

twice. Though none of these efforts succeeded in removing him from office, they effectively paralyzed the executive, eroded public trust in institutional checks and balances, and fostered a broader perception of democratic dysfunction.

The opposition also capitalized on economic uncertainty to push policies that, while popular in the short term, had deeply destabilizing effects. Chief among these was the promotion of early pension fund withdrawals during the pandemic. Framed as emergency relief for struggling families,[3] these measures injected liquidity equivalent to 35% of GDP into the

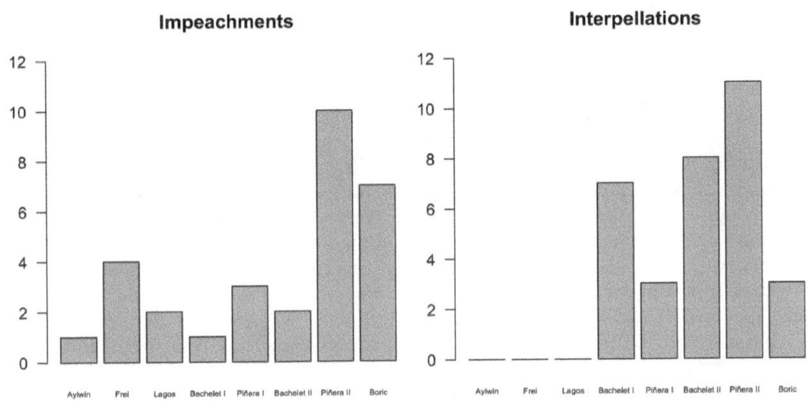

Fig. 15.1 Constitutional impeachments and interpellations (1990–2025). (*Note* To initiate an impeachment (*Acusación Constitucional*) in Chile, a minimum of 10 members of the Chamber of Deputies must sign the motion, which then follows a multi-step process involving admissibility votes and, if accepted, trial in the Senate. An interpellation (*Interpelación*, a mechanism established in 2006), by contrast, requires only 1/3 of the members of the Chamber of Deputies to request that a minister appear and respond to questions; it is a political oversight tool and does not carry legal consequences. *Source* Author with data from Tresquintos)

Health Jaime Mañalich (2020), and Minister of Education Raúl Figueroa (2021), all of whom were acquitted. Notably, former Minister of Foreign Affairs Andrés Allamand was impeached in 2022 after leaving office, but the case was dismissed on procedural grounds.

[3] See Chapter 10 for a broader discussion of the destabilization strategies employed to manufacture politically favorable conditions. One such tactic was the projection of the word *Hambre* (lit. "Hunger") onto Santiago's iconic Telefónica Tower—an

economy. However, the consequences were swift and aligned closely with expert warnings. As shown in Figure 15.2, the Consumer Price Index spiked following each withdrawal round, fueling a cycle of inflation that disproportionately affected the most vulnerable.[4] Remarkably, despite clear evidence of these harmful effects, the opposition continued to press for additional withdrawals. One proposal came while inflation was still climbing, and another followed even after the inflationary consequences had become undeniable. This persistence reflected the willingness to

event framed as a desperate public outcry, yet strategically leveraged to portray the government as indifferent to mass suffering. See: Quijada, N. 2020. "Regresan las intervenciones en la Torre Telefónica con mensajes acerca de la pandemia del covid-19." May 19. *Emol*. https://www.emol.com/noticias/Espectaculos/2020/05/19/986647/Torre-Telefonica-intervenciones-coronavirus-pandemia.html. Despite Chile's strong standing in regional health and nutrition metrics, as well as its swift and effective COVID-19 response, this visual rhetoric was used to manufacture a perception of humanitarian crisis—creating political cover for the push to allow early pension withdrawals. While the artists involved may not have acted with explicit political intent, the symbolism was quickly co-opted by opposition politicians who promoted the withdrawals not merely as emergency relief, but as part of a broader strategy to delegitimize and defund the private pension system (AFPs). The underlying objective among these political actors was to bankrupt the AFPs and pave the way for their replacement with a state-run model. The first of the three pension withdrawal laws was approved by Congress less than a month after the projection, even though the proposal had been circulating since 2019—well before the pandemic. See: Arciniegas, Y. 2020. "Chile: Senado aprueba el retiro anticipado de pensiones en medio de la pandemia de COVID-19." *France 24*. July 23. https://www.france24.com/es/20200723-chile-senado-aprueba-el-retiro-anticipado-de-pensiones-en-medio-de-la-pandemia-de-covid-19.

[4] By the time a fifth pension withdrawal was being debated in Congress, analysis showed that the cumulative impact of the previous retiros had significant macroeconomic consequence. According to *Banco Central* President Rosanna Costa, the withdrawals injected liquidity equivalent to 18% of Chile's GDP (roughly USD 50 billion), contributing to an internal demand surge that pushed inflation to levels more than triple the Central Bank's target. In response, the Central Bank had to raise interest rates sharply, while long-term rates also increased due to elevated risk premiums and capital market disruptions. Costa highlighted that the repeated nature of the measures amplified uncertainty, leading to a depreciation of the peso and increased volatility in financial markets. The pension savings of many households—particularly those in the lower and middle income brackets—were severely reduced, with national savings falling from 76% to 56% of GDP, effectively wiping out over a decade of accumulation. Additionally, the cost of housing credit rose, with mortgage interest rates increasing and loan conditions tightening. These effects, Costa concluded, were not isolated but compounding, with each round of withdrawals intensifying inflationary and financial pressures. See: Costa, R. 2023. *Impactos económicos y financieros de retiros de ahorros previsionales*. Santiago: Banco Central de Chile. [This document, *Impactos económicos y financieros de retiros de ahorros previsionales*, is available on the author's website.]

pursue short-term political gains over long-term economic stability, even if it came at the direct expense of the very sectors the policies were "meant to support."[5]

In fact, the policy reverberated across the board. Perhaps most notably, it impacted interest rates, which surged as the Central Bank moved aggressively to contain inflation (see Figure 15.3). If the spike in the Consumer Price Index hurt the purchasing power of lower-income households, rising interest rates put pressure on both the middle and upper classes, tightening credit conditions and limiting their ability to borrow, invest, or spend. Mortgages became more expensive, business loans harder to secure, and long-term financial planning increasingly uncertain. In this way, the ripple effects of the withdrawals extended far beyond what their proponents had claimed would happen. .

In the realm of public security, the opposition adopted a discourse that often delegitimized law enforcement and framed the post-2019 surge in crime—including homicide, robbery, and home invasions—as secondary to concerns about police brutality. While this narrative resonated with activist and urban youth sectors, it clashed with the growing fears of ordinary Chileans, especially in the middle class, who were witnessing a breakdown in safety. By focusing their rhetoric on the failures of the police and the executive, rather than proposing concrete public security solutions, opposition leaders contributed to a political environment in which insecurity became normalized. This was especially troubling considering the rising rate of post-social outburst homicides (see Figure 15.4).[6]

[5] All four pension fund withdrawals legislated during the Piñera administration received cross-party support. While most political coalitions were internally divided— some members voting in favor, others against—the only coalition that unanimously backed all four withdrawals was Frente Amplio. All 20 of its deputies in the Chamber of Deputies and its sole senator (Juan Ignacio Latorre, RD) voted in favor of each measure. Notably, this includes then-deputy Gabriel Boric, who justified his support in several congressional speeches. [This dataset, *Roll-call votes of Senators and Deputies for Pension Withdrawl during the Piñera administration (2018–2022)*, is available on the author's website.]

[6] Between 2015 and 2018, Chile averaged approximately 660 homicide victims per year. In contrast, post-2019 figures reflect a steep rise, with the total reaching 1,207 victims in 2024—representing more than a 100% increase over pre–social outburst levels. The homicide rate climbed from around 3.5 per 100,000 inhabitants in 2018 to 6.7 in 2023. The period also saw a marked shift in the nature of violence, including increased firearm use, a higher share of unknown perpetrators, and a growing proportion of foreign victims, which rose from 5.6% in 2020 to 18.2% in 2024. The 2025 report, which includes complete data

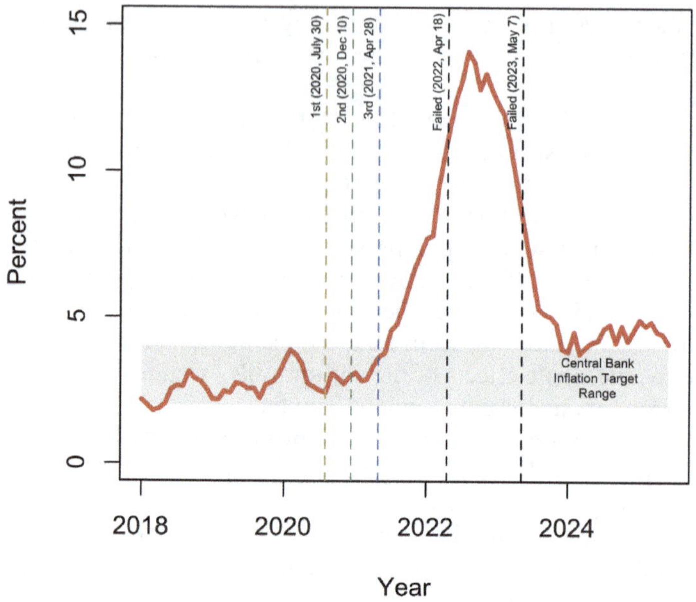

Fig. 15.2 Consumer Price Index, 2018–2025. (*Note* The solid red line shows the year-over-year change in Chile's Consumer Price Index (CPI) from 2018 onward. The shaded gray band marks the Central Bank's inflation target range of 2% to 4%. Vertical dashed lines indicate five key legislative events related to pension fund withdrawals: the first three (July 30, 2020; December 10, 2020; and April 28, 2021) correspond to successful approvals, while the final two (April 18, 2022, and May 7, 2023) represent failed attempts. *Source* Author with data from the International Monetary Fund [CL.M.PCPI_IX.PCH])

Migration became another significant political wedge during these years, especially in Chile's northern regions (e.g., Arica y Parinacota, Tarapacá, and Antofagasta). The increase in undocumented immigration, particularly from Venezuela and Haiti, became a major source of social anxiety. Rather than working toward pragmatic solutions, the opposition

up to the end of 2024, reports that the two defining years of the constitutional process—2022 and 2023—were the deadliest on record. In 2022, there were 1,330 homicides in Chile, while in 2023 there were 1,249. See: *Observatorio de Homicidios*. 2025. "Informe de Víctimas de Homicidios Consumados 2024. [This document, *Informe de Víctimas de Homicidios Consumados*2024, is available on the author's website.]

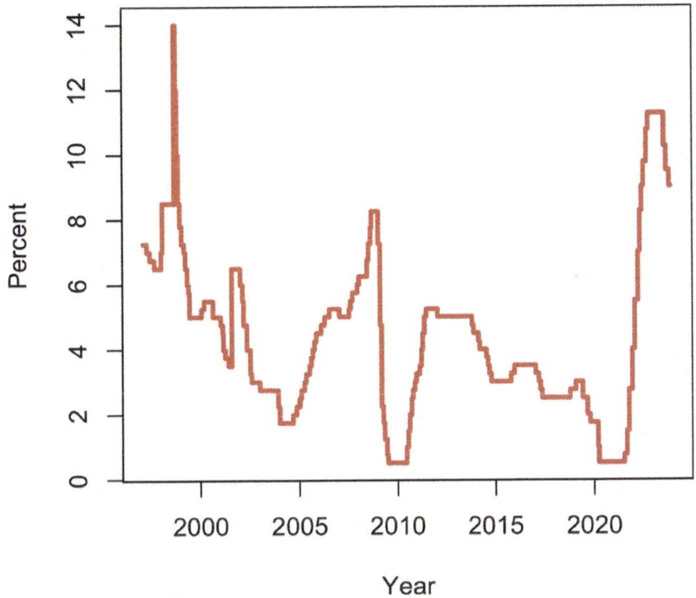

Fig. 15.3 Interest rate set by the Central Bank (1997–2025). (*Note* The solid red line shows the evolution of Chile's monetary policy interest rate (*Tasa Política Monetaria*, TPM) from 1997 onward. The TPM is set by the Central Bank and reflects its primary instrument for conducting monetary policy. The plot highlights periods of rate stability, gradual adjustments, and sharp increases, particularly during periods of inflationary pressure. The vertical axis measures the policy rate in percentage terms, while the horizontal axis spans calendar years. *Source* Author with data from the Central Bank of Chile)

treated the crisis as yet another opportunity to undermine the sitting government. This approach polarized public opinion and made it more difficult to form a consensus on migration policy, even when it was already clear that there was a nexus between illegal immigration and rising crime.[7]

[7] According to a 2023 report, the relative share of foreign-born individuals involved in crime was on the rise, with a marked uptick in violent offenses such as homicide and robbery. By 2022, foreigners were already overrepresented in homicide convictions. Their involvement in other types of crimes was also found to be steadily increasing. See: Vergara, R., and G. Ugarte. 2023. "Inmigración y delincuencia: últimas cifras." *Centro de Estudios Públicos: Puntos de Referencia* 663: 1–23. Also see: Mennickent Barros, C., and

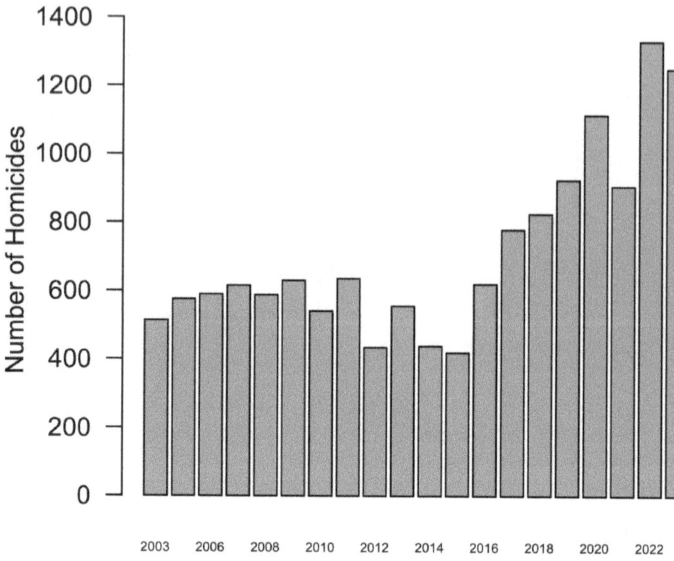

Fig. 15.4 Number of homicides by year (2018–2023). (*Note* The bars show the total number of completed homicides recorded annually in Chile between 2003 and 2023. Each bar corresponds to the absolute number of victims reported for that calendar year. Homicides are measured as individual cases of intentional killing validated by officials. *Source* Author with data from the Observatorio de Homicidios[8]

S. Martínez Tapia. 2023. "Con "bagaje de violencia superior": extranjeros formalizados por homicidios aumentan un 270% en 4 años." *Biobio Chile*. March 19. https://www.biobiochile.cl/especial/bbcl-investiga/noticias/reportajes/2023/03/19/con-bagaje-de-violencia-superior-extranjeros-formalizados-por-homicidios-aumentan-un-270-en-4-anos.shtml/. Empirical data confirms the correlation between rising homicide rates and the growth of the undocumented migrant population. Between 2017 and 2022, the foreign-born population more than doubled, while the number of foreign nationals detained for homicide rose by over 400 percent. Although the total number of cases remained low, the rate of growth was significant enough as to generate studies pushing for specific policy. See: Jofré Rickenberg, C., and M. Cofré Vásquez. 2023. "Representación poblacional de detenidos por homicidio en Chile (2017–2022)." *Revista Academia de Ciencias Policiales* 5(1): 62–78.

[8] The *Observatorio de Homicidios* is an interinstitutional body tasked with consolidating and validating official data on completed homicides in Chile. It is composed of the *Ministerio Público*, *Carabineros de Chile*, *Policía de Investigaciones*, *Gendarmería*, *Servicio*

Apart from these specific strategies, the opposition employed a cultural and rhetorical approach that romanticized chaos as a necessary precondition for political transformation.[9] A statement by Sebastián Depolo in 2021, that is, a victory by Boric would bring *instability*,[10] encapsulated this mindset. Although this rhetoric energized the opposition's base, it entrenched public distrust in governance and contributed to a sense of institutional fragility. Instead of stabilizing the country, opposition leaders embraced disorder as a political tool, further weakening the state's capacity to manage the crises at hand.

15.3 The Left with Boric in Power

When Gabriel Boric assumed office in March 2022, the left transitioned from a disruptive opposition to a governing force—inheriting a country marked by economic fragility, rising crime, and widespread institutional distrust. Rather than recalibrating to meet these challenges pragmatically, the Boric administration responded with a mix of ideological rigidity,

Médico Legal, *Servicio de Registro Civil e Identificación*, *Ministerio de la*Mujer *y Equidad de Género*, *Servicio Nacional de la Mujer y Equidad de Género*, *Servicio Nacional de Menores*, *Servicio Nacional de Reinserción Social Juvenil*, *Servicio Nacional de Protección Especializada a la Niñez y Adolescencia*, and the *Departamento de Estadísticas e Información de Salud* (DEIS) of the *Ministerio de Salud*.

[9] One example of the induction of chaos as a form of protest was the widespread chanting of "*El que no baila no pasa*" ("If you don't dance, you don't pass") at improvised roadblocks, where protesters halted traffic and required civilians to dance in order to proceed. Though often presented as playful or symbolic, this practice disrupted public order and infringed on civil liberties—recasting coercion as revolutionary performance. In parallel, the fictional stray dog *Perro Matapacos* was elevated as a moral icon of the uprising, celebrated for his perceived loyalty to protesters and defiance of authority. His image was later enshrined in the *Museo del Estallido Social* ("Museum of the Social Outburst"), a publicly funded institution under the Boric administration, reflecting the state's implicit endorsement of the protest's cultural mythology.

[10] Depolo, then campaign coordinator for Boric, stated that "vamos a meterle inestabilidad al país porque vamos a hacer transformaciones importantes," framing instability not as a risk but as an inherent feature of structural reform. He argued that such disruption was necessary to dismantle entrenched privileges and pave the way for substantive change. See: Soto, J. 2021. "Depolo y posible gobierno de Boric: "Vamos a meterle inestabilidad al país porque vamos a hacer transformaciones importantes"." *El Mercurio*, November 1. https://digital.elmercurio.com/2021/11/01/C/SN41OCPI/. Depolo would later be appointed as Chile's ambassador to Brazil by President Boric.

symbolic gestures, and strategic deflection, which only deepened public dissatisfaction and made the situation worse.

Although Boric largely avoided addressing the economic crisis—likely to avoid acknowledging the damaging effects of pension withdrawals, which the left had supported—he took a more assertive stance on public security, but not in the direction many expected. Instead of recognizing escalating violence, Boric downplayed public concerns. When confronted by a journalist about rising crime in 2022, he accused critics of "cherry-picking" statistics to fabricate a narrative of crisis, insisting that crime "could not be solved with more police, but by addressing inequality."[11] This response aligned with his progressive platform, but ignored the immediate fears of millions of Chileans facing record levels of homicide, home invasions, and robbery—particularly in urban centers like Santiago.

As crime escalated, migration became an increasingly salient concern. Yet, rather than shifting strategy, the government—under the leadership of Luis Thayer Correa—maintained an open-border stance consistent with Boric's progressive ideals.[12] Yet this position appeared out of touch with the growing public anxiety around crime and precarity linked, rightly or wrongly, to migration.

In addition to these thematic misjudgments, the Boric administration suffered a series of political gaffes that undermined its legitimacy. Most infamously, Interior Minister Izkia Siches's visit to La Araucanía descended into chaos when she narrowly avoided an armed ambush—a trip framed as a goodwill gesture but remarkably poorly

[11] The remark drew significant public attention, as many Chileans sought to understand the meaning of "cherry picking"—a term hitherto rarely used in Chilean political discourse. The contrast between the President's rhetorical framing and the public's growing anxiety over crime contributed to the moment's visibility, making the phrase symbolic of the broader disconnect between government messaging and societal sentiment. Choosing to downplay the worsening situation just one month before the 2022 plebiscite would later prove to be a poor strategic decision. See: *Biobio Chile*. 2022. "Cherry picking": Qué significa el término utilizado por el Presidente por los datos de delincuencia." August 23. https://www.biobiochile.cl/noticias/nacional/chile/2022/08/23/cherry-picking-que-significa-el-termino-utilizado-por-el-presidente-por-los-datos-de-delincuencia.shtml/

[12] Legal deportations were consistently delayed for technicalities such as not having printers at the border. See: Izquierdo, M. 2025. "La insólita explicación del director de Migraciones por demora en expulsión de extranjeros irregulares a Bolivia." *Ex-Ante*. March 18. https://www.ex-ante.cl/la-insolita-explicacion-del-director-de-migraciones-por-demora-en-expulsion-de-extranjeros-irregulares-a-bolivia/

planned and executed.[13] It reinforced perceptions of incompetence and *naïveté* at the highest levels of government.[14]

The administration further eroded public trust by closely aligning itself with the *Apruebo* campaign in the lead-up to the 2022 constitutional plebiscite (as described in Chapter 14). By transforming the vote into a referendum on his leadership, Boric inadvertently tied the fate of the constitutional project to his own administration's popularity, which was already rapidly declining due to its clear mishandling of the issues mentioned above.

Moreover, the government's relationship with several oversight institutions also became strained. This was first evident when the Comptroller General raised concerns about possible interventionism during the constitutional campaign, prompting public skepticism about the administration's respect for institutional boundaries.[15]

[13] The itinerary was coordinated by the Interior Ministry's protocol and security staff as part of a two-day tour of the La Araucanía region, a zone long marred by territorial conflict and violence. A prior site visit was carried out days earlier to evaluate risk and establish logistics. Despite these precautions, the trip unraveled when the delegation, which included then-Undersecretary Miguel Crispi, encountered an unexpected roadblock and gunfire in Temucuicui, forcing Minister Izkia Siches to retreat. The incident severely undermined her credibility during the early days of the administration. See: Browne, M., and P. Radovic. 2022. "Error de diagnóstico: La historia del viaje que empañó el debut de Izkia Siches." *La Tercera*, March 20. https://www.latercera.com/la-tercera-domingo/noticia/error-de-diagnostico-la-historia-del-viaje-que-empano-el-debut-de-izkia-siches/2JUXP4RFF5FI5PRICYEL4A4N54/

[14] Another illustrative episode occurred when Minister of the Interior Carolina Tohá visited the northern border in late 2023 with a megaphone in an effort to signal that the government was taking decisive action. Instead of generating public support, the gesture was seized upon by the opposition as evidence of the futility of the government's strategy. The incident not only weakened the administration's credibility on migration policy but also damaged Tohá's personal credibility, casting doubt on her effectiveness as a political leader. This loss of authority may have contributed to her unexpected defeat in the 2025 primary election to the Communist Party candidate, Jeannette Jara. See: Carvajal Vega, X. 2023. "Pérdida de equilibrio y ruptura de tímpano: los efectos del arma no letal tras el megáfono mostrado en la frontera." *La Tercera*. November 21. https://www.latercera.com/la-tercera-pm/noticia/perdida-de-equilibrio-y-ruptura-de-timpano-los-efectos-del-arma-no-letal-trasel-megafono-mostrado-en-la-frontera/JHVGGCUGYRBJPKP3QGZQJU25K4/

[15] The Comptroller Jorge Bermúdez's comments were interpreted as a warning shot to *La Moneda*. See: Durán, V. H. 2022. "Intervencionismo electoral: El mensaje del contralor Bermúdez que encendió todas las alarmas en La Moneda." *Ex-Ante*. July 27. https://www.ex-ante.cl/intervencion-electoral-el-mensaje-de-bermudez-que-encendio-todas-las-alarmas-en-la-moneda/

It did not help the government when Minister Giorgio Jackson—one of Boric's closest allies (see Chapter 8)—declared that his political sector and generation possessed a superior moral standard compared to their predecessors,[16] or when the President issued pardons to several court-convicted criminals for their roles in the 2019 outburst (readers may recall the "*presos del estallido*"), a move once again celebrated from the left but broadly condemned as a breach of the rule of law from the center rightwards.[17]

International missteps, such as the poorly received North American tour,[18] or undersecretary José Miguel Ahumada's resistance to the

[16] The remarks triggered immediate backlash across the political spectrum, as they were widely interpreted as dismissive of previous democratic administrations and as an expression of moral superiority by the new governing coalition. Faced with mounting criticism, the statement was later clarified, though the episode left a lasting impression on the public debate about generational divides and political humility. See: Palacios, C. 2022. "Ministro Jackson: "Nuestra escala de valores y principios en torno a la política no solo dista del gobierno anterior, sino que frente a una generación que nos antecedió"." *La Tercera*. August 3. https://www.latercera.com/politica/noticia/ministro-jackson-nuestra-escala-de-valores-y-principios-en-torno-a-la-politica-no-solo-dista-del-gobierno-anterior-sino-que-frente-a-una-generacion-que-nos-antecedio/CFUUSLEIMJD2PI7ZENKKU4YQAI/

[17] Among those pardoned was Jorge Mateluna, a former guerrilla figure—intensifying criticism from across the aisle. See: Caro, I., and I. Martínez. 2022. "Presidente Boric indulta a doce condenados en el marco del estallido social y al exfrentista Jorge Mateluna." *La Tercera*, December 30. https://www.latercera.com/politica/noticia/presidente-boric-indulta-a-diez-condenados-en-el-marco-del-estallido-social-y-al-exfrentista-jorge-mateluna/YM26BBOXEFAFPJRUH77F65OTI4/. Another pardoned inmate was Luis Castillo, who was arrested for reoffending just days before the 2023 plebiscite. The timing of his detention, amid heightened concerns over security, was seen by analysts as a potential turning point capable of swaying undecided voters toward the "Approve" option. See: Soto, M. 2023. "Kenneth Bunker y detención de Castillo: "Es un efecto Atocha, que puede volcar muchos indecisos hacia el A favor." *Ex-Ante*. December 15. https://www.ex-ante.cl/kenneth-bunker-y-detencion-de-castillo-es-un-efecto-atocha-que-puede-volcar-muchos-indecisos-hacia-el-a-favor/

[18] The North American tour, undertaken from June 6 to 10, 2022, aimed to position President Boric as a credible global actor ahead of the IX Summit of the Americas. Instead, the visit became notorious for a string of public relations misfires. In Ottawa on June 6, the delegation struggled with simultaneous translation and language confusion while addressing binational cooperation with Prime Minister Justin Trudeau. During the summit in Los Angeles (June 9–10), Boric publicly criticized the U.S. for its absence—only to be met with pointed reminders that John Kerry was in attendance representing the Biden administration. Other gaffes included avoiding key officials in side meetings and inconsistent messages about hemispheric solidarity and migration policy. Far from

TPP11 trade agreement,[19] further emphasized a government seen as symbolic rather than strategic. Late efforts to recover—including a cabinet reshuffle that replaced Siches with Carolina Tohá and sidelined key advisors like Jackson—arrived too late to reverse the damage.[20]

enhancing Chile's global profile, the tour underscored a presidency grappling with execution and coherence. See: Vargas, F. 2023. "Errores, impasses y desprolijidades: la lista de polémicas de la canciller de Boric a menos de un año de asumir." *La Nación*. January 25. https://www.lanacion.com.ar/el-mundo/errores-impasses-y-desprolijidades-la-lista-de-polemicas-de-la-canciller-de-boric-a-menos-de-un-ano-nid25012023/. Foreign Affairs Minister Antonia Urrejola, who accompanied the tour, became emblematic of these missteps and was removed from her post in early 2023 following a series of further controversies—including the leak of private audio criticizing a diplomat and remarks deemed imprudent about the President himself. See: *El País*. 2023. "Antonia Urrejola, excanciller de Chile: 'Operó en mi contra un grupo de interés empeñado en hacerme la vida imposible.'"April 5. https://elpais.com/chile/2023-04-05/antonia-urrejola-excanciller-de-chile-opero-en-mi-contra-un-grupo-de-interes-empecinado-en-hacerme-la-vida-imposible.html; also see: *La Segunda*. 2022. "A veces le digo al Presidente: 'No sé si tienes noción del impacto que genera tu liderazgo en el exterior'." June 10. https://digital.lasegunda.com/2022/06/10/A/GB44SQ6F#zoom=page-width/

[19] Subsecretary Ahumada's resistance to the TPP11 trade agreement reflected deep-rooted ideological convictions. In line with his academic background and critiques of neoliberal globalization, he publicly dismissed the treaty as offering "minimal commercial benefits" while embodying "what has been understood as neoliberal globalization." The administration was broadly sympathetic to this view—President Boric himself had voiced opposition to the TPP11 during his campaign—but the combination of doctrinal rigidity and inexperience in international trade negotiations proved politically costly. See: *El Mostrador*. 2022. "Subsecretario Ahumada apunta que TPP-11 genera «beneficios comerciales mínimos» y que «condensa lo que se ha entendido como globalización neoliberal»." October 14. https://www.elmostrador.cl/dia/2022/10/14/subsecretario-ahumada-apunta-que-tpp11-genera-beneficios-comerciales-minimos-y-que-condensa-lo-que-se-ha-entendido-como-globalizacion-neoliberal/. In any case, mounting pressure from coalition allies and business sectors led to Ahumada's dismissal in late 2022, and the treaty was ultimately ratified. Chile formally joined the TPP11 in 2023, with the agreement entering into force on February 21 of that year. See: Toledo, M. 2023. "TPP11 100% operativo para Chile: se publica en el Diario Oficial y entra en vigor este martes." *Diario Financiero*. February 20. https://www.df.cl/economia-y-politica/comercio-exterior/tpp11-100-operativo-para-chile-se-publica-en-el-diario-oficial-y-entra/

[20] The reshuffle was widely interpreted as a direct response to the resounding rejection of the constitutional draft in the September 2022 plebiscite—an implicit recognition that the Boric administration's transformative agenda had reached an impasse. Several key figures were replaced with more experienced members from the center-left coalition, marking a strategic pivot toward institutional governance. Interior Minister Izkia Siches was replaced by Carolina Tohá (PPD); Secretary General Giorgio Jackson was moved to the Ministry of Social Development, while Ana Lya Uriarte (Socialist Party) assumed his

By 2023, Boric's presidency had become synonymous with mismanagement. Rather than stabilizing Chile, his administration had deepened the very instability it had created—while maybe not through malice, at least through miscalculation or ideological stubbornness. Unsurprisingly, his presidential approval ratings would fall early in his term and, much like Piñera, never really recover in time to have any consequential effect, as Figure 15.5 shows.[21]

former role. Ximena Aguilera replaced María Begoña Yarza as Minister of Health, and Jeannette Jara (Communist Party) took over the Ministry of Labor. The reshuffle also strengthened the role of government Secretary General Camila Vallejo (also Communist), who became central to political messaging. Collectively, these changes signaled a shift in the balance of power from *Apruebo Dignidad* to the more moderate *Socialismo Democrático* bloc. See: *The Clinic*. 2022. "El desembarco de la ex Nueva Mayoría y un "frenazo" a la agenda transformadora: el primer cambio de gabinete de Boric en la mirada de cuatro expertos." September 7. https://www.theclinic.cl/2022/09/06/ex-nueva-Mayoria-frenazo-agenda-transformadora-primer-cambio-gabinete-boric/

[21] President Boric's approval ratings declined sharply early in his term, stabilizing around 30%. While not the lowest in recent democratic history— President Piñera's ratings were lower at times—Boric's fall was notable for its speed and for the isolation of his support: he retained a loyal base, but lacked broader backing. Combined with internal missteps and limited legislative influence, this led to his being widely described as a "lame duck" by midterm. See: Soto, M. 2024. "Kenneth Bunker: 'A la mitad de su gobierno, Boric ya tiene el síndrome del pato cojo.'" *Ex-Ante*. March 25. https://www.ex-ante.cl/kenneth-bunker-a-la-mitad-de-sugobierno-boric-ya-tiene-el-sindrome-del-pato-cojo/

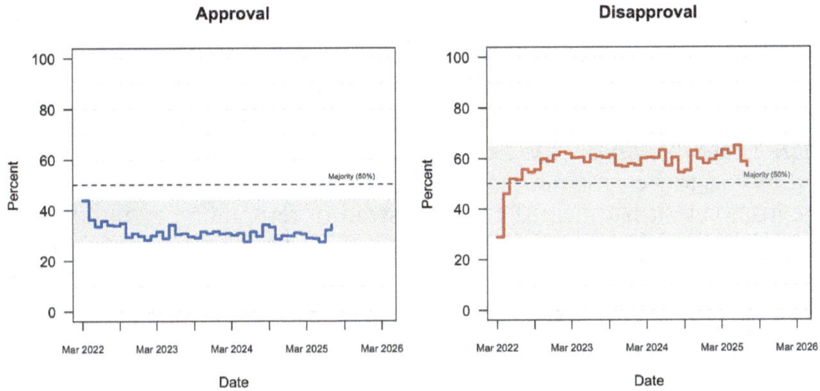

Fig. 15.5 Presidential popularity of Gabriel Boric (2022–2026). (*Note* The panel on the left displays the monthly average of presidential approval, while the panel on the right shows the monthly average of disapproval. In both panels, the staircase line represents the average for each month based on available survey data. The shaded gray area indicates the full range (minimum to maximum) of monthly averages observed during the term. Horizontal dotted lines mark this range, and the dashed horizontal line at 50% serves as a reference point for majority approval or disapproval. *Source* Author with data from Tresquintos)

15.4 Conclusion

The period surrounding Chile's first and second constitutional assemblies was defined by instability, notorious political miscalculation, eroding institutional trust, and realignment. While the constitutional process itself served as a focal point for public debate, the deeper crisis that unfolded during this time transcended the fate of any one text. What could have been a moment of institutional renewal became instead a case study in how political irresponsibility can drive a country into deeper uncertainty. The instability that gripped Chile during this period was not merely a consequence of exogenous shocks or policy disagreements but the result of strategic decisions made by political actors who likely underestimated the long-term consequences of their own actions.

In opposition, the political left embraced destabilization as a strategy. By turning impeachment into a routine tool, promoting short-term economic relief through pension withdrawals, and undermining public confidence in law enforcement, it weakened the very institutions it would later rely on. These moves may have succeeded in delegitimizing the Piñera administration, but they also left behind a more fragile state, rising public anxiety, and a polarized electorate. What was once framed as a transformative project increasingly came to resemble political brinkmanship, where disruption was treated as a virtue, not a risk.

Once in power, the new administration proved incapable of managing the instability it had helped create. Instead of responding to the public's growing concerns over crime, migration, and inflation, it prioritized ideological alignment, symbolic gestures, and internal loyalty. These failures were not isolated events, but part of a broader pattern in which political leadership appeared consistently disconnected from the urgency of the moment.

The overambitious pursuit of transformation did not simply derail reform—it redirected the trajectory of Chilean politics. As instability deepened and trust in progressive leadership eroded, public sentiment began to shift toward actors who promised order, pragmatism, and control.

CHAPTER 16

The (Second) Constitutional Council

16.1 Introduction

The 2023 Chilean Constitutional Council was conceived as a response to the failures of the first constitutional process with the objective of rectifying its excesses through a structured, rule-bound approach. After the resounding rejection of the first draft in the 2022 plebiscite, political leaders sought to design a process that would increase public trust. The new council operated under strict procedural safeguards. In contrast to the activist-driven and ideologically diverse first convention, right-wing parties, particularly the Republican Party (the leading political force in the May 2023 elections), dominated the Council (see electoral results in Chapter 14). While the process was more disciplined and predictable than the previous one, it also encountered an electorate that was increasingly disengaged from the constitutional debate and preoccupied with pressing economic and security concerns.

This chapter begins stepping back to give a description of the Council's institutional structure, highlighting the implemented safeguards to avoid the procedural instability of the first process. The discussion then shifts to the leadership of Beatriz Hevia and Aldo Valle, whose roles as president and vice president, respectively, symbolized the council's shift toward a more conventional, institutionalist approach. It also explores the ideological composition of the council with a focus on the internal dynamics of the right-wing majority and the relative weakness of the left.

K. Bunker, *Chile's Transformation Amidst Crisis*,
https://doi.org/10.1007/978-3-031-96463-3_16

Next, the chapter turns to look at the ideological alignments and voting patterns within the council to reveal the influence of the interaction among factions on the constitutional draft. As a mirror to Sect. 12.5, the chapter then turns its attention to the content of the second proposal, which reflected a significant departure from the first draft. Among other things, the new proposal prioritized institutional continuity, reinforcing the presidential system, bicameralism, and market-friendly economic policies that were already in place while also introducing several new social rights.

Finally, the chapter examines the December 2023 plebiscite, in which voters once again rejected the proposed constitution, marking the second failed attempt at constitutional change in less than two years. The ultimate rejection underscored an increasing disconnect between political elites and the electorate, which in turn ushered in doubts about the viability of any future constitutional reform in the near term. By tracing the trajectory of the second constitutional process from its inception to its failure, this chapter seeks to highlight the limits of procedural corrections in the absence of public engagement and trust.

16.2 The Safeguards

As described at length in Chapter 14, the second constitutional process was designed as a structured and disciplined response to the failures of the first attempt. The lack of specific rules and procedural safeguards contributed to the dysfunction of the previous convention, thus prompting lawmakers to establish a more controlled framework for this new effort. To prevent a repeat of previous mistakes, the process incorporated strict oversight mechanisms, including three key bodies, namely, the Experts Committee, the Technical Admissions Committee, and the plenary and its commissions. These institutions were established to ensure a structured, rule-bound process that limited uncertainty and ideological overreach.

The Experts Committee was composed of 24 members nominated by the Senate (12) and the Chamber of Deputies (12) and was tasked with drafting a preliminary constitutional text prior to the convening of the elected Constitutional Council. This measure was intended to prevent the process from beginning with a blank slate, as in the first attempt. By providing an initial framework, the committee aimed to steer discussions toward viable and legally sound proposals instead of politically extreme or impractical ideas.[1]

The Technical Admissions Committee, composed of 14 members (primarily legal scholars and constitutional experts), functioned as an oversight body. Its primary role was to ensure adherence to the 12 guiding principles outlined in the *Acuerdo por Chile* (see Chapter 14). Acting as a constitutional tribunal, of sorts, this committee held the authority to review and, if necessary, prevent any provisions that violated the core principles.[2]

Next to these two safeguards,[3] the third major body that shaped the second constitutional process was the plenary itself along with its thematic commissions. While the oversight committees provided structure and guardrails, all substantive deliberation occurred within the plenary and its commissions, which were tasked with producing the final constitutional draft.

Prior to examining the internal workings of the plenary and its commissions, addressing the significant shift in leadership is necessary, as it marked a stark deviation from the fragmented and ideological-driven governance of the first constitutional process. A key example is the election of Beatriz Hevia, a young conservative politician from the Republican

[1] The resultant preproposal was delivered to the council as a foundation for debates, which provided members with a structured starting point instead of an open-ended deliberation. The pre-proposal was signed by the 24 members of the Constitutional Expert Commission, appointed under Chamber of Deputies and Senate quotas. From the Chamber: Alexis Cortés (sociologist), Antonia Rivas, Carlos Frontaura, Catalina Salem, Domingo Lovera, Flavio Quezada, Juan José Ossa, Marcela Peredo, Máximo Pavez, Natalia González, Paz Anastasiadis, and Verónica Undurraga (all lawyers). From the Senate: Alejandra Krauss, Catalina Lagos, Francisco Soto, Gabriel Osorio, Hernán Larraín Fernández, Jaime Arancibia, Katherine Martorell, Leslie Sánchez, Magaly Fuenzalida, Sebastián Soto, and Teodoro Ribera (all lawyers), along with Bettina Horst (economist).

[2] Despite the significant authority given, the committee never needed to intervene throughout the process, a sign that the council operated mainly within its established boundaries.

[3] The effectiveness of this structured approach was evident in the high level of consensus achieved—more that 90% of the initial draft of the Experts Committee was incorporated into the final proposal. For a general overview grounded in quantitative methods, see an analysis that applies entropy metrics and voting pattern comparisons to assess levels of polarization and institutional order: Valenzuela Everke, L. 2023. "Radiografía al Consejo Constitucional." *Res Pública* 995: 1–15.

Party, as president of the Council. Her election symbolized the dominance of the right in the process as well as the departure from the activist-led first convention. Hevia's leadership reflected a pragmatic and institutional approach, in contrast to the more radical and experimental order under Elisa Loncon.

Along with Hevia, Aldo Valle (a member of the Socialist Party and a former university rector) was elected vice president. Valle's appointment ensured that the left continued to be involved in the process, but in a traditional and structured manner. Compared with the more strategic left led by Bassa, Valle represented the social democratic establishment, which indicated a return to the more moderate and traditional political style of the *Concertación*.

Together, Hevia and Valle embodied a generally centrist and controlled approach to constitutional reform. Along with the procedural safeguards, their collaboration shaped a process that was disciplined, efficient, and predictable. However, while this structure rectified many of the organizational flaws of the first attempt, it also constrained the scope of the debate, an issue that would eventually prove significant to the formation of the public perception of the final proposal.

16.3 New Rules

We now turn to look at the plenary, the central decision-making body of the constitutional council, and its thematic committees. Like in the first process, outlined in Chapter 12, the committees were responsible for producing (or curating, in this case) legislation while the plenary was responsible for determining which provisions were retained or omitted from the final draft.

It is worth reminding that one of the most significant structural changes in the second constitutional process was the deliberate reduction in the size of the plenary—from 155 members in the first Convention to 50 members in the second. As mentioned in Chapter 14, this was done to discourage fragmentation and, hopefully, expedite the legislative process.

Though initially designed for 51 members, the final composition was retained at 50 due to the exclusion of Aldo Sanhueza (Republican Party), which mirrored the expulsion of Rodrigo Rojas Vade from the first constitutional process.[4] However, this adjustment did not alter the overall distribution of members or the balance of political coalitions.

Apart from its size, the rules governing the plenary were also notably different from those of the first convention. The key distinction lied in the quorum required to pass amendments and legislation. In the first process, the quorum was a simple majority in thematic committees and a two-thirds majority in the plenary. This high threshold rendered consensus difficult, frequently leading to gridlock (even among like-minded legislators) and ideological entrenchment.

The second process retained a simple majority for committee votes but lowered the plenary quorum to three-fifths. Negotiated among congressional leaders purposely (readers may recall the *Acuerdo por Chile*), this adjustment intended to make reaching agreements easier. As a result, any constitutional provision required 30 out of 50 votes to pass in the plenary. This change played a crucial role in the formulation of legislative negotiations and coalition-building, which will be explored in the next section.

In addition to the plenary, much of the council's work occurred within the thematic committees, which functioned similarly to those in the first convention but under stricter procedural rules. In contrast to the first process, which created numerous temporary commissions—including explicitly political ones such as the Human Rights Commission—the second constitutional council streamlined its structure into only four thematic committees.

These committees were formally constituted in June 2023 and tasked with drafting (revising) specific sections of the Experts' constitutional proposal. The first committee (Political System, Constitutional Principles, and Nationality) was tasked with addressing the structure of government, electoral rules, and fundamental state principles. The second committee (Rights, Freedoms, and Constitutional Guarantees) was charged with focusing on individual and collective rights, social protection, and legal safeguards. The third committee (State Organization and Public Administration) was responsible for defining the roles

[4] Sanhueza resigned before formally taking office, following public outcry over past sexual assault allegations. See: *Ex-Ante*. 2023. "Renuncia al Consejo Constitucional Aldo Sanhueza, ex republicano acusado de abuso sexual." May 27. https://www.ex-ante.cl/renuncia-al-consejo-constitucional-aldo-sanhueza-ex-republicano-acusado-de-abuso-sexual/

and responsibilities of governmental institutions, decentralization policies, and the judiciary, and the fourth committee (Economic, Social, and Environmental Matters) was made responsible for formulating regulations on economic policy, property rights, labor laws, and natural resources.

Moreover, in contrast to the first process, in which the plenary frequently overturned or rewrote committee reports, the second council placed greater emphasis on continuity between committee deliberation and plenary decision. This aspect ensured that the work of the committees was not disregarded in later stages, thus decreasing the risk of ideological clashes that could derail the process.

Finally, one last notable departure from the first process worth mentioning, before moving on, concerns the leadership. While the first convention opted to replace its directive after six months, the second council decided to maintain a single leadership structure throughout its duration. This enabled greater political stability and ensured that the process avoided the same degree of internal restructuring experienced by the first one.

16.4 A Polarized Assembly

To fully understand the internal dynamics of the 2023 Constitutional Council, the political and ideological forces that shaped decision-making should be examined. While earlier sections explore the structural and procedural frameworks that governed the process, this section focuses on the composition of the council, the coalitions that emerged, and the voting patterns that defined its legislative behavior.

Using the same spatial voting models explained and applied in Chapter 12, the following analysis maps the ideological positions of council members to reveal patterns of polarization and coordination.[5]

[5] To assess the ideological leanings of members and the coalitions they formed, this section draws on research previously conducted. See: Bunker, K. 2023c. "¿Cuál fue el nivel de acuerdo en el pleno del consejo constitucional de 2023?" *Ideas: Laboratorio Democracia y Gobierno USS* 1(7): 1–4.; Bunker, K. 2023d. "¿Cuál fue el nivel de acuerdo en las comisiones del consejo constitucional de 2023?" *Ideas: Laboratorio Democracia y Gobierno USS* 1(8): 1–4. As explained in Chapter 5 of this book, these studies applied spatial voting models to map ideological alignments and coalition dynamics. See theoretical foundations of spatial models: See: Hinich, M. J., and M. C. Munger. 1992. "A Spatial Theory of Ideology." *Journal of Theoretical Politics* 4(1): 5–30; McFadden, D. 1973.

The reader may recall that, in contrast to other methods of ideological classification, this one identifies relative positions based on legislative voting behavior, which offers a thorough data-driven understanding of alignments from within.

The results demonstrate that although polarization persisted, its nature and intensity differed from that of the first convention. The ideological distance between opposing factions was narrower, as the structured framework of the second process—beginning with an agreed-on text and operating under strict procedural rules—encouraged greater consensus in voting outcomes.[6] However, crucial divisions remained, particularly within the dominant sector, now the right, in which the Republican Party and *Chile Vamos* (known as *Chile Seguro* in this assembly) frequently disagreed over key provisions.

16.4.1 Ideological and Value Positions of Coalitions and Members

Figure 16.1 displays the one-dimensional placement of council members based on all recorded votes. Overall, the ideological map indicates that polarization remained a defining feature. The figure illustrates that while the left was relatively cohesive, the right was divided into two distinct blocs, the Republican Party, which occupied the more conservative end of the spectrum, and *Chile Vamos*, which positioned itself closer to the center (this internal polarization is also visible in the figures in Chapter 6).[7]

The pattern on the left, in turn, contrasts with the first convention in which the dominant progressive coalition exhibited greater internal

"Conditional Logit Analysis of Qualitative Choice Behavior." In *Frontiers of Econometrics*, edited by P. Zarembka, 105–142. New York, NY: Academic Press.

[6] The observation on relative distance does not stem from a direct comparison between the W-NOMINATE scores, but from the careful consideration of other mediating factors that are described later in the book.

[7] Remarkably, all 17 members of Unidad para Chile scored between −1.0 and −0.5. On the right, all 11 members of *Chile Seguro* scored between 0.5 and 0.81, and all 22 members of the Republican Party scored above 0.82. (The lone reserved seat representative voted with the left). For reference, the most extreme members on the left were Marcela Araya and Christian Suárez, while the most extreme on the right were Antonio Barchiesi and Claudia Mac-Lean. The 30th voter (from the top-down) was Pilar Cuevas of *Renovación Nacional*. The most centrists voters (closest to 0) of each sector, were Aldo Valle and Gloria Hutt.

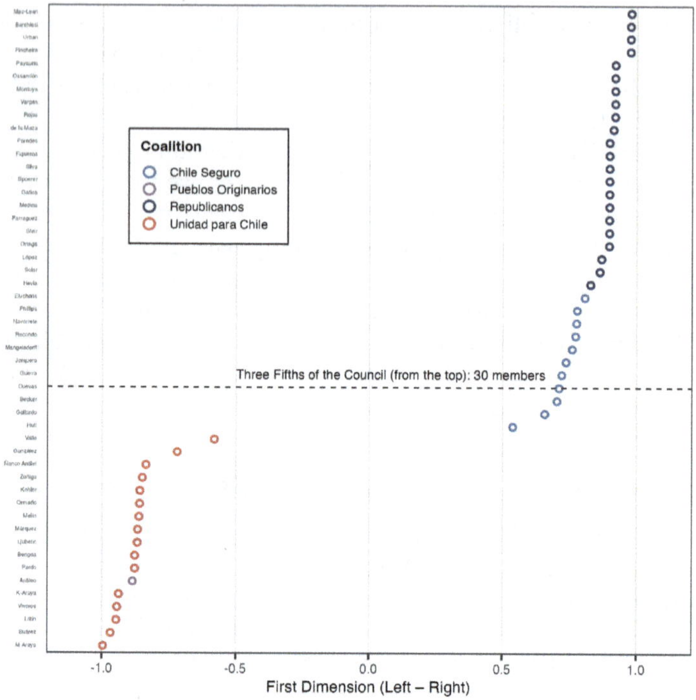

Fig. 16.1 One-dimensional ideological placement of Constitutional Council members in the plenary (*Source* Author with data from Bunker 2023c[8])

divisions. In 2021–2022, tension between the far left (represented by *Apruebo Dignidad* and independent activists) and the more moderate Socialist Party and former *Concertación* figures led to frequent disagreement over constitutional provisions. In the second process, the sector operated within a more narrow ideological range, which mainly aligned with social democratic positions.

[8] In total, 1,180 votes were cast in the plenary of the Constitutional Council. Of this total, 959 (81.3%) were approved with more than three-fifths. [This dataset, *Roll-call votes in the Plenary of the Constitutional Council of Chile, 2023*, is available on the author's website.]

Nonetheless, the number of agreed-on provisions was considerably larger than that in the first convention despite these ideological divisions. The structured nature of the process, which featured a pre-drafted text, lower quorum requirements, and stricter procedural oversight, all facilitated this. Many articles that were highly contentious in the first convention, such as those related to the organization of the state, the role of Congress, and judicial independence, were now approved with relative ease.

Figure 16.2 extends the analysis by placing council members along two dimensions to incorporate ideological positions and value orientations. It shows that the left remained relatively unified and clustered around social democratic positions with few significant internal divisions. In contrast, the right was more dispersed, revealing a clear ideological distance between the Republican Party and *Chile Vamos*. Thematically, the former maintained a strictly conservative stance, particularly on social issues such as abortion and gender policies, while *Chile Vamos* positioned itself as a flexible coalition, occasionally aligning with the center-left on governance-related issues.

The same ideological divisions were evident in the thematic committees (or commissions). Figure 16.3 indicates that the left operated as a cohesive bloc across all four committees, consistently clustered around shared positions, while the right displayed visible internal fragmentation. In Commission 1 (Political System, Constitutional Reform, and Form of the State), the distance between *Chile Vamos*, which tended to occupy more centrist positions, and the Republican Party, situated on the ideological edge, was especially marked. Nevertheless, Republican influence often nudged *Chile Vamos* toward more conservative proposals, though the final outcomes reflected a degree of moderation. A similar pattern held in Commission 3 (Principles, Civil and Political Rights) and Commission 4 (Economic, Social, Cultural, and Environmental Rights), where the right was internally divided, and the left remained unified (at least on the first dimension), allowing it to negotiate from a position of strength.

Commission 2 (Jurisdictional Function and Autonomous Bodies) stood out as an exception. Here, the ideological distance within the right was less pronounced: *Chile Vamos* and the Republican Party appeared more closely aligned, presenting a unified conservative front on key institutional matters. This cohesion allowed the right to act with greater effectiveness, shaping the discussion without the same need for internal negotiation needed in the other three commissions.

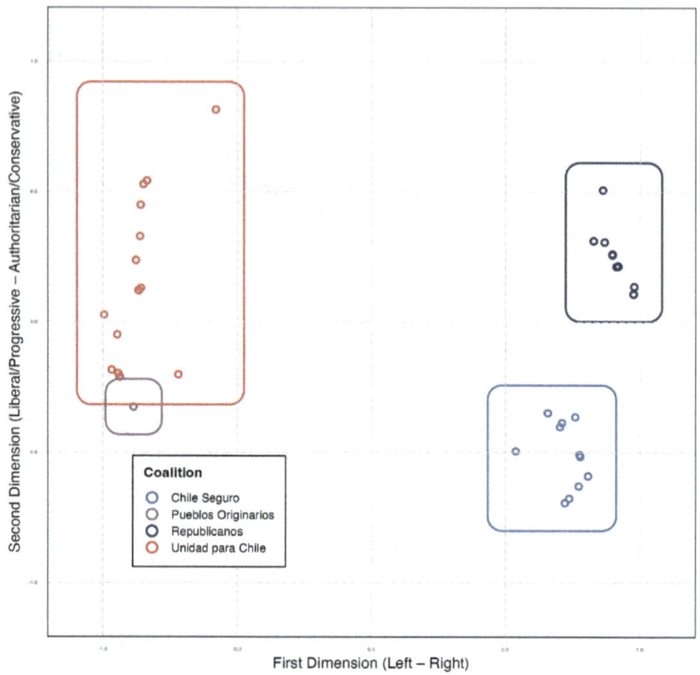

Fig. 16.2 Two-dimensional placement of Constitutional Council members in the plenary (*Note* Each point represents a member of the 2023 Constitutional Council, positioned in a two-dimensional ideological space derived from roll-call voting patterns. The horizontal axis reflects a left–right dimension, while the vertical axis captures a liberal/progressive versus authoritarian/conservative orientation. Points are color-coded by party, and rectangular outlines indicate clusters of members belonging to the same party. *Source* Author with data from Bunker 2023c)

Overall, the patterns in Figure 16.3 reflect a consistently unified left and a right that, while fragmented across most commissions, showed moments of strategic convergence, particularly where ideological proximity or shared institutional goals enabled coordinated action.

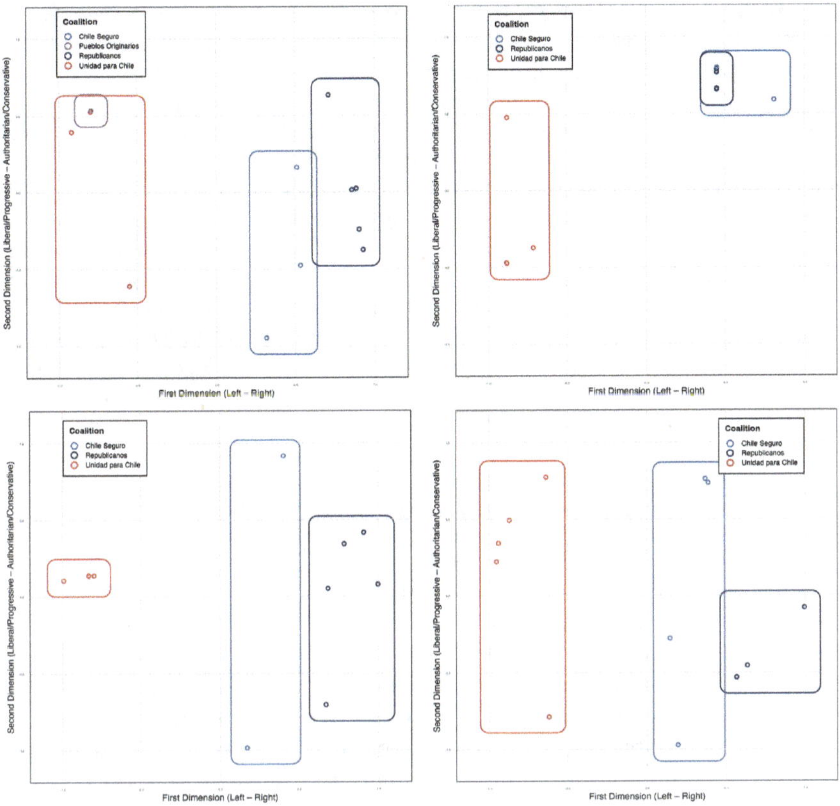
Coalition
Chile Seguro
Pueblos Originarios
Republicanos
Unidad para Chile
Second Dimension (Liberal/Progressive – Authoritarian/Conservative)
First Dimension (Left – Right)
Coalition
Chile Seguro
Republicanos
Unidad para Chile
Second Dimension (Liberal/Progressive – Authoritarian/Conservative)
First Dimension (Left – Right)
Coalition
Chile Seguro
Republicanos
Unidad para Chile
Second Dimension (Liberal/Progressive – Authoritarian/Conservative)
First Dimension (Left – Right)
Coalition
Chile Seguro
Republicanos
Unidad para Chile
Second Dimension (Liberal/Progressive – Authoritarian/Conservative)
First Dimension (Left – Right)

◀**Fig. 16.3** Two-dimensional placement of Constitutional Council members in their respective commissions (*Note* Each circle represents a member of the 2023 Constitutional Council, positioned in a two-dimensional ideological space derived from roll-call voting patterns. The horizontal axis reflects a left–right dimension, while the vertical axis captures a liberal/progressive versus authoritarian/conservative orientation. Points are color-coded by coalition, and rectangular outlines indicate clusters of members belonging to the same coalition. The names of the commissions were as follows: Commission 1 was *Sistema Político, Reforma Constitucional y Forma de Estado* ("Political System, Constitutional Reform, and Form of the State"). Commission 2 was *Función Jurisdiccional y Órganos Autónomos* ("Jurisdictional Function and Autonomous Bodies"). Commission 3 was *Principios, Derechos Civiles y Políticos* ("Principles, Civil and Political Rights"). Commission 4 was *Derechos Económicos, Sociales, Culturales y Ambientales* ("Economic, Social, Cultural, and Environmental Rights"). *Source* Author with data from Bunker 2023d[9])

16.4.2 A Cohesive Yet Divided Assembly

In summary, voting patterns reveal a broadly cohesive but internally divided assembly, in which the right held a clear majority but operated within two competing factions. While the Republican Party pushed for an ideologically rigid approach, *Chile Vamos* served as a moderating force and tempered a few radical proposals. In contrast, the left remained unified but numerically weak, which limited its ability to influence the contents in the final document beyond minor adjustments.

Given the numerical dominance of the right, the aforementioned structured nature of the second process, and the clear ideological bias of its members, a right-leaning proposal was expected.[10] However, internal ideological divergence within the right prevented the draft from fully

[9] Across the commissions of the Constitutional Council, approval rates varied notably. Commission 1, focused on the political system, recorded 400 votes, of which 297 passed with more than 50 percent, resulting in an approval rate of 74.2%. Commission 2, dealing with jurisdictional matters, saw 141 of 148 proposals approved, yielding a notably high approval rate of 95.3%. In Commission 3, on constitutional principles, 125 of 222 votes passed, or 56.3%. Commission 4, which focused on rights, had 118 votes, of which 76 passed, amounting to an approval rate of 64.4%. [This dataset, *Roll-call votes in the Commissions of the Constitutional Council of Chile, 2023*, is available on the author's website.]

[10] At least a more *traditional* proposal was expected, considering the presence of the pre-drafted text, the influence of expert oversight, and the lower quorum requirements all contributed to an efficient decision-making process. The tighter timeframe also gave the

adhering to a single, pure canon. As a result, the final text—while still conservative in principle—included a number of ideas that had emerged from the broader political debate in the years leading up to this moment.

16.5 The Second Proposal

The second constitutional proposal was made public on October 7, 2023. Comprising 17 chapters, 216 articles, and 49,882 words, the document reaffirmed a traditional vision of governance.[11] Its cover featured a sober background with a unitary map of Chile rendered in the national colors of white, blue, and red—visually reinforcing themes of tradition and continuity.[12]

Chapter 1 (pp. 7–13), entitled Foundations of the Constitutional Order, covered Articles 1 to 15 and established the fundamental principles for the State of Chile. It emphasized core values such as human dignity (Art. 1), the family unit (Art. 2), and the social and democratic nature of the state (Art. 5). In contrast to the first proposal it recognized indigenous population as part of a unitary nation (Art. 5), and mentioned national symbols such as the flag, the anthem, and traditional sports (Art. 11), as well as expressed a clear position against terrorism (Art. 15). Generally, it was considered a continuation of Chile´s historical legal foundations, though with a clearer emphasis on traditional and national values.

Chapter 2 (pp. 14–44), on Rights and Fundamental Freedoms, Guarantees, and Constitutional Duties, spanned Articles 16 to 37. It guaranteed various rights, including personal liberty, freedom of expression, decent work, access to housing, social security, and property rights. Article 16 sought to guarantee the life of those yet to be born (n. 1), and the freedom to consciously object (n. 13), while constitutionalizing private

rendezvous a sense of urgency that allowed it to elude the legislative procrastination and distractions that characterized the first process.

[11] As a reference, the 1980 constitution had 25,299 words upon its ratification in 1980, 25,360 words upon its debut in 1990, 25,649 words after it was reformed in 2005, and 25,821 words at the time of the estalldo social in 2019, the year the constitutional process began. In comparison, the 2018 Bachelet proposal had 28,119 words, the 2022 Constitutional Convention proposal had 52,924 words, and the 2023 Experts preproposal had 40,329 words.

[12] This document, *Propuesta de Nueva Constitución (2023)*, is available on the author's website.

healthcare (n. 22), education (n. 23), and the pension system (n. 28). It also specifically addressed nationality and citizenship (Art. 17–20), states of emergency (Art. 30–36), and constitutional duties (Art. 37). While the right to access water was explicitly recognized in numeral 30, it was qualified in numeral 35(i), which allowed for the establishment and transfer of private water use rights in accordance with the law. In sum, while maintaining most classical rights, the chapter also reflected the conservative spirit of the council.

Chapter 3 (pp. 45–51), titled Political Representation and Participation, included Articles 38 to 50 and provided detailed rules for referendums (Art. 39), electoral systems (Art. 40), and democratic practices within political parties (Art. 41–44). Much in line with the previous proposal, it encouraged citizen initiatives (Art. 45–46) and increased participation in public administration to ensure inclusivity in the drafting of norms (Art. 47–50).

Chapter 4 (pp. 52–79), regarding National Congress, spanned Articles 51 to 89 and established a bicameral legislature with a Chamber of Deputies and a Senate (Art. 51). While maintaining much of the existing order, Article 55 added new mechanisms against independents (n. 5) and outsiders (n. 6). Remarkably, Article 56 lowered the district magnitude to 2–6 from 3–8, and reduced the size of the Lower Chamber to 138 from 155 (in the thirtieth transitional provision). The chapter also outlined roles for legislators (Art. 57–58) and the legislative process in general (Art. 74–89). Generally, it moved in a restrictive direction, seeking to reduce party fragmentation and increase legislative discipline.

Chapter 5 (pp. 80–93), regarding Government and Administration of the State, covered Articles 90–113 and began by defining the President of the Republic as the Head of State and Government. It assigned presidential responsibilities for maintaining public order and national security and specified a four-year term limit and a cap of two nonconsecutive terms—all this much in line with the 1980 Constitution. It also listed the president's and ministers' duties and attributions. The chapter innovated by establishing the Law and Public Policy Evaluation Council (Art. 112) to enhance legislative effectiveness and policy oversight.

Chapter 6 (pp. 94–95), entitled National Defense, comprised Articles 114–116 and described the structure and duties of the Armed Forces, including the Army, Navy, and Air Force, under presidential authority. The chapter, broadly consistent with the existing order, emphasized national defense, emergency response, and border protection while prohibiting military personnel from political or union affiliations. Internal organization and appointments were assigned to legislative definitions. In sum, it maintained the traditional civilian oversight of the military, slightly modernizing its operational governance.

Chapter 7 (pp. 96–99), regarding Public Security, was composed of Articles 117–125 and addressed the operations of the *Carabineros* and the Investigative Police. Under the proposal, tasks would include maintaining national order and providing emergency collaboration. Similar to the Armed Forces, personnel would be barred from political and union affiliations with additional probity and transparency controls. Despite introducing stronger institutional accountability, it remained largely unchanged in practice.

Chapter 8 (pp. 100–113), regarding Government and Regional Administration, spanned Articles 126–154, and upheld regional governments but added significant regulatory, financial, and supervisory powers. It promoted decentralization and citizen participation, and addressed special territories such as Easter Island, Juan Fernández, and Antarctica.

Chapter 9 (pp. 114–122), on Judicial Power, included Articles 155–167 and focused on the independence of courts and judicial accountability. It introduced bodies for appointing judges and judicial prosecutors, training programs, and the Conduct Tribunal to address disciplinary issues. Transparency and probity mechanisms were emphasized throughout the chapter. These provisions continued longstanding legal traditions while introducing clearer standards of judicial conduct. It marked a drastic difference from the first draft, which had proposed a parallel justice system.

Chapter 10 (pp. 123–131), titled Constitutional Court, comprised Articles 168–173 and established an 11-member Constitutional Court appointed by the Supreme Court, the President, and the Senate (Art. 169). Consistent with the 1980 Constitution, the role of the Court was to ensure constitutional supremacy and resolve legal disputes involving bills, treaties, and governmental acts. It was also empowered to disqualify political parties and individuals from holding certain positions (Art. 172).

Chapter 11 (pp. 132–133), National Service for Access to Justice and Victim Support, spanned Articles 174–176, and ensured access to justice and support for crime victims. Just two pages long, the chapter institutionalized legal, psychological, and social assistance under the supervision of a National Director and the Superior Council (Art. 175). It also allowed for a Victims' Ombudsman Office to provide legal aid to those affected by crimes (Art. 176). This represented a break from past frameworks by formally integrating victim support into the constitutional structure.

Chapter 12 (pp. 134–140), The Public Prosecutors' Office, comprising Articles 177–189, regulated an autonomous body accountable for investigating crimes and pursuing public prosecutions. Prosecutors would be prohibited from judicial or electoral roles and would be governed by regional and deputy offices. The Senate would appoint the National Prosecutor with a Supraterritorial Prosecutors' Office to address complex crimes (Art. 178). This chapter was built on existing prosecutorial independence but added layers of complexity.

Chapter 13 (pp. 141–145), on Electoral Justice and Electoral Service, spanned Articles 190–192 and was intended to regulate the *Tribunal Calificador de Elecciones* and its oversight of elections and plebiscites (Art. 190). The chapter also established regional electoral tribunals and empowered the *Servicio Electoral* to supervise elections, political parties, and electoral expenditures (Art. 192). This did not change much in relation to the existing structure.

Chapter 14 (pp. 146–148), regarding the Office of the Comptroller General of the Republic, covered Articles 193–197 and redefined the autonomous entity that oversees legality and probity in State administration. It held that the *Contraloría* would operate at the national, regional, and local levels, auditing public funds, controlling government acts, and submitting annual accounts to the Chamber of Deputies. The chapter also established the Court of Auditors to review objections and ensured that State payments adhered to budgetary authorization (Art. 196). Overall, the structure reaffirmed classical public auditing frameworks with added procedural detail.

Chapter 15 (pp. 149–151), on the Central Bank, spanned Articles 198–205 and regulated the authority of the autonomous Central Bank over monetary and financial matters. It restricted the Bank from financing public expenditures, thus limiting its role to exceptional cases. A five-member board appointed by the President and Senate would oversee its operations with strict requirements for transparency. The chapter preserved the Central Bank's institutional autonomy, consistent with recent decades, while adding further safeguards (a major point of contention in the first proposal).

Chapter 16 (pp. 152–153), Protection of the Environment, Sustainability, and Development, covered Articles 206–213, and aimed to reinforce environmental stewardship and sustainability, and promote public–private collaboration and citizen participation. The chapter introduced ecological education, territorial sustainability, and climate change measures, supported by technical institutions and evaluation systems. Building on trends rather than traditions, it marked a break with the past.

Finally, Chapter 17 (pp. 154–156), Procedures for Constitutional Change, included Articles 214–216, and specified processes for initiating constitutional reforms. In this draft, reform proposals could only originate from the President or Congress and would require a three-fifths majority in both chambers for approval. In the case of disagreement, unresolved issues could be subject to a plebiscite (Art. 215–216). This process echoed the earlier proposal, embedding plebiscites into the constitutional reform mechanism.

In summary, while the 2023 constitutional proposal did not mark a significant departure from the incumbent constitution, it offered a substantially more conservative and institutional vision for Chile's governance than the 2022 one did. While it emphasized stability, order, and the protection of traditional values, critics noted its limited scope in addressing social demands. The focus on national unity resonated with some, but concerns about inclusivity and social rights persisted. Ultimately, the proposal not only raised questions about whether change was meaningful but even necessary.

16.6 Waning Support and a Predictable Rejection

In contrast to the first referendum, in which enthusiasm for the initial proposal decreased over time, the second process began with less public engagement. Polling data indicates that constitutional fatigue, combined with shifting public priorities (e.g., rising crime rate, economic instability, and concerns over immigration), overshadowed the importance of constitutional change. Previously considered a crucial political milestone, the constitutional debate gradually became a secondary issue, as many Chileans began to perceive it as detached from their immediate concerns.

Figure 16.4 provides a visual representation of the evolution of public sentiment toward the second constitutional proposal in the months prior to the December 2023 plebiscite. The figure depicts trends in voting intention and illustrates the proportion of valid responses to open-ended voting intention questions, thus distinguishing between approval and rejection. While low but stable support for the proposal indicates widespread disillusionment with the constitutional process, the ups and downs on the Reject side indicate the interference of specific issues (these are explored in Chapter 17).

Finally, on December 17, 2023, Chileans returned to the polls for what would be the final vote in the constitutional reform process. After months of debate and increasing public skepticism, the outcome delivered a decisive blow: the proposal was rejected. The result landed like a bucket of cold water on its supporters and political backers, marking a historic moment. Chile became the first country in modern history to consecutively reject two constitutional drafts. Table 16.1 shows the final results: 55.8% voted to reject the draft, while 44.2% approved it—closely aligning with the predictions made by most polling firms.

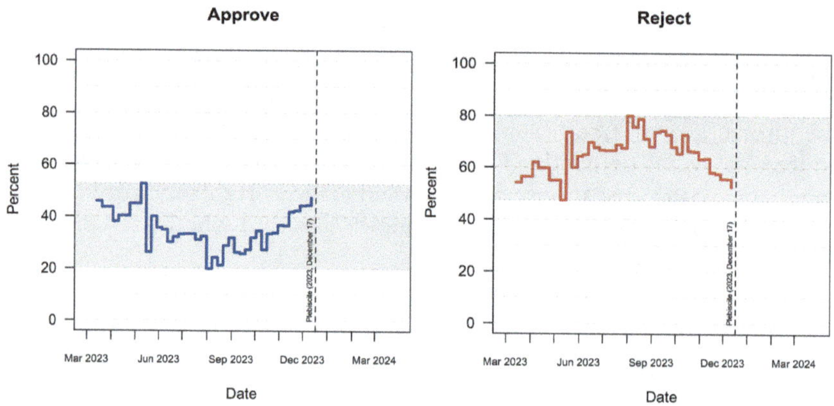

Fig. 16.4 Trends of voting intention for the 2023 constitutional plebiscite (*Note* The panel on the left displays the weekly average of support for the Approve option, while the panel on the right shows the weekly average of support for the Reject option, in the lead-up to Chile's 2023 constitutional plebiscite. In both panels, the staircase line represents the average for each week based on available survey data. Percentages are calculated using only the responses for Approve and Reject, excluding undecided or other responses. The shaded gray area indicates the full range (minimum to maximum) of weekly averages observed during the period. Horizontal dotted lines mark this range, and the vertical dashed line marks the date of the plebiscite (December 17, 2023). Note that, by law, polls could not be published during the final two weeks before the vote, and this is reflected in the absence of data during that period. *Source* Author with data from Tresquintos)

Table 16.1 Results of the 2023 constitutional plebiscite

Question: Do you approve the proposal drafted by the 2023 constitutional council?		
	Number of votes	*Percent of votes*
Approve (*A favor*)	5,472,375	44.21
Reject (*En contra*)	6,905,483	55.79
Valid Votes	**12,377,858**	**95.00**
Null Votes	**480,826**	**3.69**
Blank Votes	**169,968**	**1.31**
Total	**13,028,652**	**100**

Note Voting was mandatory. Registered voters: 15,406,352. Estimated turnout: 84.48%. *Source* Author with data from Servel

For the left, the rejection came as a relief, as it blocked what they perceived as an attempt to entrench a conservative model of governance. They had dodged a bullet. For the right, however, the outcome was a painful setback. Much like their predecessors, they had misjudged the priorities of the electorate and fallen in the trap.

For the rest, for the broader population, the rejection was neither a source of relief nor setback. It was, above all, a sign that it was finally time to close the book and move on. After four years of debate, elections, and referendums, they were simply glad it was finally all over.

16.7 Conclusion

The 2023 Constitutional Council stood in stark contrast to its predecessor. While the first constitutional convention was fragmented, experimental, and ideologically diverse, the second was structured, disciplined, and ideologically polarized. Yet despite differences and corrections in approach and tone, the outcome was the same.

One of the defining aspects of the second constitutional effort was its strict adherence to rules and oversight mechanisms, which were implemented to avoid the procedural shortcomings that characterized the first attempt. The Technical Admissions and Experts Committees played a crucial role in shaping a more structured process to ensure consensus-driven deliberations and limit radical proposals. However, the rigid framework may have hindered public engagement because it prioritized political discipline over citizen mobilization. By focusing on pragmatism and moderation, the council aligned with traditional political norms, which may have alienated just *one too many voters* who were still seeking transformational change.

Polarization within the council further underscored the complexity of the political landscape in Chile. While the right-wing majority controlled the process, internal division between the Republican Party and *Chile Vamos* revealed tension over the scope and ideological tone of the final draft. Although these divisions did not significantly obstruct legislative agreements, they foreshadowed challenges in securing unified electoral support during the referendum. Meanwhile, the left played a minor role as its influence was limited to mitigating conservative proposals instead of shaping the draft. This imbalance contributed to a proposal that leaned towards moderates, but ultimately remained out of reach for the majority of the electorate.

In any case, it is clear that the 2023 Constitutional Council represented a missed opportunity for reconciling Chile's constitutional aspiration with its social and political reality. While it succeeded in constructing a disciplined process, it failed to inspire public trust or enthusiasm. The reasons behind its ultimate failure are explored in the next chapter. For now, the lesson that remains is that successful constitutional reform requires more than procedural efficiency—it demands a genuine recognition of the tangible concerns and priorities of the electorate.

CHAPTER 17

Coming to Terms: Why the Second Constitutional Process Failed

17.1 Introduction

This chapter examines the rejection of Chile's second constitutional proposal by analyzing the reasons why it failed to gain public support despite being a restrained alternative to the first draft. While avoiding the extensive ideological overreach of its predecessor, it failed to retain key societal rights, leaving itself vulnerable to attacks and skepticism. The inability of the proposal to preserve critical issues, such as abortion rights and other social provisions, led to uncertainty and ultimately alienated moderate voters, who feared that if enacted, it could lead to regression rather than stability.

The design of the second process was theoretically intended to correct the flaws of the first and offer a moderate and institutionally stable framework. However, its practical execution was insufficiently pragmatic. While it avoided radical restructuring, it nevertheless failed to strike a balance that would reassure the majority of the electorate. By failing to explicitly guarantee rights previously enshrined in law, the proposal fostered doubts about whether it would be used to erode the existing protection under future conservative governments. Similarly, its stances on social policies reinforced perceptions that it was an ideologically rigid document instead of a unifying one. Although the second draft was less extreme, it continued to carry ideological baggage that made it politically vulnerable.

K. Bunker, *Chile's Transformation Amidst Crisis*,
https://doi.org/10.1007/978-3-031-96463-3_17

Apart from these substantive concerns, other factors reinforced public opposition. For example, the *constitutional fatigue* that had set in by the time of the second plebiscite also played a crucial role in the rejection. After four years of political division, prolonged debates, and unfulfilled promises, many Chileans became weary of the idea as a whole. What had been presented as a necessary institutional response to the 2019 crisis had muted into a prolonged and exhausting political battle without any clear end in sight. For *too* many, the promise of a new constitution had lost its urgency and been replaced by the immediate concerns of the day (see Chapter 15).

As public patience wore thin, the referendum presented voters with a stark choice: to accept the new proposal or to end the constitutional process entirely. In contrast to the first plebiscite, in which rejection was framed as a means for seeking a better alternative, the second referendum did not offer this option. By this point, and because many viewed the existing Pinochet-era constitution as flawed but functional, they opted for the latter rather than for an untested, uncertain future.

This chapter is structured as follows. First, it examines the failure of the second proposal to secure societal rights, particularly in areas that became politically contentious. It then explores the political and economic contexts of the months and days leading up to plebiscite, with a focus on *constitutional fatigue* and the *trade-off mindset* that had set in as the main driving forces shaping voting behavior. Finally, it reflects on the implications of the two consecutive rejections and argues that, in the end, both failures stemmed from the same fundamental misdiagnosis.

17.2 Extremely Ambitious, Insufficiently Pragmatic

The rejection of Chile's second constitutional proposal was a result of its failure to strike a balance between pragmatism and viability. While the draft was far more measured than its predecessor, it lacked simplicity. It avoided sweeping ideological overreach but contained details that, although seemingly minor, became an easy target for opposition campaigns. Amplified by political actors and media narratives, these details increased skepticism about whether this constitution was indeed the one that Chile needed.

One of the most significant examples of this strategic flaw was the issue of abortion. While the proposal did not explicitly roll back the existing reproductive rights, it failed to safeguard what existed in a manner that reassured the electorate. Ambiguously worded, Article 16, numeral 1 was interpreted as ushering in future restrictions on abortion.[1] Critics of the time argued that by refraining from guaranteeing the protections established under the 2017 reform, the draft left room for conservative majorities to impose greater limitations. This ambiguity created uncertainty, particularly for women's rights advocates who viewed reproductive freedom as a non-negotiable social gain.

The backlash to the introduction of the article was bold. Former president Michelle Bachelet, for example, emerged as a vocal critic, warning that the proposal could weaken the hard-won reproductive rights achieved under her administration.[2] Despite reassurance from supporters of the draft that abortion rights would not be at risk,[3] the lack of explicit protection channeled into a perception that the new constitution could actually represent a step backward.

The perception proved *fatal*. While logic dictated that the new proposal should avoid introducing controversial ideological shifts,

[1] In September 2023, the Constitutional Council approved language in Article 16 stating that "the law protects the life of the unborn," a phrasing that sparked controversy over its implications for Chile's existing abortion law. Critics argued the clause lacked sufficient safeguards and could lead to future judicial challenges against the 2017 law legalizing abortion under three specific conditions. See: Sanhueza, A. M. 2023. "El Consejo Constitucional chileno asegura "la vida de quien está por nacer" y complica los acuerdos." *El País*. September 21. https://elpais.com/chile/2023-09-21/el-consejo-constitucional-chileno-asegura-la-vida-de-quien-esta-por-nacer-y-complica-los-acuerdos.html/

[2] In late November 2023, Michelle Bachelet warned that the new constitutional draft could enable the courts to declare the existing law on abortion in three cases unconstitutional, undermining a key reform passed under her government. See: Pareja, P. 2023. "Bachelet alerta que con la propuesta de nueva Constitución la "despenalización del aborto en tres causales podría ser declarada inconstitucional"." *La Tercera*. November 28. https://www.latercera.com/nacional/noticia/bachelet-dice-que-con-la-propuesta-de-nueva-constitucion-la-despenalizacion-del-aborto-en-tres-causales-podria-ser-declarada-inconstitucional/XOBDV3WYFFGE5ALVZ2DB7OOALI/

[3] On December 6, 2023, Evelyn Matthei and several former ministers from the Piñera administration publicly countered Bachelet's concerns, insisting that the proposed text would not jeopardize the current abortion framework. Among the signers were: Isabel Plá, Mónica Zalaquett, Gloria Hutt, Karla Rubilar, and Carolina Schmidt. See: Navarrete, E. 2023. "Matthei y exministras de Piñera responden a carta de Bachelet: aseguran que texto constitucional "no pondrá en riesgo" aborto en tres causales." *La Tercera*. December 6. https://www.latercera.com/politica/noticia/matthei-y-exministras-de-pinera-responden-a-carta-de-bachelet-aseguran-que-propuesta-constitucional-no-pondra-en-riesgo-aborto-tres-causales/A352QP77ENGHDN7LCQEFEZ45AE/

Council members did so anyway. The debate over abortion overshadowed the more moderate content of the draft, which illustrates how strategic political framing can invalidate even an otherwise balanced constitutional proposal.

There were several other examples of articles that could have been moderated, but because they were not, they consolidated as a direct threat to the moderate segment of voters. For example, Article 16, numeral 28, recognized the right to social security, but its letter b) explicitly granted individuals ownership over their pension contributions and the freedom to choose between public or private administrators, while prohibiting any form of expropriation by the state. While this aligned with the right's agenda, it was seen by the ruling coalition as a constitutional entrenchment of the existing AFP system, effectively blocking future reforms toward a solidarity-based. Instead of offering a flexible framework that could accommodate multiple visions for pension reform, the proposal locked in one approach, reinforcing perceptions that the text prioritized ideological goals over pragmatic consensus.

A similar dynamic emerged in the areas of healthcare and education. Article 16, numeral 22, on the right to health, guaranteed the freedom to choose between public and private systems, a wording that, according to the center-left, effectively entrenched the ISAPREs and limited the possibility of future reforms based on solidarity. In education (Article 16, numeral 23), the draft endorsed per-student funding for both public and private schools and limited the role of the Ministry of Education by allowing institutions to define their own curricula. In both cases, what could have been framed as balanced approaches instead came across as rigid attempts to lock in a particular ideological model—once again pushing moderates away.

For the majority of voters, however, the debate pointed less to the substance of these issues and more to the political context in which they were being discussed. It was not so much about pensions, or healthcare or even education, but about the growing ideologization of the conversation. This shift increasingly worked against the right, as it reinforced perceptions that the constitutional process was being used to advance a narrow partisan agenda.

As such, the main problem of the proposal lay less with its substantive content than in the strategic clumsiness with which it was presented.[4]

[4] Ironically, many of the socially conservative, market-friendly provisions that contributed to the proposed constitution's defeat were later implemented or advanced

In broad strokes, it was a moderate proposal, but because it included provisions that created sufficient uncertainty, or enough room for doubt regarding its intentions, it allowed for critics to seize the moment and make a case for reasonable doubt.[5] With the ideological overreach of the first process in hindsight (see Chapter 12), the tactic proved effective, as voters were no longer willing to trust a proposal that carried even the slightest perception of risk.

Well aware of this sentiment, the opposition focused its campaign on these details instead of the overall framework of the draft. They selectively highlighted provisions that could be framed as a step backward and refrained from attacking the document in its entirety.[6] This strategy was successful, but only because the electorate was exhausted by the constitutional process. It is likely that under any other circumstance, it would not have worked; at least not as effectively.

through ordinary legislation by the Boric administration. This was notably the case with the 2023-2024 "reforms" in the pension and healthcare sectors (see Chapter 3), which ultimately consolidated both the AFP and ISAPRE models established during the dictatorship. This suggests not only that the draft's orientation was likely less extreme than some portrayed, but also that the left's opposition during the constitutional debate was driven more by political strategy than by genuine disagreement with the substance of these policies.

[5] Post-election analysis indicates that the decisive factor in the proposal's rejection was not the presence of radical content, but the way uncertainty, particularly around rights and institutional design, was amplified during the campaign. Opponents capitalized on this ambiguity, framing it as evidence of hidden objectives and mobilizing skepticism among key voter segments. Notably, those who voted against were disproportionately from vulnerable groups such as women, young people, and former null voters, rather than from the middle class. See: *El Pais*. 2023. "Mujeres, jóvenes y antiguos nulos: el perfil del votante que tumbó la propuesta constitucional de Chile." December 22. https://elpais.com/chile/2023-12-19/mujeres-jovenes-y-antiguos-nulos-el-perfil-del-votante-que-tumbo-la-propuesta-constitucional-de-chile.html/

[6] In addition to the issues of abortion, pensions, and education discussed above, the opposition also pointed to other articles that, in their view, entrenched right-wing policy preferences and restricted future democratic debate. These included provisions on the right to strike (Article 16, numeral 27), the recognition of water use rights as transferable private property (numeral 35), expanded protections for conscientious objection (numeral 13), and electoral rules that could reduce "political pluralism" introduced by previous reforms. For a review, see: Ávila Cárdenas, M., and G. Pizarro. 2023. "Propuesta Constitucional: los ocho artículos que impedirían la competencia democrática de todas las ideas." *CIPER*. October 30. https://www.ciperchile.cl/2023/10/30/propuesta-constitucional-los-ocho-articulos-que-impedirian-la-competencia-democratica-de-todas-las-ideas/

17.3 Additional Considerations

Similar to the outcome of the first constitutional process, which was shaped by a series of moderating variables beyond the content of the proposed constitution, the fate of the second was also influenced by several additional factors. However, unlike the first plebiscite in 2020, which was framed as a moral decision, and the second in 2022, which was ultimately perceived as an inconsequential dry run, the third plebiscite in 2023 came to be viewed as a matter of rational choice. This time, voters made their decision not with emotion or hope, but by carefully weighing the pros and cons and evaluating the gains and losses of the entire constitutional process in hindsight.[7]

At the very least, this rational approach helps illuminate two key dynamics that contributed to the proposal's failure, even without direct reference to its content. First, it sheds light on the emergence of *constitutional fatigue*, as many Chileans—after years of political conflict and unmet expectations—no longer saw reform as a pressing priority. Second, it helps explain the rise of a *trade-off mindset*, in which voters assessed whether the costs of replacing the existing constitution outweighed the potential benefits.[8]

17.3.1 Burden of Constitutional Fatigue

While the content of the second proposal played a significant role in its rejection, the political context was at least as important. By December 2023, Chileans were experiencing widespread *constitutional fatigue*—a deep exhaustion with a reform process that consumed the public debate for four years without delivering tangible changes.

[7] While the substantive content of the second constitutional proposal played a central role in its rejection, the strategic missteps by the drafting majority were arguably more consequential. Despite early optimism, a palpable sense of societal fatigue had taken hold well before the process even began. This weariness—left unaddressed—eroded enthusiasm and trust, setting the stage for another defeat. The failure to acknowledge and respond to this mood was, in many ways, the final nail in the coffin of Chile's second constitutional endeavor. See: Nugent, C. 2023. "Chileans Reject Second Attempt to Rewrite Constitution." *Financial Times*. December 18. https://www.ft.com/content/70611572-1563-47d1-b0d7-0bc9aadf9138

[8] See an original, and timely discussion in this regard: Bunker, K. 2023. "La Constitución de Kast o la Constitución de Pinochet." *Ex-Ante*. May 13. https://www.ex-ante.cl/la-constitucion-de-kast-o-la-constitucion-de-pinochet-por-kenneth-bunker/

The initial enthusiasm for a new constitution had long faded. In 2019, the process was framed as a necessary response to the social unrest, a means for addressing Chile's structural problems, and restoring faith in its institutions. However, by the time of the second plebiscite, many Chileans had lost faith in that vision. If the first proposal had exhausted the patience of the electorate, the second attempt failed to reignite their optimism.[9]

As laid out in Chapter 15, several factors underlaid the fatigue. By the end of 2023, Chile was dealing with a failing, unpopular government, unable to control inflation,[10] create jobs,[11] bring down crime,[12] or control the borders.[13]

[9] The rejection of the second constitutional draft generated widespread analysis, with commentators attributing the outcome to factors as wide as ideological exhaustion, strategic voting behavior, and a broader disillusionment with the constituent process itself. See: Rivas, C. 2023. "Nadie entiende nada... ¿Cómo interpretar el resultado del plebiscito?" *Diario Financiero*. December 19. https://www.df.cl/economia-y-politica/politica/nadie-entiende-nada-como-interpretar-el-resultado-del-plebiscito/

[10] According to a report from Consensus Forecast, Chile was projected to be tied with Nicaragua with the sixth-highest inflation rate in Latin America for 2024. See: del Solar, D. 2024. "Chile será el sexto país con la inflación más alta de Latinoamérica en 2024." *La Tercera*. November 27. https://www.latercera.com/pulso-pm/noticia/chile-sera-el-sexto-pais-con-la-inflacion-mas-alta-de-latinoamerica-en-2024/5ORCLQFRHNBF7COWO3JSZBOZ6Q/

[11] A November 2023 report by the *Instituto Nacional de Estadísticas* (INE, "National Statitics Institution") reported that Chile's unemployment rate had increased for the twelfth time in twelve months. David Bravo, director of the Centro de Estudios Longitudinales of the Pontificia Universidad Católica, considered the trend a 13-year setback. See: *Pauta*. 2023. "Doble clic a cifra de desempleo: "Tener un retroceso de 13 años es una emergencia laboral"." November 29. https://www.pauta.cl/economia/2023/11/29/doble-clic-a-cifra-de-desempleo-tener-un-retroceso-de-13-anos-es-una-emergencia-laboral.html/

[12] A global survey conducted by IPSOS found that Chile was leading the world in public concern about rising crime rates. See: *IPSOS*. 2023. "Chilenos lideran ranking mundial entre quienes perciben mayor aumento de delincuencia en su barrio." June 14. https://www.ipsos.com/es-cl/chilenos-lideran-ranking-mundial-entre-quienes-perciben-mayor-aumento-de-delincuencia-en-su-barrio/

[13] A report on Chile's immigration trends from the Ministry of the Interior revealed that the number of irregular immigrants in the country in 2023 surpassed the total from the previous four years combined. See: *El Líbero*. 2024. "Balance de los dos años de Gobierno del Presidente Boric: inmigración irregular supera la suma de los cuatro años anteriores." March 9. https://ellibero.cl/actualidad/balance-de-los-dos-anos-de-gobierno-del-presidente-boric-inmigracion-irregular-supera-la-suma-de-los-cuatro-anos-anteriores/

As such, voters began questioning whether the constitutional process was even worth it at all. The abstract debate over governance structures, legal rights, and institutional reforms was increasingly seen as a disconnected conversation among elites rather than the bottom-up process it had once been presented as. Amid soaring living costs and deepening economic uncertainty, the idea of upending the entire system was no longer making the same sense it once did.[14]

This growing disillusionment was compounded by political leadership that did little to restore confidence. If nothing else, President Gabriel Boric's controversial decision in late 2022 to pardon several individuals convicted in connection with the 2019 social outburst sent a damaging signal that would linger for years.[15] Conveniently carried out after the first constitutional process, the pardons' political effects were felt not only in the results of the May constitutional council election—which punished the left in particular—but also in the exit plebiscite, which punished the political class more broadly.

Finally, as if to confirm doubts about the country's direction and the quality of its leadership, a corruption scandal erupted in the months prior to the referendum. The revelations linked the Ministry of Housing under the Boric government to key members of *Revolución Democrática*, presidential advisors, and technocrats in the Treasury. Public trust collapsed

[14] In the lead-up to the vote, high inflation, elevated interest rates, and rising unemployment fueled public discontent, further eroding trust in the idea that the political establishment could deliver a constitutional solution without inflicting significant costs on Chiles development path. See: Lefin, D. 2023. "Altas tasas de interés, inflación y 110 mil desempleados más que en 2022: cómo llega la economía al plebiscito del 17-D." *El Mercurio*. December 3. https://digital.elmercurio.com/2023/12/03/B/UU4C3F8A/

[15] President Boric's decision on December 30, 2022, to pardon 12 individuals linked to the 2019 social unrest, along with former FPMR (Frente Patriótico Manuel Rodríguez) guerrilla Jorge Mateluna, sparked significant backlash. The move disrupted ongoing security negotiations with the opposition, prompted the resignation of the Minister of Justice, and drew criticism from the Supreme Court for encroaching on judicial authority. One of those pardoned, Luis Castillo, was later arrested for kidnapping and robbery—an episode that further eroded public trust in the government's capacity and willingness to address the security crisis. See: *Cooperativa*, 2023. "Luis Castillo quedó en prisión preventiva por secuestro extorsivo y robo con violencia." December 16. https://cooperativa.cl/noticias/pais/policial/secuestros/luis-castillo-quedo-en-prision-preventiva-por-secuestro-extorsivo-y-robo/2023-12-16/114904.html

even further, making it increasingly clear that the political path Chile had embarked on was already exhausted.[16]

17.3.2 The Trade-Off Mindset

Another factor that prompted voters to rationally reject the second proposal was the realization that the tradeoff of adopting a new constitution was simply not worth it. Compared with 2022, a time when many voters considered the rejection of the first proposal as a means for pushing for a better alternative, the second plebiscite lacked any such forward-looking motivation. As advanced above, voters now faced with a binary choice: to retain the Pinochet-era constitution or to replace it with the Kast constitution.

Despite its origins, the existing Pinochet-era constitution proved to be preferable. Over time, it had been amended *enough* to mean something different. Some even referred to it as the "Lagos Constitution," which gave solace to the harsher anti-Pinochet voters that did not want to favor Kast, but knew that they had to vote for one of the two options at the end of the day.

Aware of this, the left-wing opposition surprisingly shifted its message just weeks before the plebiscite was due to take place. While initially campaigning against anything associated with Pinochet, they were *now* suddenly willing to make an exception. Their argument was that approving the new draft would not only not solve Chile's problems, but it would also prolong political instability. However read, the reversal was

[16] In June of 2023, a major corruption scandal involving the Ministry of Housing, known as the *Democracia Viva* case, erupted, capturing national attention and severely undermining public trust in the Boric administration. The scheme centered on the irregular transfer of public housing funds to NGOs linked to members of *Revolución Democrática*, exposing conflicts of interest and misuse of state resources. Although Housing Minister Carlos Montes was not directly charged, the scandal implicated prominent party figures, including former RD president Catalina Pérez, presidential advisor Miguel Crispi, and several government-aligned technocrats, leading to arrests, indictments, and resignations. The case ultimately shattered RD's credibility and contributed to the party's dissolution, with its remnants later absorbed into the *Frente Amplio* coalition. See: Ojeda, J. M., and F. Artaza, "Democracia Viva: a un año de la pesadilla que golpeó a Boric y hundió a RD," *La Tercera*, 9 June 2024. https://www.latercera.com/la-tercera-domingo/noticia/democracia-viva-a-un-ano-de-la-pesadilla-que-golpeo-a-boric-y-hundio-a-rd/DHZMELTWLBBXLEXHVXYQIIQZIE/

striking. After years of demanding the abolition of the Pinochet constitution and writing a new one in its place, the left was now embracing it and urging voters to do the same.

This shift momentarily blurred traditional ideological lines. The irony was evident: while conservative parties urged voters to replace the constitution they did not want to change, the left—historically the strongest advocates for full replacement—asked voters to keep what remained of Pinochet's original text.

This dynamic led to an outcome of rejection that was less about the content of the proposal and more about the desire to end shenanigans. Chileans were no longer voting on whether they supported the principles of the second draft but on whether they wanted to continue their engagement with the greater constitutional debate.

The final weeks of the Constitutional Council reflected this shift in public perception. Compared with the (first) Constitutional Convention, which was chaotic and ideologically charged, the second council was methodical but *boring*. It lacked grand debates and impassioned public mobilization but featured a slow, bureaucratic process that lacked the energy and momentum to inspire public trust. By the time the referendum came, voters had disengaged and checked-out. The second plebiscite was not about hope or renewal; it was about putting an end to an overly extended and ultimately unnecessary process.

17.4 Missed Opportunity

Following the rejection of the second constitutional proposal, it quickly became clear that Chile's constitutional process had reached its end. The government, reading the political moment accurately, chose not to pursue a third attempt. After years of debate, two failed plebiscites, and deepening political polarization, no major political faction showed genuine interest in continuing. For most Chileans, the process had become exhausting. While some celebrated and others saw it as a defeat, the dominant feeling across society was relief. The country could finally move past a prolonged and divisive chapter.

As anticipated in Chapter 5, and reaffirmed in Chapter 13, the failure of both constitutional efforts cannot be separated from the misdiagnosis made by Chile's political and intellectual elite that justified the entire process. From the outset, they framed constitutional reform as a necessary solution to the country's structural problems and misread the 2019 social unrest as a clear mandate for sweeping change. Rather than addressing the real and immediate concerns of the public, they focused on an ambitious institutional overhaul and presented constitutional reform as the only viable path forward. Polling data from both before and after the unrest consistently showed that most Chileans prioritized issues such as pensions, healthcare, and public safety. Constitutional change was never a central concern for the majority. The insistence on turning it into the centerpiece of national politics ignored what most citizens were actually demanding. As a result, they indirectly helped derailed not one but two proposals, setting the country back years, if not decades, in key areas of economic and social development.

Although both processes failed, they did not do so in exactly the same way. The second proposal came closer to being approved, suggesting that some room for consensus still existed. While both processes are often described as equally polarized in opposite directions,[17] there is reason to believe that the polarization was not symmetrical.[18] This raises the possibility that a more modest, focused, and less ideologically charged proposal could have succeeded. As some suggested before any of this even began, a minimalist constitution could have been enough to seal the deal.[19]

[17] A common perception was that both constitutional drafts were equally problematic. Some organized opposition groups from civil society, such as *Una que nos una*, who had viewed the first proposal as flawed and were now campaigning against the second, reinforced the notion that the two projects represented opposite ideological extremes. See: *Cooperativa*. 2023. "Promotores de "Una que nos una" van por el En Contra." November 17. https://cooperativa.cl/noticias/pais/politica/constitucion/promotores-de-una-que-nos-una-van-por-el-en-contra/2023-11-17/162339.html/

[18] The central idea is that despite both constitutional processes being polarized, the overall distance between the two opposing sectors was lower in the Constitutional Council than in the Constitutional Convention. This moderation is evident in the higher approval rate of articles in the plenary—82.8% in 2023 compared to just 36.1% in the 2021–2022 process—as well as in the lower rejection rate in the plebiscites, with 62% of Chileans rejecting the first proposal but only 56% rejecting the second. While Figure 12.1 may lead some to believe that the Constitutional Council was more polarized than the Convention shown in Figure 16.1 due to the apparent distance between extremes, the two are not directly comparable. This is because of the methodological limitations of W-NOMINATE, as the ideological dimensions are computed on different scales—a distance between -1 and 1 in the first process could be equivalent to a distance between -1 and 0 in the second. See: See: Rivas, C. 2023. "Estudio de la USS destaca rol 'moderador' de Chile Vamos y su contribución a un mayor acuerdo en el Consejo Constitucional." *Diario Financiero*. Novemeber 29. https://www.df.cl/df-constitucional/estudio-de-la-uss-destaca-rol-moderador-de-chile-vamos-y-su

[19] See an early proposal for a minimalist Constitution: *Las Últimas Noticias*. 2019. "Kenneth Bunker: Una constitución que se pueda leer en la micro." November 22.

17.5 Conclusion

This chapter examined the failure of Chile's second constitutional proposal by analyzing its rejection within the context of the country's ongoing constitutional debate. While the second draft was rejected by a smaller margin than the first, the outcome continued to reflect widespread dissatisfaction. Two key factors shaped this result. First, the proposal failed to preserve key societal rights, particularly on issues such as abortion and other social rights, alienating moderate voters who perceived it as a step backward. Second, *constitutional fatigue* and voter exhaustion had deepened, which made the electorate increasingly skeptical of another attempt at reform. In the face of persistent economic struggle, rising crime rate, and political instability, the idea of a new constitution lost its sense of urgency, which further diminished public support.

If the first draft was rejected for extremely favoring the left, then the second was dismissed for excessively leaning in the opposite direction. While more measured than its predecessor, it continued to carry an ideological rigidity that left it vulnerable to attack.

After four years of political division, prolonged debates, and unfulfilled promises, Chileans had grown weary of a process that was seemingly detached from their immediate concerns. Their *trade-off mindset* worsened their exhaustion: the second plebiscite no longer offered the possibility of drafting a third proposal, which left voters with a basic choice between approving an imperfect document or ending the constitutional debate entirely. Unwilling to take a risk on a new framework that they observed was flawed, many opted for the latter. Thus, what was previously framed as a historic moment for change became a referendum on whether the country should simply move on.

At its core, the second constitutional failure stemmed from the same misdiagnosis that doomed the first—the belief that a complete constitutional overhaul was the necessary solution. Ironically, however, the rejection of the second proposal served not only to reaffirm the flaws in that original diagnosis, but also to vindicate the very constitutional framework that had been so heavily criticized.

Part IV: Reckoning

CHAPTER 18

Looking Back on Four Years of Upheaval

18.1 Introduction

How could a country so often regarded as a regional success story descend into widespread unrest, with citizens questioning the very foundations that once set it apart? And if constitutional change was essential to addressing the demands behind the social outburst, how can the rejection of not one but two proposed alternatives be interpreted?

These two questions, originally presented in Chapter 1, define the core of Chile's constitutional crisis. The first speaks to the apparent contradiction at the heart of the 2019 social outburst: how a nation praised for its democratic stability, economic performance, and institutional strength could become the site of mass protests, institutional breakdown, and calls for systemic overhaul. The second addresses the irony that followed: how a country that had reached consensus on the need for a new constitution ultimately fail twice to agree on what that new foundation should look like.

This chapter serves as a stand-alone piece summarizing some of the main arguments in the book, and tackles each question in turn.[1] First, it examines the structural and contextual conditions that eroded Chile's

[1] Readers following the book in chronological order may prefer to proceed directly to the final chapter. Those starting here may wish to consult the footnotes and references in earlier chapters, where many of the claims developed in what follows are further supported.

K. Bunker, *Chile's Transformation Amidst Crisis*,
https://doi.org/10.1007/978-3-031-96463-3_18

institutional capacity long before the crisis erupted. Years of political fragmentation, weakening party–voter linkages, and the gradual loss of institutional legitimacy created a brittle political enviornment. When these fragilities met a new wave of activist-led politics and rising expectations for transformation, the conditions were set for rupture.

Then, it analyzes the dynamics that led to the rejection of two constitutional proposals. The first convention, driven by ideological ambition and shaped by a new generation of political outsiders, produced a document *too* many viewed as *too* radical. The second, more restrained in tone and content, nevertheless failed to inspire trust or mobilize public support. In both cases, the problem was not merely the content of the drafts, but the inability of the political system to recover legitimacy, rebuild consensus, or respond credibly to public concerns.

Together, these two questions frame Chile's recent constitutional history not as a failed attempt at renewal, but as a broader political crisis that began in tragedy, with an elite misdiagnosis rooted in a convenient reading of an otherwise hopeful situation, and ended in farce, as major political actors not only inverted their positions multiple times over the years, but ultimately campaigned for outcomes they had initially opposed.[2]

[2] It is worth underscoring how clearly the constitutional process illustrates this tragicomic arc. The tragedy lay in the original elite misdiagnosis of the crisis: rather than identifying what worked and building on it, they fixated on a narrative that sought to tear everything down. They argued the problem was legitimacy of origin, yet voters rejected two proposals drafted under democratic conditions; they claimed it was constitutional rigidity, yet the major authoritarian enclaves—such as designated senators and the binominal system—had already been dismantled, and the last remaining one was set to disappear before the end of the first process; and they pointed to neoliberalism, yet even with reduced quorums, Boric's left-leaning government ultimately reaffirmed the "the model" they had long denounced. The farce, instead, unfolded in the form of remarkable political reversals: the Communist Party, which had refused to sign the 2022 *Acuerdo por la Paz y Nueva Constitución*, came to dominate the first convention, only to lose its draft and later endorse the Pinochet Constitution; while the Republicans, who had rejected the 2023 *Acuerdo por Chile* and opposed constitutional change altogether, led the second process, only to end up backing the kind of overhaul they had once resisted.

18.2 From Model to Mayhem

For decades, Chile was held up as a model of democratic stability and market-driven development in Latin America. Its post-authoritarian trajectory, marked by steady economic growth, robust institutions, and peaceful transitions of power, seemed to place it above the volatility that plagued many of its neighbors (see the comparative analysis in the first part of Chapter 5). Yet in October 2019, that image came shattering down. A sudden and massive wave of protests sparked by a modest metro fare increase quickly evolved into a full-scale national crisis (a crisis covered in Chapter 9). What followed was a prolonged period of political instability, economic uncertainty, and a widespread call for a new constitutional order.

Understanding how Chile arrived at this point requires moving beyond the surface narrative of a successful nation suddenly overtaken by unrest. The truth is more complex. Beneath Chile's reputation for institutional strength lay deep structural weaknesses: a fragmented party system, a declining connection between political elites and voters, and institutions increasingly perceived as unresponsive or illegitimate. These vulnerabilities did not emerge overnight—they were the result of slow-moving processes that, over time, hollowed out the foundations of Chile's democratic order.

At the same time, contextual factors accelerated this unraveling. The rise of niche political movements, the emergence of a new generation of leaders shaped by protest politics, and the cumulative effect of reforms that raised expectations without resolving long-standing grievances transformed latent discontent into a rupture. The convergence of structural decay and contextual agitation created a combustible political environment, one in which a relatively minor trigger was sufficient to produce an outsized reaction.

This section examines both layers. It first explores the structural erosion that destabilized the Chilean political system from within: the weakening of traditional parties, the fraying of voter–institution linkages, and the gradual loss of institutional authority. It then turns to the contextual accelerants that gave the 2019 outburst its intensity: generational turnover, ideological polarization, and a culture of confrontation that displaced the politics of negotiation. Together, these forces explain how Chile, long celebrated for its stability, entered one of the most turbulent periods in its modern history.

18.2.1 Structural Erosion

Chile's descent into political crisis did not emerge from sudden disruption, but from the gradual erosion of the very institutions that had once supported its democratic reputation. At the heart of this erosion was the weakening of Chile's party system and the steady collapse of its intermediary institutions. For much of the post-authoritarian period, political parties functioned as key transmitters between society and government. They organized political life, translated demands into policy, and channeled discontent into institutional forms. By the 2010s, however, those functions had largely collapsed.

The first and most visible form of structural erosion was fragmentation (see Chapter 6). Electoral reforms introduced as early as 2004 and as late as 2015—particularly this last one, a move to a *full* proportional representation system in Congress that lowered entry barriers and incentivized the proliferation of small parties. What was once a relatively stable political landscape, dominated by broad coalitions, quickly gave way to a fragmented and unstable one. With more parties vying for influence, coalition-building became more difficult, and governing majorities more tenuous. Multiplicity replaced mediation. As new parties emerged without coherent ideological programs or institutional discipline, the party system lost its capacity to generate stable policy agendas.

Notably, fragmentation was asymmetrical. While new parties and movements emerged across the spectrum, the left experienced a particularly intense internal diversification. The traditional center-left, long anchored by the *Concertación* coalition, began to collapse under the weight of generational and ideological splits. A growing number of left-leaning movements promoted more radical platforms, increasingly distancing themselves from the incrementalist legacy of the post-dictatorship period.

Simultaneously, voter–party linkages deteriorated (see Chapter 7). Chilean citizens grew increasingly detached from formal politics, disillusioned with parties they perceived as self-serving, corrupt, or indifferent to everyday concerns. This decline in political trust was long in the making, compounded by repeated scandals, policy inertia, and growing disconnections. By the time of the social outburst, political parties had long lost their legitimacy as mediators.

The result was *representation backsliding*—a situation in which citizens were becoming detached from democratic institutions, even as the party system appeared to become more open and pluaral than ever. Parties still occupied institutional space, but they no longer commanded public trust with authority. In this vacuum, institutional politics ceased to function as effective mediators for demands.

By 2019, Chile's political system was in trouble. The party system was fragmented and ideologically incoherent, while institutions were weak and uprooted. With no capacity to channel popular demands through legitimate democratic mechanisms, the country was slowly sliding into a political crisis.

18.2.2 Contextual Acceleration

If structural erosion explains why Chile's political system was vulnerable, it was the events and dynamics of the early 2010s that made the crisis irreversible. A series of contextual shifts—emerging political actors, generational turnover, shifting expectations, and a growing discourse of rupture—transformed slow-moving decay into a volatile political situation. These forces did not replace the structural weaknesses; they magnified them.

One of the most significant contextual developments was the disintegration of the *Concertación*. After losing the 2010 election, the coalition fully fractured into two camps, with the *autoflagelantes* giving way to a new political current that accepted the need for deeper and more structural changes. This internal split weakened the old coalition's ability to act as a moderating force and eroded its influence over the broader political agenda. In doing so, it left a vacuum in the center of the system—one that was captured by Piñera and the right, and which in turn created a heightened sense of urgency for the left.

At the same time, a new, more ambitious political generation was rising (see Sect. 8.3). Students and young leaders shaped by the 2006 and 2011 student mobilizations, whose formative political experiences occurred outside of institutional politics, were coming to the front. With them, came a distrust of the party system, a rejection of gradualism, and a confrontational political style that had not been seen in decades. They had risen to seize power, not to negotiate (the main party that resulted from this process was called *Revolución Democrática*—Democratic Revolution).

This generational turnover coincided with rising expectations (see Sect. 8.4). The second administration of Michelle Bachelet (2014–2018) had introduced an ambitious program of structural reforms—on education, taxation, and the electoral system—that, while incomplete, signaled a shift away from the neoliberal consensus of the post-dictatorship years. For many, these reforms suggested that deeper change was finally possible. However, it also generated frustration, particularly among younger generations, who witnessed first-hand that the system was still resisting change when Bachelet's constitutional proposal was shelved in 2018.

As a result a rupturist rhetoric began to spread (see Sect. 8.5). So, by the time the 2019 crisis erupted, the discursive and political foundations for rupture were already in place. It had become increasingly plausible to argue that incremental reform would be insufficient, and that only a complete replacement of the existing model could address the depth of the crisis.

This framing had been intentionally developed and refined by left-leaning intellectual elites in the decade leading up to the outburst. As the younger generation of student leaders rose to prominence, progressive academics were actively articulating ideas of rupture (see the second part of Chapter 5). They argued that constitutional overhaul was necessary not only to address deep inequities embedded in the neoliberal model, but also because the 1980 Constitution was considered fundamentally illegitimate, as it originated under dictatorship and was structurally designed to avoid meaningful change.

In combination, student leaders and intellectuals provided both the ground force and the justification for rupture. While the former brought political energy and mass mobilization, the latter supplied the normative and conceptual arguments that framed constitutional overhaul as both necessary and legitimate. By positioning these ideas within mainstream political discourse, they elevated demands for structural change.

The 2019 outburst did not result from an inevitable failure of the system. Rather, it was the outcome of years of democratic backsliding, during which political representation weakened and a rupturist discourse gained traction. This discourse aimed not only to overhaul the institutional order but also to replace the political actors in power. In this context, the combination of institutional reforms that lowered barriers to entry and intellectual narratives that misrepresented the country's progress both played a significant role in creating the conditions that led to the breakdown.

18.3 Reform Without Resolution

The same structural weaknesses and discursive distortions that contributed to the 2019 outburst carried over into the constitutional process, compromising its legitimacy and coherence from the outset. If the Social Outburst of 2019 was the result of accumulated institutional fragility and a degree of political and intellectual short-sightedness, the constitutional process that followed was its institutional response.

Of course, this was not immediately visible at the time. In the midst of the crisis, virtually all political actors agreed that a new constitution was necessary (see Chapter 10), both as a symbolic break from the legal framework inherited from the Pinochet era and as a material foundation for a more equitable and responsive state. The urgency of that consensus led to the 2020 plebiscite, in which nearly 80 percent of voters endorsed the drafting of a new constitutional text.

This section examines not only how the effects of misdiagnosis and political ambition contributed to the ultimate failure of each constitutional process, but also how each process, in turn, generated internal dynamics that led to its own downfall. In the case of the first, the argument centers on ideological overreach, as it pursued an expansive and polarizing vision that exceeded the bounds of public consensus. In the case of the second, failure resulted from an inability to return to the political center, combined with widespread *constitutional fatigue* and a *trade-off mindset* that prioritized closure over change.

18.3.1 The Failure to Get It Right

The first Constitutional Convention was convened in 2021 under conditions shaped as much by symbolic weight as by institutional urgency (see Chapter 12). Its formation marked a turning point: for the first time since the return to democracy, Chile would attempt to rewrite its foundational charter through a participatory and democratic mechanism. Expectations were high, and the political moment was widely interpreted as a historic opportunity for deep and lasting transformation.

The composition of the Convention reflected this sentiment. Progressive and independent candidates dominated the elections, many of them emerging from social movements, activist circles, or outside the traditional party system altogether. The outcome represented a clear repudiation of the political establishment—and an opening for a new generation of political actors who viewed the convention not as a space for compromise, but as a platform for reimagining the Chilean state.

This orientation shaped the tone and trajectory of the Convention. Rather than framing its work as a constitutional update, many delegates approached it as a foundational rupture. The 1980 Constitution was treated as illegitimate by origin and irredeemable by reform. This framing led to an expansive—and at times maximalist—approach to constitutional drafting. Delegates proposed a wide array of progressive reforms: recognition of Chile as a plurinational state, extensive social and environmental rights, a unicameral legislative system, judicial decentralization, and broad guarantees for public goods like housing, education, and health (see Chapter 12).

While many of these proposals responded directly to demands expressed during the social outburst, the Convention struggled to translate social urgency into institutional credibility. The lack of formal party discipline and the weak role of mediating institutions made internal coordination difficult. Procedural missteps, public controversies, and symbolic gestures often overshadowed substantive debate. As polarization within the Convention grew, so did the gap between its internal priorities and the broader electorate's expectations.

The Convention's progressive majority interpreted its mandate expansively—but without the institutional anchoring or political infrastructure to temper or legitimize its ambition. The absence of a unified bloc capable of internal moderation made it difficult to construct consensus, and the process quickly became a forum for competing ideological projects rather than a space for national convergence. For voters, the draft appeared less like a shared framework and more like a partisan manifesto.

Ultimately, the rejection of the first draft in September 2022—by 62% of voters—reflected not only disagreement with specific proposals but also a broader rejection of the process itself (see Chapter 12). The public had endorsed the idea of a new constitution, but it had not endorsed the vision—or the tone—presented in the final product. What had begun with overwhelming support for change ended in a decisive rebuke.

In hindsight, the first Convention was undone by its own moment. It mistook public frustration for a blank check, enthusiasm for consensus, and procedural novelty for legitimacy. It captured the spirit of rupture, but not the discipline of governance. Without the political structures to anchor its ambition or the institutional trust to sustain it, the Convention failed to produce a proposal that could unify a divided society.

18.3.2 The Failure to Correct

If the first process was characterized by overreach, the second was defined by restraint. Convened in 2023 after the rejection of the initial draft, the second constitutional process aimed to correct the missteps of its predecessor (see Chapter 16). It was more procedurally structured, politically moderated, and institutionally overseen. The new rules were tighter, the drafting process more constrained, and the balance of power shifted rightward. In nearly every respect, the second process was designed to avoid the excesses that had doomed the first.

But the context had changed—and not in its favor. Public trust, already frayed in 2021, had by 2023 largely collapsed. The very institutions tasked with facilitating constitutional reform were now widely viewed as incapable of delivering meaningful change. The earlier enthusiasm that fueled participation in the first plebiscite had given way to exhaustion, skepticism, and a deep sense of disillusionment. Even before the second convention had drafted a single article, its legitimacy was already in question.

This loss of trust shaped every stage of the process. While the Council avoided the ideological maximalism of the first, it also failed to articulate a compelling narrative about why its draft was necessary, and how it differed in purpose—not just in form. It did not inspire renewed public engagement, nor did it succeed in reframing the constitutional question. Voters no longer believed that a new text, however carefully drafted, would resolve the country's deeper political and institutional crises.

The right, which held greater influence in the second process, adopted a more cautious and technocratic approach. The draft that emerged was significantly narrower in scope than the first: fewer rights, less institutional redesign, and a greater emphasis on order, security, and economic stability. While this appealed to segments of the electorate fatigued by political instability, it also alienated many who had initially supported the idea of constitutional change. Progressive voters, still reeling from the first rejection, now viewed the second draft as *too* limited, *too* conservative, and *too* disconnected from the spirit of the original demand.

By the time the second draft was put to a vote in December 2023, the process had lost momentum. The referendum became less about the content of the proposal and more about the legitimacy of the actors behind it (see Chapter 17). Organized opposition successfully framed the draft as both unnecessary and untrustworthy. For many Chileans, the entire constitutional process had become symbolic of the broader dysfunction of their political system. A second rejection—this time by a smaller margin, but still decisive—confirmed that no political force had succeeded in rebuilding the consensus that had briefly emerged in 2020.

In the end, the failure of the Council was not about its content alone; it was the product of an exhausted public, a discredited elite, and a political process that had lost its narrative. Where the first convention failed due to overambition and fragmentation, the second failed because the conditions for recovery—trust, legitimacy, and a sense of collective purpose—were no longer present. It was, in many ways, too little, too late.

18.4 Conclusion

This chapter circled back to two of the three questions presented in Chapter 1. First: how could a country so often regarded as a success story descend into widespread unrest, with citizens questioning the very foundations that once set it apart? And second, if constitutional change was essential to addressing those demands, how can the rejection of not one, but two alternative proposals be explained?

The answer to the first lies in Chile's slow-burning institutional erosion. Long before the 2019 outburst, the political system had begun to fragment. Parties lost coherence, voter linkages deteriorated, and public trust in democratic institutions steadily declined. These structural weaknesses left the system vulnerable to shock. When contextual accelerants—generational turnover, rising expectations, and a culture of rupture—met this institutional fatigue, Chile's apparent stability gave way to a crisis that had been years in the making.

The second question can only be understood through the lens of this fragility. The failure of the constitutional process was not simply a matter of poor drafting or flawed proposals. It was the result of a political system that had lost its ability to mediate, to inspire confidence, and to govern through consensus. The first convention was too bold, unmoored from public moderation. The second was too cautious, arriving after public trust had already collapsed. In both cases, the problem was not just what was proposed, but the absence of a credible process to carry it forward.

Chile's experience is not simply one of failure, but of profound misdiagnosis and elite ambition. It demonstrates that when political change is unwarranted but imposed nonetheless, it can produce not only unforeseen and adverse outcomes, but also serious and long-lasting consequences.

CHAPTER 19

Chile's Reckoning and the Limits of Transformation

19.1 The Ship of Theseus

After looking at the transformation of Chile from historical, political, and social perspectives, this chapter turns to the subtitle of the book: the Theseus paradox—an ancient philosophical thought experiment that offers insight into enduring questions of continuity and change.

The Ship of Theseus tells the story of a vessel that embarks on a long journey across the seas. Along the way, its planks, nails, ropes, and sails are gradually replaced, one by one. By the time it returns to port, not a single original part remains. The question, then, is whether the ship that returned is the same one that sailed away in the first place. If every one of its components has been replaced, yet the vessel appears unchanged, is it the same or not?

Chile offers a real-world representation of this paradox. In 2019, following the social outburst, the country set sail on what many believed would be a one-way journey toward a new constitutional order. And yet, after a turbulent passage, the only thing that was expected to be replaced without a doubt—the constitution—was left untouched. Not once, but twice, Chileans voted to reject alternative proposals, leaving the 1980 Constitution in its place.

This brings us to the third question raised in Chapter 1: Was the social upheaval, the political turmoil, and the economic disruption ultimately worth it? Well, if the country would have fundamentally transformed

K. Bunker, *Chile's Transformation Amidst Crisis*,
https://doi.org/10.1007/978-3-031-96463-3_19

for the better, then the answer is *yes*. But if the costs of the journey outweighed the tangible benefits, then the answer is *no*. How much, then, did Chile actually change? Did the country remain the same, as the failure of both constitutional referendums might suggest? Or did something fundamental shift—even if not visible to the naked eye?

19.2 A Constitutional Stay

In terms of what remains, it seems obvious that the Pinochet Constitution—despite widespread calls for its replacement—was *de facto* ratified twice. In both 2022 and 2023, Chileans voted against new constitutional drafts, effectively reaffirming the continued validity of the 1980 text.

This outcome extends beyond the document itself. It encompasses the institutional scaffolding built around it: the presidential system, the bicameral structure, centralized Justice, and the broader architecture of governance that defined Chile beyond its transition.

Remarkably, the act of rejecting both proposals through democratic means produced an unintended consequence: the old framework, once deemed illegitimate by origin, was validated by procedure, putting an end to the legitimacy of origin question.

But the text was also compounded with unexpected elements. Among them, perhaps the most relevant was the lowering of constitutional reform quorums. What had previously required a two-thirds supermajority in Congress was modified in an unexpected twist of events when a legislative amendment entered by Senators Ximena Rincón and Matías Walker reduced the threshold to four-sevenths.[1] Together with the previous abolition of designated senators, binomial system and other *enclaves*, this reform put an end to the question of rigidity.

It is in this balance that the paradox emerges. The foundational document was neither reaffirmed nor replaced, its origin was legitimized, and its rigidity was softened. The state was not restructured, yet its capacity

[1] On August 23, 2022, the Chilean Congress approved a constitutional amendment that lowered the quorum required for constitutional reforms from two-thirds to four-sevenths. This change, led by Senators Ximena Rincón and Matías Walker, was enacted through a bill that passed in both the Chamber of Deputies and the Senate with overwhelming support. See: *Cooperativa*. 2022. "Se acabaron los 2/3: Ya rige el quorum de 4/7 para reformar la Constitución vigente." August 23. https://cooperativa.cl/noticias/pais/politica/constitucion/se-acabaron-los-2-3-ya-rige-el-quorum-de-4-7-para-reformar-la/2022-08-23/102542.html/

for evolution was enhanced. The constitutional framework returned from the journey the same, but completely different at the same time.

19.3 A Change in Sentiment

A less material, but perhaps even more revealing dimension concerns a shift not in institutions, but in national sentiment—a reckoning in spirit. The relevant change was not to the rules of the game, but to how Chileans understood them.

The early stages of the constitutional process were marked by a profound sense of rupture. The social outburst of 2019 was not presented simply as a protest against specific policies; it was presented as a collective denunciation of a "model" portrayed as exhausted.

However, the rejection of two constitutional drafts, each different in content and shape, pointed to a problem with this picture. If the model had been such a problem, then voters would have endorsed any of the alternatives presented to them. But they did not. They chose status quo. They chose the model. They reaffirmed the same system that had been in place since the 1980s and that had been presented to them as *the root of all evils*.

They also chose stability over change, coming to appreciate, albeit implicitly, the roots of order in the 1980 constitution. Change, they learned, was not risk-free. The process itself—lengthy, uncertain, and at times incoherent—exposed the costs of experimentation. Chile fell into a deep and severe security crisis and backtracked significantly in most areas linked to the influence of the state, including the economy, health, education, and pensions, which were all severely affected, in one way or another, by the ambition to reform, and those who pushed for change.

19.4 Final Remarks

The journey did not yield a new constitution, but it did produce a reckoning—politically, institutionally, and culturally. Chile returned from a period of upheaval having learned something essential: that transformation is neither linear nor guaranteed, and that the pursuit of change, while often necessary, carries costs that are not always foretold or foreseen.

Processes of this nature invite reflection. While they may generate important insights, as they did in Chile, they can also impose significant strain on a society's institutions, economy, and social fabric. In this sense, Chile was fortunate. The country emerged altered, but still afloat.

Chile remains the same, yet everything has changed. For other nations considering an overhaul, this experience is a reminder to think carefully before setting sail. The Chilean case suggests that the desire for change must be tempered by a sober understanding of context, capacity, and consequence. Change does not guarantee success. It does not eliminate uncertainty. And in moments of instability, it can deepen rather than resolve the crisis. If there is one final lesson to learn, it is that things can, in fact, always get worse.

Appendix

The following figures present visualizations that illustrate key ideological spatial positions and areas of electoral influence in post-transition Chile, offering a synthesis of how political ideologies have evolved over time. Drawing from the historical and electoral analysis developed in Chapter 6, these maps are not intended as fixed or precise boundaries but as general guides for understanding patterns of ideological alignment. They depict every political party and presidential candidate, along with the majority of major coalitions, that have participated in democratic elections since the transition in 1989. While the original spatial approach to party systems is more general in scope, the application presented here is tailored to highlight specific ideas and dynamics discussed throughout the text—particularly those related to ideological alignment, partisan continuity, and presidential contests. Figure A1 maps the general area of influence of political coalitions; Figure A2 focuses on individual political parties; and Figure A3 highlights presidential candidates. Each map includes a background layer showing the broader spatial reach of Chile's principal political sectors, offering a composite view of how electoral geography and ideological tendencies intersect. See also: Bunker, K. 2025. "Mapping party systems over time: a spatial distribution of ideological competition in Chile." *Journal of Political Ideologies* (online first): 1–18.

K. Bunker, *Chile's Transformation Amidst Crisis*,
https://doi.org/10.1007/978-3-031-96463-3

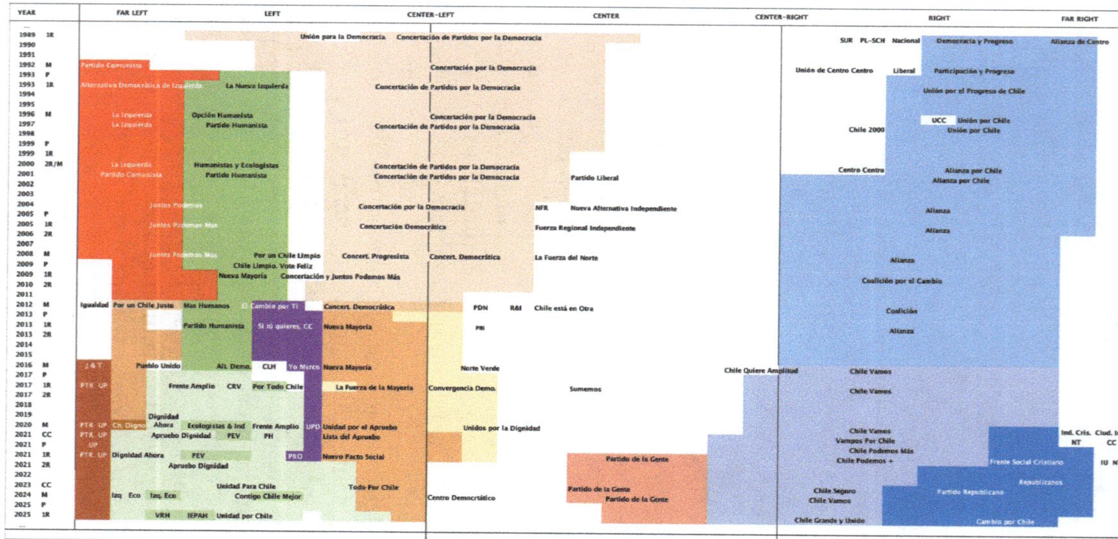

Fig. A.1 Spatial map of electoral competition in Chile (1989–2025) (*Note* Years in the figure are shown in chronological order, but some include multiple elections, which may lead to overrepresentation. The labels indicate the type of election: "1R" stands for the first round of the presidential election, "2R" for the second round of the presidential election, "P" for presidential primary, and "M" for municipal election. The colored regions represent general areas of political influence or voter alignment and should be taken as a reference, not as a classification. *Source* Author with data from Chapter 6)

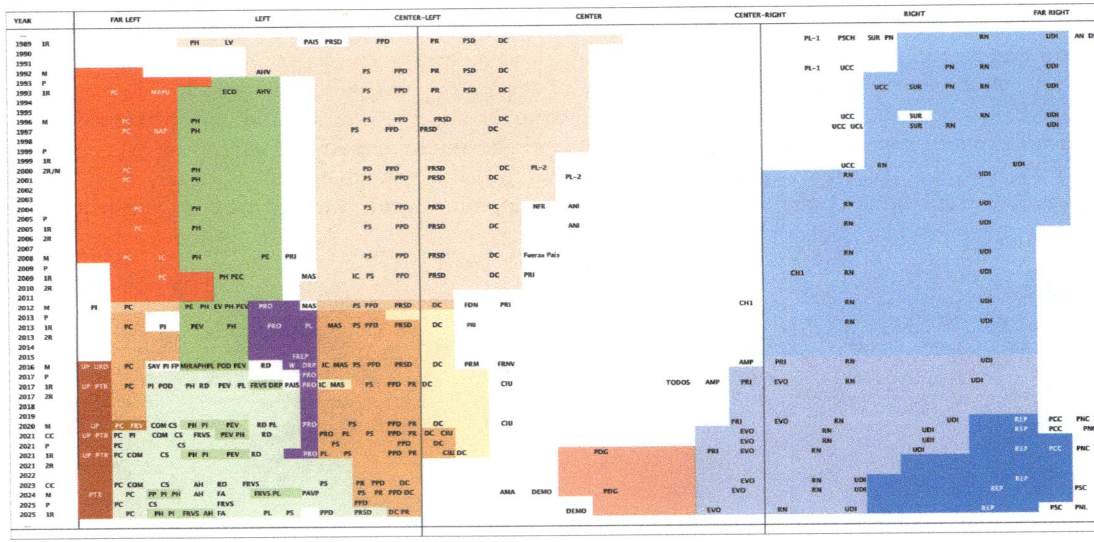

Fig. A.2 Spatial map of political parties in Chile (1989–2025) (*Note* The years in the figure are shown in chronological order, but some include multiple elections, which may lead to overrepresentation. The labels indicate the type of election: "1R" stands for the first round of the presidential election, "2R" for the second round of the presidential election, "P" for presidential primary, and "M" for municipal election. The colored regions represent general areas of political influence or voter alignment and should be taken as a reference, not as a precise classification. Also note that the 2020 municipal election was held in 2021. *Source* Author with data from Chapter 6)

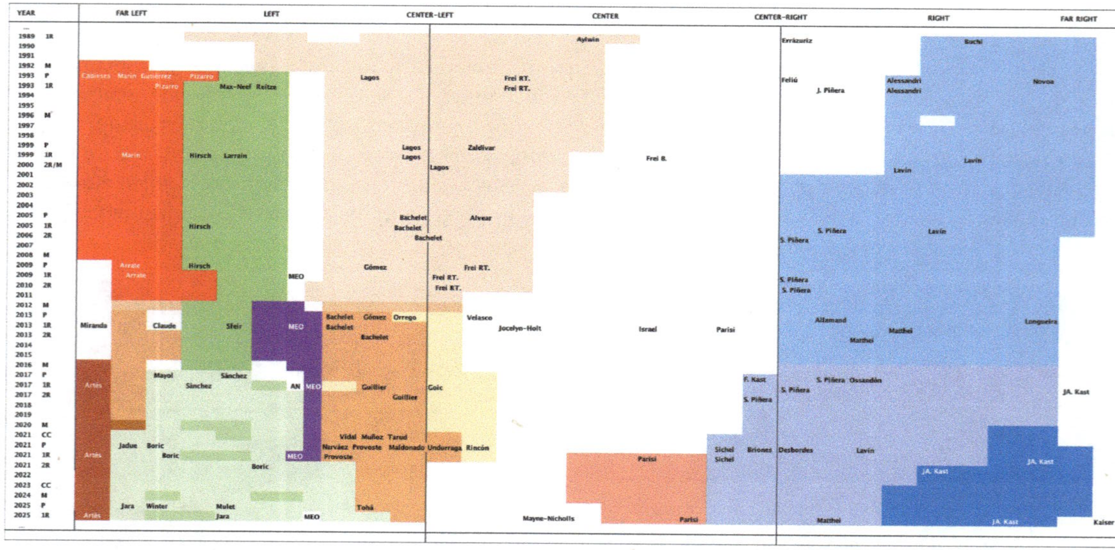

Fig. A.3 Spatial map of presidential candidates in Chile (1989–2025) (*Note* The years in the figure are shown in chronological order, but some include multiple elections, which may lead to overrepresentation. The labels indicate the type of election: "1R" stands for the first round of the presidential election, "2R" for the second round of the presidential election, "P" for presidential primary, and "M" for municipal election. The colored regions represent general areas of political influence or voter alignment and should be taken as a reference, not as a precise classification. Also note that while all primary elections before 2013 were organized by parties and not Servel, parties still organized informal primaries thereafter. *Source* Author with data from Chapter 6)

Index

K. Bunker, *Chile's Transformation Amidst Crisis*,
https://doi.org/10.1007/978-3-031-96463-3

FSC
www.fsc.org
MIX
Papier | Fördert gute Waldnutzung
FSC® C083411

Kolibri 360 GmbH
Ferdinand-Jühlke-Straße 7
99095 Erfurt, Deutschland
produktsicherheit@kolibri360.de